Administering

SAP R/3:

The Production Planning Module

Administering SAP R/3: The Production and Planning Module

International Standard Book Number: 0-7897-2274-7

Library of Congress Catalog Card Number: 99-068230

Printed in the United States of America

First Printing: December, 1999

01 00 99   4   3   2   1

Contents at a Glance

Table of Contents

II Preparing the System

3 Setting Up Bills of Material   51

4 Setting Up Work Centers   69

6 Assigning Production Resources and Tools 125

III Controlling the Production Facilities

7 Scheduling Routings 143

8 Planning and Controlling Shop Floor Production Orders   159

Credits

ASSOCIATE PUBLISHER
Dean Miller

ACQUISITIONS EDITOR
Randy Haubner

DEVELOPMENT EDITOR
Sean Dixon

MANAGING EDITOR
Lisa Wilson

COPY EDITOR
Grechen Perry Throop

INDEXER
Joy Dean Lee

PROOFREADER
Ruth Frick

TECHNICAL EDITOR
Bhanu Kuruganty

TEAM COORDINATOR
Cindy Teeters

COVER DESIGNER
Dan Armstrong

PRODUCTION
BooksCraft, Inc.

Composed in *Century Old Style* and *ITC Franklin Gothic* by Que Corporation.

I dedicate this book to my dear wife, Jennifer, and our beautiful daughter, Xanthe, who was born August 16th, 1999.

—*Jonathan Blain*

About the Authors

ASAP World Consultancy is an international SAP consulting company and is part of the ASAP International Group. It is in the business of selling high-quality products and services relating to SAP and other enterprise applications, computing systems, and implementations. The company specialises in " Enterprise Transformation Management" delivering integrated business solutions. ASAP World Consultancy is part of the global ASAP Group whose activities include the following:

- Introductory SAP Courses for corporate clients globally
- SAP Implementation Consultancy
- SAP Permanent Temporary and Contract Recruitment
- Business Process Re-engineering, Renewal, Change Management and Transformation Consultancy
- SAP Human Issues Consultancy
- SAP Internal & External Communications Consultancy
- SAP Project and Resource Planning Consultancy
- SAP Skills Transfer to Your Employees
- SAP Education and Training
- SAP System Testing Consultancy & Resourcing
- SAP Documentation Consultancy
- SAP Procurement Consultancy
- SAP Access and Security Consultancy
- Hardware and Installation Consultancy
- Development of SAP Complementary Solutions
- SAP Market Research
- SAP Product and Services Acquisitions, Mergers, and Joint Ventures

ASAP World Consultancy operates all over the world.

The company is known for:

- Accelerated Skills Transfer
- Maximising Retained Value
- Transformation Management
- ASAP World Consultancy Implementation Methodology
- ASAP Institute

The company prides itself on the quality of its people. It uses a combination of its own employees, sovereigns and associates, who bring a wealth of experience and skills to meet the needs of its customers.

ASAP has a commitment to quality and is focused on meeting the business objectives of its clients through a number of highly specialized divisions and companies. ASAP specializes in technology driven change and in particular the ERP & CRM Markets.

ASAP World Consultancy can be contacted at the following address:

ASAP World Consultancy
ASAP House
P.O. Box 4463
Henley on Thames
Oxfordshire
RG9 1YW
UK
Tel: +44 (0)1491 414411
Fax: +44 (0)1491 414412
e-mail: enquiry@asap-consultancy.co.uk
Author Comments: authors@asap-consultancy.co.uk
Web site: http://www.asap-consultancy.co.uk/

ASAP - 24 Hour - Virtual Offices
New York City, NY
Voice Mail: (212) 253-4180; Fax: (212) 253-4180

Sydney, Australia
Voice Mail +61 (0)2 9475 0551
Fax: +61 (0)2 9475 0551

Brussels, Belgium
Voice Mail: +32 (0)2 706 5004
Fax: +32 (0)2 706 5004

See the advertisements at the back of this book for more details.

Jonathan Blain is the founder of the ASAP group of companies. He has been working in the SAP market since 1991. He has a strong business background, having spent 10 years in the oil industry working in a variety of different roles in the downstream sector for the Mobil Corporation before becoming a Management Consultant. He has specialist knowledge of large-scale SAP implementations, project management, human issues, planning, communications, security, training, documentation, and SAP recruitment. He has benefited from professional business training with the Henley Management College and other institutions.

As a management consultant, he has specialized in matching corporate business strategies to IT strategies. He has a special interest in business engineering and the effective management of change when implementing large-scale IT systems.

Coming from a business rather than systems background, he is focused on providing business solutions. He believes that the implementation of SAP can improve the way that companies do business and that, provided common sense and logical thinking are applied, SAP implementations need not be daunting.

Jonathan is a keen yachtsman. He has been instrumental in the development of the "Hy-Tech Sprint" yacht, a revolutionary 43-foot light displacement, water-ballasted ocean cruiser.

Bernard Dodd, after graduating in psychology at Aberdeen University, Bernard Dodd built and directed an industrial training research unit over a period of nine years at the Department of Psychology, University of Sheffield. Two years with an international business consultancy lead to an open competition direct entry to the specialist Civil Service where he served the Royal Navy for seventeen years to become the senior psychological advisor to the Second Sea Lord.

Since 1990 he has specialized in technical interviewing of experts and the writing of system documentation and user handbooks for the computer-intensive industries.

Acknowledgments

In writing this book we have benefited from the help and support of many people. There would not be space here to acknowledge everyone. They have each given their time and effort freely to make this book thorough, accurate, and useful to the readers. Equally, there are many companies who have given us much of their valuable time and shared their thoughts and opinions.

Our heartfelt thanks go to everyone who has helped. The writing of this book has been a team effort, and just praise should go to each and every team member.

Tell Us What You Think!

As the reader of this book, *you* are our most important critic and commentator. We value your opinion and want to know what we're doing right, what we could do better, what areas you'd like to see us publish in, and any other words of wisdom you're willing to pass our way.

As a Associate Publisher for Que, I welcome your comments. You can fax, email, or write me directly to let me know what you did or didn't like about this book—as well as what we can do to make our books stronger.

Please note that I cannot help you with technical problems related to the topic of this book, and that due to the high volume of mail I receive, I might not be able to reply to every message.

When you write, please be sure to include this book's title and author as well as your name and phone or fax number. I will carefully review your comments and share them with the author and editors who worked on the book.

Fax: 317-581-4666

Email: opsys@mcp.com

Mail: Associate Publisher
        Que
        201 West 103rd Street
        Indianapolis, IN 46290 USA

Exploring R3 PP

Using PP Within an R/3 Environment

SAP R/3 runs as a Basis core system into which are integrated a number of functional components. The actual components that are installed and configured depend on the requirements of the client company. This discussion will assume that the manufacturing functions will be of most interest.

The Basis core components are classified according to their main functions according to the following scheme:

- Database Administration
- Basis—Services and Communications
- ABAP/4 Development Workbench
- Business Engineering Workbench

An administrative component—Basis—is used to set up the necessary links between the various databases used by a particular implementation. Successive releases of R/3 have extended the functionality of the Basis module system so that the following additional components can be configured with release 3.1G:

- Business Framework
- Business Information Warehouse
- Business Self-Service Application

Releases 4.0 and 4.5 have extended the Internet and intranet functionality and added more specialized functions to the main applications.

In summary, the core R/3 system will be servicing the Basis module in all implementations. Most implementations will also have the core system with the financial accounting (FI) application installed and configured, together with components of the logistics system, such as materials management (MM) and sales and distribution (SD).

Deploying PP in Different Industries

The production planning and control (PP) application depends on the R/3 system. However, not all of the PP components may be needed in a particular company. The manufacturing companies are traditionally classified as follows (many companies employ all four types of manufacturing):

- Continuous process
- Repetitive manufacture
- Assemble to order
- Engineer to order

Each company will require cost accounting and materials management. Most companies will also use some form of resource planning and document management. Naturally, there will be a human resources function. Any or all of these functions can be integrated by configuring the appropriate R/3 modules.

If your manufacturing plant is complex, then you may need to have the progress of the products monitored and displayed across departments and between plant locations so that the linked activities may be smoothly managed. Your manufacturing and data processing systems will generate their own administration and maintenance workloads.

It is a design policy for all SAP systems to share a common and intuitive method of control and reporting, so that users may transfer easily from one type of task to another. Functions to model and simulate planned actions are often provided, and the system is primed to offer reasonable suggestions for all data input and control entries.

It has to be recognized that every software system will be under continuous development, even though the introduction of new functions will normally be arranged as a succession of software releases. The R/3 policy is for all software and master data changes to be strictly controlled by the system of authorizations and automatically documented under a change management discipline.

The complexity of the basic R/3 and its associated applications is managed by using a range of organizing techniques. For example, each data element is defined as an example of an abstract formal definition. The formal definition determines how the system will interpret and process any particular instance of the element. These data elements can range in complexity from a calendar date to a structure of technical information from which a complex assembly can be manufactured.

If the system of standard data formats has been standardized across all instances of R/3, the functions that handle this data can also be standardized and reused. When a particular element has to be handled differently according to circumstance, a table of parameters can be passed to the function so that the particular activities can be determined. For instance, the preferred format for displaying a date can be established according the login profile of the user who will read it.

The benefit of a standardized method of data storage and processing is that the user may rapidly adapt to new functions as they are introduced. The cost of this approach is that all data formats and processing controls have to be established when the system is first established, then followed exactly. The system will not accept inputs that do not conform to the structure expected.

The benefit in terms of system reliability is that the standard functions can be thoroughly tested and proved before the component is released. The only difficulty remaining should then be a matter of setting up the correct control parameters and master data for the implementation in which the system is going to operate.

SAP provides a comprehensive system of implementation guides (IMG) that direct the implementation engineers through the processes of setting a system up to work. The process is referred to as customizing, and includes entering the particular texts and labels that will be used in the various display screens.

In the context of particular industries, the system of standard programmed components is able to embody the best accounting and industrial management practices and make them available as options to be selected as appropriate during customizing.

Thus a specific user interface in a particular company will be supported by a number of generic building blocks, and perhaps some building blocks developed for a particular industry sector. There will be generic functions available and perhaps some functions developed specifically for the industry, or even for the individual company. Finally, the details of the processing will be controlled by the particular application modules that are active. Thus the screen from PP will look slightly different from a screen from PM, even though they are both integrated into the same R/3 implementation. The differences will include a particular set of menu paths and the use of terminology appropriate to the industrial activity. The customizing intention is to make the user's screen intuitive and helpful according to the activity in process.

Recognizing Differences Between Manufacturing Companies

There are many ways in which business data processing will be the same, whatever the company, and whatever the industrial processes. However, there are distinctive processes that are identified as such because they are significantly specialized in the data they require and the control actions that have to be exercised.

Process manufacturing tends to be identified with the following activities:

- Process management
- Process data documentation
- Process data evaluation
- Electronic batch recording (EBR) of production and quality data
- Batch management
- Integrated quality management
- Integration with a laboratory information management system (LIMS)
- Processing of coproducts and by-products
- Links to process control systems (PCSs)
- Links to process instruction (PI) sheets used by plant operators

Repetitive manufacturing or make-to-stock production is identified with the following activities:

- Orderless production, or internal order production not based on specific customer orders
- Revision-level handling to accommodate changes in constituents
- Backflushing to post goods issued some time after they have been withdrawn from stores for processing
- Reporting points set up to improve the control over a variable process
- KANBAN, or just-in-time (JIT) delivery, from one stage to another and self-regulating production control
- Automatic production authorization by schedule
- Period-based controlling

Assemble-to-order manufacturing is distinctive in the following ways:

- Order-driven configuration
- Releasing procedures, status maintenance
- Cost controlling per order
- Reworking to achieve specification if necessary
- Ordering confirmation
- Quality management
- Link to plant data collection (PDC) systems

Engineer-to-order manufacturing is exemplified by shipbuilding and toolmaking. Both types of manufacturing, although different in physical size and manufacturing timescale, depend on designing what the customer requires and building it on time to the required specification. The following processes are prominent in successful engineer-to-order production:

- Project management
- Project-specific MRP run
- Project-specific or customer-specific inventory
- Sales order BOM
- Product data management (PDM)
- Manpower planning
- Preliminary order
- Cash management
- Project-specific supply chain

The larger engineer-to-order companies will clearly benefit if their system includes the following integrated R/3 applications:

- Sales and distribution (SD)
- Project system (PS)
- Production planning and control (PP)
- Materials management (MM)
- Human resources (HR)

Emphasizing Different Aspects of Manufacturing

The requirements of a complex company may well include several types of industrial and commercial processes. For instance, a chemical production company will possibly require a process control system for the manufacturing stages, yet the packaging may be a matter of managing discrete items that have to be documented in terms of identified batches and numbered packages. Within the plant, the development and maintenance of the production facilities will probably be managed using projects and engineer-to-order where the customers are internal departments.

By contrast, an automotive company may be focused on assemble-to-order production of standard cars. Specific parts may be made to order, and production tools will be engineered to order. However, the painting of the vehicles may be more akin to a process manufacturing line.

A heavy- or high-technology engineering company will perhaps emphasize the design process and control it by a project system that may well extend into the stage of building a prototype. Production may be on an engineer-to-order basis using the prototype as the basis for the particular variations required by the customer. Some products may reach the stage of being assembled to order from fairly standard component subassemblies. Some large items may have to be preassembled under controlled conditions and shipped to the destination for final assembly. Yet within the production company, there may be several lines devoted to repetitive manufacture of the company's standard components. The on-site service of a complex system will perhaps be offered as a standard product. This would justify the use of a service management system that has access to the product data that was used in its initial production.

Designing SAP R/3 Components

From the point of view of the SAP system designer, there are some modules that are going to share some functions regardless of the method of manufacture or assembly they are serving. Cost accounting and materials management are examples. Some functions, such as resource planning and document management are similar for all the manufacturing types.

From the point of view of the customer company, a manufacturing support system should be able to show where all the various processes are throughout the plant and, indeed, across all plants. Some industries also need to know the production progress of their key suppliers. A dedicated subsystem may serve this function, or it may be necessary for particular employees to be assigned the task of tracking the supply chains of the key component materials.

The customer also will need to be assured that the whole system is going to be reliable and easy to maintain. In fact, the reliability of the SAP system is very high. What needs to be assured is the availability of a dedicated team of system professionals who can maintain the system and adjust it to changing circumstances.

If you are looking at a system from the end user's point of view, the following factors will need to be considered:

- Can the system be easily tailored for repetitive tasks so that the user gets as much help as possible and no irritation, such as unnecessary entry of data that is already in the system?
- Does each subsystem and task offer the same methods of getting help and advice throughout the company?
- Does each module use the same technical and commercial style and language, even when the terms are translated into the sign-on language?
- Is every function as intuitive or natural as possible, and are functions consistent in their controls?
- Will the intended users be able to understand what is required of them?

■ Can the tasks and dialogs be adjusted so that they accurately reflect how business is conducted in the company?

■ Can the displays and dialogs be given the particular terms and presentation conventions used by the company?

The presentation of the R/3 components will naturally be directed at the intended customers and users. However, there are some aspects of the SAP programming style that are best appreciated by considering the entire R/3 range of products.

Computing can often be more efficient if it is arranged to work at a high level of abstraction. In practice, there may have to be several levels of abstraction. At the bottom level will be particular data items, such as the trade name of a material. This name is always used in the format defined for it. However, this data element can be used in many different places. The function that seeks out this trade name is probably responding to the material number sent to it by a function at a higher level of abstraction—which is itself being called by still higher level processes. The format for a data item will be assigned from a predefined list of formats, so that the processing function will correctly interpret the data fields

All SAP R/3 processes work under this principle of abstraction. Each action uses building blocks that may themselves be structures of other building blocks, and so on. One of the ways in which the abstraction principle is demonstrated is in the process of customizing an application so that it exactly fits the company that is to use it. An implementation management guide (IMG) will ask for all the levels of abstraction to be defined so that the software will work correctly when needed. Thus you will have to decide how many types of material you intend to differentiate, how you will name them, and what codes you will use. When you declare an interest in a particular material, you will have to assign it to one of the material types you defined in customizing.

If you do not wish to define the levels of abstraction, the system will adopt the default or model structures so that the system will work correctly, if not at its most efficient.

A generic model is a pattern from which a family of similar patterns can be derived by copying the generic model and then making adjustments to the copy without disturbing the master. The R/3 system is delivered as a generic model from which the implementation team copies one or more instances, or instantiations, that are then customized to suit the client company.

Each component of R/3 is constructed as a generic model that can be used to generated variants. This modeling and copying procedure is used at all levels. If you need a new data format, for instance, the best way to create it is usually to copy and rename an existing standard format that you can then adjust to suit your purpose.

Standardizing functions is another SAP technique. If you have gained experience with one function, you will probably be able to find your way about another, especially if it is in the same business application area.

In addition to offering standard formats for data and software functions, R/3 tends to encourage the standardization of manufacturing processes. Each manufacturing process will be documented and managed in the same way as far as possible. This may not accord with the way your manufacturing processes have been managed in the past. Some process redesigning or at least reengineering may be needed to ensure that the full benefits of the R/3 system are made available.

Functions tend to be reused wherever possible. Thus the same list function will be used in many contexts. A report function may be used to alter data because it is already programmed to sort through the database and select particular items. The output of the report may be restricted to just a confirmation that the intended alterations have been made.

Architecture in the context of business data processing tends to refer to the way data is stored and processed. An appropriate architecture is designed for the benefit of the mechanisms that will access this data rather than the convenience of the mechanisms that are storing it.

In the context of a manufacturing concern, you might argue that all data should be stored according to the customer's order. Yet this might entail searching through orders to determine what stock to replenish. If your buyers can strike better bargains at certain times in the market cycles, perhaps you will purchase to stock and hope that orders will arrive to consume it. Your particular interest might be the maintenance of the plant. You could argue that all data should focus on plant items. Orders are relevant only insofar as they document the timetable of demands on the plant.

Architecture may also affect how work is performed. Your company may need to employ many staff on only some of the business functions. Alternatively, you may expect almost all staff to be able to handle a very wide range of functions; for example, whatever the customer needs at the moment when you are in contact with him or her.

Thus R/3 and its various component applications may have to be configured in different ways for different working structures. Clearly there has to be control over who is authorized to access each function, data type, and perhaps customer. This is managed by a system of profiles that allow access to specified data and functions. A particular employee may be assigned several profiles. Each profile is restricted by a time period of validity.

Although a particular user may need only a few functions, these functions may call upon many elements of an integrated R/3 system. It has to be possible to configure whatever applications have been installed so that they work together in what hopefully will be a seamless way that does not hold up the user, nor impose unnecessary work. One of the techniques to assist integration is to insist that master data is stored at an appropriate level. If some information is never going to be needed outside a particular application, it can be stored there. If the information is going to be needed at a known destination, then a specific interface can be defined to control the communication. However, if some information might be needed anywhere in the company, then it should be stored and maintained up to date in a database that is routinely available to all.

The final way in which the design of R/3 is directed at the client company is in the support and maintenance of the system itself. There is a system of online help and support that is managed in the same way for all applications. New software releases are controlled throughout the SAP R/3 user community.

Identifying the Building Blocks of Manufacturing

The fundamental components of manufacturing software are divided into three groups according to their main purpose:

- Product data management
- Planning
- Execution

Product data management includes the following concepts:

- Bill of materials
- Product documents
- Product configuration
- Product classes

Planning includes the following concepts:

- Forecasting
- Master scheduling
- Allocating materials and resources
- Material and resource planning

Execution includes the following types of manufacturing activity:

- Repetitive manufacturing
- Flow control
- Process management
- Materials management
- Quality management
- Plant maintenance

Manufacturing systems can be supported and modeled by an integrated system of building blocks, each specialized for a certain type of business data processing. There are some generic functions that are largely adopted from R/3 Basis because they can be applied in most applications. In addition, there are functions that are specific to manufacturing enterprises.

The more important generic functions are concerned with the following processes:

- Effectiveness determination of a process or product
- Status management
- Material availability check
- Scheduling
- Confirmation of significant events elsewhere in the system

- Cost calculation and settlement
- Change documentation and management
- Where-used lists for plant items and materials

The following processes are largely confined to manufacturing concerns:

- Computer assisted production planning (CAPP)
- Action control
- Trigger point management
- Production campaign planning and control
- Material quantity calculation

The main business process areas are as follows:

- Sales and operations planning
- Production planning
- Manufacturing operation management
- Product data management (PDM)
- Product configuration
- Integrated sales and manufacturing
- Integrated quality management
- Integrated reporting and decision support
- Integrated controlling

The following specific products are used according to the type of manufacturing process:

- Project System Graphical Planning Board
- Repetitive Planning Board
- Process Sheet (Automotive)
- Process Instruction Sheet (Process)

Building a Product Data Management System

Product data management (PDM) is a term that emphasizes a particular way of organizing information, namely, according to products. There are generic building blocks of functions available to all applications, and there are some functions that are specialized for product data management.

The generic PDM functions can be found in the R/3 system under the following topic headings:

- Material master
- Material specification
- Classification

- Bill of materials
- Document management
- Engineering change management
- Workflow
- Product configuration

The specific PDM functions can be found in the PP module under the following topic headings:

- CAD integration
- Engineering workbench
- Customer order BOM
- Line design
- Recipes
- Resource networks
- Substance database

Arranging R/3 Systems in Manufacturing Networks

The three main activities of product data management, planning, and execution can be supported by a central R/3 system. A large system may be configured as a network of three R/3 systems, one for each of the main activities. If there are many production facilities, they may be controlled in decentralized clusters, each with its own R/3 system specialized in execution.

Configuring R/3 According to Industry Sector

When a standard R/3 is delivered, it is a fully operational system. But it is not fine-tuned for a specific company. The customizing process affects this adaptation under the implementation management guide (IMG). However, several companies in the same industry sector may well end up with similar customizations. SAP has recognized this possibility and now markets preconfigured R/3 systems that are directed at specific industry sectors.

Each of these industry solutions is delivered with the full standard customizing functionality, so that local variations in terminology and business practice may be accommodated. However, a specialized R/3 industry solution will be delivered with specific customizations already in place and fully documented. For example, the material database will probably be set up with the classes and categories of product usual in the target industry.

Preconfigured systems are available that have been optimized for a specific type of business. Industry solutions are available for the many industry sectors, for example:

- Automotive
- Chemical
- High tech or electronics
- Aerospace and defense

- Process manufacturing
- Repetitive manufacturing (make-to-stock)
- Assemble-to-order
- Engineer-to-order
- Consumer packaged goods
- Mechanical and plant engineering
- Pharmaceuticals
- Banking
- Construction
- Education and training
- Healthcare
- Environmental health
- Insurance
- Investment management
- Oil and gas
- Public sector
- Real estate
- Retail
- Sales and distribution
- Telecommunications
- Transportation
- Utilities

The industry solutions require relatively little customizing to become fully adapted to an individual client business.

In the aviation industry, the SAP R/2 mainframe system has been used in the for the following purposes:

- Production planning and control
- Materials management
- Maintenance planning and processing
- Sales, dispatch, and invoicing
- Financial accounting
- Assets accounting
- Human resources administration and payroll accounting
- Cost accounting and profitability analysis with order accounting
- Project management and control

The SAP R/3 IS-Aviation industry solution provides a client/server configuration to cover the same areas. It includes the following enhancements:

- Spec2000 communication standard applied to real-time logistics modules
- Serialized parts management
- Manufacturer part number management

The marketing strategy of offering R/3 in a largely preconfigured form has been extended beyond the essentially modular industry solution concept. The idea is to offer a company a complete data processing and management support system that is optimized for its particular type of enterprise and that has extended the customizing so as to include all the applications that are needed in a comprehensive system. These industry business units (IBU) are identified by the inclusion of the word SAP in their titles, for example:

- SAP Chemicals
- SAP Consumer Products
- SAP High Tech and Electronics
- SAP Oil and Gas
- SAP Pharmaceuticals
- SAP Banking
- SAP Insurance
- SAP Public Sector
- SAP Automotive
- SAP Healthcare
- SAP Retail
- SAP Telecommunication
- SAP Utilities
- SAP Aerospace and Defense
- SAP Engineering and Construction
- SAP Metal, Paper, and Wood Products

These industry business units comprise an R/3 system with which has been integrated the following types of element:

- Core components, such as R/3 Basis
- Core building blocks, such as logistics and financial accounting
- Core functions, such as change management
- Industry templates that set up a particular customizing framework
- IBU add-ons, such as numbered component tracking that may be used in more than one IBU
- Additional third-party components to provide any functionality not available from SAP

Many of the IBUs have been installed with one or more of the following SAP applications:

- Engineering Workbench
- Business Framework
- Business Information Warehouse
- Business Engineer
- Business Self-Service ●

CHAPTER 2

Introducing the Concepts and Components of PP

Production Planning and Control

Versatility is the distinctive feature of the production planning and control (PP) module. It is designed to be used in any sector of industry. All modules are real-time applications, that is, quantities and values are saved immediately so that all users of the system have access to the same data that is always up to date.

There are standard interfaces between PP and the following R/3 applications:

- Sales and distribution (SD)
- Materials management (MM)
- Controlling (CO)
- Project system (PS)
- Personnel planning and development (PD)

These standard interfaces are completely integrated into SAP and can be modified to fit any company's needs.

The PP module is organized into the following groups of components:

- Basic data (PP-BD)
- Sales and operations planning (PP-SOP)
- Master planning (PP-MP)
- Capacity planning (PP-CRP)—formerly capacity requirements planning
- Material requirements planning (PP-MRP)
- Production orders (PP-SFC)—formerly shop floor control
- KANBAN (PP-KAN)
- Repetitive manufacturing (PP-REM)
- Assembly processing module (PP-ATO)
- Production planning for process industries (PP-PI)
- Plant data collection (PP-PDC)
- Information systems (PP-IS)

Each of these components contains subcomponents that are defined in the sections that follow.

The functions of the production planning and control system support planning for the types and quantities of products as a demand program as well as planning for their production. Production planning includes procurement, warehousing, and the transport of materials and inter-mediate products between one stage of production and the next. PP also includes the resource allocation to complete the production processes in a timely manner.

Storing Basic Data

The PP-BD component contains the master data needed for production planning in discrete manufacturing. The master data tends to remain constant and is always used in the same way.

Using Bills of Material

The PP-BD-BOM component supports the use of the bill of material concept in a wide range of circumstances where there is a tree structure of associated items. For example, BOMs can be generated in the following forms:

- Material BOM
- Equipment BOM
- Functional location BOM
- Document structure
- Sales order BOM

In each instance, the BOM comprises a structured list specifying each component needed: name, quantity, and unit of measure, for example.

Each industry sector may have its own preferred name for the structured list that is maintained by R/3 as a BOM; recipe, list of ingredients, and furnish are examples of list names.

The role of the BOM, or its equivalent, is to provide master data for such organizational areas as the following:

- Materials planning
- Staging of materials for production
- Product costing
- Plant maintenance

PP-BD-BOM has to be installed, not only for production planning, but also if you intend to maintain complex document structures or technical specifications that require a hierarchical structure, as in assembly processing and plant maintenance. The document management submodule can be installed and configured to provide a wide range of facilities for manipulating all types of drawings and other document resources.

Setting Up Work Centers

The work center component (PP-BD-WKC) defines the organizational units where operations are carried out that produce outputs of work. Each work center is assigned to a cost center for specific time periods.

The work center can be used to specify which machines or people take part in the operations and to collect the information needed to determine costs, capacities, and dates for the operations.

If you are linked with the personnel planning and development module (PD), you can assign qualifications, positions, and people from the PD module to particular work centers.

Referring to Routings

A routing defines a sequence of work steps and resources required to produce a material item or quantity without reference to an order. The routing component (PP-BD-RTG) allows you to refer to a stored routing when planning and executing a production order.

The following routing types are defined in production planning and control:

- Routings and reference operation sets
- Rate routings and reference rate routings

The standard values for the planned times for the execution of individual operations have to be entered in a routing. These standard values are used in a production order for the following operations:

- Lead-time scheduling
- Product costing
- Capacity planning

The standard values suggested by the system can be altered in the production order if necessary. A product costing submodule is available to extend the range of functions.

A routing is akin to a task list because it defines what has to be done. Master recipes in PP-PI and networks in the project system (PS) serve a similar purpose.

Using Computer Aided Production Planning

Computer aided production planning (PP-BD-CAP) is a component that uses the computer aided process planning functionality (CAPP) to derive standard values for work scheduling. Tables and formulas are provided that can calculate the standard values for a routing.

Assigning Production Resources and Tools

Production resources/tools (PP-BD-PRT) is a basic data component in which all movable operating resources are specified. These PRTs can be devices used to form objects that become finished or partially finished products. The PRT category also includes tools and fixtures that are used in measurement and inspection to check the size, structure, or efficiency of products being manufactured. A set of technical drawings and specifications is also defined as a PRT.

Planning Sales and Operations

The sales and operations planning component (PP-SOP) is used to forecast and plan sales and the production operations needed to meet the planned targets. SOP can also be used to set up targets for any link in the supply chain. You can carry out rough planning to arrive at a reasonable prediction of the amounts of resources and the capacities you will need at the various work centers included in the plan.

The data for these plans can be developed from historical records, or you can begin from the existing production data. Alternatively, you can work on estimated future production and create a plan to achieve it.

The PP-SOP component can produce plans that address each level of a complex planning hierarchy through the supply chains to the production resources, including staff. The component can also produce detailed plans based on the targets of finished products.

You can use the bottom-up method to find out what is needed to produce your targets; or you can see what could be produced given your existing or planned financial, plant, and energy resources—the top-down method.

The system can be configured to accept target key figures at any organizational level. These targets will then be distributed automatically and consistently to all the other organizational levels up and down the hierarchy.

Standard sales and operations planning is delivered as a preconfigured procedure that is customized only so as to fit your company. Standard planning is based on product group hierarchies and is always carried out level by level.

Flexible SOP can be freely configured. For example, any hierarchies containing any chosen organizational levels can be targeted by a single plan. Thus you could develop a plan for a particular sales organization, distribution channel, material, and plant.

In the flexible planning option, you are able to specify the content and layout of the planning screens to suit your users. If your planning hierarchies stretch across a distributed environment, your customizing must also configure Application Link Enabling (ALE).

The PP-SOP component comprises four subcomponents, all of which are essential for standard sales and operation planning:

- Basic data (PP-SOP-BD)—contains the administrative and technical functions
- Sales plan (PP-SOP-SP)—allows you to set sales targets for product groups or finished products and submits planned sales quantities to demand management
- Production plan (PP-SOP-PP)—allows you to set the production quantities required to meet your sales targets and submits planned production quantities to demand management
- Distribution requirements planning (PP-SOP-DRP)—allows you to optimize inventory replenishment in a network of warehouses

Master Planning the Production Quantities

The role of the master planning component (PP-MP) is to define the production quantities for a stated interval. Four subcomponents are needed for this kind of master planning:

- Material forecast (PP-MP-MFC)—uses known rates of consumption to forecast what should be available for production. The forecast values are submitted to the demand management component or to the consumption-based material requirements planning component, where they can be used to calculate the reorder point and the safety stock levels automatically.
- Demand management (PP-MP-DEM)—defines future requirement quantities and dates for finished products and important assemblies, including items procured elsewhere. The demand program can be created automatically from preceding sales planning, SOP, and material forecasts. A demand program can also be created under manual control.

■ Master production scheduling (PP-MP-MPS)—allows you to mark certain parts or products as master schedule items for special attention because they take up critical resources or dominate profits. Includes functions for separate planning, planning time fence and fixing logic, interactive planning, and a special evaluation layout for master schedule items.

■ Long-term planning, or simulation (PP-MP-LTP)—uses current operations data to anticipate the detailed consequences of the master plan. The module calculates capacity requirements, activity requirements for the cost centers, and the number of purchased parts required.

The long-term planning functions allow you to generate both annual plans and a rolling quarterly plan that previews the future stock and requirements. The system can automatically use future requirements for materials to suggest production details such as reorder point materials, bulk material, or KANBAN materials.

The purchasing departments will also use long-term planning results when negotiating delivery schedules and contracts with vendors.

Capacity Planning

The capacity planning component (PP-CRP) has the role of determining available capacities in relation to the capacity requirements, and, if necessary, leveling the assignments between work centers.

Capacity planning differentiates between the following time frames:

■ Long-term rough-cut planning
■ Medium-term planning
■ Short-term detailed planning

The following applications can use the capacity planning functions:

■ Sales and distribution (SD)
■ Production planning and control (PP)
■ Plant maintenance (PM)
■ Project system (PS)
■ Personnel planning and development (PD)

The CRP component comprises the following subcomponents:

■ Scheduling (PP-CRP-SCH)—uses standard times from task lists and may operate lead-time scheduling disregarding capacity loads and finite scheduling which does take account of capacity loads. PP-CRP-SCH is used with production orders, for example.

■ Capacity loads (PP-CRP-LD)—calculates as a percentage the ratio between requirement and availability of each capacity.

■ Capacity evaluations (PP-CRP-ALY)—prepares the data for capacity leveling by comparing available and required capacities.

- Capacity leveling (PP-CRP-LVL)—distributes the capacity underloads and overloads to work centers. Also suggests the optimum commitment of machines and production lines and selects appropriate resources.

The ALY and LVL subcomponents are not needed if capacity leveling is a manual task that uses the capacity load outputs of the LD function.

Ensuring that Materials Are Available by MRP

The material requirements planning component (PP-MRP) has to guarantee material availability for sales and distribution and for internal purposes. In particular, stocks have to be monitored and replenished by timely purchasing and production, preferably by automatically creating order proposals for purchasing and production.

Materials planning can be seen from two aspects: the amounts of materials and other resources consumed over recent similar periods, and the planned production levels for the future. The module is able to support planning across more than one production or storage plant.

Overall, materials planning entails finding optimum levels for two interacting factors:

- Level of service to the internal or external customers
- Profitability, by minimizing costs and capital lockup

MRP can take place for all the relevant materials that are planned for a particular plant—total planning—or for a single material or product group—single-item planning.

The MRP component uses the following subcomponents:

- Basic data (PP-MRP-BD)—maintains the data used in MRP controlling, lot-sizing, and special procurement types
- Planning execution (PP-MRP-PR)—executes MRP for all materials or assemblies whose requirement or stock situation has changed since the last MRP run
- Procurement proposal (PP-MRP-PP)—takes manual entries from the MRP controller or the quantities and dates suggested automatically by the MRP component, and compiles proposals for in-house (internal) procurement and external procurement
- Planning evaluation (PP-MRP-PE)—provides checks on the planning results

Checks on the MRP results are provided by the PE subcomponent in the following formats:

- MRP list
- Current stock/requirements list
- Comparison of the MRP list and the stock/requirements list
- Planning situation, in a format that can be configured to provide the most useful evaluation
- Planning result, also configurable
- Comparison of the planning situation and the planning result
- Pegged requirements that are limited by requirements defined higher up the BOM
- Order report on relevant orders still open

Part
I

Ch
2

Managing Production Orders

A production order is a specification of what is to be produced and on what dates, the dispatching point, and the production costs. The production orders module (PP-SFC) was formerly the shop floor control module. SFC accepts a planned order or an internal request posted at a previous MRP planning level, to which the shop floor control adds order-specific data, such as dates and quantities.

The production orders (PP-SFC) module comprises the following components:

- Order planning (PP-SFC-PLN)
- Order execution (PP-SFC-EXE)
- Order close (PP-SFC-CPL)

Order Planning

Order planning (PP-SFC-PLN) selects a routing, explodes a bill of material, reserves materials and resources, determines planned costs, generates capacity requirements for work centers, and identifies nonstock components and external processing operations, both of which will require purchase requisitions.

The PP-SFC-PLN component automatically schedules a production order as soon as it is created. The basic order dates are used as starting points for the schedule. You can arrange for the order to be automatically rescheduled if any relevant changes occur or you can trigger rescheduling manually at any time.

The order planning component is further subdivided into the following subcomponents:

- Header/operation
- Components
- Production resources/tools
- Trigger points

The header screen of the header/operation component displays the main order elements of an order. These material production data elements will be automatically copied from master data, if it exists.

The header data for each material includes the following information:

- The material number of the material to be produced
- The order quantity
- The basic start or finish date, depending on scheduling type
- The expected scrap quantity
- The order priority
- The order status
- The plant in which the material is to be produced

The operation overview screen of the header/operation component includes the following information:

- The operation and suboperation numbers that specify the sequence in which operations are to be performed
- The work centers at which the operations are to be carried out
- The current status of the operations
- The start and finish dates of the operations
- The control key of each operation to identify its purpose, such as external processing, completion confirmation, printing, scheduling, costing
- A short description of each operation

The components of a production order represent the materials that are required in production. If their details already exist as master data, they will be automatically copied to the order by the PP-SFC-PLN components software. These components will be automatically copied to the first operation when the order is created, unless they have already been allocated to the appropriate operation by the routing document. These allocations of components to operations can be revised manually.

Production Resources/Tools is a functional module that manages the production resources and tools (PRT) used in production, but which can be moved from one work center to another. PRTs include technical drawings and specifications, measurement and inspection tools, and operating tools and fixtures that are needed in the production operation. An numerical control program (NC) would also be classified as a PRT. A movable rig that is used to test a product for structure or efficiency would be another example of a PRT.

Production resources/tools can be assigned to operations in task lists or to the production orders for which they are needed.

Trigger Points is an optional function that is used in the automation of operations. A trigger point is a data object that is allocated to an operation so as to initiate another activity. This other activity may be part of the operation itself, in which case the trigger will be allocated to a particular step. The effect may be to alter a status indicator when a certain stage is reached. A trigger point can also be configured to create an order, perhaps for replenishment, or for preparations that should begin for a subsequent operation. There may be the requirement to control operations so that they are released only at defined moments in time or logically defined moments, in which case a trigger point can be employed.

A complete workflow structure of tasks may be initiated by a trigger point. You may also wish to arrange a trigger in completion confirmation so that any defects in the operation can be reworked.

The order execution function (PP-SFC-EXE) begins when an order is released. The shop floor papers have to be generated. Goods movements have to take place. And the results of completing the order have to be confirmed.

Shop floor papers are printed or displayed electronically. They can include some or all of the following:

- Operation control ticket
- Job ticket
- Pick list
- Time ticket
- Confirmation slip

Goods movements include taking the materials needed from stock and delivering the finished product back into stock, which entails posting a goods receipt. Alternatively, you can arrange for goods movements to be posted automatically when the completion of an operation is confirmed. Backflushing is the process of posting a goods issue document for component goods that were previously released from stock for production. The confirmation of an operation or an order is the trigger for backflushing its constituent material components.

The confirmation of an order entails posting the actual order data that are obtainable only when the operation or order is completed. The scrap, the yield, and the processing time are normally recorded in the confirmation document.

The order close function (PP-SFC-CPL) controls some accounting actions. The costs incurred by manufacturing to a production order are settled on one or more cost objects. For example, the costs of the material mentioned in a sales order will be settled on that sales order. At the same time, an offsetting entry is generated automatically to credit the production order. Some of the costs may be settled on other cost objects, according to the accounting procedure established in customizing.

Controlling Production and Material Flow with KANBAN

The KANBAN technique is a method of holding up the production or replenishment of a material until the moment when it is actually required. "Just-in-time" is another term for this method of production management. There are some obvious advantages in avoiding nugatory work on products that may not be sold; and there can be advantages in not holding reserves of stock or raw materials. The disadvantages center on the risk of a delay in delivery should anything go wrong in the procurement or production processes.

The KANBAN just-in-time technique can be applied to single-stage production or to a chain of production processes, in which case the demands or releases have to be linked in a backward direction from the required delivery date.

The purpose of the KANBAN module (PP-KAB) is to support a self-regulating environment controlling production and procurement in which manual administrative effort is at a minimum so as to promote minimal lead times and zero inventories.

KANBAN may not be worthwhile. Cost-effectiveness depends on the following conditions:

- There should be a relatively constant consumption level of the material that is to be controlled by KANBAN, at least for longer than it takes to replenish the stock.

- The production processes should have minimum setup times.
- Production should be reliable.
- Production should tend towards many small lots within a short period.

The KANBAN module depends on the following functional components:

- Control cycle—KANBAN (PP-KAB-CC)
- KANBAN control (PP-KAB-CRL)
- KANBAN board (PP-KAB-KPB)
- Creation of master data, or backflushing (PP-KAB-BF)
- Evaluations (PP-KAB-KE)

Part
I
Ch
2

A KANBAN control cycle is a specification of the relationship between the supply source and the demand source. A control cycle defines the following elements:

- The replenishment strategy
- The number and contents of the circulating containers
- The format of the KANBAN card printout
- The delivery address
- User-defined data elements

The KANBAN control component (PP-KAB-CRL) manages the status change trigger signals for the containers so that they are set to "full" or "empty." This KANBAN signal may be derived from scanning a bar code. The system then acquires the control cycle information so that it can automatically post the data to initiate a replenishment. When a container has been filled, the system posts the appropriate goods receipts for the replenishment.

The KANBAN board (PP-KAB-KPB) is a component that displays the control cycles sorted according to the supply areas to which they are allocated. You can see all the containers in use and their status as full or empty. The board can also be used to trigger the KANBAN signal.

The creation of master data component (PP-KAB-BF) is responsible for controlling backflushing. When a product is completed, backflushing automatically posts the goods receipt for it and, at the same time, posts the goods issue for the components used to manufacture it. The effect is to maintain the accounts in balance with a minimum of effort.

The method of replenishment affects the cost accounting procedure for in-house production using KANBAN. There are three possibilities:

- If the process operates with run schedule quantities, the costs are collected at a so-called production cost collector and can be settled periodically by product costing.
- If manual KANBAN is operating, the costs are also collected at a cost collector.
- If replenishment control is operating with production orders, the costs are assigned to the production order.

You can monitor the success of a KANBAN operation with the evaluations component (PP-KAB-KE). The following tools are provided:

- Error display
- Plant overview per control cycle, with user-selectable format
- Evaluations from other areas

Managing Long Period Repetitive Manufacturing

The repetitive manufacturing module (PP-REM) is designed to manage planning and control for repetitive manufacturing environments that are characterized by the following features:

- Master plans are created and processed. They specify periods and quantities of the materials to be produced. These master plans are typically released automatically for production.
- The quantities in the master plans are processed by easy-to-use backflushing functions.
- Constituent materials are dispatched to production lines.
- Planning includes both capacities and quantities.
- Information is maintained on the range of coverages expressed as the number of days for which an adequate supply of material is available for a particular production activity.
- Materials are typically procured for more than one order at a time.
- Material allocations are not usually firmed, so that activities may use whatever is necessary.
- The planning and control of the manufacturing is normally period based.

PP-REM is supported by the following functional components:

- Run schedule header (PP-REM-ORD)
- Planning for repetitive manufacturing (PP-REM-PLN)
- Planning run schedule quantities (PP-REM-PLN)
- Planning partial orders (PP-REM-PLN)
- Creation of master data (PP-REM-ADE)
- Evaluations (PP-REM-ALY)

Most repetitive environments will require all of these functions to be installed and configured, especially if production is both to stock and to specific order.

Understanding the Run Schedule Header

The run schedule header function in PP-REM-ORD creates a run schedule (RS) header document, which is essential if a material is to be planned for repetitive manufacturing. This header is also required for settling the finished and semifinished products as they are produced over a long period.

The RS header does not contain production quantities or any dates. The system accepts the RS quantities assigned to the RS header and creates the necessary plans with quantities and dates.

The RS header does not have to be assigned an individual production cost collector. Costs can be settled in the following ways:

- Via a production cost collector per RS header
- Via a production cost collector that is created for several RS headers
- Via production orders

Planning for Repetitive Manufacturing

The planning for the repetitive manufacturing in PP-REM-PLN functional component works with the master plan. The PLN component displays the master plan as a periodic planning table showing all run schedule headers, materials, product groups, production lines, and groups of production lines.

The PLN planning table shows all the important information, in particular, the capacities and available quantities of necessary materials. You can access this planning table interactively and use it to control the production lines.

Planning with Run Schedule Quantities

The planning run schedule quantities component in PP-REM-PLN allows you to specify the production quantities for a run schedule header that are to be produced in a certain period. When the production takes place, the actual data and cost settlement data are collected by the production cost collector.

Your company will probably conduct planning with run schedule quantities if the same routings and same work centers are deployed as production lines that continue repetitive manufacturing over a relatively long period.

Planning with Partial Orders

The planning partial orders component in PP-REM-PLN is designed to support planning partial orders in a run schedule header. Part of the RS header planned quantity is converted into a production order to be delivered on certain dates.

Planning a production order with partial orders is often used when producing complex, multi-level products, each with a separate routing to be settled separately. Another reason to use partial orders is if each production lot is to be settled using a separate production order.

Backflushing

The functional component responsible for controlling backflushing in repetitive manufacturing is creation of master data in PP-REM-ADE. The following backflushing options are provided to post the accounts to the production cost collector:

- Post goods receipts with automatic reduction of the open master plan
- Post goods issues
- Post actual costs to the production cost collector
- Update the statistics without any financial transaction

If a production cost collector is not to be used, the following options are available to initiate backflushing in repetitive manufacturing:

- Post goods receipts
- Post goods issues
- Post confirmations

Evaluating Repetitive Manufacturing Progress

The purpose of the evaluations component in PP-REM-ALY is to provide the following progress reports:

- Pull list
- Reporting point overview of goods in process
- Component reprocessing list
- Document log
- Controlling reports

The following statistics and analyses can be accessed from the logistics information system (LIS):

- Goods receipt statistics
- Reporting point statistics
- Material consumption analysis
- Production costs analysis

Assembly Processing in Make-to-Order Production

Assembly processing is a method of providing a make-to-order service to the customer. It has the particular advantage of offering reliable delivery dates because the finished product is managed as an assembly of components. And each component is automatically checked for availability to promise at the time the sales order is being considered. Automobiles and personal computers are examples of products that are beneficially managed by assembly processing.

The logistics system cooperates with the assembly processing module (PP-ATO) to automatically create a procurement element, such as a planned order, when creating the sales order. Furthermore, should any changes arise in either delivery dates or quantities, the alterations are immediately apparent in the sales order document. By the same mechanism, if the customer requires any alterations in the sales order, the changes are automatically submitted to the production system.

Production by lots and projects is supported in the context of repetitive manufacturing.

Assembly Processing in Repetitive Manufacturing

The repetitive manufacturing component (PP-ATO-REM) allows you to use the planning and control tools from the repetitive manufacturing module. When you create a sales order, the system automatically creates a planned order. This means you can take materials from a repetitive manufacturing run that is under control of a run schedule header and use them to meet a make-to-order sales order. When the order is delivered, the backflushing process of the RS header will post the outcomes directly to the sales order.

Assembly processing in repetitive manufacturing is a technique that is most effective under the following conditions:

- The production process of the finished product is simple with clear production processes.
- The production of the assemblies is carried out in a constant flow through the production lines.
- Simple routings are used, or the assembly can be carried out without routings.
- The components are anonymous—any example will suffice.
- The components are procured using KANBAN production techniques and consumption-based planning or via assembly planning.
- The production control effort is to be kept to a minimum and backflushing is to be simplified.

Assembly Processing in Production by Lots

The production by lots component (PP-ATO-LOT) is able to use production orders to control the production. When a sales order is posted, the system automatically creates a production order. Alternatively, a planned order can be created that will later be converted to a production order when the manufacturing capacities have been confirmed.

Complex production procedures are beneficially controlled by the PP-ATO-LOT component. The advantages of using production orders include the option of adopting the following control techniques:

- Collective orders
- Status management of the production order
- Using various business operations at operation level

Using assembly processing with production orders for individual lots is typically associated with the following situations:

- Process flow production
- Manufacture of coproducts
- Production with parallel production lines

Production Planning for the Process Industries

Some industries are obliged to manage and document their products in batches because conditions and raw materials may change during a production run to such an extent that the characteristics of different batches may vary considerably. The application module Production Planning for Process Industries (PP-PI) is designed to apply the PP techniques of planning, control, and execution management under the particular circumstances of batch-oriented process manufacturing.

Four examples define the scope of PP-PI:

- Chemicals
- Pharmaceuticals
- Food and beverages
- Process-oriented electronics

The functions that are particularly emphasized in PP-PI are as follows:

- Integrated planning of production, waste disposal, and transportation within a plant
- Integration of plants vertically within the company by continuous information flow management
- Integration of plants horizontally within the company by coordinating planning between production plants, recycling, waste disposal facilities, and production laboratories

The following higher-level planning components are usually integrated with PP-PI:

- Sales and operations planning
- Master planning
- Material requirements planning

PP-PI may need data and services provided by other functional modules, such as the following:

- Material master (Logistics, General, and Basic Data) and materials management for the planning of input materials required and products to be manufactured
- Batches (Logistics, General) for batch-oriented manufacturing
- Classification system (cross-application functions) to search or select classified data more easily
- Engineering change management (Logistics, General) to create a change history as well as to implement a release procedure
- Variant configuration (Logistics, General) enabling you to create different production variants using material master formulas (recipes)
- Quality management, to carry out in-process inspections
- Controlling, to carry out order settlement

Storing Master Data in PP-PI

The basic data component in PP-PI-MD controls the storage of the PI data that is unlikely to change over time and is used in the same form in many places. Some of the master data items in PP-PI correspond to similar items in the discrete manufacturing data stored in Basic Data (PP-BD). Table 2.1 illustrates this correspondence.

Table 2.1	Corresponding Master Data in PP-PI and PP-BD
PP-PI process manufacturing data	**PP-BD discrete manufacturing data**
Resource	Work center
Master recipe with material list	Routing and bill of material (BOM)

Defining PI Resources

A resource is an object or person that is involved in the production process and that has specific capacities allocated to it. Resources identify units of capacity and, therefore, are allocated to operations and phases in the master recipe and process order. As a result of collected data or shrewd experience, the assumption is that the resources assigned to the master recipe and process order will be just sufficient to ensure that the product successfully meets the delivery deadline and the quality standards.

The resources component of PP-PI-MD allows you to define resources and then assign them to master recipes and process orders. This resource data is used as the basis for the calculation of costs, capacity requirements, and dates.

The work center is equivalent to a PI resource. However, the PI module will allow you to create a resource network that specifies the sequence in which the various resources are to be used. A work center in discrete manufacturing is not able to represent a network, although it can be an element in a network.

Storing Master Recipes

A master recipe is a scheme that details how a company's various manufacturing processes are to be deployed in order to produce the intended product. The master recipe does not depend on the requirements of any particular production order or customer order. It is intended to define the most efficient way of manufacturing one of the company's standard products.

A master recipe can also be used to specify what has to be done to clean out a production facility and prepare it for another batch of product or to effect a changeover in preparation for using the facility for another product.

Each company will have its own master recipes that may differ because they produce different materials and because they may use different resources, even to manufacture the same product. Indeed, parallel production lines in the same plant may use different master recipes for the same reasons.

The master recipe component in PP-PI-MD enables you to maintain and assign master recipes.

The scope of the data held in a master recipe in the R/3 system is defined in accordance with the following standards authorities:

- The International Standards of the European Batch Forum (EBF)
- The Norms Working Committee for Measuring and Control Techniques in the Chemical Industry (NAMUR)
- Standard S88 of the Instrument Society of America (ISA)

In summary, the master recipe data will normally include the following information:

- The individual steps in the production process defined as operations and phases.
- The sequence in which the steps are to be carried out.
- The planned durations as standard values.
- Other activities associated with the production process, such as plant cleaning, defined with standard values.
- The resources required for the individual steps in the production process.
- The ingredients required for production, specific in a material list.
- Instructions for in-process quality inspections, such as the characteristics that are to be monitored and the scheduling of inspections.
- Parameters relevant to the control of the production process defined as process instructions. These parameters are specified during process planning and have to be communicated to process control for each run.

The master recipe is used as the main source of information when creating a process order.

Planning and Executing a Process Order

The process order function in PP-PI-POR takes the information from the master recipe and creates a process order for a production run or for the output of a service. The process order is the principal document used in the detailed planning and execution of process manufacturing.

The process order becomes the repository of the following kinds of information:

- Planned quantities
- Planned dates
- Planned resources
- Control data for the process order execution
- Rules for the account assignment and settlement of the costs incurred

Specifying the Steps of Process Order Execution

The order execution function in PP-PI-POR manages the central processing steps entailed in process order execution. These steps are as follows:

- Creating process orders using a master recipe, creating reservations or copying them from planned orders, calculating planned costs, creating capacity requirements for the resources needed
- Scheduling from the basic order dates, with the option of subsequent automatic or manual rescheduling
- Releasing process order to begin process order execution and process management
- Creating and downloading control recipes (optional)
- Printing shop floor documents
- Carrying out material withdrawals under control of goods issues from the warehouse
- Recording confirmations
- Carrying out in-process quality inspections (optional)
- Posting goods receipts—initiating delivery of the manufactured product to the warehouse by posting a goods receipt

Control recipes have to be created during process order execution if you use process instruction sheets and/or process control systems. In this case, you must also install the corresponding components from Process Management.

If you intend to carry out in-process quality inspections for your orders, you must install the relevant components from Quality Management.

Closing a Process Order

The order close function in PP-PI-POR manages the following steps that are needed to close a process order after it has been executed:

- Process order settlement
- Archive process orders

To be able to settle a process order, you must install the special functions for process manufacturing within Product Cost Controlling.

Manipulating Process Capacities

The capacity planning component (PP-PI-CAP) is able to determine the available capacity and carry out capacity leveling to meet capacity requirements. Three levels of capacity planning are available:

- Long-term planning
- Medium-term planning
- Detailed planning

Interfacing PP-PI with Process Control

The process management component (PP-PI-PMA) provides a flexible interface between the PP-PI and the process control facilities. The component can link to manually operated production lines, to automated lines, and to partially automated lines.

The PMA interface performs the following tasks:

- Receive control recipes with process instructions from released process orders
- Transfer control recipes to the corresponding line operators or process control systems
- Edit process instructions in natural language in PI sheet format so that they can be displayed and maintained on the screen by the line operator
- Receive, check, and transfer process messages with actual process data
- Accept manual entry of process messages

Sending Process Messages from Process Control

Process Message is a functional component that maintains a message structure that can be dispatched to one or more of the following types of destination:

- R/3 function module or component, such as inventory management (MM-IM)
- User-defined ABAP/4 tables such as are used for process evaluation purposes
- Users of the SAP office mail system, particularly, the shift leader
- External functions, such as a third-party process control system

A process message can update an existing data record, as well as contribute to batch and production records. The content of each process message can be determined individually by assigning predefined characteristics and characteristic values. Thus the potential content as well as the destinations of process messages are customized specifically for a particular plant.

A process message can arrive via the PI-PCS interface from an external system, or it can be created when an R/3 PI sheet is maintained. Process management then consults its records to identify the destinations for this message.

Directing Control Information to the Operator

The control recipe function prepares a control recipe that contains all the information needed by a particular process control system or line operator. In particular the control recipe includes the following items taken from the process instruction sheet:

- Information on the processing steps to be carried out during process control
- Information on the actual data to be reported

After a process order or a phase of one has been released, the relevant process instructions are repackaged into control recipes and transferred to the control system or line operator destinations as specified in the process order.

Reading the Process Instruction Sheet

The process instruction (PI) sheet function allows the process instructions contained in a control recipe to be formatted as a PI sheet for display and maintenance from the screen. This facilitates communication between supervisors, the PP-PI module, and line operators where the lines are not fully automated.

The content of a PI sheet will depend on the process instructions contained in the control recipe. The following possibilities are supported:

- Displaying control information in natural language
- Recording of actual process data
- Calculating values
- Reporting entered and calculated values using process messages
- Recording inspection results by jumping directly to QM
- Calling R/3 function modules to access, for example, order confirmation, document management, or material quantity calculation

Archiving Process Data

The process data documentation (PP-PI-PDO) component is responsible for listing and optically archiving order-related and batch-related process data. The key factor is that these records cannot be manipulated. Thus an electronic batch record (EBR) can be produced for any product batch, should the need arise after delivery.

The content and format of these archived lists are based on international standards such as those defined in the guidelines on good manufacturing practices (GMP). Customer-specific enhancements to the GMP standards are possible.

Evaluating Process Data

Process data evaluation (PP-PI-PEV) is a component that can be configured to evaluate collected process data using standard evaluation procedures and user-defined calculations.

The following data can be analyzed from the shop floor information system:

- Resources
- Business transactions
- Materials
- Process orders
- Materials consumption
- Product costs
- Process message evaluation—displays message data using SAP business graphics or transfers it to Microsoft EXCEL for further processing

If you have installed the ODBC software interface, process data may be extracted from the database for evaluation by third-party analysis tools.

Integrating PP-PI with Higher-Level Systems

When PP-PI is part of a decentralized production planning configuration, it can use the integration with higher-level systems (PP-PI-LHL) component to exchange data with higher-level or central-planning systems in the following matters:

- ID number of the material to be produced
- Delivery date
- Requirement quantity

These requirement specifications may be accepted from an R/2 system or from a third-party system.

Through the data exchange facility, the process data may take part in cross-application cost processing and efficiency studies, for example.

Linking to Other Systems

The mainframe SAP system R/2 may be used for central planning and financial management. The link to R/2 (PP-PI-LHL) component can be installed to exchange order information with one or more R/3 installations using PP-PI.

Links to third-party systems are enabled by the link to external host systems (PP-PI-LHL) component.

Collecting and Displaying Plant Data

Plant data includes messages related to the work of the line operators and the automated or partially automated machinery. Collecting plant data provides up-to-date information on machine utilization, order situation, and quality. The collected data also contributes to the stored statistics.

If you have installed external or third-party systems, the collection and display of their plant data is controlled by the plant data collection component (PP-PDC), which is able to provide functions under the following headings:

- Check
- Processing
- Editing
- Evaluation
- Transfer

Recording Time Worked on Production Orders

A production order will have been planned on the basis of standard times. If you can record the actual times of the process phases you can make comparisons and arrive at an estimate of the effectiveness of the process in relation to the time planned for it.

The work order time recording component (PP-PDC-WOT) collects and evaluates all the time-related messages arriving as a result of work done on the particular order. The component has to be integrated with an external subsystem, such as a time recording system, which has been configured to communicate via a standard SAP interface.

Work Order Time Recording for PM Orders (PP-PDC-MOT) is a component that manages work order time recording and evaluation against standard times for a plant maintenance order.

The personnel time recording component (PP-PDC-LTR) has the task of recording all labor-related messages that are associated with particular production orders. The time messages signal when a line operator arrives and leaves or takes a break. The evaluated time data may be used in performance-related or time-related payment systems. Time Management is extensively covered in the QUE book, *Administering SAP R/3: HR-Human Resources Module*.

Personnel Time Recording has to be linked to a time recording system through an SAP standard interface.

Project Time Recording (PP-PDC-PTR) is a component that collates collected time data in relation to a specific project.

Consulting the PP Information System

The information system component (PP-IS) provides a shop floor information system for monitoring, controlling, and planning your business operations relating to production. The particular features of the PP-IS are that it provides a choice of points of view on the data and you can control the level of detail displayed. The system is also referred to as the shop floor information system (SFIS).

The display of production information is based on key figures. A standard key figure is provided for many of the measurements that can be derived from collected plant data. The PP-IS looks after the collation of records and the calculations for the following types of key figures, for example:

- Lead times
- On-time delivery performance
- Capacity load utilization
- Costs
- KANBAN evaluations of just-in-time manufacturing

You can accept the standard evaluation procedures or specify flexible analysis in which you can modify the evaluation logic and parameters online or in customizing.

The shop floor information system (PP-IS) contributes to flexible planning systems, the early warning system, and the logistics information library (LIL). LIS also integrates with the purchasing information system (PURCHIS) and the inventory controlling system (MM-IM). All information systems in LIS use similar techniques of analyzing data and they are all controlled in the same way by the user.

PP-IS can be linked to external data from third-party systems.

Reporting (PP-IS-REP) is the component that provides reports from the PP-IS information system. Analysis options take the following forms:

- Standard analyses—allow targeting of specific key figures for analysis, graphical display, and selective levels of detail.
- Flexible analyses—allow grouping and aggregation of key figures to your specification followed by standard analysis and display.

The R/3 standard analysis and display functions include the following:

- ABC analysis of important, less important, and relatively unimportant result sources
- Cumulative frequency curve
- Correlation curve
- Previous year comparison
- Planned/actual comparison

Linking PP with Sales and Operations Planning

The role of the planning (PP-IS-PLN) component is to link with the planning functionality of the logistics information system (LIS). LIS is integrated into the central component Sales and Operations Planning (SOP).

The SOP system is a flexible forecasting and planning tool with the following areas of applicability:

- Sales
- Production
- Supply chain

You can use the SOP to set targets on the basis of historical, existing, and estimated future data. Rough-cut planning forecasts the amounts of the capacities and other resources required to meet these SOP targets. You can conduct high-level planning of complex planning hierarchies and the detailed planning of finished products. Standard SOP is configured to use product group hierarchies planned level by level. Flexible SOP allows you to determine the structure of the planning hierarchies.

By configuration, you can arrange for target key figures set at one level of the organization to be distributed automatically and consistently to all the other organizational levels in the hierarchy. Alternatively, you can arrange that each level is planned separately.

Linking PP to the Logistics Information Library

Interface to Logistics Information Library (LIL) is the component (PP-IS-LIS) that allows a PP user to create, classify, and find key figures in the area of logistics and the information systems connected with it.

A simple search will elicit all the key figures that are available in the LIL with their associated calculation procedures. You can arrange your own structured catalog of any key figures of interest. From the LIL, you can also build integrations of the reports, transactions, information systems, and tables from different areas of logistics, such as purchasing, sales, and production.

Building a Logistics Data Warehouse

Data Collection (PP-IS-DC) is an essential component of the logistics information system. You can use the PP-IS-DC component to define your own logistics data warehouse.

The technique of "self-defined information structures" is used to ensure that any local data structure can be used without explicit modification by other user groups who can assign specific data to them. Updated groups and updated rules are used to help standardize the data warehouses across user groups.

Setting Up Early Warning Systems

The early warning system (PP-IS-EWS) component is integrated in the shop floor information system so that you can use it to select weak points in the production processes and have them monitored. The results are expressed in terms of selected key figures. You can also define exceptions that will initiate follow-up actions, such as a mail or fax message accompanied by a display of the critical data.

Integrating Supply Chain Management

The classical material requirements planning approach (MRP II) takes as its starting point a plan of the operations to be carried out, whether in sales or orders and projects. From this stage, the system offers accepted methods of planning and control of materials through to delivery of the products.

Now that online management of all aspects of business is becoming the norm, and not only in medium-sized and large companies, it has become essential for a company to link the MRP II disciplines to the sales and controlling functions. In the context of the SAP standard business functions and integrated applications, the linking of MRP II and SAP takes place in three stages that are linked seamlessly together:

1. Customer order details are passed automatically to the sales information system (SD-IS) and to the profitability analysis system (CO-PA).
2. The sales and operations planning system (PP-SOP) selects the necessary information from the sales information system and the profitability analysis component.

3. The sales and operations plan is passed to the demand management functions. From here the material requirements planning component (PP-MRP) can initiate the MRP II planning chain that ends with the generation of the necessary order proposals.

New customer orders are offset with the orders previously planned, and the next cycle of the optimized planning run can begin. The integrated quality control provided by the SAP R/3 quality management system (QM) is applied to all the operations of the production planning and control module (PP).

Defining Basic Data for Production in the PP-BD Component

The objects of interest to production planning are obviously the products and the methods by which they are produced and managed. The SAP R/3 system is designed for medium-sized and large organizations. The same products and production processes might appear in different divisions, so the organizational structure must be defined and then referenced in the basic data records for production and production planning.

Assigning Data to Organizational Units

The SAP R/3 general organizational units relevant to production planning are taken from the SAP R/3 Enterprise Data Model:

- Author Instance is the highest level in R/3 and is identified by code sysid. It is at this level that some data is managed because it can be set up for all lower levels. Currencies and units of measure are examples.

- Client is the second highest level. Client 000 is updated only by SAP. A copy of 000 is created as client 001, and this may be customized. The data of one client may not interact with another client. There is often a training client and a testing client, in addition to the client code that represents your group or corporate identity and under which the SAP system runs normal business. Some data is managed at the client level because everyone in the corporate group of companies will want to refer to exactly the same information and be certain that it has been maintained as up to date and correct. Vendor addresses would be an example of data managed at the client level.

- Company Code signifies a legal unit under the client that produces its own financial documents, the balance sheet, and the profit-and-loss statement, and may well maintain them continuously reconciled.

- Plant is an organizational unit that is seen as central to the production planning concept. A plant can be a production site or a group of storage locations that share materials. Plant is the unit for which MRP prepares plans and maintains the inventory. It is the focus of Materials Management (MM). Each plant will have been given planning and control elements such as material, inventory, operations, work centers, and so on.

Planning can take place across plants. For example, products manufactured in different plants can be combined for planning purposes into a product group. Manufacturing can also take place and be controlled on a cross-plant basis.

The stocks held in individual storage locations within a plant can also be managed separately with respect to inventory and can be planned using MRP.

You may have defined other organizational units to suit your own planning and production needs. These user-defined organizational units can be used to focus materials requirements planning:

- Planning Plant is the one plant chosen as the central unit when you are engaging in cross-plant material requirements planning.

- Work Center is the central planning element to use when you are applying shop floor control and capacity planning. The system will allow you to build work center hierarchies and use them for MRP.

- Planner Group is a definition of people who are chosen, not by name necessarily, but by their personnel group, which is assigned by the human resources functions. This way, the members of a planning group can be selected from those who are available on the day they are needed and who have the necessary experience and qualifications. You can define other planning groups. Three planner groups are commonly assigned materials, resources, and production tools.

- MRP Controller Group is an identification for those who are experienced at materials requirements planning.

- Work Scheduler Group is an identification of those with experience in the scheduling of work resources including people.

- Shop Floor Controller Group is an identification of those with experience in the detailed management of shop floor personnel and the places where they work.

Defining a Material

It is standard throughout the SAP R/3 system to define *material* to include whatever is used in the production process. The following are examples of materials in the SAP R/3 system:

- Finished products
- Intermediate assemblies
- Unfinished products
- Raw materials
- Part-processed materials
- Resources such as energy, air, and water
- Packaging
- Services

Storing Information as a Material Data Structure

Two principles apply to the storage of data in the SAP R/3 system:

- Information that is expected to remain constant for a long time is entered in one place only, and the latest change to it is logged.

- Local information is stored at the level encompassing all the operational units for which it is pertinent but can be made available elsewhere.

You have the following range of options:

- At the level of the client or the company code, maintain general data valid for the whole organization—for example, material code numbers, multilingual text concerning each material code, and classification rules applicable to material.
- At the plant level, maintain the data for material requirements planning and for production planning and control and also valid bills of material and routings.
- Maintain inventories at the level of the individual storage location, of which a plant may have more than one.
- Maintain the sales data at the level of each purchasing organization and distribution channel.

You can define individual access authorizations as create, change, or display only. These can be specific to each user and each organizational level. If you are authorized to create transaction data, you can obviously display and change it unless the item is reserved as read-only. At the intermediate level of authorization comes the permission to alter a record but not generate a new one. For example, a sales representative might be allowed to change the address of a supplier, but not to create new suppliers or delete existing addresses.

The Basis team that maintains the databases has to ensure that the authorizations determined by the management team are set up as mechanisms that use the profiles to control an employee's access to the various types of data.

Confining Materials to User Departments

Sections of the information on a material master can be allocated to different user departments, such as the MRP department, the work scheduling department, and so on. By doing this, you can give each department access to just the information it needs about a specific material.

Establishing Material Types

Material data is maintained centrally. Different views of the master records can be called for by making reference to the material type. For example, you could maintain data for work scheduling in the case of a material of the type "semi-finished goods," but you cannot schedule raw materials.

The material type determines certain other control parameters:

- Which user departments can maintain the data for a material of this type
- Procurement type, which indicates how this material is procured—in-house manufacturing or external procurement
- Type of inventory control to be used—for example, whether by quantity, value, or both

You may create and configure material types to suit your business.

Recognizing Industry Sectors

If a material is used in more than one industry, you may decide to create industry sectors in which the material type is configured in a special way for each sector.

Managing Batches and Special Stock

Batches of a material are managed at the storage location level, but you may want to differentiate between, for example, special stock and batches:

- A batch is a full or partial quantity of material. The material in the batch is managed separately on the inventory. It may be a production lot or a delivery lot, for example.
- Special stock may be designated as vendor special stock, for example, because it is a consignment from a particular vendor.
- Customer special stock might be the designation of, for example, packaging materials returnable by the customer.
- Activity-related special stock may be identified because it is going to a particular customer on a make-to-order product, for example.

Using Departmental Profiles for Materials

An existing material master record can be used as a reference when creating a new material master. The data necessary on the user departments of your company can be maintained in the form of user department profiles, which contain no reference to any specific material, but you can reference them when creating a new material master. Each user department can set individual options to control how this data is applied.

Creating Bills of Material

The bill of material (BOM) is an instrument for describing the structure of a product for any of the following production types:

- Repetitive manufacturing
- Manufacturing products with variants
- Process manufacturing
- Make-to-order production

You can also maintain bills of materials for sales orders, projects, equipment, and documents.

The BOM is used in central planning functions, such as materials requirements planning and product costing. Five forms of the basic BOM are supported in Production Planning and Control (PP). They may be created at any time by extending a simple BOM:

- Simple BOM—one rigidly defined bill of material associated with one material.
- Variant BOM—several similar materials associated with one bill of material.

■ Multiple BOM—a set of bills of materials describing each of several different production processes, constituents, or relative quantities of components, all of which produce the same material. There are several ways of making the same thing.

■ One-time BOM—a bill of material for a specific sales order that is used in make-to-order production.

■ Configurable BOM—a bill of material that is configured automatically on the basis of logical links. It is used for complex variant structures or process-dependent BOM configuration in continuous flow production.

Exploring the BOM Data Structure

The BOM has a header and one or more items. The header indicates that the BOM is assigned to one or more plants and specifies its validity period. The header also carries its status indicator, which determines whether the BOM is released for production in its current form.

The BOM items each describe a component of the assembly in terms of the following categories, which you can subdivide as the need arises:

■ Stock items are components kept in stock.

■ Nonstock items may have purchasing data that you have maintained and that can be used to link with purchasing in MM.

■ Variable-size items must have the quantity to be used calculated automatically from the sizes entered.

■ Document items include drawings or safety instructions integrated into the BOM.

■ Text items are available for you to store all types of text in association with the BOM.

By-products and scrap can be represented on the BOM by negative quantities that will be processed in Material Requirements Planning (PP-MRP) and Product Costing (CO-PC).

Parts of a BOM can be marked for the attention of a particular department, or a separate BOM can be used for each department.

Maintaining a BOM

You can update a BOM from the CAD system or directly in Production Planning and Control. Copy and editing functions are available. The standard SAP R/3 classification system can search for suitable materials quickly.

Engineering change management is facilitated by mass changes to bills of material. The integrated engineering change management functions allow you to track the complete history of changes to a BOM.

Using BOM Explosion Numbers

A BOM explosion is the process of identifying each item in a bill of material. Each item in turn is then examined to determine its constituent parts, and each part is examined for its constituents, and so on, until the lowest level units are those managed in the inventory.

A BOM explosion number is a method of making particular subsets of this extra information available to the users of a BOM in a controlled manner. The BOM is given a master record that indicates whether it applies specifically to one product or to many. The BOM explosion number may go through several revision levels, each of which will carry the fixed key date (the date on which that particular version of a BOM explosion should come into force). From that date, the content of the BOM explosion number has to be taken into account by the production scheduling and routing functions.

The BOM explosion number is a reference to a technical document that can serve a range of functions—for example:

- Notifying the details of product liability obligations
- Referencing ISO standards for quality assurance
- Documenting an engineering change made during the production process
- Referencing the relevant technical drawings and pointing out the salient features
- Documenting the technical status according to which a product is manufactured for all BOM levels
- Ensuring that the correct BOM and the corresponding routing are used in orders for spare parts

Directing the Materials

The BOM can be used to control production in several different plants, if they have the necessary resources. The R/3 system documents production resources in terms of work centers through which the material is routed. Thus different plants may employ different work centers and therefore need individual routing instructions.

Defining Work Centers

A work center is both a place where a process is carried on by means of activities and a technical concept in the production planning and control system. The real work center has people, machines, production lines, assembly lines, and all the paraphernalia of industry. The work center in SAP R/3 is a data object.

In the data object of the type "work center" you can specify the data for the scheduling, costing, and capacity planning of operations. Formulas held there can compute execution times, costs, capacity requirements, and so on.

The SAP customizing module allows you to specify the data at your work centers so as to serve your company's needs. The system will supply default values for a work center to simplify and speed up work scheduling, or you can copy or reference from one source to another. The work center will have standard texts to assist you in maintaining the correct operation descriptions in routings. Any parameter unit held at a work center can be given up to six standard values to speed up complex costing or duration calculations, for example. You just specify by a key the value to be used on each occasion.

Work centers are assigned to a cost center during work center data maintenance. This provides the link to the controlling system (CO).

Every aspect of activity at a work center can be assigned a capacity value, which will then take part in capacity planning, production control, and the scheduling of routings. Not only can you define capacities for machines and labor, you can set up capacity parameters to define virtually any resource that you might need to improve the value added by each work center. Here are some examples:

- Energy consumption
- Emissions
- Reserve capacities for rush orders ●

Preparing the System

Setting Up Bills of Material

Specifying Basic BOM Data

The basic data component (PP-BD) contains the master data needed for production planning in discrete manufacturing. The master data tends to remain constant and is always used in the same way.

Defining Bills of Material

The PP-BD-BOM component supports the use of the bill of material concept in a wide range of circumstances where there is a tree structure of associated items. For example, BOMs can be generated in the following forms:

- Material BOM
- Equipment BOM
- Functional location BOM
- Document structure
- Sales order BOM

In each instance, the BOM comprises a structured list that specifies what is needed in each of the components—name, quantity, and unit of measure, for example. The advantage of holding a single master BOM is that all departments can refer to the same product specification.

Each industry sector may have its own preferred name for the structured list that is maintained by R/3 as a BOM; recipe, list of ingredients, and furnish are examples. The PP-PI module for the process industries uses master recipes rather than bills of materials to define the constituents and processes of manufacture for the various products.

The role of the BOM, or its equivalent, is to provide master data for such organizational areas as the following:

- Materials planning
- Staging of materials for production
- Product costing
- Plant maintenance

PP-BD-BOM has to be installed, not only for production planning, but also if you intend to maintain complex document structures or technical specifications that require a hierarchical structure, as in assembly processing and plant maintenance.

Establishing Control Data for Bills of Material

The control data are the modification parameters and default values for your BOM management system. All types of BOM structure are controlled in the same manner. You should not attempt to change them once you have started using BOMs in the productive R/3 system. The standard system is delivered with default values.

A modification parameter is a value that you can adjust to control the standard BOM functions. For example, if you wish to maintain the validity date, you can specify a valid-from date when maintaining BOMs. The standard options are to create bills of material as of the current date or using the system low date (1/1/1990)—you have to activate one or the other.

If you activate engineering change management during customizing, you can thereafter make historical changes to BOMs. The system will store the status of the BOM before and after the change, which will be recorded as a numbered change event. At a later stage of implementation, you can decide whether to configure BOM history as a requirement for certain types of BOM.

Your company may have a computer-assisted design (CAD) function, in which case you can set the *CAD active* indicator to allow the BOMs to be maintained through CAD. An indicator field will then appear to signal when a BOM header or a BOM item has been maintained from a CAD system.

One of the modification parameters that you will probably wish to customize will be the units of measure used in your BOMs. Standard R/3 defaults to the value "piece" in the field unit of measure "piece," at all levels of a BOM. You can change these values to accord with your company structure and products.

Thus you have to supply a parameter value for each unit if you do not wish to accept the R/3 defaults. The BOM headers require a base unit of measure for each of the following types of BOM:

- Equipment BOM
- Functional location BOM
- Document structure
- Standard BOM

The BOM items require a component unit of measure for each of the following types of BOM item:

- Text item
- Document item
- Nonstock item without a material master record

When the system is working with a bill of material, it may discover that individual items are themselves complex structures that have been defined with BOMs of their own, and so on. If you are working out how much an order will cost, or how long it will take to manufacture, you may well need to explore each component down to the lowest level of constituent that is managed by your inventory. This expanding search is known as a BOM explosion.

There can be various types of BOM explosion. When you are setting up the basic data for a BOM type, you must establish what type of BOM explosion is to be permitted.

One complication with BOM explosions is the matter of validity periods. For example, you may have to change an item in a BOM. This will probably be associated with a change number,

Part

II

Ch

3

which will have a validity defined as the period between the valid-from date and the valid-to date, during which the alteration is to be accepted. This item validity period may not correspond with the validity period of the BOM as a whole, which is defined at its header level. As a consequence, your production line may have to handle products defined by the old BOM, the changed BOM over the validity of the change, and the BOM after the change validity has expired.

For example, you would not want to use Christmas wrappings for products to be delivered after December 25.

A sequence of validity periods of a change item in a BOM can enjoy or suffer from the following variations:

- Negative validity—the valid-to date is before the valid-from date.
- Two validity periods overlap—in the overlap period, two versions of an item exist with two different change numbers.

You have to settle for one of these values to control how the system conducts a BOM explosion, for all BOM categories:

- Value " " (blank)—all versions of an item are equally acceptable. They are given the same item number, but show their relevant change numbers.
- Value 1—the system finds the latest version according to its creation date.
- Value 2—the system finds the latest version by choosing the latest valid-from date.

Of course, you could deactivate the engineering change management function (ECM), in which case changes to bills of material would not get recorded.

If you accept the standard default settings, the following conditions will apply:

- Validity date maintenance is active.
- Engineering change management is active.
- BOMs assume the current system date is the default valid-from date.
- CAD is active.
- The BOM explosion type for BOM items is blank, signifying that items adopt the same validity rules as the BOM headers.

Defining BOM Default Values

When you are creating or maintaining BOMs, the system will make various assumptions that have to be either predefined or accepted as the standard system defaults. These values apply to all types of BOM structure—material BOMs, document structures, and equipment BOMs, for example. In particular, the following values will probably need to be maintained to suit your company:

- Base quantity—the amount of material to which the standard values apply, such as volume, weight, cost, and so on. Routings also apply to base quantities.

- BOM status—defaulted to a value that can be consulted by related applications, for instance, to find out which BOM is current.

- The size unit (mm)—proposed for items that are always the same size, unless you define another unit of size.

- The variable-size item unit (pieces)—if items can be of different sizes.

Setting Out the BOM Status Structure   The purpose of the *BOM status* indicator is to identify whether a particular BOM can be used by another application. When these applications are themselves being implemented, the BOM status indicators that they will recognize are specified. The acceptable status is defined as a minimum by nominating which status values are valid.

For example, material requirements planning will look only at BOM records that carry at least one of the following status indications:

- Explosion in MRP
- Released for orders

It is clearly dangerous to delete a status indicator if the possibility exists that some BOMs in the system have been assigned it.

A BOM status can have an exception message attached to it. This will cause it to be automatically presented to the MRP controller. The reason for doing this may be to warn the controller that a straightforward explosion of this BOM may not be good enough for planning—perhaps the controller will have to make a manual intervention.

One application is if a product includes sensitive material that should always be planned manually, even though the rest of the BOM can be exploded automatically.

The text of these exception messages has to be defined under control of the implementation guide for material requirements planning, which will arrange for them to be uniformly defined and grouped.

Defining General Data for BOM Headers

Every item in a BOM is subject to the rules and defaults defined in General Data.

Further readings:

Define BOM usages

Define default values for the item status

Define copy default for item status

The BOM usage parameter declares who will be interested in the BOM. You can create a separate BOM for each organizational area or department that will have an interest in the product, material, technical object, equipment, or functional location. A BOM is a data structure, recipe, description; so you could arrange for the BOM data to be filtered to suit each readership—design, production, costing, distribution, for instance. The design BOM need not contain the same information as the distribution BOM, although some data items will be of interest to both.

Part

II

Ch

3

When you are defining BOM usages, you have to configure the status for each BOM item using indicators that are interpreted as "relevant for engineering/design," or "relevant for production," and so on.

This enables the production department to be given a planned order, and later a production order that contains only those items that have been assigned the status "relevant for production" in the BOM from which they have been copied.

There are some restrictions on what you can do with BOM usages. You cannot delete the BOM usage if an existing BOM has been assigned it. You cannot assign the indicator relevant to plant maintenance unless the BOM is actually to be so used.

A BOM for production could have the following allowed usage pattern:

- Production—Essential
- Engineering/Design—Can be relevant
- Spare parts—Can be relevant
- Plant Maintenance—Not relevant
- Costing—Can be relevant

A BOM for engineering/design could have the following allowed usage pattern:

- Production—Can be relevant
- Engineering/Design—Essential
- Spare parts—Can be relevant
- Plant Maintenance—Not relevant
- Costing—Can be relevant

When you are creating new BOM items, the possible status indicator values will be proposed. You then select those that are of relevance for this item. In practice, it is usual to define BOM usage patterns that are likely to be true most of the time, and then alter the entries when the items are created if necessary. Thus an item relevant for production is almost always going to be relevant for costing.

One way of generating a BOM is to copy one you already have in the system. You can define a copy default for item status to control whether some or all of the defaults are copied when the rest of the BOM is copied. Those that are copied are then offered as defaults when maintaining the new BOM.

Defining Allowed Material Types for BOM Headers

For each material type used as the BOM header material, you can control which BOM usages are allowed. If you enter the generic indicator "*," then all BOM usages are allowed for that material. You can also specify which material types are allowed for BOM headers.

Similar control over BOM item usage and material combinations is available.

Standard R/3 is delivered with no restrictions on any material types with respect to BOM usages.

Associating BOMs and Particular Laboratories

You can control which laboratories, design offices, persons, or groups are to be responsible for particular bills of material. A laboratory, for instance, may have a special interest in testing the quality of a particular material, wherever it is used. The lab may also be assigned responsibility for any BOM in which it appears.

Configuring BOM History

You can specify whether a bill of material with a certain BOM usage and BOM status should be changed only under the control of engineering change management so that the alteration can be timed and documented. You can add a requirement for change history to a BOM that has been created without it—but you cannot cancel a requirement for a BOM to be maintained only with ECM history.

The history requirement entails activating both validity date maintenance and engineering change management.

Defining BOM Item Data

An item in a BOM may itself be a BOM, and so on. Therefore, it is important to maintain a proper control over the structure of BOM items as well as their parent BOMs.

Further readings:

> Define item categories
>
> Define object types
>
> Define allowed material types for BOM items
>
> Define formulas for variable-size items
>
> Define spare part indicators
>
> Define material provision indicators
>
> Define explosion types
>
> Item Data from Related Application Areas

Defining Item Categories

The item category defines the attributes and functions of a BOM item. When you enter an item in a BOM, its category has to be identified because this will control field and screen selection for detail screens when maintaining the BOM. The following aspects of the item are controlled by its category:

- If a material number is required
- If the item is to be used in inventory management on a quantity basis
- If the item is a text item, with no other functionality
- If the item is to be used as a variable-size item with the option of entering individual sizes
- If the item is a document that you have created using the system

■ If the item is a class item in a configurable material BOM that will be automatically replaced by an instance of the class that has the specified characteristics

■ If subitems are supported

■ If the item is a plant maintenance structure element, in which case the material of the item will not be checked to see if it is maintained in the plant

■ If the item is a master recipe intramaterial that comes into existence between two processing units

■ If negative quantities are supported as when the item is a coproduct that is kept in stock and can therefore be entered, not as a positive material requirement, but as a negative requirement that will increase the stock of the coproduct

The item category is also used to specify which detail screens and fields appear and which can be maintained by the user.

You can design new item categories, although the system will refuse to allow certain combinations of attributes and functions that are incompatible. It is essential to assign a new item category the correct item screen control key, so that it is compatible with the existing categories.

The standard item categories are as follows:

■ Document item

■ Class item for configurable BOMs

■ Stock item

■ Text item

■ Nonstock item

■ Variable-size item

■ PM structure element (only for plant maintenance)

■ Intramaterial (only for master recipes)

Assigning Object Types   Each BOM item category can have assigned to it an object type. For example, the following are objects that can be used as BOM items:

■ A material

■ A document

■ A class

■ An intramaterial

■ No object (for example, text item or nonstock item without a material master)

You will see the standard object types in the general item overview screen, as follows:

■ M Material

■ D Document

■ C Class

- I Intramaterial
- " " No object (blank)

You can alter the abbreviation of the object type during customizing.

Understanding BOM Item Objects

BOMs and their equivalents such as master recipes notify the planning and production facilities what is needed to create the intended product. The descriptions in a BOM data structure are necessarily terse yet precise. However, there can be a slightly different interpretation of the various objects according to the application using the BOM.

The following sections recapitulate the formal definitions of the standard object types.

Defining Material

In an industry solution application such as Retail (IS-R), a material is the smallest unit or customer pack that can be ordered independently and that cannot be split further into any smaller units. These units are normally ordered for a particular plant, such as a warehouse, and sold as individual units.

From the logistics–general (LO) application a material is any product that takes part in a business activity. It is traded, used in manufacture, consumed, or produced.

A material is classified as a business object. The data relating to a particular material is stored in the form of a material master that is associated with a particular element of the organizational structure. A typical organizational structure will comprise the following levels, with one or more instances at each level:

- Plant
- Storage location
- Warehouse complex
- Distribution chain

The same material master may be accessed with different views according to the department that is using it:

- Materials planning
- Costing
- Purchasing
- Warehouse management
- Accounting

Each of these departmental views may adopt different parameters to define how activities such as materials planning or quality inspection are carried out for this material. And, although a base unit is defined for the material master, a conversion factor can be defined so that each departmental view can include the units of measurement most convenient for its purposes.

Some units of a material may be identified by a European Article Number (EAN). It may be necessary to maintain serial numbers that uniquely identify each individual piece of a material. If there is more than one way of producing a material, each method can be identified as a production version of the material.

A batch is a subset of a material that has been manufactured in a particular production run and stocked separately from other subsets of the same material. The batch where-used list shows you which batches make up which finished products.

The possible uses of a material may be suggested by the R/3 classification categories to which it is assigned. For example, it may have parameters that indicate its material type and industry sector. A material can also be identified as a member of a material group on the basis of the attributes it shares with other members.

In the production planning for process industries module (PP-PI), a material is defined as any substance or object dealt with on a commercial basis or used, consumed, or generated during production. Thus it could be a chemical element or a compound.

If your R/3 implementation has not configured the personnel administration and payroll accounting application (PA), you can use a material master to define an employee.

Defining Document

From the point of view of the controlling application (CO), a document is defined as a proof of a cost accounting posting. The document can prove a posting within the controlling application, such as an account distribution, or it can be proof of a posting elsewhere, such as a primary cost posting in financial accounting (FI).

A document may be identified with a document type and a document class.

There are many software components that are so much used throughout an implementation of an integrated R/3 system that they are presented as a separate module of cross-application functions (CA). In the CA context, a document is treated as any data storage medium that holds information for the user or for transferring to another system. Thus any of the following would be classified as a document:

- Design drawing
- Program
- Photograph
- Data disk
- Text

One of the modules within CA is documentation tools (CA- DOC). This module enables the formatted text system SAPScript, which is used for online documentation. This type of document is accessed by the Help functions and may be independent or attached to a particular object in the R/3 system.

The document has a particular role in financial accounting. A document in FI is taken as a proof of a business transaction. A distinction is drawn between original documents and data processing documents.

Original documents include incoming invoices, bank statements, and carbon copies of outgoing invoices. DP documents include, for example, accounting documents, sample documents, and recurring entry documents.

An accounting document represents the original document and may be used for legal purposes. All other documents are taken as mere data transfer facilities.

The implementation guide component (BC-BEW-IMG) controls how a first implementation of an R/3 system shall be customized. In particular, the IMG defines the following document classes because they represent textual or graphical information held in special tables:

- BOOK
- CHAP—Chapter in a book
- SIMG—Step, for example, in a procedure
- NOTE

The R/3 word processor is SAPScript, installed as module BC-SRV-SCR. Its task is to apply styles and layout sets to text and so create a document for output to a screen or to a printer.

In the sales and distribution application (SD), a document is interpreted as a printed record of a business transaction in sales and distribution processing. Three kinds of printed SD document are recognized:

- Sales document
- Shipping document
- Billing document

Defining Class

A class is managed by the cross-application functions (CA) as the key element in the R/3 classification system. In particular, materials, batches, and documents can be assigned attributes that can be used to retrieve them through the classification function.

The environment, health, and safety module (EH&S) uses classes to identify characteristics of substances, either singly or in groups of different characteristics. The substance database will accept any number of properties as the definition of a class.

The concept of class has yet another use in workflow management, which is controlled by module BC-BEW-WFM. There are two primary classes of object that can appear in a user's integrated inbox:

- WF—workflow
- SO—SAPoffice

The user selects which class of inbox item is of interest, and the screen will offer only those functions necessary for the class.

Defining Intramaterial

There is one item category that is normally needed only in production planning and control. This is the intramaterial—a material that is entered in a bill of material or recipe, but which exists only temporarily between stages of a technical process.

Defining Allowed Material Types for BOM Items

When you are defining what types of material are to be allowed in BOM headers and BOM material items, you can enter the generic "*" to signify that there are no restrictions. You can do the same in the BOM usage field.

This control is designed to ensure that a BOM or recipe intended for a particular usage will not contain material types that are not appropriate. The system will issue an error message if you attempt to create a BOM that violates these restrictions.

You can specify any number of combinations of conditions to control BOM usage with material header and item types.

Standard R/3 defaults to no restrictions on material types for BOM usages.

Defining Formulas for Variable-Size Items

A raw material may be delivered in various sizes, loads, or dimensions. These materials must be identified as variable-size items and there will have to be formulas specified to calculate the quantity of material included in each size of delivery. The default calculation when no algorithm has been entered is to multiply the dimensions to arrive at a cubic volume.

Defining Spare Part Indicators

A spare parts list can be developed as a BOM. Each item that could be a spare part has to be identified by the *spare part* indicator. In a BOM explosion, you can use the spare part indicator to restrict the display of items to the spare parts only.

You can define a variety of spare part indicators, for instance, so as to be able to view the parts that are to be replaced after successively longer periods of operation.

Defining Material Provision Indicators

The *material provision* indicator is used to identify a BOM item as a material to be provided for production. This indicator is read in MRP. There are two provision filters:

- Provision of material by a customer free of charge.
- Provision of material by a vendor through special procurement or subcontracting in which all the materials needed are provided free of charge for the subcontractor to carry out part of the production process. This indicator is not required if the materials are already at the subcontractor's premises.

Defining Explosion Types

The MRP1 screen of a material master allows you to define special procurement keys that are used to indicate when the BOM explosion should be of a particular type.

The following three special procurement keys are relevant to explosion types:

- Phantom assembly off—controls whether the BOM header material requirements will cascade down through successive levels generating additional material requirements as planned orders or purchase requisitions.

- Switch off planning—used when dependent materials are not needed because there is no final assembly or where there are materials already planned for assembly. The finished product is made by assembling components only when a sales order is received. Bought-in parts may not need to be planned.

- Collective order—the components are produced directly for the superior assembly and will have been planned as part of a "direct production" planning segment.

You can also define for an explosion type whether the item is relevant to long-term planning and in which form the dependent requirements are to be displayed. Long-term planning can simulate MRP and be used in parallel to immediate productive planning, although there will be computer system overhead that may make it necessary to omit some items from long-term planning.

Specifying a Distribution Strategy by a Distribution Key

A distribution strategy is a scheme of sharing materials or resources. You can also distribute production targets. The particular pattern for a distribution is selected by a four-character distribution key that has to be customized to suit your company. In particular, the distribution strategy for each defined key has to associate the following parameters because they are needed for processing the planning table:

- Distribution function—specifies the percentage of the quantity to be produced or consumed after a percentage of the production time has elapsed. These distribution functions are customized by adjusting standard functions.

- Distribution type—determines whether the requirement is to be distributed discretely to the points defined for the distribution function or linearly according to the definition in the distribution function.

Each distribution strategy is saved in the material master record and identified by a production version code.

Defining the Relevance of a BOM to Other R/3 Applications

A BOM text item will usually carry a usage indicator key that suggests how it can be used in sales and distribution. The other BOM items might also be useful in SD. A single BOM or BOM item might be of relevance to several other R/3 applications.

Part
II
Ch
3

During customizing, there is the opportunity to define a range of single-digit indicators that will signify how a BOM or a BOM item might be of relevance outside the PP module. A textual description of their possible use is appended to the master record of each indicator.

When an application accesses a BOM, the usage indicator can serve to filter out any information that is not relevant. All BOM explosions will automatically take account of any usage indicators that are in the active status.

Interpreting a Multiple BOM

A collection of BOMs that specify alternative combinations of materials or components for the same product can be defined in a multiple BOM. Each of these BOMs contains a complete description of the product.

One of the reasons for using a multiple BOM is so that each user application in the usage list can access a BOM that is confined to the information needed for the work to be done by that application. Thus a costing BOM need not contain the same data as a BOM for sales, even though they both refer to the same product. Even within one usage target, several different BOMs can be defined if the user department would find this helpful.

Another use for a multiple BOM is where there is an alternative production specification for the same product.

Defining Automatic Alternative Determination

If there are different BOMs for the same product, the system must be given a method of choosing which one to use in a BOM explosion.

The first part of the alternative definition is to select a BOM for the usage it is intended for. Thus a related application area, such as MRP, will automatically select a BOM marked with an indicator that is interpreted as relevant for MRP. The second parameter is a choice of which BOM to use if there is more than one for the intended usage. The following application areas are normally assigned parameters to control automatic alternative BOM determination during customizing:

- Inventory management
- Production
- MRP
- Costing
- Sales and distribution
- Plant maintenance

For example, inventory management (IM) will normally be configured to initiate automatic determination of BOM alternatives in the following processing circumstances:

- When you create an order, network, or project, IM will automatically reserve stock materials.

■ When a goods issue with reference to a BOM is posted, stock materials are automatically copied from the BOM to the goods issue transaction.

■ When subcontracting is indicated for the header material of a material BOM, the material is ordered from the supplier by a subcontracting item in a purchase requisition, purchase order, or scheduling agreement.

■ When a subcontracting item has subitems, these subitems are marked with a material provision indicator for each of their constituent or component BOM items, and so on.

When a subcontract order is posted, the system automatically determines the components for the subcontracting items, using the default values that have been specified in inventory management.

The other related applications use multiple BOMs under the same types of controls, although standard R/3 allows only one BOM application for plant maintenance. A BOM for a plant or piece of production equipment that is intended for use only by the plant maintenance application (PM) is not allowed any other usage indicators.

Defining an Order of Priority for BOM Usages   When the system has identified a BOM usage in terms of the application it is intended for, it will then seek a definition of the order of priorities to be applied to any alternative BOMs that may exist within that usage. The definition of priorities will have an ID. You can control BOM explosion by specifying the ID of the priority list that is to be used. Such a list is needed, even if there is only one item on it.

Product cost planning with reference to quantity structure is also controlled by specifying the ID of a stored data structure. In this case the choice of ID will determine the quantity structure that is used in the particular plant. Each material will have a designated quantity structure that is used in costing.

Pricing for sales and distribution can be determined from the BOM, and there can be alternative determination if different methods of product pricing are in use, perhaps for different sectors of the market, perhaps for items of different categories. The item category also controls how invoicing and inventory posting are performed.

The standard item categories include the following:

■ Inquiry item for the presales period—setting SD01 includes the specification of which BOM alternative will be referred to as per a certain date

■ Standard item

■ Free-of-charge stock item

■ Text item for standard orders

Defining Applications for Alternative BOMs

The system has to know which applications might call on a BOM because each application may need a different BOM explosion. However, a material master record can contain settings that control the automatic determination of alternative BOMs.

For example, you can have BOMs chosen according to any of the following criteria:

- Order quantity or lot size
- Date
- Production version

The order of priority of BOM usages that is specified by a selection ID will be overruled if the material has been assigned for BOM selection according to date in the material master record. You can also arrange for any order of priority selection ID to be rendered inactive for a specific material.

Defining Settings for Individual Users of BOMs

Each user that is working with BOMs can have an individual screen profile for BOM maintenance and reporting. You can define a profile for the user *Dummy* that will apply if there are no individual profiles. A user can alter the settings at any time.

The following parameters can be set for BOM maintenance:

- Item increment
- Item category for "New material items" screen
- Item category for "New document items" screen
- Item category for "New class items" screen
- Material provision indicator
- PM assembly for plant maintenance BOMs

The following parameters can be set for BOM reporting functions:

- Dialog print option
- Display subitems
- Display subassemblies
- Direct where-used list
- Where-used list via classes
- Display objects allocated to classes

Using BOM Tools on Legacy Data

It may well be the case that your company holds a great deal of valuable information about your products and production methods in databases held in SAP R/2 systems or in third-party systems. A suite of BOM tools is provided to facilitate the transfer of this data to the R/3 PP application.

The data transfer functions have to support the following logical processes:

- Identify the database fields in the existing system and their counterparts in the target system.
- Compare the fields and field contents.

- Identify which fields can be copied directly.
- Define rules for processing any fields that cannot be copied directly.
- Decide whether copying shall be under manual or automatic control.
- Create a transfer program in your existing system to build a sequential file that contains the extracted data.

The standard R/3 BOM tools will copy only simple BOMs. Variant or multiple BOMs have to be assembled manually from simple BOMs after the transfer has taken place.

Maintaining the Structure of the BOM Transfer File

The description of the table structures in the existing source database in a programming language defines the transfer structures that will be written to the sequential transfer file. The following programming languages can be used in R/3 to define the source table structures:

- COBOL
- C
- PL/1

You can arrange to transfer BOMs with or without long texts, and you can arrange to transfer only those changes to BOMs that you have transferred previously. If a BOM has already been transferred, you can choose to transfer any variants to it. ●

Part

II

Ch

3

CHAPTER 4

Setting Up Work Centers

In this chapter

Defining the Role of Work Centers

The work center component (PP-BD-WKC) defines the organizational units where operations or work steps are carried out that produce outputs of work. Each work center is assigned to a cost center for specific time periods that are defined in the Work Center Master Records.

The amount of work that can take place at a work center is represented as a capacity. If this capacity is not assigned to an order, it is an available capacity.

When a capacity is used, the activities performed at the work center are valuated by charge rates. A charge rate is selected according to the activity type and the work center at which it is performed.

A work center can be defined to include any combination of the following resources:

- Machines
- People
- Production lines
- Groups of craftsmen

If your R/3 implementation includes the personnel planning and development application (PD), a work center is interpreted as the physical location where certain tasks are carried out, and to which one or more employees can be assigned for a specified period. Each work center is assigned to a cost center for a specified time.

The PD work center as a physical location can be as large as a geographic location or as small as a particular work station that is equipped with specified tools and equipment and is located in a particular building.

Within the PD application, work centers are used in building comprehensive job descriptions. PD also allows a particular profile of qualifications to be associated with a work center. These qualifications can then be used to identify suitable persons to assign to the work center.

Another role of a work center is to be a reference point in the logistics (LO) application to which materials can be delivered and from which products may be collected.

Workflow Management (BC-BEW-WFM) is a component that allows defined work centers to be specified in workflows through which orders pass as part of the production process. In a similar fashion, the basic data (PP-BD) component refers to work centers in managing the routing through which a material must go in production processing.

The Work Center Master Record stores data that will be used in the following business functions:

- Costing
- Scheduling
- Capacity planning
- Printing shop floor papers
- Shop floor control
- Confirmation

By having data stored in work center records, you can carry out the following business operations:

- Schedule operations in task lists
- Cost operations in task lists
- Carry out capacity planning for the work center

Although you can arrange work centers to suit the size, complexity, and production methods of your company, the following business areas are normally served by work centers:

- Routing management
- Order processing
- Costing

Work center records and bills of materials are the vital master data elements in R/3 production management. However, interfaces are normally configured to any of the following applications that are active:

- Sales and distribution (SD)
- Materials management (MM)
- Controlling (CO)
- Project system (PS)
- Personnel planning and development (PD)

These supporting applications are discussed further under "Integrating Production with Supporting Applications."

The following data objects need to refer to work centers that have been previously defined:

- Routing
- Rate routing
- Reference operation set
- Inspection plan
- Maintenance task list
- Standard network

All of these data objects adopt the same SAP structure and they can be referred to as examples of the generic term *standard task list*, or simply *task list*. Thus a work center can appear in a task list or a work order. The term *operations* includes the activities named in standard networks.

Once you have defined a work center, you can find out which machines or skilled people are to be used in the operation or operations to be carried out there. And you can also calculate the costs of these operations because you will know the capacities to be consumed. There will also be enough information to determine the dates when the work center will be expected to complete each work item.

Maintaining the General Data for a Work Center

The general data stored in a work center specify the category, usage, location, and personnel.

The category of a work center determines what types of data may be stored and maintained there. The nature of this data limits the functions, such as costing and scheduling, for which the work center may be used. Each work center category is associated with one or more applications that are allowed to use any work centers assigned that category. Separate standard work center categories are provided for statistical work centers, production work centers, and maintenance work centers.

You can also specify whether work centers of a particular category have to be maintained under the discipline of engineering change management (ECM) so that all alterations are timed, dated, and documented.

A default or model work center is normally defined for each work center category so that it can be copied when creating work centers of that category. A work center cannot be used in scheduling until it has been assigned at least one defined capacity.

Controlling Interaction by the Work Center Category

The work center category also determines the sequence of screens that will be available for maintaining the work center so that it contains exactly the information that the permitted user applications will need. Each of these screens can be adjusted to display only those fields needed by the particular user. You are provided the following standard groups of screens from which you can select particular fields:

- Task lists
- Header screens
- Sequence screens
- Operation screens
- PRT overview
- PRT details

Fields are categorized as *modifiable* and *influencing*:

- Modifiable fields can be defined for input, required entry, display only, hidden, or highlighted.
- Influencing fields are displayed according to conditions, such as the type of order being processed.

You have to accept that all screens in a screen group will adopt the same field display controls if the influencing field is active.

The usage of a work center or production resource/tool is a notification of the task lists in which the work center or tool may be used. For example, you may restrict the usage of inspection work centers to inspection plans, whereas other work centers may be used in general task lists without restriction. Each usage pattern is defined as a usage key that can be assigned an appropriate selection of task list types. And each work center can then be assigned the corresponding usage key.

During customizing, the control data for human resources (HR) integration is set up for each work center to establish whether it can be used by both the HR and the PP systems. If these two systems are integrated, you can refer to work centers already set up in HR. Similarly, HR functions will be able to refer to work centers defined in PP.

Assigning R/3 Objects to Work Centers

A work center has to be assigned to a cost center; but most of the other R/3 objects that could be assigned to a work center are located in the personnel planning and development (PD) module of the HR application.

The following sequence will display the Work Center Assignment Overview from which the existing associations can be inspected: Goto→Assignments→Overview.

A work center can be assigned to just one cost center plus any number of the following PD objects:

- Qualifications
- Positions
- People

Assigning a Cost Center

The following sequence will initiate the assignment of a work center to a cost center: Goto→Assignments→Cost center. You have to specify the validity as a time period over which the assignment is to be effective. The cost center must have been previously defined in the controlling area that includes the work center, usually the plant. By default, standard values will be used for costing, unless you define other types of internal processing, in which case you have to enter the activity type that is to be used in the calculation, and you have to specify the formula.

If you create a work center in Logistics, the system automatically creates a work center in the personnel planning and development system. If you create a work center in PD, you are invited to declare whether the work center is also relevant to Logistics, in which case you have to nominate the plant location and usage.

Assigning a Qualification

The normal process of creating a work center will invite you to define a qualification by presenting the Assignment of a Qualification screen. The following sequence will access the same screen: Goto→Assignments→Qualifications.

The following object types can be assigned to a work center:

- Qualification
- Requirements profile

Part II Ch 4

The following information might be needed to complete the assignment:

- The priority of an object type in relation to other qualifications
- A proficiency defining how well a person must meet a specific qualification
- Experience in years of the employee at this work center

During capacity planning, a hit list is created that displays the suitability of the people who are assigned to the work center and capacity category. Their suitability is a combination of the elements of the requirements profile, the capacity, and the operation to be carried out.

Assigning a Position

The following Work Center Maintenance sequence will access the Assignment of a Position screen: Goto→Assignments→Positions.

You have to specify the validity period of this assignment of a position to the work center. The system will then automatically assign persons holding the position to the work center.

Assigning a Person

The following sequence will allow you to assign a person to a work center on the Assignment of a Person screen: Goto→Assignments→People. You have to enter the employee's personnel number and the time period that defines the validity of the assignment.

Maintaining Work Centers

Work center maintenance functions are provided so that you can associate tasks, functions, and reports with a work center. The following sequence will reach the initial Work Center menu: Logistics→Production→Master data→Work centers.

The Work Center Capacity Menu includes the following options:

- Work centers—allows you to create, change, or display a work center; or replace one with another in all task lists where it is used. It allows you to create capacities that are not pooled with other work centers. This option allows you to make the initial assignment of a work center to a hierarchy, but not to alter this position thereafter.
- Capacity—accesses the capacity menu to create, change, or display capacities. It allows you to maintain pooled capacities.
- Hierarchy—allows you to create, change, or display hierarchies. This option must be used if you wish to maintain the position of a work center in a hierarchy after the initial assignment.
- Reporting—accesses the standard SAP reports that are delivered with the system. You can call for where-used lists that show where a work center appears in task lists, or where capacities are managed as pooled capacities. The reporting option accesses change documents in order to list or print changes to fields.

■ Extras—allows you to create standard texts that are included in the task list. Extras allows the archiving of work centers.

As a user, you will be given an authorization that determines which of the following processing types you will be allowed to perform in relation to work centers:

■ Create

■ Change

■ Display

You will probably be advised to create work centers by using only the appropriate default work center as a model.

The following sequences will allow you to access the Work Center Maintenance screens:

■ Logistics→Production→Master data→Work centers

■ Logistics→Plant maintenance→Work centers

Building the Basic Data for a Work Center

The Work Center Basic Data screen is presented automatically when you create a work center. You can also access this screen by a function key in Work Center Maintenance or by the following sequence of menu options: Goto→Basic data.

The following information is entered and maintained on the Basic Data screen:

■ Short text describing the work center in the logon language or in another language.

■ Person responsible for the work center.

■ Location for the work center.

■ Usage specifying the task list types in which the work center may be used.

■ Standard value key.

■ Performance efficiency rate key.

■ *Backflush* indicator that causes the system to automatically post the goods issue when you confirm the operation, if this decision has been delegated to the work center by the MRP 2 screen. Otherwise, components are always backflushed if this is indicated in the routing or production order.

When you are maintaining a work center, the menu symbols Next screen and Previous screen can be pressed to access the screens in the predefined sequence. The menu option Skip leaves the contents of a screen unchanged.

Creating Language-Dependent Short Texts

The following sequence will allow you to create short texts in several languages from the Basic Data screen in Work Center Maintenance: Extras→Short texts. You are not permitted to delete the original language version of a short text.

Part

II

Ch

4

Assigning Standard Values

From the Work Center Basic Data screen, you can associate a key word with a maximum of six standard values using the standard value key. This key shows you the available standard values and their key words. When you are assigning a key word to a work center, you have to specify a dimension such as time or area for each of the standard values. You can also declare whether a standard value must be maintained in the task list.

The standard value key depends on units of measure defined in the default values screen. This screen will be offered in the sequence during work center creation, or you can use Goto→Default values when you are maintaining the work center.

The performance efficiency rate key specifies the ratio of an employee's actual output to the theoretical average output. The default value assumed in a routing is 100%. For example, a group of employees in a work center that can complete its task in only 66% of the standard time will be accorded a performance efficiency rate key of 150%.

Referencing Default Values

The following default values can be stored in a work center:

- Wage data, such as wage type or wage group
- Suitability of an employee to work at this work center
- Control key to influence an operation or suboperation in a task list or work order
- Standard text key
- *Reference* indicators to specify whether each default value can be changed in a task list or not

Setting Control Key Indicators

When a work center is being customized, the following indicators can be set in the control key:

- *Scheduling*—schedules an operation or determines the earliest or latest dates for a suboperation. If you do not set this indicator, the duration of the operation is set automatically to zero. This can be used to designate the work center for documentation purposes, for example. The order passes through the work center but consumes no resource capacities.
- *Capacity planning*—creates capacity requirements records for the operation or suboperation, if there are suitable formulas for calculating the amounts.
- *Costing* indicator—shows whether the operation or suboperation can be costed.
- *Confirmation*—shows whether and how the operation or suboperation can be confirmed.
- *Time tickets*—signifies that time tickets are printed for the operation or suboperation.
- *Print operation*—signifies that shop papers are printed for the operation or suboperation.
- *External processing*—signifies that the operation or suboperation is to be performed by a third-party. A requisition for this work is generated during order creation.

Creating Standard Texts

You can enter a standard text key to assign a previously created standard text to an operation or suboperation. This text can be a description or a procedure included for reference. The text can be altered as necessary.

The following sequence will allow you to create and maintain standard texts within Work Center Maintenance:

1. Select Logistics→Production→Master data→Work centers→Extras→Standard texts.
2. Enter the name of the standard text and choose what you intend to do with it—create, change, delete, display.

You can also select Routings in place of Work Centers to maintain standard texts.

Defining Capacities for a Work Center

A capacity is a unit that represents the ability to perform a task. A particular work center may be able to provide various services and so will be recorded as having corresponding capacities. The amount of work in a unit of capacity will usually be defined by reference to a certain time period.

The standard capacity categories that can be assigned to work centers include the following:

- Machine capacity
- Labor capacity
- Reserve capacity for rush orders
- Emissions
- Energy

For example, internal labor costs are calculated per unit of finished product. These costs are thus assigned to the work center as a cost object that accumulates the costs according to the output of product. Accounting then proceeds by considering the work center cost records.

The labor costs are determined during planning for each type of activity and recorded as standard values.

If a work center is to be used in Scheduling, the execution times for the activities performed there have to be recorded. Again, standard values are determined at the planning stage and applied in conjunction with the quantities planned or produced. Given these execution times, or the formulas to derive them, the system can calculate the start and finish times for any particular operation.

When it comes to capacity planning, the various capacities available from the work centers are used to select how one or more work centers can be used to provide the capacities needed for any particular order or batch of orders. Standard values are used to convert the order quantities into work center capacity requirements.

Work centers can be structured in hierarchies; and their available capacities can be cumulated upwards through these structures, or the capacity requirements can be distributed downwards.

Setup times will also be specified as standard times at the relevant work centers, if necessary.

A standard value key is an indicator code that can be used to specify which standard values are mandatory for an operation and which are optional in the work center. This key can also determine the units of measure to be used for the standard values.

A Work Center Assignment is a linking of a work center with any of the following objects:

- Another work center
- A cost center
- A qualification
- A position
- A person assigned an ID in the personnel planning and development (PD) application

The purpose of assigning qualifications to a work center is to define the minimum level of education or skill required of an employee who is to work there.

If you assign a position, such as an established and approved post, to a work center, any employee who is available and is currently holding that position will be automatically assigned to the work center.

An employee who is documented in the PD module and has therefore been assigned a unique personnel ID number can be assigned to a specific work center.

Using Work Center Default Values

Default values maintained in a Work Center Master Record are automatically copied to the operations to be processed using that work center.

If you use work center default values as references in task lists, you have to accept them; you cannot change work center default values from the task list itself.

Using Work Center Formulas

You can adjust copies of standard formulas or create your own to calculate the following work center values:

- Costs of operations carried out at the work center
- Execution times in the production order for each operation—setup, processing, teardown
- Times for other types of internal processing such as networks and maintenance orders
- Capacity requirements for each operation—setup, processing, teardown

A formula may include a split. This is a refinement of the calculation to accommodate such factors as variable lot size and partial lots.

You have to signify the formula you intend to use by selecting a formula key that will identify a formula and the parameters needed by it.

The parameter ID determines the following:

- The parameter's definition and key word
- The parameter's dimension
- The parameter's name in a formula

Parameters can be formed from the following origins:

- Standard value—a standard value is assigned to the parameter used in the formula by a standard value key.
- Formula constants stored in the work center—a fixed value taken from the Work Center Master Record is assigned to the parameter.
- General operation value—a field is directly assigned to the parameter from the general operation data, such as lot size, base quantity, number of splits (partial lots), number of employees. The value in this field is entered into the formula.
- User-defined field from the operation—a user-defined field is assigned to the data field in the operation. The value in this field is entered into the formula.
- Value from production resource/tool (PRT) assignment—a field is assigned to the parameter during PRT assignment. The value in this field is entered in the formula. This value can be either the quantity or the usage value of the production resource/tool.
- Production resource/tool constants—a fixed value is assigned to the parameter in the master record of the PRT. This value is then entered into formulas.

Using Standard Formula Keys

Table 4.1 shows how three standard formula keys are defined. Table 4.2 shows the description and origin of each parameter used in Table 4.1.

Table 4.1 Work Center Standard Formula Keys

Formula key	Formula
F1	SET
F2	RUN * LOT / B
F3	SET + RUN * LOT / B

Table 4.2 Origin of Work Center Formula Parameters

Parameter ID	Parameter description	Origin
SET	Setup time	Standard value
RUN	Processing time	Standard value
LOT	Lot size	General operation value
B	Base quantity	General operation value

Part
II

Ch
4

Creating Formulas for Work Centers

A standard formula can be assigned, or new formulas can be created in customizing if you have the necessary authorization. The parameters used in a formula must be standard or defined in customizing. You can assign an indicator to a formula to control where and how it is used, for example, in the following business procedures:

- Scheduling
- Costing
- Calculating capacity requirements
- Calculating production resource/tool requirements

The basic operations and functions that can be used in formulas are as follows:

- Basic arithmetic calculations, such as +,-,* and /
- Trigonometric functions with SIN and COS
- Division of integers with remainders using DIV or MOD
- Calculation of square roots with SQRT
- Exponential function with EXP
- Natural logarithm with LOG

The length of a formula is limited to three lines. There must be at least one blank space between the operand and the operator, except where the operand is enclosed in brackets, for example, SIN (X + 2). Units of measure are automatically converted and do not have to be included in the formula.

There are three methods of displaying formulas:

- From the Scheduling, Capacity Overview, or Cost Center Assignment screens, position the cursor on the formula and select the menu options Extras→Formula→Display....
- On the Scheduling screen, click the Information symbol after the formula you are interested in.
- On the Capacity Overview screen, press the function key Formula.

The following sequence will allow you to test a formula in the Scheduling, Capacity Overview, or Cost Center Assignment screens:

1. Position the cursor on a formula and select the menu options Extras→Formula→Test.
2. In the dialog box Test Formula, enter the testing data, such as the key words for user-defined fields, the operation quantity, standard values, and such values as the normal duration for other types of internal processing.
3. Press the function key Calculate.

You can define a parameter value in a work center that will then be used in any formula at that work center that contains the key word for that parameter.

Providing Work Center Technical Data for CAPP   CAPP is computer aided process planning. This function module provides calculation services that begin with the computation of standard values. These parameters define the capabilities and resource needs of a manufacturing or other business process. An activity that is assigned to a work center can use the data provided there, which can included the following:

- Technical data, such as machine type and sort strings for finding formulas and processes by matchcodes

- CAPP planner group ID to identify the person or people responsible for maintaining CAPP elements and technical data

- Additional values and rounding categories entered as a predefined key and used to adjust the computed values so as to accord with the policy or practice in quantity estimating for this work center

- Processes, chosen from a list of processes that have already been assigned to the work center

This data is entered during work center maintenance by the sequence Goto→Technical data. The standard values computed from the technical data are copied to the routing and then used for planning and scheduling.

If you need to assign a process to a work center, you select Extras→Process assignment from the Technical Data screen. A standard indicator is normally maintained for each process so as to streamline data entry. The CAPP cannot calculate standard values for a work center unless at least one process has been assigned to it.

Part

II

Ch

4

Understanding a Work Center Hierarchy

Two work centers can have the relationships *superior* and *subordinate*, respectively. This pair of work centers constitutes a simple work center hierarchy. There is no limit in R/3 to the complexity of a hierarchy.

You can set up any number of hierarchies; one work center can appear in more than one hierarchy. The justification for defining a work center hierarchy can include any of the following purposes:

- Locate work centers in plant configurations
- Cumulate available capacity during capacity requirements planning
- Cumulate capacity requirements in capacity planning
- Locate work centers when creating task lists
- Structure a graphic display of work center master data

Assigning a Work Center to a Cost Center

A cost center is defined as a part of a company delimited according to responsibility, location, or billing areas. The cost center is assigned to a controlling area.

If the plants are all assigned to the same company code for accounting purposes, work centers from various plants can be assigned to one cost center. Assignment will be for a defined period of time.

A cost center may have more than one work center assigned to it. But each work center must be assigned to only one cost center at any moment.

Establishing the Activity Types for a Cost Center

The different activity types within a cost center can be divided into categories, such as production and maintenance; and within a controlling area, you can define activity types that will be used as necessary in this area.

An activity type is evaluated by assigning it a value that depends on the cost center, the period, and the charge rate. The charge rate is made up of a fixed portion and a work-related portion. Not all activity types need be valid for a particular cost center.

Understanding Work Center Capacity Data

A capacity can be maintained as exclusive to a particular work center, or you can define capacities that are independent of any work center. The following capacities are differentiated:

- Work center capacities
- Pooled capacities
- Reference capacities
- Default capacities

Typical work center capacities are as follows:

- Machine capacity
- Labor capacity
- Reserve capacity for rush orders
- Emissions
- Energy consumption

Each capacity category appears only once per work center.

A *pooled capacity* can be assigned across several work centers. Thus a particular group of employees can be assigned to several work centers so that they can work in any of them.

A *reference capacity* is used for copying during the creation of new capacities. A reference capacity is maintained independently of any work center.

A *default capacity* is a combination of a capacity and a plant that is copied when a new capacity is being created. Default capacities are maintained only in customizing.

Defining Available Capacity

The Capacity screen enables you to define the operating time and daily available capacity at a work center. These available capacities can be defined for individual work centers or for all work centers. You have to define the available capacity for each individual capacity category at a work center in terms of the number of working hours. This value is used in Scheduling, although not before it has been modified by some or all of the following factors:

- Break times
- Technical malfunctions
- Organizational problems

The net result is a value of the productive working hours or theoretically available hours. This number of productive working hours is called *operating time*. You can derive the capacity utilization and thus the percentage of operating time that is productive in a shift for each capacity.

The total available capacity for a work center capacity is the operating time multiplied by the number of individual capacities for each capacity category. This computation can exist in several versions, of which only the active one is used in scheduling and capacity planning. A standard version is used by default unless you specify otherwise.

A *reference available capacity* can be defined as a model to use when creating capacities.

A *standard available capacity* can be used to record the normal work start and finish times, break times, and the capacity utilization. This standard is valid every workday unless a particular interval of available capacity has been defined. When the system needs to calculate the overall lead time for a routing, the standard available capacity data is used, and no reference to an order is needed.

An *interval of available capacity* is an available capacity that has been assigned a defined validity period. This interval has a cycle length and it is repeated as required. Thus you can define the shift values for one cycle of an interval of available capacity and the pattern will be automatically repeated.

Part
II

Ch
4

Defining Shift Values

Shift values are needed to calculate the total available capacity in a shift when using intervals of available capacity. The shift values are as follows:

- Capacity utilization—the ratio, as a percentage, of the capacity actually used to the theoretically available capacity for all individual capacities, per capacity category
- Number of the individual capacities in a shift
- Operating times

Using a Shift Definition

A *shift definition* includes the start, finish, and break times in a shift for all work centers. Thus if you alter the values in a shift definition, the change will affect all capacities that refer to it in all work centers.

A *shift sequence* is a defined succession of shift definitions that can be repeated over a period and will apply to all work centers. The sequence can be accessed when maintaining available capacity in a work center.

A *profile of available capacity* is an overview of the available capacity for a work center. You can define up to three versions of available capacity or capacity categories. The display will show the capacities available on each day. SAP presentation graphics can be used on these profiles.

Cumulating Available Capacity

When work centers are arranged in a hierarchy, the available capacity of different work centers can be cumulated to the superior work center level. Capacity categories are differentiated. You can use a different version of available capacity if a work center forms part of more than one hierarchy.

Using Period Pattern Keys

Available capacity is cumulated according to a period pattern key that defines a time frame and an increment.

A period pattern key comprises any number of consecutive segments. Each segment is built from periods defined by period length and period type. Typical period types include:

- Calendar days
- Workdays
- Weeks
- Months
- Years

Available capacity is cumulated per period as an average for each available capacity. The averaged available capacities for one period are then cumulated.

Using Capacity Assignments

A capacity assignment is a relationship or association between the capacity and another object. If you have the PD application installed and configured in your system, and if you have set the *CapCatPers* indicator in customizing for the corresponding capacity category, you can assign a capacity to the following types of object:

- People
- Qualifications
- Positions

If you did not set the indicator, or you do not have PD, you can still create a capacity and store it as an individual capacity.

Creating Individual Capacities

The following sequence will allow you to define individual capacities: From the Capacity Header screen, select the menu options Goto→Assignments→Indiv. capacities. An individual capacity belongs to the same capacity category as the capacity itself. If an individual capacity *Maintain(ed)* indicator is set, the available capacity of this individual capacity has been maintained.

Individual capacities are used to plan resources and commitments in more detail within capacity planning. For example, you can associate part of a work center available capacity with an individual machine and so manage the capacity requirements for that facility. If you have not entered particular data during individual capacity maintenance, the system will use the operating time of the corresponding capacity to calculate the available capacity.

Assigning People to Specific Work Center Capacities

If you have PD, each employee or external contractor will have a unique ID, which you can assign to a capacity where they are to work.

The following sequence from the Header screen for the capacity will access the Assignments to People screen where you can assign people to the capacity: Goto→Assignments→People.

Restricting People Assignments by Qualifications

A qualification or qualification requirements profile assigned to a capacity will restrict the people who can be assigned to that capacity. The following sequence from the header screen for the capacity will access the Assignments to Qualifications screen: Goto→Assignments→Qualifications.

A qualification is defined by the following parameters:

- The priority of an object type in relation to other qualifications
- A proficiency defining how well a person must fulfill a specific qualification
- Experience in years of the employee at this work center

Using Positions

A position can be assigned a qualification or qualification profile. You can then assign this position to a capacity as a way of representing the role or accepted title of a person who is suitable for performing the particular work. The qualifications associated with the position will then limit the selection of employees for the capacity.

The following sequence from the Header screen for the capacity will access the Assignments to Positions screen from which you can assign a capacity to a position: Goto→Assignments→Positions.

Part
II
Ch
4

You will not be allowed to refer to a position unless it has been defined in the personnel planning and development (PD) application.

Assigning Capacities

The following sequence will access the Capacity Maintenance screen: Logistics→Production→Master data→Work centers→Capacity. A Copy from... function key allows you to create a new capacity by copying the details from one previously defined. There are various ways you can find the capacity to imitate:

- If you want to use a pooled capacity or a reference capacity, enter the capacity and its capacity category.
- If you want to copy a capacity that belongs to a work center, enter the work center key and its capacity category.

You can select how much data to copy from a model or reference capacity:

- Header data
- Short descriptions
- Intervals of available capacity

You can access the same Capacity Maintenance dialog from the Detail screens of Work Center Maintenance. Your authorization will control whether you are allowed to create, change, or only display capacities.

During customizing, your system will have been given a default capacity containing setting of default values for each combination of capacity category and plant that your company is likely to need.

If you need to create a new capacity using the Create function, you have to enter the following header information:

- A plant where the capacity is located
- A name by which the capacity is known in the system
- A capacity category, such as labor or machine

Maintaining Data for Capacity Planning

The Planning details area of a capacity record includes the following indicators:

- *Relevant to finite scheduling*—causes the system to use the available capacity and the capacity load in finite scheduling.
- *Can be used by several operations*—allows the available capacity of this capacity to be used by several operations. For example, if the capacity represents a person, you can plan that they will perform various operations. You can also set this indicator when the capacity you are planning is the available capacity of a defined group of machines. If this indicator is not set, any portion of the capacity remaining available cannot be assigned to another operation.

■ *Long-term planning*—allows you to mark this capacity for use in long-term planning (LTP), where the material requirements and capacities are calculated after consulting a planned demand program.

The planning details area also allows you to enter an overload percentage, which will permit the system to accept a load that exceeds the available capacity. To achieve this, you might have to arrange for the work center to carry on through breaks, for example.

Maintaining Capacity Data in the Work Center

A work center may have a category that allows you to alter the capacities assigned to it. If so allowed, you can access the Capacity Overview screen during the work center creation procedure, or by the following sequence from Work Center Maintenance:
Goto→Capacity→Overview

The header data for a capacity used for general scheduling is not related to specific orders. This header data includes the following types of information:

■ General data

■ Available capacity

■ Standard available capacity

■ Planning details

The general data for a capacity includes an identification of the planner group responsible for maintaining this capacity and the group to which the capacity is assigned for maintaining daily work schedules. Groupings 1-50 are used for Employee Management and groupings 51-99 are for Logistics.

Distributing Capacity Requirements

The distribution of capacity requirements over the duration of the operation refers to the way in which the various available capacities are consumed. For example, a manufacturing process that uses a machine capacity for several shifts will probably need to call on some labor capacities to check that it is working properly at intervals throughout the run. On the other hand, there might be a requirement for continuous periods of a labor capacity for the setup and teardown operations. Thus each capacity category has its own distribution over the duration of the whole operation. These distributions are assigned using a distribution key during capacity planning. You can maintain the following kinds of distribution keys:

■ A key specifying the distribution of capacity requirements according to the operation segments setup, processing, and teardown, for example, in a production order.

■ A key specifying the distribution of capacity requirements for other types of internal processing, for example, in networks or maintenance orders.

Setting Data for Scheduling

You can access the Scheduling screen during work center creation, or you can access it directly by the following sequence: Goto→Scheduling.

Part
II

Ch
4

The scheduling data is as follows:

- Scheduling basis—determines which capacities are used for an order
- Execution time—calculated from the operating time of the capacity
- Interoperation times
- Dimension and unit of measure of work

An available capacity will not be considered for scheduling unless it has been assigned the dimension "time."

Reviewing Available Capacity

A display of available capacity is generated according to the search parameters that you define as a user or during customizing. An available capacity has to contain references to the following types of information:

- The factory calendar ID that the available capacity is based on—the plant factory calendar will be assumed by default
- The active version of the available capacity— causes a display of the Details icon that you can click to find out about the version of available capacity if it is different from the standard available capacity
- Base unit of measure, which must have the dimension "time"

Converting the Base Unit of Measure

If you need the available capacity in units other than time, such as pieces or tons, you can set up the conversion calculation and then use it to convert a capacity to or from units of time.

The following sequence on the Header screen will allow you to make conversion arrangements: Extras→Units of measure. The dialog box Units of Measure for Conversion offers you the chance to select a base unit of measure in the time dimension. Then, you have to enter the number of units of capacity that corresponds. For example, you could select *10 seconds* and enter *1 piece*. The system would then automatically store a conversion factor that would apply to any time interval and any number of pieces. If you enter an amount of product against a time interval, the system will similarly store a conversion factor that applies to any amount of product.

Specifying a Standard Available Capacity

A standard available capacity requires the following data:

- Work start and finish times of a shift
- Length of breaks
- Capacity utilization
- Number of individual capacities, such as the number of machines or people

The system uses this information to calculate the following values:

- Operating time of the capacity in hours
- Available capacity in the base unit of measure or in one of the units of measure for which you have entered a conversion factor

This standard available capacity is valid for all versions unless you have defined an *interval of available capacity* to restrict its scope.

You can use a model or reference to create an available capacity record by copying the details from a capacity that belongs to a work center or from a pooled capacity record that has been created for reference purposes. The copying operation will transfer both the standard available capacity and the interval of available capacity to the new capacity.

You can edit the details you have copied. However, if you do make any changes, the reference will not be altered, nor will your new capacity reflect any changes that are subsequently made to the reference capacity. If you copy a capacity from a capacity that cites a reference, your new capacity will copy this reference directly.

Consulting the Profile of Available Capacity

Part
II
Ch
4

The *Profile of Available Capacity* screen allows you to compare different versions of available capacity and/or different capacity categories. The display will accept a maximum of three versions of available capacity and/or capacity categories at the same time.

You can filter the data by nominating the capacity category and version number of the capacity of interest, and you can limit the search by entering the earliest date from which the valid intervals of available capacity are to be displayed.

A standard available capacity is valid for an unlimited period. However, within an interval of available capacity, you can define an available capacity that has a limited validity period.

Displaying Intervals of Available Capacity

The system will default to version 1, all dates, when you display the *Intervals of Available Capacity* screen, unless you can select available capacities according to their version numbers and their validity dates. The standard available capacity is the first interval in the overview.

The *Intervals of Available Capacity* screen shows the following data:

- Validity period for the interval of available capacity
- Indicator showing whether the standard available capacity is valid for the interval
- Shift sequence for the interval of available capacity you have specified
- Cycle length specifying the number of days over which the available capacity is repeated within the interval of available capacity
- Maximum number of shifts in one day within the interval of available capacity
- Indicator showing whether the days in the interval are working days

You can inspect another version by the following sequence: Goto→Version→Another cap. Version.→Enter version number→Press Continue.

Defining Shifts

After you have created an interval of available capacity, the system will automatically display the Shifts screen on which you can maintain the following information:

- Shift definition—used to copy the details from a shift that has been previously defined
- Shift start
- Shift finish
- Length of break
- Capacity utilization
- Number of individual capacities in this shift

You can use Edit to add shifts as new entries before the shift indicated by your cursor. You have to insert new shifts consecutively so that the start and finish times do not overlap.

You can also use Edit to copy a shift and insert as directed by the weekday and shift number you enter.

Displaying Available Capacity with SAP Business Graphic

SAP Business Graphic may be used to display the Profile of Available Capacity screen by following this sequence:

1. Goto→Graphic
2. Consider the dialog box Time Frame for Period Pattern and Selections
3. Enter a period pattern key to specify a pattern of consecutive time segments
4. Enter the dates you wish to inspect as a 3-D graphic
5. Press the function key Continue

Cumulating Available Capacity

Cumulation uses a capacity hierarchy to collect available capacity at the superior work center level from the capacity in the subordinate work centers. You might need to do this in requirements planning if you have not maintained available capacity directly for the superior work center level.

The technique is used in both capacity maintenance and work center maintenance. There is a *Stop explosion* indicator that can be set in a branch to control the extent of the cumulation up a hierarchy.

Cumulated available capacity is used in capacity planning. The system automatically defines the operating time for the superior work center as the greatest operating time of the subordinate work centers involved.

One work center can be included in several hierarchies. You can define a version number if you cumulate available capacities using a different hierarchy. You then have to specify which version is to be used for capacity planning.

Administering Work Centers

You can copy a work center and edit the copy to create a new work center. You have to select the work center you intend to use as a reference, and this will entail identifying the plant in which the model is located.

If you initiate the copy from the work center initial screen, all the data will be copied by default. If you are in another screen, such as the Default Values screen, then only the values on the screen will be suggested for copying.

There is a Work center→Change procedure available during work center maintenance that you can use to rename an existing work center and reassign a work center key. You can then edit any data before saving the work center under its new name. The act of saving a renamed work center will automatically change all applications where the old name or old work center key is used.

Finding a Work Center

The following search specifications can be used to find a work center using a matchcode:

Part

II

Ch

4

- Work center category
- Class
- Work center name
- Technical data
- Person responsible

Classifying Work Centers

If you have assigned some work centers to a predefined work center class, you can maintain data in the class and it will be applied to all member work centers.

The following sequence will create a class:

> Logistics→Central functions→
> Classification→Class→Create

When you are assigning work centers to a class, the system will automatically recognize that you are dealing with the work center class type, although you can choose another class type if there is more than one assigned to the work center. The following sequence will allow you to build a work center class from the Basic Data screen:

> Extras→Classification→Values

From the Values screen, you can choose a characteristic value to be entered.

Assigning Work Centers to Subsystems

A work center can be associated with one or more subsystems, such as a plant data collection (PDC) system. This subsystem can be included in work center maintenance so that the work center data is automatically transferred to the subsystem. The following sequence will identify the destination:

1. From the work center Basic Data screen, select Extras→Subsystem link→Subsystem Grouping screen.

2. Enter the subsystems where the work center data should be sent.

You can have the work center data checked for completeness so that processing will be successful. The work center can be locked against further changes or usage. You can then unlock it at a later date.

Deleting Work Centers

Deleting a work center on the Basic Data screen will remove it from the system and it can no longer be archived for later use or analysis. You can set a deletion flag for a work center that is currently in use so that it will be removed when the next reorganization run takes place. You cannot assign a work center that has a deletion flag. However, you can archive and delete a work center with a deletion flag. You can also remove the flag.

Limiting Work Center Assignment Validity Periods

You can specify validity periods so that a work center is assigned to different cost centers according to the time periods defined. Similarly, you can establish validity periods for any of the following work center or capacity assignments:

- People
- Positions
- Qualifications

Understanding Work Center Administrative Data

The following information can be obtained from the Administrative Data dialog box:

- Technical info on the work center, including the system's internal key for the work center
- Last change in the work center, when it took place, and who did it
- Status of the work center—active, locked, or marked for deletion

The ability to make alterations to work center data is controlled by the standard SAP system of authorizations, in which each user is assigned a user master record during customizing. The permissions are structured as follows:

- Activity authorization according to the create, change, display, and delete processing types

- Plant authorization
- Work center category authorization

Displaying Work Center Change Documents

You can see what changes to work center data have taken place if various conditions can be met:

- For each work center category you are interested in, there must be an indicator set that allows the data to be displayed.
- The fields you want to see must be marked for display in the Data Dictionary.

If you then ask about changes, the system will display all changes to the field for each posting. It is prudent to limit the amount of data you collate. For example, you can ask for reports on change documents for only specific work centers. You might need to limit the scope by setting the *hierarchy explosion* indicator to stop at a certain level. An additional search frame could be built using values for the following parameters:

- Person responsible
- Location
- Task list usage
- Changes made from a certain date and time
- Changes made to a certain date and time

The results will be a list of change documents in which each document refers to the changes made at the same time.

Archiving Work Centers

The work center archiving process will not delete pooled capacities and reference capacities. Otherwise, all work center data and work center capacities will be deleted, whether deletion flags are set or not.

Using Default Work Centers and Capacities

The purpose of a default work center is to enable you to establish a set of default values that can be copied when creating instances of work centers in the same work center category and plant. Copies from a default work center cannot include a long text or a description. No ID key is set up for a default work center.

Default capacities may be established and used in the same way as default work centers.

Using Field Modification in Work Centers

When a work center is being customized, you can determine how each data field shall be modified when it is displayed. The following are standard field modifications:

- Input fields
- Required entry fields
- Display fields
- Hidden fields
- Highlighted fields

Fields can also be identified according to whether they are *modifying* or *influencing*. For example, standard screen groups have been defined for the following types of information:

- Basic data
- Default values
- Scheduling
- Capacity overview

The work center category is also an influencing field in that you can arrange for a standard value to be entered in certain fields automatically according to the work center category.

Creating Work Center Hierarchies

An SAP hierarchy is a data structure that is similar to a family tree in that there can be many branches, and each branch can have its own branches, and so on. Each hierarchy has to be defined in the master records.

A work center hierarchy is a tree structure that links work centers into whatever groupings are useful. For example, you might want to have each manufacturing plant defined as the owner of some work centers that correspond to departments. Each department could have a number of work centers that correspond to sections, and each section could have one or more physical work centers where one or more employees do the actual work. Thus an individual worker could be traced along the following hierarchical path:

Employee works in a

Work center that belongs to a

Section that is part of a

Department that belongs to a

Plant that is accounted under a

Company Code that is consolidated as part of the

Client that represents the highest level of the enterprise

If you want to have a work center hierarchy with all these levels, you have to create it during customizing. After that, you can define one or more work centers at each of the various levels of the hierarchy. One use of a work center hierarchy is to represent the physical location of each working unit. For instance, if you look for the details of a work center defined as a particular department, you will find the address and similar administrative information. You will also discover that the departmental level work center comprises some sectional level work centers, and so on down the levels.

The master record for this departmental level work center will also show that the department is responsible to the management of a specific plant that is owned by a company or company code unit, which is in turn owned by a particular corporation.

Apart from using a work center hierarchy to classify administrative information, you can have the system examine the entire hierarchy to cumulate available capacities at each level. This gives you the basis on which to plan how much work can be scheduled.

The same work center hierarchy structure can be used to cumulate the capacity requirements for a given production output.

The following sequence will create a work center hierarchy:

1. Select Logistics→Production→Master data→Work centers→Hierarchy→Create
2. Enter the name of the hierarchy and the plant ID
3. Enter a short text to describe the hierarchy
4. If you do not want to maintain any additional data, save the hierarchy by selecting Hierarchy→Save

When you have created a work center hierarchy, you can assign a work center to it during Hierarchy Maintenance or during Work Center Maintenance. A work center can be assigned to several different work center hierarchies if they have been created for particular purposes.

You can assign a single work center to a hierarchy by entering just the plant and the work center IDs. If you have several work centers that can be identified by a generic search code such as "Packing*", they can all be assigned in one operation. Another search possibility is to assign work centers according to the person responsible for them. The system reminds you of any assignments that have already been made if you attempt to create a duplicate assignment to the same hierarchy.

When you have identified the work centers you wish to assign, you can use the Work Center Assignments Graphic to point to the exact position in the hierarchy to which the assignment is to be made.

If you are maintaining data for a particular work center, you can assign the work center to a specific place in another work center hierarchy by the following sequence:

1. Select Goto→Hierarchy→Relationships.
2. Examine the display of the existing relationships between this work center and any hierarchies to which it belongs.
3. Select Edit→New entries.
4. In the dialog box Another Hierarchy, enter the plant and the key for the hierarchy to which you want to assign the work center.
5. Press Continue to show the Hierarchy Detail screen.

Part
II
Ch
4

6. Set the *root* indicator if you wish this work center to become the root at the highest level of the hierarchy. This will not be allowed if the hierarchy already has a root.

7. Enter a superior work center to which the work center will be assigned.

Using the Hierarchy Structure

If you select the Graphic screen in hierarchy maintenance, you can control the arrangement of the display so as to be able to carry out any of the following procedures:

- Connect Work Centers—by dragging a dashed line with the cursor
- Delete Work Center Connections—by using the function *Split* when you have marked the subordinate with your cursor
- Display Hierarchy Structures—by Goto→Hierarchy structure, from the Header display in hierarchy maintenance
- Limit the Hierarchy Structure Display—to specified levels, *All after* or *Up to* an indicated work center level

The system stops you from assigning a work center as a subordinate to another if you have already defined it as being a superior. You have to delete the previous relationship if you want to make this kind of reassignment.

The hierarchy graphics are controlled by standard SAP Graphics functions that allow you to make various adjustments to the colors and the ways objects are selected in the displays.

Identifying the Work Center Additional Functions

The following additional functions have been defined for specific purposes when managing work centers:

- Displaying where-used lists for work centers
- Displaying where-used lists for capacities
- Replacing work centers
- Replacing work centers in operations
- Replacing work centers using the menu
- Defining the object overview—to select data such as the header, sequence, operation and suboperation, and the fields within those objects
- Maintaining default values
- Displaying and changing objects in task lists
- Defining replacement control
- Replacing work centers
- Displaying error logs
- Displaying work center lists
- Displaying cost center assignments

- Displaying work center capacities
- Displaying work center hierarchies
- Reporting

Displaying a Work Center Hierarchy

The following sequence will produce a list of work centers displayed in a hierarchy:

1. Select Logistics→Production→Master data→Work centers→Reporting→Work ctr hierarchy.
2. To restrict the search, enter the plant and the work center, or work center category.
3. Enter the hierarchy plant and hierarchy name for the hierarchy to be displayed.
4. To confine the report to particular levels of the hierarchy, enter the numbers of the levels you are interested in.
5. Select Program→Execute, or press the function key Execute.

Work Center Reporting

The Reporting menu choice offers a choice of standard reports delivered with the system. Alternatively, you can select any reports that have been specifically designed for your user company. These *user-defined reports* access the logical database for work centers in order to assemble and collate the information pertaining to the selected work centers.

The standard work center reports are as follows:

- Work center list
- Cost center assignment
- Work center capacity
- Work center hierarchy

Displaying a Work Center List

The following sequence will generate a work center list:

1. Select Logistics→Production→Master data→Work centers→Reporting→Work center list.
2. Enter the work center key if you know it. Otherwise, you can enter a generic string containing * to signify *any characters*. Another search tactic is to enter the plant where you think the work center is located and restrict the search by nominating the work center category and, if necessary, the person responsible for the work center.
3. Set the hierarchy explosion indicator if you want the report to include work centers on the lower branches of a work center hierarchy that you have identified by its hierarchy name. If you have entered a work center key, the explosion will begin at the work center specified by the key.
4. Select Program→Execute or press the function key Execute.

Displaying the Assignments of Work Centers to Cost Centers

The following sequence will produce a list of cost center assignments:

1. Select Logistics→Production→Master data→Work centers→Reporting→Cost center assignmt.

2. If you do not want all the cost center assignments to be reported, enter a work center key. Alternatively, nominate the plant and the work center and search for particular controlling areas or cost center assignments. You can limit the search by entering a work center category, controlling area, and/or cost center.

3. Select Program→Execute, or press the function key Execute.

Displaying Work Center Capacities

The following sequence will list the selected work center capacities:

1. Select Logistics→Production→Master data→Work centers→Reporting→Work center capacity.

2. To restrict the search, enter the plant and the work center or work center category.

3. Enter the capacity category for the search.

4. Select Program→Execute, or press the function key Execute.

Displaying User-Defined Reports

Any additional reports you require have to be defined in customizing. For example, you can use the work center list report program RCRA0010 as a reference model and create a variant of it. ●

CHAPTER 5

Routing the Steps of the Production Processes

Distinguishing Routings from Other Task Lists

The step-by-step production of a finished product from raw materials is represented in SAP R/3 by a *routing*. The master record of a routing takes the format of a task list because it specifies the sequence of individual operations needed. A routing is considered to be a master record because it does not take into account any requirements arising from a particular order.

The routing specifies the tools and resources necessary for production and how these production resources and/or tools (PRTs) are deployed among the work centers where they are used. The routing can also specify the individual work steps that have to take place at each of these work centers.

In addition to the sequence of work centers with their particular PRTs, a routing records the standard times that are used when planning the individual operations.

A routing is built from elements known as *routing objects*, of which the following are the most important:

- Operations
- Material components
- Production resources/tools
- Inspection characteristics

The same master routing can be used by the R/3 system in any of the following activities:

- Production ordering
- Scheduling
- Capacity planning
- Costing

The order of processing steps for a production order is determined by consulting the appropriate routing, and the execution time of each operation is calculated by applying the scheduling procedure.

Scheduling from a Routing

The aim of the scheduling procedure is to calculate the date, and perhaps also the time, when each operation is to be carried out. Each operation is assigned values for the time taken for each of the following stages:

- Setup
- Processing
- Teardown

The total of these stages is stored as the *execution time*. Clearly the quantity of material to be processed in a work step can have a profound effect on the processing time, although some processes will always operate on the same quantity of material, such as a single piece of material.

Apart from the execution time of the actual processing, a material may spend some time at a work center before work on it begins. This waiting before execution time begins can be allowed for by assigning a *queue time*, which may be a standard value computed from the records.

The *move time* is defined as the time taken to move a material from one work center to the next in the sequence defined in the routing.

The *wait time* is the period when a material has undergone all the work allocated to that work center and is waiting to begin the move to the next work center.

The following types of scheduling are differentiated:

- Lead time scheduling, which assumes that a work center will always have sufficient capacity to complete the operation on the quantity specified
- Finite scheduling, which takes into account possible limitations in the available capacity

Capacity Planning from a Routing

The purpose of capacity planning is to determine the capacity requirements needed to complete the operations specified in a routing. The capacity planning function also compares the capacities needed with those actually available in the work centers.

The capacity requirements are calculated using the standard values and quantities specified in the routing, to which may be applied particular formulas that are stored in the Work Center Master Records.

Costing

When a material is produced or processed in-house, your company has to calculate the internal costs because they are needed in the following business processes:

- Pricing
- Valuation
- Cost controlling
- Profitability analysis

Part
II

Ch
5

When the production of a material is defined by a routing, cost accounting can use the information to compute the cost. Each work center in the routing will have been assigned one or more activities that are to take place there. Each activity will belong to an activity type. This activity type will control such factors as whether an activity is to be costed according to how long it takes or according to the quantity of material processed. Some activities may cost the same regardless of the quantity of material or the time taken.

Each work center is linked to a cost center in which all similar activities are costed in the same way by applying predefined cost rates. Thus the system of activities and activity types allows the cost centers to put a cost value on the work entailed in executing a master routing for a specific work order or customer order. The cost center can apply the formulas to deal with the actual quantities involved and any adjustment that has to be made to the various execution times and the delays between operations.

Understanding PP Routing Types

The processing steps needed to produce a material may be different according to the circumstances in which the routing is required. For example, your company may use a different routing according to the size of the lot to be processed. Another usage difference may be where a particular routing is assigned to direct the material if it has to be reworked, or if a prototype material is being processed.

The following variants of a routing are recognized by the PP module:

- Reference operation set, which is a set of operations that can be copied as many times as needed to build up a routing for a large quantity of one or more materials
- Rate routing, in which the data specifies how much of a given material can be processed in a standard time interval—the production rate—for each operation
- Reference rate routing, which is a set of operations for which the production rates have been maintained in the data so that the set can be copied to build a rate routing

Yet another variant of a simple routing is to arrange for alternative combinations of reference operation sets, materials, and plants. The particular configuration of the routing is determined at execution time. For example, both a left- and a right-handed component may be specified in the master routing.

If rate routings are used, the work centers concerned must have standard keys assigned to them that specify standard values for production, setup, and teardown times.

Using a Routing as a Task List

The following data objects in R/3 share the same structure and may all be referred to as *task lists*:

- Routing
- Rate routing
- Reference operation set
- Inspection plan
- Maintenance task list
- Standard network

Configuring the Routing Maintenance System

The process of customizing includes setting up the control data for routings and other types of task list. A routing is identified by a task list group and a group counter. Thus the following groups may each include one or more task list structures that are identified by their group counter numbers:

- Routing, which can also be accessed via a material
- Reference operation set
- Rate routing
- Reference rate routing

The task list groups can be identified by a code assigned by the system or by an alphanumeric ID assigned by an authorized user. Within each group, the system administrator can define the number ranges to be assigned to the members of the group.

Identifying General Data for Routings

The general data for a routing controls how a link to Materials Management should be configured and installed and other configured application modules can access routings.

The general data also specifies the groups of people who are responsible for particular task lists, including routings.

Defining Material Type Allocations

The constraints on a task list include the types of material on which it may operate. In particular, you cannot create a routing for a material if the material type has not been assigned to the routing task list type. The R/3 system is delivered with standard assignments of material types to task list types that cover most requirements.

Defining Routing Statuses

A *routing status* is an indicator that controls the work areas in which that routing may be used. There is a routing status indicator for the following work areas:

- Release for usage in orders or for reference in other task lists (reference operation sets or reference rate routings)
- Release for costing
- Automatic consistency check before the routing is saved

You can use a routing status indicator to select all routings ready for a particular work area.

Defining Task List Usage

Another indicator used to select task lists automatically is the task list usage. A set of standard usage indicators is provided, and new usages can be defined in customizing. Thus you can create several task lists or routings for the same material, but each list has a different usage and hence a different pattern of processing. For example, one routing may be used only by Plant Maintenance, and another only for Goods Receipt.

In each plant a planner group is defined for the maintenance of routings. This is indicated on the routing master records and can be used in task list selection.

Defining Overview Variants for Routings

An object overview is a list of the variables to be displayed for a particular purpose. Thus an overview variant can be created that will generate a particular screen containing the required selection of the following objects:

- Operations or sequences
- Fields displayed for each object, such as dates and quantities

Where-used lists can be customized in a similar way, as can the screens to be used in *mass replacement* in which defined work centers and reference operation sets are replaced by others.

Defining Relevancy to Costing

The product cost controlling module (CO-PC) collects data on the operations performed in manufacturing. This data collection is controlled by a parameter stored in the operation master record as an indicator called *relevancy to costing*.

The relevancy to costing indicator serves the following purposes:

- Controls whether an operation or suboperation in a routing is costed
- Controls whether a BOM item is costed
- Determines what portion of the fixed and variable costs are used in costing

The relevancy to costing indicator can be assigned price factors that are used according to the valuation variant. A price factor is used to modify the stored cost data of an operation under defined circumstances. A price factor is ignored in the following calculations:

- Standard cost estimate
- Calculation of the production order in the task list
- Calculation of the production order for the actual data.

Price factors can be applied to both the fixed and variable costs of an operation.

Defining Standard Trigger Point Usage

A *trigger point* is used in PP to mark the point in a production sequence where particular functions are to be executed if the status of an operation changes. A trigger point can be assigned to an operation in a routing, which will ensure that it is always active when the routing is used, or in an order, which will confine the trigger to that one occasion.

A trigger can be used, for example, to engage extra resources if the status of an operation signals a possible scheduling problem. These extra resources could be defined by a reference operation set that is copied into the routing if the status indicator goes critical. A condition record has to be specified to define what parameter values are to be considered when judging whether a trigger should be activated.

Standard trigger points are delivered in the system. A set of standard trigger points can be assigned to a trigger point master record and given a group name. If you group trigger points and associate them with particular usages, the system will suggest trigger points according to the usage when the user is assigning a trigger point to a routing or an order.

Selecting a Routing

The PP system will identify a task list, such as a routing, when you activate any of the following procedures:

- Creating a task list using the copy function
- Creating an order
- Scheduling
- Costing

The system has to decide which task list to select by consulting one or more of the following parameters:

- Task list application
- Task list type
- Selection ID

A selection ID points to a set of criteria that have been defined for the automatic selection of routings. You can arrange selection priorities for each selection ID so that the following criteria are searched in a particular order:

- Routing type
- Routing usage
- Routing status

Assigning Production Resources/Tools

An individual operation can be assigned a specific combination of materials, production resources, and tools. This assignment can take place in task lists or in specific work orders, where the default task list assignment will be overruled.

A PRT assignment is specified by attributes. You can define default values for these attributes in the master data records of the PRTs. These assignments can be activated by predefined PRT control keys and formulas.

A PRT control key determines which of the PRTs that have been allocated to a task list or an order are to be included when each of the following business functions is executed:

- Scheduling
- Costing
- Printing production orders
- Confirming completion

Formula parameters and formulas are used when the master records of production resources/ tools are being maintained. The calculations determine the total quantity or total usage value of a PRT needed during the operation. It may also be necessary to have different formulas for different production situations, such as when the operation is used on different lot sizes.

The operation formula parameters are also needed during work center maintenance to define standard values and formulas that apply to the work center in which the operation takes place. The work center formulas calculate capacity requirements, lead times, and costs for use in the following activities:

- Capacity planning
- Scheduling
- Costing

Transferring Routing Data from Third-Party Systems

Your routing data may be held in an existing system that is not integrated with your R/3 implementation. In these circumstances a transfer structure has to be generated that will read the source database into a sequential file that can be batch processed to transfer the information.

The SAP system is able to generate a transfer structure in the following programming languages:

- COBOL
- C
- PL/1
- ASSEMBLER

Report RCPTRA01 is able to process the data elements into the following standard table structures:

- Session record
- Material allocation
- Task list header
- Long text Task list header
- Sequence
- Long text Sequence
- Operation
- Long text Operation
- PRT allocation
- Long text PRT allocation
- Material component allocation
- Header record per transaction—contains the transaction code of the transaction to be processed
- "CA01"—create routing
- "CA11"—create reference operation set

Creating and Maintaining Routings

Although a routing is assigned to a specific plant, you can assign individual operations in a routing to another plant if necessary, provided this plant belongs to the same company code.

A material can have a routing assigned to it. The following configurations are allowed:

- A material has routings in more than one routing group, for example, if there is more than one method of producing it.
- Routings for a material belong to the same routing group and are distinguished by their counter numbers.
- A routing can handle different materials, from different plants, if necessary.
- A routing can be created without reference to a material; the material is identified later.

When you create a routing for a material, the system will automatically display a list of all the routings already created for this material.

Understanding Routing Groups

A routing group can be created because the members of the group employ similar production processes. Another grouping basis is that the routings produce similar materials.

If you have different routings for various lot sizes, you can combine them into a group. Similarly, you can form a group out of the routings for all the plants that produce the same material.

Within a group, the routings are distinguished by the group counter number assigned to them. During routing maintenance, the system will load all members of a routing group together. Therefore it is best not to form large routing groups. If your routings have usages to associate them with particular application modules, you should create a new group for each usage and ensure that the same production alternative is given the same group counter number in each group so that automatic production alternative selection may be activated.

Exploring a Routing

The master records of a routing are accessible at various levels:

- Header—organizational and material-related data such as the plant, usage in production or engineering/design, material produced, validity period
- Sequence overview—standard ordered list of operations, plus alternative and parallel sequences
- Operation overview—shows work centers and short descriptions of the work performed in each and provides access to all other screens
- Detail screens—where the operations are maintained through overview screens for material components, production resources/tools, inspection characteristics, and trigger points
- Object overview—a configurable list of all objects and assignments in the routing, providing access to all other screens

Using Routing Profiles

Where some fields in routings have the same values, it is convenient to create a profile made up as a collection of default field values. A profile can be created for the routing header data or for operations. The default values can be changing in routing maintenance.

A data field in a routing master record may be an influencing field such as the indicator for the routing type. The value in this field can influence how the record is processed and perhaps the interpretation of other data fields. A modifiable field is amenable to the display controls.

The modifiable fields that are displayed during routing maintenance can be controlled by specifying characteristics for each data field from the following options:

- Field is ready for input.
- Field is a required entry.
- Field is displayed.
- Field is hidden.
- Field is highlighted.

Checking Authorization for Routing Access

A system user is represented by a user master record in which a profile of authorizations is recorded. User access to routing data is controlled by the following scheme of authorization objects:

- Authorization for an activity—authorizes creating, changing, displaying, and deleting routings
- Authorization for a task list type, such as routings or reference operation sets
- Authorization for a plant—authorizes maintenance of materials and routings (headers, operations, and suboperations) within a certain plant
- Authorization for a status
- Authorization for a usage
- Authorization for generating where-used lists
- Authorization for using the mass replace function
- Authorization for updating the material master
- Authorization for archiving routings
- Authorization for other purposes as defined in customizing

For example, the standard authorization object C_ROUT for routing maintenance allows the following actions:

- Action 01: Insert new data
- Action 02: Change data
- Action 03: Display data

- Action 24: Create archive files
- Action 41: Delete data from database

If your profile includes the authorization C_ROUT_MAT, you can also update the material master from routing maintenance.

Creating a Routing

You can create a routing with reference to a material, but if you do not specify a routing group, the system will assign one automatically, using the next free number in the range allocated in customizing to the type of task list you are creating.

You are allowed to copy a routing, a rate routing, reference operation set, or a reference rate routing. You do not have to copy from the same task list type. Then you can edit the data you have copied before saving the routing.

The following fields are available for data entry when creating a routing:

- Material and plant
- Sales document
- Group
- Change number—to access a change master record that records all changes and their effective dates
- Key date—to select the data that is valid at that particular time

The Header Details screen for a routing shows data that is valid for the entire routing, as follows:

- Group counter—number within the routing group
- Deletion flag—to mark this routing for deletion during the next archiving run, unless the flag is removed beforehand
- Planner group—the planner group and the production scheduler are identified in the material master record
- Status—of a reference operation set
- CAPP order—to select Production order, Planned order, or Standard value calculation using CAPP
- Header unit—to identify a unit of measure to be used throughout the routing for the material to be produced. The unit must be convertible to the base unit of measure specified in the material master record.

Saving the first routing in a group will determine the header unit for all subsequent routings in the same routing group.

An operation can allow dynamic modification of individual characteristics so as to inspect and control the quality level of the product. You have to specify the parameters for Dynamic Modification/Inspection Points during routing maintenance.

The following sequence will create a routing:

Part

II

Ch

5

1. Select Logistics→Production→Master data→Routings.
2. Select Routings→<TASK LIST TYPE>→Create.
3. Maintain the data on the initial screen.
4. Press Enter.

If there are no existing routings for the material, you will be able to go on to maintain the Header Details screen. However, if the system already has one or more routings in the same routing group for the material, you will be shown the overview screen.

If the system finds that there are routings for this material in various routing groups, you will be shown a dialog box that lists all groups and their routings.

When you find a suitable routing, you can select it and maintain the data or use it as a model from which to make a copy. The system checks all changes and edited copies. You will be branched to a detail screen from which the error can be corrected.

Classifying a Routing

If you have already created a class within the R/3 classification system, you can assign routings to it so as to be able to locate routings by searching the class.

The following sequence will assign a routing to a class:

1. Select Details→Header during routing maintenance.
2. Select Extras→Classification→Header.
3. Enter the class to which you want to assign the routing.
4. If necessary, select Edit→Values and maintain the characteristic values.

The following sequence will create a class:

1. Select the menu options Logistics→Central functions→Classification.
2. Select Class→Create.

Defining Matchcodes for Routings

Standard matchcodes are delivered in the system to facilitate locating data objects. You can select which matchcodes are to be associated with routings, and you can specify which fields taken from the routing master records are to be used with the matchcodes. You can also generate new matchcodes in customizing.

Displaying Administrative Data

The following sequences will call up administrative data for routing objects:

■ Header—from the header overview, select the routing and the menu options Details→Header.

■ Operation or suboperation—from the operation overview, select the operation or suboperation and the menu options Details→Operation.

- Sequence—from the sequence overview, select the sequence and the menu options Details→Seq.

- Material component allocation—from the material component overview, select the material component and the menu options Details→Mat. components→Administrative data.

- Production resource/tool—from the PRT overview, select the production resource/tool and the menu options Details→Prod.resources/tools →Administrative data.

- Inspection characteristic—from the characteristic overview, select the characteristic and the menu options Details→Insp. characteristic→General data→Administrative data.

The administrative data concerning routing objects and their assignments includes the following information:

- The item number by which the material component is identified in the bill of material, its item category (for example, variable-sized item), and its quantity

- The validity period of the routing object and its assignments as well as when and by whom the object or its assignments were created

- Whether the routing object or its assignments were changed using a change number as well as when and by whom the last change was made

Understanding Operations

An operation is the molecular unit of a routing. The operation details the individual processing steps that make up the production process. A routing is a task list and the tasks are represented in R/3 as operations.

The operation master record identifies the work center where it can take place. Each operation is maintained with an operation text that describes how the work step is to be performed. A predefined control key can be used to signify which functions are to be carried out in the operation. A sequence of operations is defined by an ordered list of operation numbers.

When the Operation Details screen is displayed, you can enter specific information such as data on external processing, splitting, overlapping, standard values, and the calculation of standard values. The materials needed in the operation and any production resources or tools can be detailed in the operation record. You can also specify any inspection characteristic and, if necessary, the inspection tools needed to perform the checks.

Setting Up Operation Data

An operation is the fundamental component in a task list or routing. Yet the operations of one company will differ from those of another. The R/3 system allows for this by customizing the data in each operation master record.

The details of a routing are maintained in the operation records of the work centers that take part in the routing. Defaults can be established so that all new operations at a particular work center are assigned the same data. The routing records define the attributes for which the values have to be obtained from the work centers concerned.

During customizing, the following data elements are defined to assist in the entry of routing data:

- Control key
- Setup type
- Wage type
- Wage group
- Suitability
- Type of standard value determination

Using the Control Key for Business Functions

The control key specifies the business functions to be carried out by the operation, and how R/3 will process the operation. The following are examples of business function indicators that can be specified in a control key assigned to a particular operation:

- Scheduling—to nominate the operation for inclusion in scheduling
- Capacity planning—to generate capacity requirements records when the operation is scheduled
- Time tickets—to cause time tickets to be printed for the operation
- Rework—to disable the automatic goods receipt indicator so that you manually post the goods receipt for the exact quantity that has to be reworked
- Costing—to include the operation in costing
- Confirmation—to specify whether and how an operation is to be confirmed
- External processing—to indicate whether the operation is internally and/or externally processed

If you change the specification of a control key, all records in which the key has been used will be changed to reflect the alteration. You can create new control keys to avoid this and select the *long text* indicator for the control key so that you can enter explanatory comments.

Defining Setup Types

The purpose of defining a setup type is to define how a machine or work center is to be set up and who is to do this. Setup types are defined for each plant. Thereafter you can reference or copy the setup type for use in routings or work orders. In particular, the setup type can be used in determining the optimum setup times when planning sequences of operations.

Defining Wage Types

A wage type is used when calculating the wages or salaries of employees. You can associate a wage type with a specific operation by referencing or by copying. Thereafter the person performing the operation will be credited with the corresponding remuneration. A person will only be remunerated if this particular wage type is included in Infotype 0008 of his or her employee master record in personnel administration in the PA module.

A wage type record includes the following information:

- Country grouping
- Wage type and salary type defined in the payroll accounting in the PA module to recognize the legal and technical requirements relevant to particular types of work
- Start and finish dates to define the period over which the wage type record is valid

Wage types have to be separately created only in systems that do not include the PA module.

Defining Wage Groups

A wage group is used to assign a value to a particular kind of work at a specific plant. The first stage is to establish the criteria to be used. For example, you could define a scale that represented the amount or duration of training needed by a typical employee in order to be competent at a specific operation.

Thus you could associate a value with work that needed several weeks of supervised training, and a much lower value if the training could be accomplished in a few hours. In this illustration, your wage groups would correspond to the length of training needed.

Defining Suitability for a Task

If certain operations in a particular plant should be performed only by employees who have been correctly trained, you can define a set of suitability indicators that can be assigned to the critical operations.

Employees must have personnel records that include the data fields for these suitability indicators so that they can be automatically considered by the system as candidates for assignment to any operation that includes a suitability key.

The system allows you to specify whether a suitability indicator is automatically copied to an operation or used only as a reference offered by default when the operation is being created.

The following factors can be used in assessing suitability and in defining suitability requirements:

- Certificates
- Courses of study
- Short-term training

Suitability records are valid only in a specific plant, although their data can be copied for use elsewhere.

Defining Types of Standard Value Determination

You may be able to have standard values calculated for an operation by the computer assisted process planning CAPP function. For some operations you may need to specify other methods. If your company uses more than one method, you can define types and use indicators to select the method.

Identifying Standard Processes as Operation Sequences

Your company will probably employ some sequences of operations over and over again. You can define such a sequence as a *reference operation set* and provide it with all the necessary data. Then you can simply refer to this set when building a routing, and all the details will be automatically copied to your new routing.

The Operation Overview screen is where you create operations and specify the data for each operation and suboperation. For example:

- Operation number—used to form the sequence of processing. The system will suggest the next number according to the increment set in the operation profile so as to allow for some later insertions.
- Suboperation number—used to create one or more suboperations to each operation if necessary.
- Work center—used to signify that the control key, the standard text key, and the default values are to be copied from the work center record to the operation or suboperation record.
- Control key—used to specify the processing for the operation from costing, scheduling, capacity planning, confirmation, and printing shop papers.
- Standard text key—used to identify a process description.
- Description—used to hold a short description of the operation; defaults to the first line of the standard text key if one has been specified.

If you identify a work center when you are maintaining an operation, the following default values will be copied from the work center:

- Control key
- Standard text key
- Suitability
- Setup type
- Wage type
- Wage group
- Number of wage tickets
- Number of confirmation slips
- Printer for shop floor papers
- Units of measurement of standard values

If these values have been copied from a work center that is marked by a reference indicator, you cannot subsequently alter them in the operation.

Exploring the Operation Details Screen

If you have marked the operation or suboperation in the Operation Overview screen and selected Details→Operation, the Operation Details screen will allow you to maintain data in the following areas:

- Operation
- Standard values
- Standard value calculation
- CAPP
- Interoperation times
- Splitting
- Overlapping
- Start and end of usage (suboperations only)
- General data
- Required qualification
- External processing
- Quality management: general
- User-defined fields
- Administrative data

Standard values are planned values for the operation and suboperation execution times. You can enter the activity types for each standard value so that the system will be able to calculate costs, execution times, and capacity requirements. The performance efficiency rate key from the work center will also be consulted in these calculations.

There are some default values copied from a work center to an operation that you are not allowed to alter. For example, the performance efficiency rate key is never maintained in the operation. If you do not specify a work center for an operation, the system will hide the standard value fields and set their values to zero.

The following standard values can be maintained in the operation:

- Base quantity—quantity of the material to be processed to which the operation standard values refer.
- Operation unit—unit of measure used in the operation for the material to be produced. An operation unit can differ from the work center header unit if you have specified how one unit of measure can be converted to the other by calling the function Unit of measure conversion.
- Standard values—planned values for the execution of the operation. Work center maintenance rules control whether standard values and the associated activity types can or must be maintained in the routing.
- Units—defaults to the standard value units from the work center.

- Activity types—system defaults to the activity types from the work center unless you assign other activity types to the standard values for calculating the costs for in-house production.
- Break—enter the break time available to an employee during the operation.

Calculating Standard Values

In the Standard value calculation area of the Operation Details screen, you enter data needed if standard values are to be calculated automatically. For example:

- Type of standard value calculation—CAPP or estimation
- Year in which the standard values were calculated
- Basis used for calculating the standard values—a formula
- Standard value code used for calculating the standard values

The standard value code may signify which tables containing planned times are to be used. Once the standard values have been calculated or copied from tables, they are displayed in the Operation Details screen.

The CAPP area will show whether the standard values are to be calculated in response to a dialog with the user during order creation.

Maintaining Scheduling Data for Operations

Scheduling data for suboperations cannot be separately maintained. For operations, the significant areas of the Operation Details screen are titled Interoperation times, Splitting and Overlapping.

One of the problems encountered in scheduling is where the basic dates for the start and finish of a manufacturing process cannot be adhered to because the various operations in sequence take too long. The first corrective measure is to reduce the interoperation times between one or more operations, if possible. Each operation can be assigned a reduction strategy to facilitate shortening the lead time.

A reduction strategy can be defined at up to six levels. Each level can be associated with specific reduction measures that are to be activated if it becomes necessary to apply the reduction strategy to that level.

The following reduction measures are standard:

- Reduction of the queue time by a percentage amount down to the minimum queue time
- Reduction of the lead time by splitting an operation between capacities of machines or people
- Reduction of the lead time by overlapping
- Reduction of the move time by a percentage amount down to the minimum move time

Interoperation times are calculated after consulting the following indicators:

- *Reduction strategy*—a reduction strategy key can be entered to assign a predefined set of reduction measures.
- *Teardown/wait simul.*—indicates that the wait and teardown times are scheduled to run simultaneously.
- *Max./Min. wait time*—sets boundaries to the shortest and longest time allowed before a material is processed in the next operation. Scheduling is always based on the minimum wait time.
- *Std./Min. queue time*—buffer time used to compensate for interruptions in production, if necessary.
- *Std./Min. move time*—between work centers or from one location group to another.

Splitting

If the operation lead time becomes critical, you may be able to split the work between production units in the work center.

The splitting area of the Operation Details screen is used to maintain the following data:

- Required splitting—an indicator that splitting is necessary.
- No. of splits into partial lots—scheduling is based on the smaller of the number of splits (partial lots), and the number of individual capacities in the operation's work center.
- Min. processing time.

Overlapping

The Overlapping area of the Operation Details screen is used to record overlap data. The operation that holds the overlap data allows the next operation to begin before it is finished. The overlap data is stored in the following structure:

- Required overlapping
- Optional overlapping
- Continuous flow prod.—signifies that operations can overlap without regard to their duration, although there may be a minimum send-ahead quantity needed to justify starting the subsequent operation
- No overlapping
- Min. overlap time
- Min. send-ahead qty—records the amount of product that has to be completed and sent ahead to the next operation before this operation can be scheduled to begin

Part
II

Ch
5

External Processing

By definition, external processing is an operation processed by a vendor. A control key can be used to signify this situation in the external processing area of the Operation Details screen. If such an operation is included in a routing, the system will respond to the external processing key and automatically create a purchase requisition for the external work and store it in the order with the quantities and dates taken from the external processing area of the Operation Details screen. The purchasing department then creates a purchase order in response to the purchase requisition.

Identifying the Data for External Processing

The External processing area of the Operation Details screen includes purchasing information or references to data objects where the information can be obtained.

A purchasing info record is a master record containing details of the relationship between your company and a vendor of goods and services. You can identify the purchasing info record and the purchasing organization that owns it in the operation details so that the up-to-date details can be transferred to the operation from the purchasing info record:

- General data—sort string
- Data for purchase order price processing—price unit, net price, and currency
- Data on the purchasing organization
- Planned delivery time
- Vendor account number
- Material group
- Purchasing group

If you transfer data from a purchasing info record, you are not allowed to make any alternations in the operation. If you are not using a purchasing info record, you have to make manual entries for the sort string, material group, planned delivery time, and cost element.

Using Suboperations

A suboperation is an operation that is subordinate to another operation. Suboperations are used to represent a more detailed level of planning in the production process. You can assign any number of suboperations to an operation.

Suboperations are often defined where several work centers are needed to carry out an operation. You can create a work center to represent a single employee, so that you could have several employees, each with different qualifications, working on the same operation. Each employee would be represented by a numbered suboperation.

A suboperation does not have to be assigned to the same plant as its parent operation. However, you cannot assign material components, PRTs, or inspection characteristics to suboperations. Nor can you maintain splitting or overlapping for suboperations.

A suboperation is created when maintaining the parent operation by entering the operation number and adding the suboperation number. If you select this combination, you can maintain the details of the suboperation in the Operation Details screen.

You can reassign a suboperation to a different parent operation by calling the operation overview and overtyping the number of the parent operation.

Cumulating Standard Values

Standard values are identified by parameter IDs. The standard values of suboperations are cumulated in the parent operation according to their parameter IDs. You can correct this cumulation if necessary.

If you delete an operation, all its suboperations will also be deleted. The delete is a logical operation because the records will not be physically deleted from the database until the next archiving run.

You cannot delete an operation that marks a branch or return for an alternative or parallel sequence.

The following criteria can be used to locate operations:

- Operation and suboperation numbers
- Work center
- Plant
- Control key
- Standard text key
- Operation description

Creating Operation Text

You can use a standard text key to generate a textual description of what is to be achieved in the work step defined by the operation. This text can be edited. Alternatively, you can use a WP facility to generate a text.

Part
II

Ch
5

If you use a standard long text, you have the option of referencing it using the command INCLUDE or copying it. An INCLUDE reference will extract the latest text each time it is used, whereas a copied text will not be affected by alternations in the original.

Creating a Standard Text

A standard text can be created for frequently used texts such as process descriptions. This text is associated with a standard text key that can then be entered in operations or suboperations. The following sequence from the routing maintenance initial menu will create a standard text:

1. Select Extras→Standard text.
2. Enter the standard text key.
3. Enter the name for the standard text.
4. Select Standard text→Create.
5. Enter the text.
6. Select Text→Save.

Creating Long Text for an Operation or Suboperation

The following sequence will create a long text for a particular operation or suboperation:

1. From the Operation Overview or the Operation Details screen, select Goto→Long text.
2. Enter the desired text.
3. Select Text→Save.

The Operation Overview screen includes the indicator *Txt* that you can set to show that a long text is available. If you then press Enter, you will reach the editor where you can enter a text or change the standard text key from which the long text was copied. You can alter some or all of a standard text copied into a long text, but the standard text key will remain on view as a reference to the original.

Using a Reference Operation Set

Reference rate routings are managed in the same way as reference operation sets.

A reference operation set differs from a routing because it is not assigned to a particular material. Therefore it can be used as part of several different routings, each processing a different material.

The reference operation set cannot include alternative or parallel sequences; it has to be a single sequence of operations. Similar reference operation sets can be grouped and assigned group counter numbers to distinguish them.

You can reference a reference operation set or you can copy it. The difference becomes apparent if the details of the reference operation set are changed. A reference operation set that has been used as a copy will not cause any updates to the routings to which it has been copied. By contrast, an updated reference operation set that is included in a routing as a reference will cause a "live link" update of all the routings in which it is cited as a reference.

Once a reference operation set has been included in a routing, you cannot insert any additional operation in that section of the routing. However, if you unlock the reference function, the operations in the referenced operation set are copied to the routing and the live link functionality is abandoned. You can then make insertions.

A reference rate routing specifies an operation sequence and computes the production quantity and reference time in addition to the production rate for each operation. The reference rate routing uses a base quantity, the requirements, and the corresponding units.

Unlocking a Reference Operation Set

The following sequence will unlock a reference operation set and copy the reference operations to the routing where they can be altered as necessary:

1. In the operation overview, select an operation in the reference operation set you want to unlock.
2. Select Extras→Reference→Unlock.

Assembling Operation Sequences

A sequence of operations is processed in order. Each sequence has a predecessor and successor relationship so that complex production processes can be represented.

Three types of sequence are distinguished:

- Standard sequence
- Alternative sequence
- Parallel sequence

Reference operation sets and reference rate routings cannot include alternative or parallel sequences.

The first operation sequence in a routing is automatically defined by the system as the standard sequence for that routing. This standard sequence becomes the reference sequence for parallel and alternative sequences that are developed later. The start and finish dates of parallel and alternative sequences are defined in relation to the standard sequence and its operations.

Alternative sequences are used if there are different ways of producing a material, or if you need different sequences for different lot sizes, for example. You may have alternative sequences that are used to avoid bottlenecks.

A *branch operation* is defined as the operation from which the alternative sequence is to replace the standard sequence.

The *return operation* is the operation up to which the alternative sequence is to replace the standard sequence.

A parallel sequence is a special form of overlapping sequence that is processed at the same time as the standard sequence. Again, a branch operation and a return operation have to be specified.

Using the Sequence Overview

The Sequence Overview screen in routings shows all sequences contained in a routing. Select Goto→Sequence overview from the operation overview, or use the function key Sequence overview from the initial screen for displaying or changing routings. Use the object overview to see all the objects in a routing at the same time.

The sequence overview displays the following data for a sequence:

- The sequence key that identifies the sequence
- The sequence category
- The branch and return operations
- A description of the sequence

If you mark the standard sequence and select Details→Seq., you can maintain the sequence administrative details, the description, and the alignment key that controls all parallel sequences in the routing by permitting floats at the start or finish.

Part

II

Ch

5

Creating an Alternative Sequence

The following sequence will create an alternative sequence from the sequence overview:

1. Select Edit→New entries.
2. From the Choose Sequence Category dialog box, select *Alternative sequence*→Continue.
3. Enter the data in the Sequence Details screen.

The data includes the following:

- Sequence—the system assigns consecutive numbers to sequences, whatever their category. You can overwrite the suggested number key to identify another sequence.
- Text describing the sequence.
- Alignment key.
- Number of the branch operation from which the alternative sequence is to replace the standard sequence. Branch or return operations cannot be chosen from a reference operation set apart from the first operation, unless you have unlocked the reference operation set.
- Number of the return operation up to which the alternative sequence is to replace the standard sequence.
- From lot size/to lot size—to identify a lot size range effective for the alternative sequence. The lot size automatically selects the correct alternative sequence during order creation. A lot size range for an alternative sequence must overlap, at least partially, with the lot size range in the routing header.

The details of the operations in an alternative sequence are maintained from their Operation Overview screens.

A parallel sequence is created using a similar sequence to the creation of an alternative sequence. An alignment key has to be specified to determine how floats are to be allowed.

Deleting a Sequence

Alternative or parallel sequences in a routing may be deleted from the sequence overview; but the standard sequence can be deleted only from the routing header. The sequence records are deleted physically during the next archiving run.

The objects in a deleted sequence, such as the PRTs, material component allocations, and inspection characteristics, are not available until released by the next archiving run.

Changing a Routing

Routing objects can be changed with or without a change history record being created to document the change. If you make a change without identifying a change number, the alterations will be valid for the same period as the routing in which you are making the change, although you can specify a key date from which the change is to be effective, or you can refer to the date from the change number with which the routing object was previously changed.

If you change a routing with a history, you enter the change number to access the master record on which the details of the changes are recorded, together with the person responsible. The change history record can document changes to more than one routing object, and will identify which fields were changed. All task lists in the relevant group will be evaluated.

When a change number is being used, the changes become effective on the exact date specified in the change master.

Changing a Work Center for an Operation

When you create a new operation and associate it with a work center, the system copies the following values from the work center to the operation:

- All default values including the units of measurement for standard values, such as minutes
- Standard value parameters
- Activity types
- Performance efficiency type key

When you replace a work center in an operation, the system does not copy all of these values. The following rules control which values are copied from the replacement work center:

- Default values, activity types, and the performance efficiency rate key are only copied from the new work center if a reference indicator is set for them in the old work center. However, the standard text from the old work center always stays the same during replacement.
- Units of measurement for standard values are not copied.

The rules for choosing data from the new work center are copied from the old work center. For example, if the setup time for the operation is classed "must be entered" then it must be copied from the new work center. If essential data is lacking, the system displays messages for you to maintain certain standard values after replacement.

Checking a Routing

When you are building a routing, the system does not automatically check consistency between operations and sequences. Therefore you can create several operations with the same number and assign a sequence order to them later.

However, you can customize for routings so that a consistency check is automatically carried out under control of the routing status indicator before saving a changed or created routing. The following conditions are checked:

- The validity period of the standard sequence must agree with the validity period of the header.
- The same operation or suboperation number must not be assigned more than once.
- A branch operation number must be greater than the return operation number.
- Branch operations must match with return operations.

- An alternative sequence must have a number larger than the branch operation in the standard sequence.

- The largest operation number of an alternative sequence must be smaller than the return operation number in the standard sequence.

- The unit of measure of the routing must agree with the unit of measure of any referenced operation set.

- The lot size range of an alternative sequence must not exceed the lot size range of the routing header.

- The lot size range of the header or of an alternative sequence must not exceed the lot size range of a referenced operation set.

The system also checks the consistency of an operation's inspection characteristics.

While a task list is being maintained, the system writes a checking log where system messages are displayed. You can decide whether these messages justify saving the routing in spite of the inconsistencies. If you have the consistency check run in background, the routing is saved along with the log.

Checking Material Allocations

If a routing has been found to be without inconsistencies it will be saved with an internal marker that prevents further checking during order creation. However, if you have saved the routing in spite of inconsistencies, or if the validity period of any change numbers has expired, then the system will check for consistency when an order is created.

If a configurable material is allocated to the routing, the system will check the consistency of the routing for the configuration you have chosen. ●

CHAPTER 6

Assigning Production Resources and Tools

Defining Production Resources/Tools

Production Resources/Tools (PP-BD-PRT) is a basic data component in which all movable operating resources are specified. These PRT can be devices used to form objects or continuous materials that become finished or partially finished products. The PRT category also includes tools and fixtures that are used in measurement and inspection to check the size, structure, or efficiency of products being manufactured.

Any of the following items is essentially portable and can be defined therefore as a PRT:

- Tools
- Jigs and fixtures
- Measurement and inspection devices
- NC programs for numerical control of machine tools
- Documents, specifications, and drawings

A PRT can be assigned to internal or external (contractor) operations. As part of the assignment, you have to define the following parameters to specify the PRT needed for the operation:

- Quantities
- Operating times
- Dates

PRT Categories

PRTs are represented as master records of different categories according to the use or origin of the PRT. The materials management (MM) module can create and maintain a PRT as a material master record. This includes the following functional options:

- External procurement
- In-house manufacture of the PRT
- Inventory management of quantities and values

You can create a production resource/tool with a PRT-specific master record as a miscellaneous PRT. This requires less maintenance than a PRT created in MM, but you cannot use the R/3 system to procure such a PRT, nor can you subject it to inventory management.

A PRT can be associated with a document information record. This can be, for example, a drawing or NC program. This type of PRT can be managed by the document management system, with full editing and engineering change history control.

If you create a PRT with an equipment master record, you can apply to it the functionality of the plant maintenance (PM) module. Using an equipment PRT makes sense if the PRT itself has to be regularly maintained and documented. You may also need to keep records of the time the PRT has been in use, or the number of occasions, so as to manage the maintenance. Any PRT that suffers significant wear and tear would fall into this category.

Assigning a PRT to Operations

A PRT can be assigned to several operations, and several PRTs can be assigned to the same operation. From this information, the system determines the usage dates on which a PRT has to be staged every time a routing is scheduled. The required quantity of the PRT and its usage value are also calculated for each scheduling of the routing.

The usage value of a PRT is a factor that takes account of the fact that a PRT has a limited life and must be costed for replacement.

Maintaining PRT Master Data

The master data required for a PRT will depend on the PRT category, of which the following are standard examples:

- Material PRTs
- Document PRTs
- Miscellaneous PRTs with their own PRT master record

PRT general data includes the following central control parameter elements:

- Category and usage in master data management
- Processes in master data management
- Operational usage in production resources/tools

During customizing, your system administrator will define a PRT authorization group and assign it so as to protect PRT master records from alterations by those not qualified. In fact, the authorization is checked before accepting any of the following PRT commands:

- Create
- Change
- Display
- Delete

The PRT authorization applies only to miscellaneous PRTs that have their own PRT master records. Materials and document PRTs require separate authorization.

The status of a PRT controls which maintenance tasks can be carried out upon the miscellaneous PRT master records. During customizing, each status is defined so as to signify whether the PRT can be used for planning or for production.

The usage of a PRT is indicated by specifying the task list or work center in which it may be used. A usage key is defined to facilitate the entry of this information when creating new PRT records. The usage indicator controls whether the PRT may appear in production routings, maintenance routings, inspection plans, or any combination of these task list types.

The PRT usage key that defines allowable task list types is applicable to the following PRT categories:

- PRTs with material master records (material PRTs)
- PRTs with PRT master records (miscellaneous PRTs)

Instances of these types of PRT can be grouped under a group key that can be assigned matchcodes or used in printing PRT information.

A where-used list of PRTs can be displayed in overview variants that have been customized for particular purposes. The same variants can be used for replacing PRTs if necessary. An overview variant defines which objects are shown. For example, the fields of parameters for operations and sequences can be selectively displayed so that one variant may show standard values, another lot sizes.

To maintain data for production resources/tools with material master records or PRT-specific master records (miscellaneous PRTs), you have to access the Production Resources/Tools screen. There you can maintain basic data and default values.

Establishing PRT Basic Data

PRT Basic Data includes the following general data:

- Base unit of measure—use in managing stocks of a PRT with a material master record. Cannot be changed after being assigned to an operation.
- Unit of issue—used as the default unit of measure when assigning a PRT to an operation. Cannot be changed after being assigned.
- MM/PP status—indicates the business functions in which the PRT may be used. Verified when the PRT is assigned to an operation.
- PRT usage—defines the task list types, such as routings and standard networks, in which the PRT can be used.
- Load records—causes a load record to be created during scheduling to store the start and finish dates of PRT usage, the required quantity, and the usage value, such as depreciation through use.
- Grouping key 1 and Grouping key 2—used to select and sort PRT records during maintenance.

Establishing PRT Default Values

PRT default values are copied when the PRT is assigned to operations in a routing. The defaults appear in the PRT detail screens. A *not changeable* indicator can be set for a default value in the material master record or PRT master record. This prevents the default value being changed in the routing.

The PRT control key determines how the PRT is processed in the task list after it has been assigned. For example, scheduling, confirmation, and costing are processing types that can be selected by a control key.

You can generate a description of the PRT and assign it to a standard text key that can be assigned to appropriate PRTs as a default. You might label a PRT with its usage description in the form of a standard text indicated by a key. A PRT master has a place for a long description that will be automatically assigned the standard text key. You can then amend or amplify the standard text, although the key will remain in the record to indicate what standard text first appeared there.

A PRT is assigned a formula named *Total qty formula/Usage value*. This formula is automatically used to calculate the required quantity and the usage value of the PRT.

Keys are used to define the usage start and usage finish dates. The usage period determines when the PRT must be available for use in the operation and when it will be free to be used elsewhere. For example, a particular PRT may be needed only during the setup time for the machine that is to perform the operation to which it is assigned. You can specify the PRT usage period by quoting an offset to start or an offset to finish. These offsets are taken from the reference date for the operation, which is usually the start date of the production phase.

The following sequence will allow you to enter or change additional data for PRT assignments to an operation on the detail screens for production resources/tools:

1. From the routing overview screen, select PRT Overview.
2. Select a production resource/tool.
3. Select Details→Prod.resources/tools.
4. Select the detail screen you need.

The PRT General View screen offers the data entered when the PRT was created, the usage value, and the formulas. The PRT Usage Dates screen shows default values used in scheduling. The PRT Administrative Data screen shows the validity period of the PRT assignment to the operation, the date of this assignment, the most recent change, and the person who made it.

Specifying Formulas for PRTs

A PRT formula calculates the quantity and the usage value of a PRT. Each formula is assigned to a formula key by which it is accessed. If you are defining a particular formula for your company, you have to identify each parameter in the formula by selecting a parameter ID. This ID specifies the following attributes:

- The definition and the key word of a parameter
- The dimension of the parameter
- The name used to identify a parameter in formulas

The values used by formulas depend on the origin of the parameters used in them. The following are examples of origins from which a parameter value can be obtained:

- Standard value in the work center
- Formula constant in the work center—assigned to the parameter in the work center
- General operation value recorded in the operation data—lot size, base quantity, number of splits (partial lots), number of employees, and so on
- Value from a user-defined field in the operation

- Value from the PRT assignment record
- PRT constant taken from the PRT master record of a miscellaneous PRT

Formulas must be created in customizing from parameters that have previously been defined in customizing.

Creating and Deleting a PRT

There are four categories of PRT, as follows:

- Materials
- Equipment
- Documents
- Miscellaneous

The SAP classification system allows you to work with classes of PRTs. For example:

- Define a PRT class by nominating certain characteristics, such as particular dimensions or weights.
- Build a class of PRTs by assigning specific PRTs to the class and then maintaining characteristic values for them.
- Search for PRTs on the basis of specified characteristics.

Creating a PRT with a Material Master Record

A PRT can be represented by a material master record in the materials management (MM) module. You have to access the material master record and maintain a separate Prod.Resources/Tools view record for each plant to which the PRT belongs.

The following alternative sequences will create a PRT as a material:

1. Select Logistics→Production.
2. Select Master data Prod.resources/tools.
3. Select Prod.resources/tools.
4. Select Material→Create (general).

Or

1. Select Logistics→Materials management.
2. Select Material master→Material.
3. Select Conventional→Create (general).

The initial screen for creating a materials PRT includes the following data elements:

- Material—a key that uniquely identifies the PRT.
- Industry sector—a key that assigns the PRT to a branch of industry.

■ Material type—controls which data and which views you can maintain. Not all material types allow you to maintain a Prod.resources/tools view to establish the material as a PRT.

If you press Continue in the PRT view, you will be shown the Organizational Levels/Profiles dialog box in which you must identify the plant to which the PRT is assigned. Then you can select Data and maintain the basic data and the default values for task list assignment in the PRT screen.

Creating a PRT with an Equipment Master Record

The following sequence will record a PRT created as equipment:

1. Select Logistics→Production.
2. Select Master data Prod.resources/tools.
3. Select Prod.resources/tools→Equipment→Create.
4. Maintain the equipment.
5. Maintain the equipment category as "P" or another category for PRTs if you have created one in customizing.
6. Maintain the data on the screen.
7. Select Goto→PRT data.
8. Maintain the PRT data.
9. Select Equipment→Save.

Creating a PRT with a Document Info Record

The following sequence will create a production resource/tool as a document:

1. Select Logistics→Production.
2. Select Master data Prod.resources/tools.
3. Select Prod.resources/tools→Document→Create.
4. Maintain the document, document type, document part, document version.
5. Maintain the basic data for the document.
6. Select Document→Save.

In customizing for document management, you can specify which document types may be used for PRTs.

Creating a PRT as a Miscellaneous PRT

The following sequence will create a production resource/tool with its own PRT master record as a miscellaneous PRT:

1. Select Logistics→Production.
2. Select Master data Prod.resources/tools.

3. Select Prod.resources/tools→PRT master (misc.)→ Create.

4. On the initial screen for creating a PRT, enter the key assigned to the PRT and press Enter.

You then have to maintain the basic data as follows:

- Authorization group
- Status
- PRT usage
- Base unit of measure
- Load records
- Location
- Grouping keys

The following sequence will then allow you to maintain the default values to be used when assigning a PRT to a task list:

1. Select Goto→Defaults.

2. Select Prod.resources/tools→Save.

Creating a PRT by Copying

A PRT can be created by copying an existing PRT and then editing before saving. However, if the master records for the PRT belong to the materials management (MM) application or the plant maintenance (PM) application, you have to carry out this copying with the authorization appropriate to that application.

Within PP, you can copy a miscellaneous PRT if you have the authorization to display the PRT master record. The following sequence is suitable:

1. Select Logistics→Production.

2. Select Master data Prod.resources/tools.

3. Select Prod.resources/tools.

4. Select PRT master (misc.)→Create.

5. Enter the key for the new PRT.

6. Enter the key for the PRT from which you want to copy.

7. Press Enter.

8. In the Copy From dialog box, select the data you want to copy.

9. Press Copy.

10. Overwrite the data if necessary.

11. Select Prod.resources/tools→Save.

The Basic Data screen also allows the same functions, by selecting Prod.resources/tools→Copy from.

Deleting Material and Equipment PRT Master Records

The following sequence will mark a material or equipment PRT for deletion in the next archiving run:

1. Select Logistics→Production.
2. Select Master data Prod.resources/tools.
3. Select Prod.resources/tools→Material (or Equipment)→Change→Schedule, **or**
4. Select Material (or Equipment)→Functions.
5. Select Set deletion flag→Set.

The deletions will be flagged when you activate the schedule of items for deletion.

Deleting a Document PRT Master Record

In order to delete a PRT that has a document info record, you must also mark the PRT for deletion. The following sequence will mark a document PRT for deletion:

1. Select Logistics→Production.
2. Select Master data Prod.resources/tools.
3. Select Prod.resources/tools→Document→Change→ ENTER.
4. Select Edit→Change deletion indicator.
5. Select Document→Save.

Deleting a Miscellaneous PRT Master Record

A miscellaneous PRT with its own PRT master record can be deleted directly. You have to ensure that it does not have documents assigned to it. If the PRT is still being used, you can mark it for deletion on the next archiving run after it is no longer needed.

The following sequence will directly delete a production resource/tool:

1. Select Logistics→Production.
2. Select Master data Prod.resources/tools.
3. Select Prod.resources/tools→PRT master (misc.)→Change.
4. Select Prod.resources/tools→Delete.

The following sequence will flag a miscellaneous PRT for deletion:

1. Select Logistics→Production.
2. Select Master data Prod.resources/tools.
3. Select Prod.resources/tools→PRT master (misc.)→Change.
4. Press Enter **or** select Goto→Basic data.
5. Select Edit→Deletion indicator.

Part
II

Ch
6

Assigning PRTs to Operations

Before a material PRT can be assigned to an operation, the material status must be checked to confirm that the material may be used as a PRT, and the PRT view in the material master must be maintained.

A miscellaneous PRT must have a status that permits resource planning.

The following sequence will assign a PRT to an operation:

1. In the operation overview, select the operation to which you want to assign the PRT.
2. Select Goto→PRT overview to inspect any PRTs that are already assigned to the operation.
3. Select Edit→New entries.
4. Select the PRT category that you want to assign.
5. In the New PRTs dialog box, choose the PRT category.

The item number of the assigned PRT can be altered and you can maintain the key identifying the PRT to be assigned. You can also enter basic data for the PRT at this stage by accessing the detail screens.

To assign more PRTs to the same operation select Insert line. Otherwise, select Back. You can choose a different category of PRT by using function keys in the NEW PRTs dialog box.

Press Cancel to end PRT assignment to this operation.

Deleting a PRT Assignment

The following sequence will delete a PRT assignment to an operation:

1. In the operation overview, select the operation whose PRT assignment you want to delete.
2. Select Goto→Prod.resources/tools to reach the PRT Overview screen and view all existing assignments.
3. Select the PRT whose assignment to the operation you want to delete.
4. Select Edit→Delete and confirm the deletion.

Using Material Allocations in Routings

The allocation of a material component to an operation in a routing will ensure that this material is staged so as to arrive at the work center just in time for the operation that needs it.

You can also allocate several materials into what is called a *phantom assembly*, which is a logical grouping of materials.

The grouping for a phantom assembly can be based on the requirements of design or engineering. But in the context of production, the components of a phantom assembly are managed together because they will be assembled into a higher-level assembly.

You can also use a phantom assembly to accelerate the entry of data.

A bill of material (BOM) comprises material components and phantom assemblies. The BOM will be assigned a routing, and by default, all the material components will be assigned to the first operation in the routing. However, you may prefer to have some of the components delivered to the specific work centers at the time they will be needed in the operations being carried out there.

Staging material allocations within a routing depends on the material components or phantom assemblies being assigned to specific operations. You can assign a material component or a phantom assembly to only one operation in the routing.

If you do not allocate a material component, it will be automatically assigned to the first operation in the routing when you create a production order.

It is not necessary to select components or phantom assemblies from a single BOM. When you are creating a production order, you select the BOM that controls whatever materials are to be allocated to particular operations in the routing.

When you allocate a phantom assembly to an operation, the system automatically allocates all of the material components in the phantom assembly to the same operation. However, if you first allocate individual components from a phantom assembly to different operations, the system will automatically allocate the phantom assembly to the first operation in the routing, together with any if its constituent material components that you have not already allocated elsewhere in the routing.

By this technique, you can identify all the constituents needed and have some or all of them allocated precisely where they are needed.

Checking Consistency

Although you normally allocate a material component to only one operation, you are allowed to assign the same material component to different operations if they belong to alternative sequences. This is permitted because only one of the alternatives will be chosen and there will be only one consumption of the material component.

Nevertheless, it is possible to make mistakes in allocating material components. For example, you could allocate the necessary material component twice without realizing your mistake. If you assigned a component to a routing, it would be automatically assigned to the first operation. If this routing included a reference operation set that already had the same material allocation, double the necessary material would be allocated to the routing.

Another source of allocation error occurs when a routing with a change history is being maintained.

You can initiate a check of the consistency of allocations to identify these kinds of error. From the material component overview, select the menu options Extras→Check consistency.

Allocating Material Components to Reference Operation Sets and Reference Rate Routings

If the operation to which you want to allocate a material component is a workstep in a reference operation set or reference rate routing you have to identify the material whose BOM would be appropriate.

The following sequence will specify the material:

1. Select Goto→Comp. alloc.—gen.
2. From the Choose BOM Material dialog box, select a material from the list of materials and the plants to which they belong.
3. If there are no material components allocated to the operation, the system displays the Material component allocation dialog box. Create a BOM for the material you want to use.
4. If you do not want to select any of the materials displayed, press the function key Other material to view the BOM dialog box where you can specify the desired material.

Allocating Material Components to Routings and Rate Routings

A routing or a rate routing must have a material allocated to it. The material may already be allocated to the plant or to a BOM already associated with the routing. If there is no unambiguous default or previous material allocation to the routing, you must make one from the overview screen. The allocation requires the following specifications:

- Material
- Plant
- BOM
- BOM change number, if one exists

Specifying the Details for Material Allocations

The following sequence will reach the detail screens:

1. Call up the material component overview in the routing.
2. Select a material component.
3. Select Details→Material components.
4. Select one of the detail screens.

The General Data detail screen allows you to maintain the backflush indicator to ensure that a material withdrawal in a production order is posted once the operation is confirmed. If necessary, you can record cutting measures in the operation records for an allocated material component. These measures do not have to be the same as the size specified in the BOM.

However, material requirements planning uses size from the BOM rather than the cutting measures maintained in the routing.

The Administrative Data detail screen contains information on the material component allocation, its validity, and the last change made to the allocation of the component.

Understanding the Backflush Indicator Logic

The backflush indicator can be set in any of three places in the master records:

- In the routing—preferred if the material is sometimes backflushed
- In the material master record—preferred if the material is always backflushed
- In the work center

If you set the indicator in a routing, backflushing will always occur, but if the system finds no indicator in the routing, it will consult the material master record. The material master can have any one of the following characteristic settings:

- Always backflush
- Backflushing decided by the work center
- Backflushing indicator not maintained—do not backflush

If the system has to consult the work center, the backflush indicator will be obeyed if it has been set.

Using the Material Component Overview

All the material components allocated to a routing are shown in this view, and you can rearrange the display to suit your purposes. You can define how the items are to be sorted and you can filter in or filter out material components.

For example, you could arrange separate views for material components according to the following characteristics:

- Not allocated
- Item for production
- Spare part

The material component overview is used for reallocating material components by marking the component and then selecting Edit→Reallocate. The destination of the reallocated component is specified by overwriting the operation number to which it is currently allocated.

Alternatively, you can call the Operation list function from the New Allocation dialog box and select the destination operation.

You can delete all the allocations you have marked in the material component overview. Select Edit→Delete. You may then reallocate these material components, although the previous allocation records will not be deleted until the next archiving run.

Part
II

Ch
6

Filtering Material Components in the Overview

The following sequence will filter material components from the material component overview display:

1. Select Edit→Filter.
2. Select the desired filter criterion in the Filter Item List dialog box.
3. Press the function key Choose.
4. Select All items to restore the display.

Maintaining a Bill of Material from a Routing

It may happen that a material needed in a routing is found to be lacking a complete bill of material. In such cases you can interrupt routing maintenance to edit a BOM.

The following sequence will change a bill of material from a routing:

1. From the material component overview, select Extras→Edit BOM.
2. Enter the change number of the BOM if necessary.
3. Make the desired changes in the BOM item overview.
4. Press Back to return to the routing.

The changes made in the BOM are saved when you save the routing.

Assigning Inspection Characteristics to Operations

Inspection characteristics are normally divided into two characteristic categories: qualitative, quantitative. An inspection characteristic defines the basis on which an inspection is to be performed. The R/3 quality management (QM) module is specialized in the creation and monitoring of inspection characteristics.

To ensure that a particular inspection takes place, the relevant inspection characteristic is assigned to an operation from the Characteristic Overview screen.

The following sequence will assign inspection characteristics to an operation in a routing:

1. From the operation overview, mark the operation that is to be inspected.
2. Select Goto→Insp. char. overview.
3. Mark the inspection characteristic.
4. Select Details→Insp. Characteristic.
5. Select the detail screen required.
6. Maintain the details.

The following sequence will delete inspection characteristic assignments to operations:

1. From the operation overview, mark the operation whose inspection characteristic assignments you want to delete.

2. Choose Goto→Insp. char. overview.

3. Select the inspection characteristic whose assignment you want to delete.

4. Choose Edit→Delete.

5. Confirm the deletion.

The deleted assignments remain on the database until the next archiving run.

Using Trigger Points

A trigger point is arranged by associating a condition record with an operation in a routing or in a production order. If the status of an operation changes when the operation is confirmed, the condition is examined to see if the trigger point should be activated.

The consequent action from a trigger point can be an extra operation or the inclusion of a reference operation set. The following functions can be controlled by trigger points:

- Release succeeding operations in the sequence.
- Release up to stop indicator—to release all operations up to and including the next operation for which the *RelStop* indicator is set.
- Release preceding operations.
- Create a new order without reference to a material by copying a reference operation set.
- Insert a reference operation set in an existing order between the operations you nominate.
- Start a specified workflow task such as sending a mail message to a specific user.

You can create a trigger point by copying a standard trigger point, which will ensure that the same condition data is copied. You can create a trigger point group of standard trigger points. You can then have all the trigger points copied to the operation by simply attaching the group key.

Trigger points can be created in customizing.

The following sequence will place a trigger point in a routing:

1. From the operation overview, select the operation for which you want to assign a trigger point.

2. Select Goto→Trigger pnt overview.

3. Inspect the existing assignments in the Operation Trigger Points screen.

4. Enter the usage and/or description.

5. Indicate the function the trigger point should serve.

The following indicators are available and may be used together:

- Functions—the trigger point initiates the functions specified on the detail screen for trigger points.
- RelStop—the operation is the last in a series of operations released by the trigger point.

Part
II

Ch
6

The following details have to be maintained on the detail screen:

- The system status that triggers the function
- The status change that triggers the function (reset status and/or set status)
- The *once* indicator if the function is to be triggered one time
- The type of event that triggers the function (manually and/or by a change in status)

The following sequence will create a trigger point by copying:

1. From the operation overview, select the operation for which you want to assign a trigger point.
2. Select Goto→Trigger pnt overview.
3. Inspect the existing assignments in the Operation Trigger Points screen.
4. Select Edit→Create by copying→Stand. trigger point, **or**
5. Select Edit→Create by copying→Trigger point group.
6. Enter a standard trigger point or a trigger point group.
7. Press Continue. ●

PART III

Controlling the Production Facilities

Scheduling Routings

Finding Out When an Operation Begins and Ends

An order or a task list such as a routing is scheduled to determine the dates when each of its operations are to begin and end. At the same time, the system examines the capacity requirements needed at the various work centers.

Planned orders and work orders are subjected to *order-related scheduling*. A routing is always used if the order is a work order, but planned orders can be scheduled using the in-house production time stored in a material master record or in the routing.

Non-order-related scheduling is carried out using routings to calculate the in-house production time of a material. For example, you might want to compare the in-house production time for a particular lot size with the production time stored in the material master record, which might be independent of lot size. You can arrange for the material master to be updated automatically, or adjust it manually.

Calculating How Long an Operation Takes

A predefined control key is assigned to each operation to supply the control parameters that enact the following logic:

- If the control key of the operation specifies that the operation can be scheduled, the system calculates the duration and the dates of the operation segments.
- If the control key of the operation specifies that the operation cannot be scheduled, the system assigns a duration of zero for all operation segments.
- If the control key of the operation specifies that the operation is processed externally, scheduling is carried out using the number of delivery days specified on the External Processing screen of the operation.

The following rules are applied if the calculated scheduling times happen to correspond to work start, work finish, or midnight:

- Start times are scheduled for work start or 0:00.
- Finish times are scheduled for work finish or 24:00.

In order to make sure that the finish time is not calculated to come before the start time, the following rules have to be applied if an operation with a duration of zero is scheduled for work start, work finish, or midnight:

- For forward scheduling, the start and finish times are scheduled for work finish or 24:00.
- For backward scheduling, the start and finish times are scheduled for work start or 0:00.

There are various other considerations that can influence the scheduling of a routing and the operations within it. These are discussed in the sections that follow.

Recognizing Scheduling Types

The standard scheduling types are as follows:

- Forward scheduling—forward from the basic start date.
- Backward scheduling—backward from the basic finish date.
- "Today" scheduling—forward scheduling using the current date as a basic start date.
- No scheduling—the operations are not individually scheduled but the system uses the floats before and after production to calculate the scheduled start and finish and enters these dates in all operations.

Each scheduling type requires that you supply one or both basic dates. If you enter both dates, the system will try to arrange that both forward and backward scheduling will fit between them. Should there be any difficulty, the system will automatically start to apply the preconfigured reduction measures that have been ordained for this purpose.

If the scheduling type is forward scheduling:

- Given the basic start date, the system calculates scheduled start, scheduled finish, and basic finish date.
- Given the basic start and basic finish dates, the system calculates scheduled start and scheduled finish dates.

If the scheduling type is backward scheduling:

- Given the basic finish date, the system calculates the basic start date, scheduled start date, and scheduled finish date.
- Given the basic finish and basic start dates, the system calculates scheduled start and scheduled finish dates.

If no scheduling is specified, and you supply the basic start and finish dates, the system will calculate the scheduled start and scheduled finish dates.

If you specify "today" scheduling and offer no other dates, the system will calculate the scheduled start, scheduled finish, and basic finish dates. If you offer a basic finish date, the system will calculate the scheduled start and scheduled finish dates.

You can set up other scheduling types for routings during customizing for capacity planning.

Using Floats Before and After Production

In order to allow for a certain amount of malfunctioning and other disturbances during production, the system carries out scheduling using a float before and a float after production.

A float before production can accommodate delays in the staging of the material components. This float can be used for moving forward production dates in the future if capacity bottlenecks are anticipated in the work centers. The float before production can thus act as a float for capacity leveling.

A float after production can be used to prevent a delay of the scheduled finish if there are any unexpected interruptions in the production process.

Part
III

Ch
7

The scheduled start date is the basic start date plus the float before production. The scheduled finish date is the basic finish date minus the float after production.

The system finds the length of the before and after production floats by consulting the scheduling margin key in the material master record.

Calculating Operation Dates from Operation Lead Times

Scheduling can take place in units of one day or in units of hours or minutes within the working day. The operating time per working day can therefore take account of start and finish times and the allowed breaks.

Operation dates have to take account of holidays and rest days, and the usual reference is a work calendar that identifies each day by its classification. How many different types of day comprise the client company's work calendar is a matter that can be arranged in customizing.

Each operation in a routing is defined by one or more capacities that are available for a specified time. The total time taken by the segments of an operation is called the execution time. The execution time is made up of a setup time, a processing time, and a teardown time.

If these operation segments are all timed in days, then the operation can be scheduled in days. However, if the setup, processing, or teardown segments are timed in hours or minutes, the scheduling has to be conducted in the same units.

The operating time of each operation segment capacity is cumulated to determine the execution time of the operation capacity.

Before an operation begins, the materials may have to queue until a suitable capacity is available. After the processing has finished, there may have to be a waiting period, for instance, to allow the material to cool.

Then there may be a further time period that has to be allowed for the partly finished product to be moved to the next operation in the routing. The move time between two operations is always added to the operation that is performed first.

If you are taking account of the actual time that a work center can be operating in a working day, the operating time will be less than 24 hours. If the records contain no operating time for a work center, the system will use an operating time from 0:00 to 24:00.

Computing Operation Lead Time

The lead time of an operation is defined as the time period between the beginning of the queue time to the end of the wait time. The lead time excludes any move time allowed before the next operation can begin.

Thus the lead time is a linear sum of the following operation segment times:

- Queue time
- Setup time

- Processing time
- Teardown time
- Wait time

The execution time is the linear sum of the following segment times:

- Setup time
- Processing time
- Teardown time

The interoperation time is the linear sum of the following elements:

- Wait time of operation 1
- Move time to operation 2
- Queue time of operation 2

The interoperation time comprises the time period between the execution completing for operation 1 and the execution beginning for operation 2. This period represents a nonproductive segment of the available capacities because the material is either waiting, moving, or queuing.

For some operations, you can allow the wait time and the teardown time to run concurrently. For instance, the material can be cooling down while it is being emptied from the production plant, if this emptying is all that has to happen in the teardown segment.

In the Operation Details screen of the operation, you can set the *teardown/wait simul.* indicator in the interoperation times section to allow the system to treat teardown and wait as simultaneous rather than consecutive. This obviously reduces the lead time of the operation.

Calculating the Duration of Individual Operation Segments

The system has access to various data elements in the routing and in the various work centers that can be used to compute the duration of the individual operation segments.

The following information is stored in the routing:

- Standard and minimum queue time
- Minimum wait time
- Standard and minimum move time
- Number of splits (partial lots)
- Standard values

The following information is stored in the work center:

- Standard and minimum queue time
- Formulas for calculating individual operation segments of execution time (setup, processing, teardown)
- Location group

Part
III

Ch
7

When the system is calculating the operation segments other than wait, the operating time per working day as defined in the work center is taken into account. The work center or the operation may have its own work calendar that is different from the calendar of the parent plant.

Queue, setup, processing, and teardown are computed in relation to the working time per working day in the work center where the operation takes place. The following data is required in order to calculate the operating time of the individual capacity:

- Work start and finish
- Break times
- Capacity utilization rate

The capacity utilization rate is a percentage value. It allows for the fact that productive operating time may be only a percentage of the theoretical operating time due to technical malfunctions and possibly organizational defects. In a complex operation, only one of the capacities may be used for scheduling. You have to identify this capacity in the Scheduling screen for the work center and maintain a value of the capacity utilization rate for it.

If the work center has its own calendar, it takes precedence. If the work center does not have a calendar, the calendar of the operation is used. If the operation does not have a calendar, the Gregorian calendar becomes the default.

Using Queue Time

If you define a queue time as an operation float, the system will use it to calculate the earliest and latest dates of the operation and of the individual operation segments. You can maintain a queue time in the work center, but the system will only consult it if there is no queue time for the operation.

One of the reduction measures that can be taken to meet a scheduling constraint is to reduce the lead time of the operation by shortening the standard queue time down to the minimum queue time.

Formulas for Calculating Setup, Processing, and Teardown

You can enter a separate formula for the setup, processing, and teardown segments in the work center. The following sources for the formula parameters are available:

- Standard values depending on the standard value key
- Formula constants from the work center
- General operation values, such as lot size, base quantity, number of splits (partial lots)
- Values from user-defined fields in the operation

The time units in which the segment times are calculated are the smallest of the units of the standard values. If no value or no formula has been maintained for calculating the duration of an operation segment, the system will allocate a duration of zero. The duration of a segment is not necessarily the same as the separate values maintained for calculating the capacity requirement for the work center.

Calculating Move Time

The move time to the next operation is added to the first operation. You can maintain a value for this move in the operation. An alternative is to refer to location groups in a move time matrix where values are stored for standard and minimum move times between each pair of location groups. This is the procedure if you have not maintained individual interoperation times.

In the interoperation times section of the Operation Details screen, there are maintainable fields for a minimum and a standard move time. If it becomes necessary to apply reduction measures to the operation lead time, the system schedules the operations using the minimum move time.

Location groups of nearby work centers are defined in customizing. You can use the Scheduling screen of a work center to assign it to a suitable location group. The move time matrix of minimum and standard move times between location groups is maintained in customizing.

Specifying Move Time

The operating time for a move is determined using the parameters in the move time matrix. The system consults the Calendar field to determine the source of the operating time to be assigned to a particular move. The possible sources for a value of a move time are as follows:

- Source work center
- Target work center
- Move time matrix

When using the move time matrix, you have to identify the shift start and shift finish in the move time matrix to determine the operating time per working day for a particular move.

Wait time is scheduled without taking the factory calendar into account. A wait can therefore appear on a schedule on any day between 0:00 to 24:00.

External operations are scheduled using a delivery time specified in days, based on the Gregorian calendar.

Scheduling Suboperations

A suboperation is not separated into individual operation segments during scheduling. The system consults the Operation Details screen to find the reference date for a suboperation, and then it calculates the start and the finish of the suboperation using the specified offset.

If the offset is positive, forward scheduling is carried out starting from the reference date. If the offset is negative, backward scheduling is carried out starting from the reference date.

If you have not maintained any data for scheduling a suboperation, the system will assign the start date of setup and the finish date of execution of the parent standard operation.

Aligning Parallel Sequences

The lead times of parallel sequences in a routing will often differ. In these situations, some of the sequences will have floats to make up the difference with the longest sequence. The alignment key controls how these floats should be arranged by the system, as follows:

Part
III

Ch
7

- If the sequence is aligned with the earliest possible date, the float is at the finish of the sequence.
- If the sequence is aligned with the latest possible date, the float is at the start of the sequence.

An alignment key has to be assigned to the standard sequence and to each of the parallel sequences.

Taking Reduction Measures on the Lead Time

Reduction measures are taken step by step with a check each time to see if the calculated dates have been reduced to within the basic dates.

Each operation can be assign a particular reduction strategy by a suitable entry in the interoperation times section of the Operation Details screen. The reduction strategy is assembled in customizing. It determines how many reduction levels may be applied to an operation, up to the maximum of six. The strategy also defines which reduction measures are to be applied at each level.

Identifying Reduction Measures for Operations

The following lead time reduction measures are available:

- Reduction of the queue time by a specified percentage for each reduction level, down to the minimum queue time
- Splitting an operation between several employees or machines, saving time at the expense of extra setup and teardown
- Overlapping operation processing, taking into account the minimum send-ahead quantity and the minimum overlap time
- Reduction of the floats before and after production by a percentage assigned for each reduction level
- Reduction of the standard move time, down to the minimum move time

The minimum wait time cannot be reduced.

Overlapping in Continuous Flow Production

Continuous flow production occurs when operations are completely overlapped without regard to their duration. As soon as the first operation has processed the minimum send-ahead quantity, the second operation can begin, and so on throughout the sequence.

When the system is scheduling in continuous flow production, the system calculates the start and finish dates on the time required to produce the minimum send-ahead quantity. If there are any brief operations in a completely overlapped sequence, they may have to be assigned a longer duration than their calculated execution time so as to accommodate to the continuous flow schedule.

Transferring Scheduling Results to a Material Master Record

If you have scheduled a routing, you can update the material master. If there has been no scheduling, the material master will probably contain a value for the in-house production time of the material. There may be several production times stored for different lot sizes.

Transferring scheduling results will set to zero the existing operation time for in-house production time dependent on lot size. You require suitable authorization to do this.

The scheduling data in the material master have to accord with the scheduling data in the routing. The following parameter values can be updated in the material master record:

- Setup time
- Processing time
- Interoperation time
- Assembly scrap—determined from the total operation scrap in the routing
- Base quantity—the lot size used in scheduling the routing

Releasing Scheduled Routings

The benefit of scheduling using a routing is that the work scheduler can check the lead times and adjust the routing before it is released for use with an order.

The following sequence will schedule a routing:

1. Call up the operation overview for the routing.
2. Select Extras→Scheduling→Schedule.
3. Maintain the data in the Scheduling dialog box.
4. Press Continue to accept the system proposal of forward scheduling for the scheduling type.
5. Enter the overview variant you want to use to display the scheduling results.
6. Press Continue.
7. Inspect the Schedule Overview screen containing the scheduling data.
8. Select Extras→Scheduling→Results to display the scheduling results, a Gantt chart, the scheduling log.

The scheduling results comprise the following data:

- Basic start and finish dates
- Scheduled start and finish dates
- In-house production time from the material master record
- Scheduled in-house production time

You can select Update mat. Master to have the assembly scrap determined by the system and displayed in the results.

Part

III

Ch

7

Calling Where-Used Lists

If you create where-used lists you can see where the routings are using specific objects of the following types:

- Work centers
- Reference operation sets
- Reference rate routings
- Production resources/tools

One occasion when you might want to do this is if you intend to delete a work center, for instance, and want to check whether it is going to be needed if any of the current routings are called on to complete an order.

If necessary, you can create a where-used list of routings that have been deleted online, but which have not yet been archived from the database.

Where-used lists can exist in several variants so that you can indicate the variant that will give you the display most suited to your purpose.

Replacing Data in Routings

The mass replace function is useful if you want to replace an object in many routings. For example, you might need to substitute an old work center with a new one.

The mass replace function effectively finds out where the object is used and rapidly replaces it according to your directions. You can mass replace any of the following objects:

- Work centers
- Reference operation sets
- Reference rate routings
- Production resources/tools

The system will generate a list of the routings in which it intends to make the replacement and allow you to change your mind. You can give the mass replace a change number if you want to alter the validity period of the replacement objects.

The following sequence will display a where-used list of the routings using the specified work center:

1. From the routings menu, select Reporting→Where-used→Work centers.
2. Identify the work center and the plant.
3. Enter a key date or accept the default, which is to display all operations in which the work center is used.
4. The system displays all valid operations.
5. Enter individually the task list types for which you want to generate a where-used list.

6. Narrow down the search by entering status, usage, routing plant, planner group, material number, or material short text.

7. If you also want to see routings that have already been deleted online but still exist on the database, set the *Extended log* indicator.

8. Select Goto→Execute.

The following sequence will access more detailed information:

1. Mark any routing of interest and select Goto→Details.

2. Mark a routing object and select Goto→Choose.

Displaying a Where-Used List for Reference Operation Sets

The following sequence will display a where-used list of the routings in which a reference operation set or a reference rate routing is used:

1. From the routings menu, select Reporting→Where-used→Ref. operation sets.

2. To display a where-used list for a reference rate routing, set the *ref. rate routing* indicator.

3. Enter the group and group counter of the reference operation set/reference rate routing.

4. The system displays all routings valid on the key date you enter. If you do not enter a key date, the system displays all routings in which the reference operation set or reference rate routing is used.

5. Enter individually the task list types for which you want to generate a where-used list.

6. Narrow down the search by entering status, usage, routing plant, group, material number, or material short text.

7. Set the Extended log indicator to include deleted task lists.

5. Select an overview variant.

6. Select Goto→Execute.

Displaying a Where-Used List for a PRT

The following sequence will display a where-used list of the routings in which a specific PRT has been assigned:

1. From the routings menu, select Reporting→Where-used→Prod. resources/tools.

2. Select Settings→PRT category or press the corresponding function key if you want to change the suggested material PRT category.

3. Enter data specific to the PRT category.

4. Select an overview variant.

The data needed for each PRT category is as follows:

- Document PRT—document number, document type, document part, document version
- Equipment PRT—ID number of the equipment

- Material PRT—material number, plant ID
- Miscellaneous PRT—ID key of the PRT

Once you have in view a list of all the assignments for the PRT, you can mark one, a routing, for example, and select Goto→Choose to view the details.

By a similar sequence you can also inspect a log of the usage of the PRT in routings that have been marked for deletion, provided they have not yet taken part in an archiving run.

Using Mass Replacement on Routings

If you need to replace a work center in a large number of routings, select Routings→Extras→ Mass replace→Work centers. You have to identify the work center and the plant that is to be the target, and you have to identify the source of the new work center and its plant. You can also use a change number so that the validity period of the changes can be controlled.

A further control is to specify a key date to ensure that the system will offer for your selection only those operations valid on this date.

The mass replace function will generate a where-used list, which you can control by entering a task list type and a search specification using any of the following data elements, entered as individual values rather than generically:

- Status
- Usage
- Routing plant
- Group
- Material number
- Material short text

You can use the object overview to select an overview variant. When the system has displayed a list of all routings and routing objects in which the work center is used, you can specify the changes to be made and set up a batch input for them. You can also change the data in the replacement objects before they are copied to their targets. The system will copy the corresponding old values if your replacement does not specify any particular field values.

A comparable procedure is available to set up a mass replacement of reference operation sets and for changing PRTs.

If there is a problem in a mass replacement, an error log is generated containing the following information:

- Total number of messages
- List of messages issued by the system—you can sort and group these messages
- Notification messages

- Warning messages
- Error messages
- Termination messages

The log displays only the data fields predefined with field selection, and the text of the messages is not displayed unless you have asked for it.

Building a Super Routing for a Configurable Material

Configured material is a material that has been assigned to a standard product. The characteristic values of the materials assigned to a product define a variant of the product.

The product is known as configurable material because it can be produced in one or more variant forms. The automobile industry provides many examples of configurable materials at all levels in the assemblies and subassemblies.

A BOM for a configurable material has to include all the components needed to produce at least one variant. The routing for this configurable material must include all the operation sequences needed for at least one of the variants.

You can manage variants by maintaining separate variant-specific configurable BOMs and routings, or you can create a super routing that includes all the materials, PRTs, and operations that are needed for all the variants. When you configure the material in response to a particular order, the system selects only the components and operations that are required for the particular variant you have specified.

A routing for a configurable material has to include *object dependencies* for:

- Sequences
- Operations
- Suboperations
- Production resource/tool assignments

The purpose of maintaining object dependencies is to define the connections and limitations when a complex product can include many variants. An object dependency represents logical constraints such as the fact that the parts and manufacturing process of a subassembly are perhaps only needed in some variants. If one subassembly is included, then perhaps it is impossible or unnecessary to include certain others. If your new car is not to have air conditioning, then it does not need the equipment nor the driver controls.

Configurations are managed with the aid of standard networks that can be grouped into configuration profiles that can be assigned to specific plants. The sales and distribution departments will also adopt different procedures for configurable materials, so the SD activities can be represented by standard networks that are controlled by a configuration profile.

Part

III

Ch

7

The operation overview of a configurable routing includes an indicator field *OD* that signifies that object dependencies exist for this operation. You can double-click this indicator to access the assignment maintenance procedure for this operation.

The following objects can be accessed from the object dependencies, and their characteristic values can be changed to control the routing:

- Operations routing table PLPOD—change Standard value, Unit of measure, Operation text
- Production resources/tools routing table PLFHD—change Quantity of the PRT
- Operation sequences routing table PLFLD—change Lot size from...to

Assigning Actions to Operations

An action is a predefined process, assigned to an operation, that will alter the value of a field when the operation is selected.

If you are creating an action, you have to create a characteristic that refers to the field you need to alter. Then you have to specify what value should be assigned to that field when the action is initiated. The alteration of a field value by an assigned action takes place only when the operation is selected.

Creating Local Object Dependencies for an Operation

The following sequence will create a local object dependency:

1. Select an operation in the operation overview.
2. Choose Extras→Object dependencies→Editor.
3. To add a new dependency, press New entries.
4. Enter the name of the new object dependency.
5. Press Dependency editor.
6. Enter a change number.
7. Press Continue.
8. Choose a dependency type.
9. Press Continue.
10. Enter the details and save.

The following sequence will create global object dependencies in an operation:

1. Select an operation in the operation overview.
2. Choose Extras→Object dependencies→Assignments, **or**
3. Double-click on the OD indicator.
4. Enter the name of the dependency.
5. Enter the dependency type.
6. Save the routing.

The result will be a routing that always carries the global dependency assignment.

Archiving and Deleting Routings

Routings can be marked for deletion and then finally deleted in the next archiving run. This process is controlled by the archiving object PP_PLAN, which allows you to archive and delete either a group of routings or individual routings specified by their group ID and group counter number.

The following sequence will begin the process from the routings menu:

- Select Extras.
- Select Delete task lists→With archiving.

Selecting Routings for Archiving and Deleting

The following attributes of task lists such as routings may be used to select them for deletion:

- Plant
- Material—several within one plant, if necessary
- Task list type, group, and group counter
- Status
- Usage
- Group
- Last time the task list was called
- Deletion flag
- Customer-specific selection criteria

Checking Dependencies Before Archiving and Deleting

The system will not let you mark a routing for deletion if is currently in use; for example:

1. Usage in a production version—the routing is stored in the material master record as a part of a production version.
2. Usage in an inspection lot—the routing used on an inspection lot for the quality management (QM) system.
3. A reference operation set or a reference rate routing is referenced in a routing or rate routing.
4. Usage in a run schedule header—the routing is needed for confirmation and other details.
5. Other usages defined through the SAP Enhancement CPRE0001.

The archiving and deleting function therefore needs to access the following types of record:

- Material master records with production versions
- Run schedule headers
- Inspection lots (archiving object QM_CONTROL)

Part
III

Ch

7

The archiving run can react to an archiving error in the following ways:

- The archiving run is terminated, and you are informed which routing is still being used.
- The archiving run is completed and then you receive a log with a list of all routings which could not be archived or deleted because of the usage check. Set the *Log* indicator in variant maintenance if you want this reaction.

Setting the Deletion/Archiving Criteria

Delete over Entire Period will select all routings that satisfy your search specification. You can also select routings that are flagged for deletion. The default is to select without regard to the deletion flag.

Delete for Key Date identifies all routing change status records ending before the key date. Deletion flags are ignored for this period. The system also looks for change status records on or after the key date and deletes those routings that have been marked for deletion. If a change status does not carry a deletion flag, the system will not delete any subsequent status records, even if they have been flagged for deletion. There must be no gaps in the validity periods of current routings.

Using the Deletion Flag and Online Deletion Indicator

There is a significant difference between a deletion flag and an *online deletion* indicator. You can remove a deletion flag at any time, but an online deletion indicator is set internally during processing and you cannot clear this indicator. However, the object, such as a routing, is still present in the database until the deletion run. You can still access it for reference purposes.

If you always maintain routings or routing objects with change numbers, the object will have several change statuses. If you never make changes with a change number, the routing and its objects have only one change status, representing the most recent alteration.

You can delete a change status online. The change status and all its subordinate objects will be locked for further processing. For example, if you delete a routing change status, the validity period of the header will be consulted. Subordinate change objects, such as sequence and operation change status objects, will also be deleted insofar as they fall within the validity period of the header.

But if the routing has more than one change status, you will still be able to access the other statuses.

By contrast, if you set a deletion flag for a change status in a routing that has several change statuses, the system will also set deletion flags on the others and so flag deletion of the entire routing. Similarly, if you remove a deletion flag, the entire routing will be preserved from archiving and deletion. In these cases, you set or remove the deletion flag in the routing header.

Alternatively, you can specify the complete routing in the selection criteria for the archiving run and remove the selection indicator *Over entire period*.

Deletion without archiving is possible, but this procedure should only be used on routings that have been created purely for testing purposes. ●

CHAPTER 8

Planning and Controlling Shop Floor Production Orders

Introducing the PP-SFC Functional Components

A production order is a specification of what is to be produced, on what dates, the dispatching point, and the production costs. The production orders (PP-SFC) module was formerly the shop floor control module. SFC accepts a planned order or an internal request posted at a previous MRP planning level, to which shop floor control adds order-specific data, such as dates and quantities.

The PP-SFC production orders module comprises the following components:

- Order Planning (PP-SFC-PLN)
- Order Execution (PP-SFC-EXE)
- Order Close (PP-SFC-CPL)

Order Planning

Order Planning (PP-SFC-PLN) selects a routing, explodes a bill of material, reserves materials and resources, determines planned costs, generates capacity requirements for work centers, and identifies nonstock components and external processing operations, both of which will require purchase requisitions.

The PP-SFC-PLN component automatically schedules a production order as soon as it is created. The basic order dates are used as starting points for the schedule. You can arrange for the order to be automatically rescheduled if any relevant changes occur; or you can trigger rescheduling manually at any time.

The order planning component is further subdivided into the following subcomponents:

- Header/operation
- Components
- Production resources/tools
- Trigger points

The Header screen of Header/Operation displays the main order elements of an order. These material production data elements will be automatically copied from master data, if it exists.

The header data for each material includes the following information:

- The material number of the material to be produced
- The order quantity
- The basic start or finish date, depending on scheduling type
- The expected scrap quantity
- The order priority
- The order status
- The plant in which the material is to be produced

The Operation Overview screen of Header/Operation includes the following information:

■ The operation and suboperation numbers that specify the sequence in which operations are to be performed

■ The work centers at which the operations are to be carried out

■ The current status of the operations

■ The start and finish dates of the operations

■ The control key of each operation to identify its purpose, such as, external processing, completion confirmation, printing, scheduling, costing

■ A short description of each operation

The components of a production order represent the materials that are required in production. If their details already exist as master data, they will be automatically copied to the order by the Components software. These components will be automatically copied to the first operation when the order is created, unless they have been already allocated to the appropriate operation by the routing document. These allocations of components to operations can be revised manually.

Production resources/tools is a functional module that manages the PRT, production resources and tools, that are used in production, but which can be moved from one work center to another. PRTs include technical drawings and specifications, measurement and inspection tools, and operating tools and fixtures that are needed in the production operation. An numerical control (NC) program would also be classified as a PRT. A movable rig that is used to test a product for structure or efficiency would be another example of a PRT.

Production resources/tools can be assigned to operations in task lists or to the production orders for which they are needed.

Trigger Points is an optional function that is used in the automation of operations. A trigger point is a data object that is allocated to an operation so as to initiate another activity. This other activity may be part of the operation itself, in which case the trigger will be allocated to a particular step. The effect may be to alter a status indicator when a certain stage is reached. A trigger point can also be configured to create an order, perhaps for replenishment, or for preparations that should begin for a subsequent operation. There may be the requirement to control operations so that they are released only at defined moments in time or logically defined moments, in which case a trigger point can be employed.

A complete workflow structure of tasks may be initiated by a trigger point. You may also wish to arrange a trigger in completion confirmation so that any defects in the operation can be reworked.

The Order Execution (PP-SFC-EXE) function begins when an order is released. The shop floor papers have to be generated. Goods movements have to take place. And the results of completing the order have to be confirmed.

Shop floor papers are printed or displayed electronically. They can include some or all of the following:

- Operation control ticket
- Job ticket
- Pick list
- Time ticket
- Confirmation slip

Goods movements include taking the materials needed from stock and delivering the finished product back into stock, which entails posting a goods receipt. Alternatively, you can arrange for goods movements to be posted automatically when the completion of an operation is confirmed. Backflushing is the process of posting a goods issue document for component goods that were previously released from stock for production. The confirmation of an operation or an order is the trigger for backflushing its constituent material components.

The confirmation of an order entails posting the actual order data that are obtainable only when the operation or order is completed. The scrap, the yield, and the processing time are normally recorded in the confirmation document.

The Order Close (PP-SFC-CPL) function controls some accounting actions. The costs incurred by manufacturing to a production order are settled on one or more cost objects. For example, the costs of the material mentioned in a sales order will be settled on that sales order. At the same time, an offsetting entry is generated automatically to credit the production order. Some of the costs may be settled on other cost objects, according to the accounting procedure established in customizing.

Controlling Production and Material Flow with KANBAN

The KANBAN technique is a method of holding up the production or replenishment of a material until the moment when it is actually required. "Just-in-time" is another term for this method of production management. There are some obvious advantages in avoiding nugatory work on products that may not be sold; and there can be advantages in not holding reserves of stock or raw materials. The disadvantages center on the risk of a delay in delivery should anything go wrong in the procurement or production processes.

The KANBAN just-in-time technique can be applied to single-stage production or to chain-of-production processes, in which case the demands or releases have to be linked in a backward direction from the required delivery date.

The purpose of the KANBAN (PP-KAN) module is to support a self-regulating environment controlling production and procurement in which manual administrative effort is at a minimum so as to promote minimal lead times and zero inventories.

KANBAN may not be worthwhile. Cost-effectiveness depends on the following conditions:

- There should be a relatively constant consumption level of the material that is to be controlled by KANBAN, at least for longer than it takes to replenish the stock.
- The production processes should have minimum setup times.

- Production should be reliable.
- Production should tend towards many small lots within a short period.

The KANBAN (PP-KAB) module depends on the following functional components:

- Control cycle—KANBAN (PP-KAB-CC)
- KANBAN control (PP-KAB-CRL)
- KANBAN board (PP-KAB-KPB)
- Creation of master data—Backflushing (PP-KAB-BF)
- Evaluations (PP-KAB-KE)

A KANBAN control cycle is a specification of the relationship between the supply source and the demand source. A control cycle defines the following elements:

- The replenishment strategy
- The number and contents of the circulating containers
- The format of the KANBAN card printout
- The delivery address
- User-defined data elements

The KANBAN control (PP-KAB-CRL) component manages the status change trigger signals for the containers, so that they are set to "full" or "empty." This KANBAN signal may be derived from scanning a bar code. The system then acquires the control cycle information so that it can automatically post the data to initiate a replenishment. When a container has been filled, the system posts the appropriate goods receipts for the replenishment.

The KANBAN Board (PP-KAB-KPB) is a component that displays the control cycles sorted according to the supply areas to which they are allocated. You can see all the containers in use and their status as full or empty. The board can also be used to trigger the KANBAN signal.

Creation of Master Data (PP-KAB-BF) is responsible for controlling backflushing. When a product is completed, backflushing automatically posts the goods receipt for it and, at the same time, posts the goods issue for the components used to manufacture it. The effect is to maintain the accounts in balance with the minimum of effort.

The method of replenishment affects the cost accounting procedure for in-house production using KANBAN. There are three possibilities:

- If the process operates with run schedule quantities, the costs are collected at a so-called production cost collector and can be settled periodically by product costing.
- If manual KANBAN is operating the costs are also collected at a cost collector.
- If replenishment control is operating with production orders, the costs are assigned to the production order.

You can monitor the success of a KANBAN operation with the Evaluations (PP-KAB-KE) component. The following tools are provided:

- Error display
- Plant overview per control cycle, with user-selectable format
- Evaluations from other areas

Administering Production Orders

Although the production order is an essential part of the PP production planning and control system, it can be successfully managed only if integrated with the SAP logistics system. In particular, PP and its components are fully integrated with the following application modules:

- Sales and distribution (SD)
- Materials management (MM)
- Controlling (CO)

A production order is a data object that specifies the material to be produced by largely internal processes. It also defines what activities have been carried out and the date when the material is to be available for delivery. The production order also specifies what resources are needed and how the various costs are to be settled on specific cost objects.

The life of a production order begins with a planned order or an internal request that has been generated by a planning process such as Materials Requirements Planning (MRP). Another source can be an assembly order, where the components already exist so that the task is to put them together. If there has been no previous planning stage, a production order or assembly order can be created manually.

When the available production resources are considered, it becomes possible to add data to the planned production order that are specific, such as the dates and quantities that will be produced against this particular order.

The planned dates and costs now associated with the production order allow it to be used to monitor the progress of the production activities and to calculate the costs of the various activities entailed. The production order also shows where the outputs of the various production facilities will become available for dispatch.

The act of posting a production order causes the PP system to carry out the following activities:

1. Select a routing.
2. Transfer the operations and sequences of the routing into the order.
3. Explode the bill of material (BOM).
4. Transfer the BOM items into the order.
5. Create reservations for all the order components kept in stock.
6. Calculate planned costs for the order.
7. Create capacity requirements for the work centers involved in the routing.
8. Create purchase requisitions for all nonstock order components.
9. Create purchase requisitions for all externally processed operations.

Using the Production Order Menu

The following sequence will reach the initial screen for production orders:

1. Select Logistics→Production.
2. Select Production orders→Select from.

The production order menu options are as follows:

- Order
- Control
- Confirmation
- Period end-closing
- Environment
- Tools

Order allows you to create, change, or display an order, subject to authorization. You can access the Collective release and Print options from this screen.

Control provides access to the following information systems that create various evaluations of production orders:

- Capacity planning
- Backorder processing
- Information on pegged requirements and pegged receipts

Confirmation allows you to create, display, change, or cancel completion confirmations and call up the plant data collection subsystem.

Period end-closing obtains data on overhead costs, work in process, and variances. You can settle orders. You can process more than one order at a time.

Environment provides access to the following functional components:

- Material provision of the SAP Warehouse Management System.
- Enter data on goods movement.
- Process incorrect records on goods movement, such as errors in automatic goods receipt and backflushing.
- Create, change, or display a batch search strategy.
- Access reports for the order from a cost accounting point of view.

Tools allows you to archive orders and create or manage archives for settlement documents.

Creating a Production Order

There are three basic ways of creating a production order:

- With reference to a material
- Without reference to a material
- By converting a planned single or collective order

The following sequence will create a production order with reference to a material:

1. Select Logistics→Production→Production control.
2. Select Order→Create→With material.
3. Enter the material you want to produce.
4. Enter the plant in which the material is to be produced.
5. Enter the order type to identify whether the internal or external order number range is to be used.
6. Enter the order number if you have indicated that you do not wish to have the system assign an internal number.
7. Press Enter to reach the Main Header screen.

The Main Header requires the following data:

- Total qty—use the unit of measure that is suggested from the material master; a fixed lot size may be suggested
- Order Start Date or Order Finish Date

Production orders are generally scheduled backwards from the finish date. The type of scheduling is indicated by the SchedType key. For example, the margin key or the scheduling margin key specifies the margin or float before production, margin after production, and the release period in days. You can enter the values using a predefined key or edit the individual fields.

The header data can also include the following information:

- Scrap portion—an estimate for the order.
- Priority—level of priority assigned to the order for management information. It has no effect on the processing.
- Long text—created in the SAP editor.

When you press Enter after completing a production order header, the system automatically searches for a valid routing and bill of material. The order type will control whether the system can adopt alternative routing sequences, if they exist.

The Operation Overview screen is displayed after a successful search for a routing and BOM. You can then change the data, if necessary, before saving the production order.

Creating a Production Order Without a Material

If you intend to use an existing order as a reference, you must choose one that is also created without a material.

The following sequence will generate a production order without referencing a material:

1. Select Logistics→Production→Production control.
2. Select Order→Create→Without material.
3. Enter the plant and order type.
4. Enter an order number if required by the order type you have entered.
5. Identify the MRP Controller.
6. Identify the production scheduler.
7. Press Enter to reach the Main Header screen.
8. Enter a short text for the order.
9. Specify the total quantity and the unit of measure.

You have to enter the Order Start Date or Order Finish Date according to the scheduling type before saving the header. Scrap portion, a level of priority, and a long text can also be entered.

A pop-up screen will offer you the chance to specify whether you want to use a reference operation set. If you do not, the system will generate a standard sequence with one operation.

The system then searches for a suitable routing and BOM.

You have to select an account receiver and maintain the settlement rule before you save the production order.

Changing Operation Data

The following sequence will allow to you change operation data:

1. Select Goto→Operation overview.
2. Select Operation.
3. Select a detail screen and update the order.

The operation detail screens are as follows:

- General view—includes scrap percentage, the number of shop papers to be printed, wage type, setup group, key to indicate whether the operation is relevant for costing
- Standard values
- Interoperation times
- External processing
- Standard value calculation
- Operation splits
- Overlapping
- Operation dates
- User fields

- Suboperation dates
- Capacity splits
- Qualifications

You can inspect but not change the details in the detail screens Quantities/Activities and Confirmed dates.

Allocating Components in Production Orders

A component can be allocated to an individual operation in a routing. If a production order is posted, any necessary components that are not already allocated to particular operations will be automatically allocated to the first operation in the routing for the production order. You can also reallocate components in the order to different operations by changing the component data.

Allocating PRTs in Production Orders

A PRT is an operating resource that is not tied to a specific work center—it can be used in different places in the plant. A PRT must always be allocated to a specific operation in a production order. This may have been prearranged in the routing.

Allocating Trigger Points in Production Orders

A trigger point is a versatile switching mechanism that can be configured to initiate a specific function when a specified logical condition is satisfied.

Such a trigger point must be associated with a particular operation in a routing.

Converting Planned Orders to Production Orders

In order to be able to create planned orders, your system has to have the following components active:

- Material requirements planning
- Routings
- Bills of material

The following information has to be stored in a planned order:

- Required quantity
- Start and delivery date
- Material number
- Material components

When the goods are required, the planned order is converted to a production order. The associated BOM is not exploded at this stage; but the dependent requirements of the components are converted into reservations. Details of the necessary operations and PRTs are obtained from the routing of the material to be produced.

You may need to change the required quantity or one of the order dates when you convert the planned order. If you do, an entry is made in the MRP file so that a new planning run will be initiated for this material and its components when the next MRP run takes place.

The following sequence will convert a single planned order:

1. Select Order→Create→With planned order.
2. Enter the Planned order number.
3. Enter the Order type of the production order you intend to create. The order type may also require you to enter the number of the production order that will be created.

The system will then select a routing and display the date for you to alter if necessary before saving the production order.

The following sequence will initiate collective conversion of several orders provided they are in the same plant and belong to the same MRP group:

1. Select Order→Create→With planned orders.
2. Enter the Plant, the MRP group, and the Order type of the production orders you want to create.
3. Specify the From and To dates of the period if you want to select planned orders according to their creation period. If your user master record includes an opening period, this will be used to propose the dates.
4. From the display of the planned orders that have been selected by your search specification, mark the orders you intend to convert. You can delete those that are not required as an alternative procedure.
5. If necessary, change the order type of the selected planned orders, and enter the order numbers for any that are external orders.

When you have saved the conversion screen, the updated and converted production orders can be individually inspected by marking the entry on the list and selecting Environment→Display order.

Converting a Planned Order to a Requisition

If you have a planned order that is not assigned for in-house production, you have to generate a purchase requisition so that the work may be executed by a suitable contractor.

The following sequence will convert a planned order into a purchase requisition:

1. Select Logistics→Production→MRP.
2. Select Planned order→Convert→Pur.req.
3. Select Individ./ Collect. conversion.

Selecting a Routing

The main use of a routing is to specify the operations and suboperations required in a production process. The individual operations and suboperations specified in the routing become part of the production order.

There are occasions when you have to create a production order without the benefit of a routing. A production run may end with a requirement that some of the work should be done again. You have to create an order for rework that, by definition, could not have been preplanned.

However, on most occasions, a suitable routing probably exists that is capable of controlling a production order. What you have to do is to set up the parameters that will find this routing in the database. Your system administrator will probably determine through customizing which types of orders are to be given a routing.

Customizing will also determine the following possibilities:

- Which routing types are allowed, such as routings, reference operation sets, or both
- Whether routing selection will be automatic or manual

A routing is associated with a transfer date, and this date is used to determine which routings can be considered for transfer. The system will not allow you to use a routing that has passed the end of its validity period. The order start date is the obvious moment to assign as the transfer date. However, if you have entered an order finish date, the system is allowed to calculate the transfer date by counting back the in-house production time if it is defined in the material master as being independent of quantity. Otherwise, the system calculates a production time for the lot size specified in the material master.

If you are presented with a list of all feasible routings that are valid on the transfer date, you have to manually select an appropriate routing from this list. If the system is assigned to automatic selection it will choose the most suitable, using the assigned selection priorities, or present you with a list of those of equal suitability from which you must make a choice.

The following criteria for automatic routing selection are applied in order:

1. Material—search for all routings available for the material.
2. Quantity—search for all routings that have a lot size range that corresponds to the specified order quantity. If there are none, disregard lot size.
3. Order dates—calculate the date on which the routing must be transferred into the order.
4. Reject routings that are not valid on the transfer date.

If the production order was created by converting a planned order that specified a production version, the system looks for a routing that is suitable for that production version.

Following the Routing Selection Priorities

Customizing will set parameters that specify how the system is to proceed if no routing exists for the material and no reference operation set can be assigned.

In these circumstances, the system automatically creates an operation. Your system may have default values to be used for generating an operation automatically and placing it in the production order. If no default values have been maintained, an operation number "0010" will be created with "0001" as the control key. If a routing has been called for and none can be found, then the system will issue a termination message and you must restart the order creation process.

Once a routing has been successfully selected, the data is transferred to the production order. If the parameters of the order type require it, you will be shown a series of detail screens on which you can check and, if necessary, amend the details.

The following data elements are transferred from the routing into the production order:

- Operations
- External processing data
- Parallel sequences
- Work centers
- Activities
- Activity types
- BOM allocations
- PRT allocations

A sequence is an ordered group of operations. Sequences can be linked by defined relationships to create networks. The following sequence categories can be processed if they appear in routings:

- Standard sequence
- Alternative sequence—alternative to a standard sequence
- Parallel sequence—parallel to a standard sequence

The first sequence to be created in a routing or a production order is recognized as the standard sequence. This may suffice if all the operations are to be sequential.

If there are alternative or parallel sequences, then there must be logical condition records that can be referenced to determine which pathway through the network is to be used in a particular production order. The operation from which a parallel or alternative sequence may be followed is identified as the branch operation.

The return operation is the first operation following a parallel or alternative sequence.

You cannot change or create alternative sequences once a production order has been created. A typical use of an alternative sequence is to cope with various ranges of lot sizes. You may also have an alternative sequence of operations that are only called into play if there is a shortage of the standard sequence capacities that might otherwise create a bottleneck.

However, you can have an alternative sequence transferred to the production order if the type definition of this order allows it. The following conditions are also checked by the system:

- The branch and return operations specified for the alternative sequence must exist in the standard sequence.
- The operation numbers specified in the alternative sequence must fit into the number interval specified in the standard sequence.
- The alternative sequence must not overlap with any other alternative or parallel sequences.

You will be invited to exchange the standard sequence for any alternative that meets these conditions, having inspected the details of the operations entailed.

If the routing selected for a production order contains any parallel sequences, they will be automatically transferred to the production order, where you will have the opportunity to make any changes via the operation overview.

Creating Parallel Sequences

The following sequence will allow you to create a parallel sequence:

1. Select Goto→Sequence overview.
2. Inspect the list of alternative and parallel sequences that already exist in the production order.
3. Select Edit→Insert.
4. Enter the parallel sequence.
5. Enter a branch operation and a return operation.
6. Enter a descriptive text for the sequence.
7. Save your entries.

Any alterations that are made to the routing or the work centers involved after a production order is created will not be updated in the order.

When a production order has been created, you can choose different master data, that is, bill of material and routing, provided the production order has not been released for production. If you opt for a different BOM, then all existing material components will be deleted and so will all purchase requisitions items for nonstock components. If selecting a different routing, then all existing sequences, operations, production resources, and tools and trigger points are deleted. Allocations of material components to operations will be deleted. Purchase requisition items for external operations will also be deleted.

The change of master data is controlled by the function Read master data. You can elect to read a different BOM, a different routing, or both.

The master data selection can be associated with a particular production version of the material to be produced, provided the version is valid on the date the BOM explosion is scheduled. If a revision level has been maintained for the material, the master data may be selected according to this revision level and so control the choice of routing, BOM alternative, or both.

The following sequence will select new master data:

1. Branch to a Header screen of the production order.
2. Select Order→Functions→Read master data.
3. Mark the master data that you want to select: routing, bill of material, or routing and bill of material.
4. Enter the desired explosion date.
5. If required, enter a production version or a revision level. These options will not be offered if the master data does not exist.
6. Press Continue.

Selecting a BOM

The bill of material is a store of data about a specific material such as an in-house manufactured product. The BOM structure can also be used for other purposes such as storing a complex of related documents.

The essential data in a BOM is the specification of the components needed to respond to a production order. The BOM information is taken into the production order.

During customizing, each order type is allocated an application. *BOM usage* refers to the application in which a particular BOM is normally used and maintained. This application is then searched when seeking a suitable BOM for a production order that is being created.

A BOM may have several usages that are represented as variants of the BOM. You can assign selection priorities during customizing to the various possible usages. For example, you can establish that the production usage BOM should be suggested before the engineering or plant maintenance BOM for the same material.

You would probably arrange for automatic BOM selection, in which case the following selection logic would be applied:

■ If there is only one BOM usage defined for the material, then select it.

■ If no usage assignment exists, select a usage according to the selection priority established during customizing.

■ Consider the status per application of each BOM and apply any existing conditions or rules. For example, a production order can only use a BOM that has the status *Released for production*.

■ Review the MRP indicator *AlternSelection* on each BOM if there are several that could otherwise meet the requirement. This indicator directs selection according to such characteristics as order quantity and hence lot size, explosion date, production version.

The production version record can be used to specify different production techniques for a material that is being produced by converting a planned order. It can also specify the BOM alternative, usage, lot size range and the validity period to be selected.

If the selection logic has been applied to the candidate BOMs and there is still no unique choice, the first alternative is transferred to the production order.

Your system may fail to find a suitable BOM for a production order. In these circumstances you have the choice of manually entering the necessary components in the production order, or you can identify a different material and allow the system to choose a suitable BOM. You may then have to modify this BOM to suit the material you really wish to produce.

Exploding a BOM into a Production Order

The system will automatically explode a BOM over just one level and copy the BOM items into the production order as components. The BOM may contain phantom assemblies, in which case the system will explode the BOM down to the first level of items that can be manufactured.

However, the system will not copy a BOM item into the production order if the item status signifies that it is not relevant to production, or if the item category indicates that it is a plant maintenance structure element or a document item. BOM subitems are not copied into the production order.

Exploding Multilevel BOM Structures

The individual assemblies in a complex BOM structure may have different explosion dates. If there have been any changes in the components used or the production technologies, new assemblies might be available with quite different BOM compositions. You can specify a BOM explosion number in the planned order, and this number will be associated with a particular explosion date that can be used for all the components. This technique is identified by a *fixed key date* that is specified in the BOM revision level. You can only use a fixed key date and a BOM explosion number with a planned order. You cannot change the BOM explosion number once it has been transferred to a production order.

Scheduling a Production Order

The purpose of scheduling a production order is to calculate the production dates and capacity requirements for all operations within the order. The system begins by scheduling the basic start and finish dates that are taken from the planned order or entered manually on the Header screen of the production order.

In customizing, you can establish whether a particular type of production order is to be automatically rescheduled each time the user saves changes relevant to scheduling.

The following scheduling types are standard:

- Forward scheduling—from the order start date
- Backward scheduling—from the order finish date
- Scheduling to current date—forward using the current date as the start date
- Only capacity requirements—the system calculates the capacity requirements of the production order

If you ask the system to calculate only the capacity requirements, it adds the *float before production* to the order start date and subtracts the *float after production* from the order finish date. The results of this arithmetic constitute the scheduled start and finish dates. These dates are then assigned to each operation as if all the operations were to be performed in parallel.

If your production order has to be created by converting a planned order, the material requirement planning will have been recorded in the planned order and the production order can take over the basic dates and the scheduled start and finish dates of the production order will be calculated on the next scheduling run. Reduction measures can be called upon if there are any problems in meeting delivery dates.

You may have to create a production order manually. The scheduling type you assign will determine which basic date you have to enter. If you enter both start and finish, the system will try to keep to these dates.

Using the Scheduling Parameters

The scheduling type, such as backwards or forwards, is proposed in the Order Header screen according to the entry made in customizing for the type of order you are creating. You can overwrite this suggestion.

"Today" scheduling can be used to reschedule an order automatically as soon as any order of a particular type is delayed by a specified number of days.

Order floats are assigned before and after production to plan an allowance for malfunctions and interruptions. You can use the float before production to tolerate some delays in the provision of necessary material components. Or you can abandon this float so as to bring forward the start date if you anticipate a bottleneck at any of the work centers needed for the production order. This can be a valuable contribution to capacity leveling.

The float after production is a reserve against unexpected malfunctions in the production process so that these affect the scheduled finish of the order.

The magnitude of these floats is specified per material as a scheduling margin key. You can alter the values in the Production Order Header screen.

The release date of the order is calculated by subtracting the release period defined in the scheduling margin from the scheduled start date of the order. Any dates that you enter manually are taken as fixed dates on which the scheduling has to be based. The order floats are not considered and therefore the basic dates are not changed. Your manual intervention merely moves the operations within the basic order dates.

A collective production order contains one or more components that are manufactured under control of their own production orders. The requirements date of a second production order is taken as its basic finish date. This logic is extended as necessary down each subtree of components and subcomponents.

The top order contains the basic order dates and the system takes them as guidelines for scheduling, which is normally of the backwards type for collective orders. The basic start date of the earliest production order equals the outline start date of the collective order.

If the scheduling run cannot meet the requirements date of any constituent order, you are informed via the scheduling log. If you decide to save the orders anyway, a system status indicator is placed in the corresponding order.

Timing Operation Segments

The lead time of an operation comprises the following segments:

- Queue time
- Setup time
- Processing time
- Teardown time
- Wait time

The execution time comprises the following segments:

- Setup time
- Processing time
- Teardown time

Move time between two operations may be added to the preceding operation so that the interoperation time comprises the following segments:

- Queue time
- Wait time
- Move time

The interoperation screen of an operation displays a field in which an indicator can be placed to determine whether wait time and teardown time are to be scheduled as simultaneous or consecutive operation segments.

The queue time is the difference between the earliest dates and the latest dates of the operation segment. The queue time is calculated for each operation segment on the basis of its earliest and latest dates.

Data relevant to scheduling can be maintained in the work center or in the routing for each operation segment. The following data is automatically copied into the production order from the routing for each operation:

- Standard and minimum queue time
- Minimum wait time
- Standard and minimum move time
- Number of splits
- Standard values

The following data is copied from the work center for each operation:

- Standard and minimum queue time
- Formulas for calculating the individual operation segments which make up the execution time (setup, processing, teardown)

The queue time from the work center is used only if there is no queue time maintained in the operation. The work center can hold formulas to be used to calculate setup, processing, and teardown times. These formulas can use the following elements:

- The standard values of the operation
- The performance efficiency rate—the ratio between the predefined planned time and the actual time needed per standard value
- The lot size of the operation
- The base quantity to which the standard values refer
- Number of splits
- Formula constants
- User fields—maintained in the detail screen of the operation

The default duration of any operation segment is zero.

The work center can also store formulas for calculating durations and capacity requirements. These formulas are maintained in the Scheduling screen of the work center.

Calling up Scheduling

When you are creating or changing a production order, you can call up the production order and select Order→Functions→Schedule. The system will then create a scheduling log to record the results of scheduling. You can display all the error messages or simply an overview.

The following sequence will display the date overview for the production order:

1. Call up the production order.
2. Select Header→Date/quantity overvw.

The following sequence will display the detail screen of individual operation segment dates:

1. Mark the operation of interest on the operation overview screen.
2. Select Operation→Operation dates. The detail screen contains the dates and times for the operation.

Managing Production Order Components

If you have suitable master records, the component data will be transferred automatically when you create a production order. There are three sources of this master data: a BOM, the routing, and the material master record.

When a BOM item is taken into a production order, the item category is also transferred:

- L—kept in stock, create a reservation for this item when the production order is created
- R—variable-sized item kept in stock
- N—item not kept in stock, create a requisition for this item when the production order is created
- T—text item
- D—document item of a particular type, such as engineering drawings, graphics, photographs
- I—plant maintenance (PM) structure element, PM assembly

Documents and PM items are not taken into a production order.

The following indicators are also taken per item:

- Costing relevancy—indicates that the component is fully relevant to costing.
- Bulk material indicator—indicates that the material is provided at the work center.

A bulk material item is not issued from stock for the order and is not relevant for material requirements planning or costing.

A routing for the material to be produced can include components allocated to specific operations in the routing. The component indicator *Backflushing* set for a component in a routing will cause the withdrawal posting for the component to be carried out automatically when the completion confirmation of the operation is posted. You can set this indicator on the general data screen of the component, in the work center, or in the material master.

The material master record can also yield data to be taken over to the production order in the form of the *Phantom assembly* indicator. This appears as a special procurement key in the first MRP screen.

Allocating and Changing Components in a Production Order

If the production order has the status *created* or *released*, you can allocate, change, or delete components in the order. However, once a component has been created in a production order, you cannot change its item category. If you delete a component in the production order that has been allocated to a released operation, the system will continue to display the item, but you will not be allowed to enter data for this component because it will carry the *Deletion* indicator.

The following sequence will allow you to inspect and change component data:

1. Select Goto→Operation overview.
2. Mark the operation to which the component is allocated.
3. Select Goto→Objects f. operation→Components.

The system lists all components that are allocated to the operation. You can then mark the component and choose a data screen that contains the information you intend to alter. The detail screens for components are as follows:

- General data
- Variable-size item data
- Purchasing data
- Text item

The following information is shown on the general data screen:

- Material—description of the material component.

- Phantom item—an indicator identifies the material as a phantom assembly marked by a special procurement key in the material master record. Used to organize other components.

- Long text—an indicator that shows that a long descriptive text has been stored for this item.

- Status—a line item that displays any system statuses active in the component.

- Storage location—where the material component is stored.

- Batch—used to record the batch number if this material is produced in batches.

- Plant—the plant to which the material's storage location is assigned.

- Sort string—an alphanumeric code used to sort a display of components, defined during customizing.

- Bulk material—indicates that the material is provided directly at the work center and is not relevant to costing.

- Costing relevancy—indicator that assigns the material component to costing.

- Follow-up time—number of days that the material component *must* be available prior to production. If the follow-time is negative, the material component *may* be available this number of days prior to production.

- Backflushing—an indicator to show that the withdrawal of the material is not posted until the corresponding operation is confirmed.

- Cuttg. measures—an indicator to show that cutting measures have been entered in the routing for the material component. Select Component→Cutting measures to inspect the values.

- Shortfall qty.—how much of the component quantity needed is not shown in the availability check for the date on which it will be required.

- Issue quantity—component quantity already issued from stock for the order.

- Quantity unit—unit of measure used for the material component.

- Operation scrap—percentage of the component quantity to be processed in an operation. The operation scrap percentage represents an estimate of the proportion of the quantity processed by the operation that will not meet the quality requirements. This percentage is maintained in the routing or in the bill of material.

- Component scrap—percentage of the component quantity that is assigned to scrap during the production of the assembly. The component scrap percentage represents an estimate of the proportion of the component quantity that will not meet the quality requirements. This percentage is maintained in the bill of material.

- Fixed quantity—an indicator specifying that the component quantity required does not change in proportion to the order quantity.
- Net price—an indicator showing that operation scrap percentage refers to the input quantity of the material. If operation scrap quantity is maintained in the routing, then this indicator is automatically set.
- Reservation—number of the reservation created automatically for the components in the order.
- Item—item number of the reservation for the requirement quantity of the material.
- Date required—when the input required quantity of the material component must be available for production. A positive requirement quantity is aligned with the operation start date: a negative requirement quantity is aligned with the latest finish date.
- Movement type—a key to specify the type of goods movement.
- Debs/Creds indicator—material movement is an inward stock movement with a debit posting or an outward stock movement with a credit posting.
- Val. perm.—an indicator that permits goods movements for the material component.

The Variable-Sized Item screen for a component of item category "R" is reached from the component overview. The Variable-Sized Item screen includes general data for the component and the following additional information:

- Size 1–Size 3—maintain the sizes used to calculate the variable-sized item quantity.
- Formula—nominate a standard formula for calculating the variable-sized item requirement quantity by entering a key.
- Number—enter the number of variable-sized items needed in the assembly.

The Purchasing Data screen is reached from the component overview of components of items of the "N" category. General data for the component is included, with the addition of the following information that is needed for nonstock components:

- Purchasing group—a key to identify the buyer or group of buyers responsible for the procurement of the material component
- Vendor—unique vendor number of the supplier of material component
- Del time (days)—required for delivering the material
- Material group—customized group ID
- GR process.time—number of days required after goods receipt to check and place the material component into stock
- Valuation price—used per price unit to valuate the nonstock component
- Price unit—number of quantity units to which the valuation price refers
- G/L account—ID number of the general ledger account to which the value of the item is credited

The Text Item screen for a component of item category "T" is reached from the component overview. You can enter general data and a descriptive text.

Allocating Components to Operations

Any operation in a production order can have components allocated to it, either by means of the routing or directly in the production order. Any component that has not been allocated to a specific operation in the routing will be allocated to the first operation in the production order when it is created.

You have the option of reallocating components to different operations.

Creating Components

The following sequence will create a component:

1. Select Goto→Operation overview.
2. Select the operation to which you want to allocate the new component.
3. Select Goto→Objects f. operation→Components.
4. Select Edit→Insert.

You must enter the following data for every new component:

■ The required quantity of the component
■ The unit of measure of the component
■ The item category
■ If necessary, the material description

The system will offer you the appropriate detail screen for any further data that is necessary.

The following sequence will reallocate components:

1. Select Goto→Component overview.
2. Inspect the list of the components contained in the production order.
3. Select the component which you want to reallocate to another operation.
4. Select Edit→Reallocate.
5. Enter the operation number to receive the reallocated component, or press the function key Operation list and mark the destination.
6. Press Continue.

Sorting Components in a Production Order

The following component sorting criteria are standard:

■ Operation number
■ Item number
■ Item category
■ Reservation number
■ Component
■ Date required

You can sort the list of components repeatedly by using the following sequence:

1. Select Goto→Component overview.
2. Select Edit→Sort.
3. Select the sorting criterion.
4. Press Enter.

Filtering components are used to restrict the display to components that meet the criteria, such as missing part, phantom assembly, or a specified item category.

The following sequence will filter components:

1. From the component overview select Edit→Filter.
2. Select the filtering criterion.
3. Press the function key Select.

You can retrieve the full list of components by filtering for All components or by accessing the component overview.

You can delete components from a production order up until it is released. You mark the unwanted components in the component overview screen and then select Edit→Delete.

Handling a Backflushing Error

Backflushing is a technique used in the materials management (MM) application module that allows the formal posting of goods issue documents to be delayed until the moment when their use in a manufacturing operation has been confirmed. The system will automatically post the goods issue documents for all backflushed components.

The material components will normally have been dispatched to the work center in time for the work on them to be carried out. But if there is a shortage of materials at the work center, the backflushing procedure cannot initiate goods issue because the operation will not be confirmed. A backflushing error message will be generated and the missing component will be assigned a corresponding status indicator in the production order.

One thing you might be able to do is to withdraw the component manually from the production order by following this sequence:

1. From the initial menu of the production orders, select Environment→Goods movement.
2. Select Comps.ErrorHandling to elicit a list of all components that should have passed through automatic goods issue when the respective operations posted their completion confirmations.
3. Position the cursor on the component for which you want to post a withdrawal.
4. Complete any missing data, such as storage location or batch number.
5. Select Issue items→Save.

Using the MRP Discontinuation Functions

A component may have some dependent requirements that have been discontinued and are no longer available from stock. However, you may be able to transfer some or all of these outstanding dependent requirements to one or more follow-up materials.

The *Simple discontinuation* procedure requires you to assign a follow-up material to the material that has been discontinued. Whatever the missing requirement quantity was, it will be automatically assigned to the follow-up material. Assigning a follow-up material can be performed in the material master or in the bill of material, but any assignment of a follow-up material made in the BOM will take precedence over an assignment in the material master.

The *Parallel discontinuation* procedure depends on a main item in a group of parts to be discontinued. A group key is assigned to the main material in the BOM. The missing quantity of the discontinued material is assigned proportionally to the planned quantity of the follow-up materials.

A discontinued material and its follow-up material must both be planned deterministically, that is, in detail, with specific items identified. They must share the same base unit of measurement.

Triggering Batch Management in a Production Order

When a component of a production order is managed in batches you can manually trigger the batch determination process. This selects all batches that meet the conditions set up in customizing and which will have stock available to meet the requirements date of the component.

There are some preconditions for batch determination for a component:

- The component must be kept in stock.
- The component must be managed in batches as shown by the indicator on the first Work Scheduling screen of the material master.
- A search strategy for batch management must have been assigned in customizing as an order type dependent parameter.

The following sequence will carry out batch determination for a component:

1. Branch to the Component Overview screen.
2. Select the component that you wish to split.
3. Select Component→Batch handling→Batch determination.
4. If no batches are suitable, select Batch determination→W/o class selection.

The system lists all batches that meet the selection criteria and have available stock on the requirements date of the component. Press the function key Copy.

Batch Splitting is used when you want to assign more than one batch to a component. The system will display each batch as a separate component in the component overview. These batch splits have to be triggered manually in the production order. The following sequence will carry out a batch split:

1. In the component overview screen, select the component that you wish to split.

2. Select Component→Batch handling→Batch determination.

3. Distribute the required quantity as required over the existing batches that have stock available on the component requirements date.

4. Press the function key Copy.

Each batch is copied as a separate component into the component overview screen.

Managing Production Resources and Tools

PRTs are mobile, unlike machines and plants. Different work centers may be able to use the same PRT. The PRT list can include the following:

- Tools
- Jigs and fixtures
- Measurement and inspection devices
- Numerical control programs for machine tools

PRTs are managed through their master records, which are classified according to their properties and business functions as follows:

- Production resource/tool with material master record (material PRT)
- Production resource/tool with PRT-specific master record (miscellaneous PRT)
- Production resource/tool with document info record
- Production resource/tool with equipment master record (equipment PRT)

Chapter 6, "Assigning Production Resources and Tools," discusses the association of PRTs with routings and operations.

There are some rules for controlling how PRTs are allocated to operations:

- A PRT with a material master record can be allocated to an operation only if you have maintained the PRT view in the material master.
- The status of the material must permit the allocation.
- A miscellaneous PRT with a PRT-specific master record must have a status that allows resource planning for the PRT.

The following sequence will allocate a PRT:

1. From Operation overview, select the operation to which you want to allocate a PRT.

2. Select Goto→Objects f. operation→PRTs for operation.

3. View the list of the existing PRT allocations to the operation in the PRT Overview screen.

4. Select Edit→New entries.

5. Decide whether you want to create a PRT with a material master, a PRT-specific master (miscellaneous), or as a document.

6. Change the suggested PRT category if necessary.

7. If necessary, maintain the item number of the PRT, the key of the PRT, and the main data of the PRT.

8. Select the function key Insert.

9. If you have finished allocating PRTs, press the function key Cancel.

Using Trigger Points

A trigger point is represented by a master record that can be allocated to an operation. The purpose of the trigger point is to initiate a function, which can be any R/3 function that has been defined and specified in the trigger point master record.

The trigger point record includes the logical or arithmetic conditions that will act as the trigger. The reason for a trigger can be positive, such as the completion of an operation, or negative, such as a failure to meet the planned delivery date. For example:

■ A specified status indicator in a particular operation changes either way between active and inactive.

■ The operation is confirmed.

■ Variance in the operation has been detected by the system and the trigger is linked to a particular reason for variance.

When a trigger condition is detected, there are various consequences that can be set up for automatic execution; for example:

■ The next operation in the sequence can be released.

■ All operations directly after the triggered operation up to a stop indicator can be released.

■ All operations preceding the triggered operation can be released.

■ A new order is created using a reference operation set without reference to a material.

■ A reference operation set is inserted into the existing order after an order that has to be specified in the trigger record.

■ A workflow task such as mailing a standard message to the user can be executed.

■ A task that has previously been defined as a workflow can be initiated by a trigger point.

Creating Trigger Points

Standard trigger points and trigger point groups can be predefined to streamline the use of trigger points in production orders. You can create a standard trigger point in the routing or in the production order. The purpose of a standard trigger point is to provide a model or reference that can be copied and, if necessary, edited for use in the production order.

The following sequence will allow you to create a standard trigger point:

1. Select Logistics→Production.
2. Select Master data→Std. trigger point.

If you need to allocate several trigger points to the same operation, it may be convenient to create a trigger point group that can be allocated by a single entry.

The following sequence will allow you to create trigger point groups:

1. Select Customizing→Production.
2. Select Shop floor control→Master.
3. Select Trigger points→Defining trigger point groups.

The following sequence will create a trigger point in a production order:

1. Call up the Operation Overview screen in the order.
2. Mark the operation to which you want to allocate a trigger point.
3. Select Goto→Objects f. operation→Trigger points.
4. Inspect the list of existing trigger points.
5. Enter a usage and/or a description.
6. If the trigger point is to be used to trigger a function, set the function indicator.
7. If the trigger point is to be used as a release stop, set the RelStop indicator.

The release stop indicator marks the operation as the last to be released following an earlier trigger containing the indicator *Release up to stop indicator*. The same trigger point can serve both as a release stop and a trigger for a function.

Creating a trigger point can proceed in the following ways:

■ Copy a standard trigger point—press function key Incl. std trigger pt, then select and copy a standard trigger point.

■ Copy a group of standard trigger points—press function key Incl. trigger pt grp, then select and copy a trigger point group.

■ Create a trigger point manually by entering a usage and a description for the trigger point.

The following sequence will allow you to develop the details of a trigger point:

1. Mark the trigger point.
2. Select Trigger point→Details.
3. Select the function that you want the trigger point to carry out.
4. Enter the status to trigger the function.
5. Specify whether the function should be triggered when the status is activated, deactivated, or in both cases.
6. Specify whether the function is only to be triggered once.

Most of this information may already be suggested as defaults if you have copied a standard trigger point or trigger point group.

Setting Trigger Point Parameters

If you press the function key Parameters, the system will display a pop-up window containing the fields required to execute the intended function of the trigger.

For example, if the trigger point has to insert a reference operation set into the production order, you might have to maintain the group and the group counter number that identifies the set you need. You will also have to check that the system knows the number of the operation after which the reference operation set is to be inserted.

You can have the system work with a selection profile that lists several status indicators that all have to be matched for the trigger to activate.

When you have finished adjusting the trigger point parameters, press the function key Back, and save the production order.

Checking that Resources Will Be Available

The main resources needed for a production order include the material, the production resources and tools, and the various capacities at the work centers.

The system can check the availability of the material components of a particular production order if this material is kept in stock, although it cannot check bulk materials. A phantom item is obviously not checked for availability.

For each order type and plant, your company can specify whether availability shall be checked automatically or manually. The checking for availability can take place during order creation, and again at order release, as necessary. You can always initiate an availability check manually.

Each material can be assigned to a checking group, which will be shown in the material master. The checking scope applied to the checking group is determined by a checking rule that is specified in customizing. The checking group and its associated checking rule server control the scope of the availability check, as follows:

- Which MRP elements are taken into account in the check
- Which inventory categories are taken into account
- Whether the replenishment lead time is taken into account
- Whether the check should also be carried out at storage location level

If a material is going to be checked for availability, it must be assigned to a checking group with an appropriate entry in its material master record. The definition of the checking group can include a *materials lock* indicator to signify that the materials must be locked during the checking process. This causes the quantities of the material already committed to be kept in a lock table. Even if you have not saved the order you are working on, the availability check will immediately reserve the quantities of any materials that you need if they belong to a checking group marked with the lock indicator.

The specification of a checking group will also include an indicator to control whether the normal available-to-promise (ATP) quantity or the cumulative ATP quantity is used. You may prefer to have the system consider the cumulative ATP quantity of a particular material because that will take account of any changes in the expected dates of goods receipts that could affect the commitment situation and the ATP quantity.

If necessary, you can switch off the availability check for a particular checking group.

Maintaining Availability Checking Rules

Each order type can be customized by specifying two checking rules:

1. Availability transaction 1—checking rule for created orders, used in manual checks on a created order and in automatic checks during order creation
2. Availability transaction 2—checking rule for released orders, used in manual checks on a released or partially released order and in automatic checks during the release of an order

The checking rule for backorder processing is defined per plant and is used only in availability checks for backorder processing.

The checking scope of a checking rule assigned to a checking group controls what shall be checked, as follows:

- Which types of stock/goods receipts/goods issues should be taken into account in the check
- Whether the check should take into account the replenishment lead time
- Whether the check should only be carried out at plant level, regardless of whether a storage location is specified in the reservation

Materials produced in-house are assigned to checking group IN. This group does not need to have purchase orders or purchase requisitions included in the checking scope.

A material that is produced externally by a contractor or vendor will be assigned to checking group EX. The checking scope for this group does not include a check of the sales or production orders because they do not affect the availability of materials produced externally.

The available-to-promise (ATP) method is used when checking availability. In particular, the system checks:

- Whether the material requirements can be fully covered on the requirements date
- When the requirements can be covered, if a full coverage of the requirements is not possible on the requirements date

If the ATP quantity of a material is sufficient, the system will normally try to commit the entire requirements quantity of a component. However, it is possible to commit only partial quantities during availability checks. What you have to do is to create a production scheduling profile during customizing that will direct that only a specified percentage of the requirements quantity is to be assigned as a partial commitment.

Each material master record can store an indicator to show whether a material is to be checked for availability per storage location or per plant. A material reservation can refer to a particular storage location, but the checking scope for this material may overrule this and cause the availability check to cover the entire plant.

An availability check may discover that the material is required for a sales order or project. In such circumstances, the availability check will consult the individual planning section of the sales order or project.

There are two ways of phasing availability checks, as follows:

1. An overall check determines the availability of all components needed for an order or collective order. It can be triggered automatically or manually.

2. An individual check determines the availability of a single component. It can only be triggered manually.

The production order information system allows you to perform a collective availability check, which is an overall check for several orders together.

Customizing per order type can establish whether an availability check is to be carried out automatically and whether the check is to take place during order creation or upon order release.

A *missing part* is defined as a material component that is not going to be available on the required date. This prediction is shown as a status indicator in the order header. A subsequent overall check or individual check may discover a suitable component that is available to promise, in which case a reservation can be made and the missing part indicator deactivated.

Viewing the Results of an Availability Check

The availability log displays the following information:

- Whether all components are available
- A list of the missing parts
- A list of the reservations that could not be checked, for example, because the necessary information had not been maintained in the material master

The availability log is not stored when you exit the production order.

The missing parts overview displays a list of the missing parts and the date on which all components will be available. From the missing parts overview, you can process the missing parts in certain ways. For example, you can nominate a different storage location to source the requirement. You can also alter the requirements quantity.

Whenever you consult the missing parts overview, you will see the results of the most recent availability check carried out in the order, even if you have exited the order. The overview contains the following information:

- A list of the missing parts
- A list of the reservations that could not be checked, for example, because the necessary information had not been maintained in the material master

If you select View→Check result→All components, you will see a list of all components checked and the date on which all components will be available.

The missing parts list is not stored when you exit the order. However, if an availability check is carried out when the order is released, the system writes the results in the release log.

You may well make changes to the dates or quantities in a production order that could impact on the availability of some of the components. However, such changes will not automatically trigger a fresh availability check. You must manually trigger an availability check.

Defining Criteria for Collective Availability Checks

The details of a collective availability check can be customized by copying the standard availability checking profile and modifying it where necessary. In particular, the orders on an individual object list for availability checking are processed from the top down. You can use the production order information system to group and sort the orders in this list before the collective checks begin. You can also mark individual orders and confine the checks to those you have marked.

It might be informative to reset the availability data from the previous check before you try out a fresh collective check. The reset operation will delete the following data:

- The committed quantity in each material component
- The *missing parts* indicator in the material components of any production order in the list
- The *total committed* date in the order header
- The committed quantity in the order header
- Any *missing parts status* indicators (MPST) active in the production order

You can perform the reset of availability data in one step or in individual steps dealing with each order in turn. Orders are locked while the data is being reset, so you have to decide whether to have the orders locked one at a time or have the whole collective locked until the last one has been reset. The reset of availability data is normally a background task, and it will take less time as a collective than dealing with each order separately.

Availability logs can be generated using different levels of message. *Abend* is the highest level, *information* the lowest. A log is generated only if there are any messages at or above the specified level. W is the code for the log to write warning, error or abend messages.

The results of collective availability checking that has been conducted under control of the standard profile are presented as follows:

- Results key—shows whether an order is fully committed, not fully committed, and so on.
- Messages—if any issued, each level will be notified by a results key that indicates the highest level of message issued during the availability check. You can see what these messages were by selecting Goto→Availability log. A log is generated for planned orders or for collective availability checks carried out in background processing.

Part

III

Ch

8

- Commitment ratio—shows a percentage relationship between the committed order quantity and the order quantity.
- Commitment difference—shows the number of workdays between the planned basic finish date and the committed basic finish date of the order.
- Total committed date—shows the date on which the entire quantity can be delivered.
- Committed quantity of the order.
- Missing parts status for production orders with missing parts.

Carrying out an Availability Check

The following sequence will check the availability of material components for the entire order:

1. Select Order→Availability check.
2. Select Material.

The status *material shortage* will be activated in the production order if any material is not going to be available in the requirement quantity on the requirement date.

You can check an individual material component from the component overview, from the missing parts overview, and from the missing parts list. The following sequence will check from the component overview:

1. Select Goto→Component overview.
2. Inspect the list of all the material components in the order.
3. Mark a material component for availability checking.
4. Select Component→Availability→Recheck.

You receive a message stating whether or not the marked component will be available on its requirement date.

The following sequence will check the availability of several orders at the same time in online mode:

1. Select Logistics→Production.
2. Select Production control→Control.
3. Select Information systems→OrderInfoSystem.
4. Select Object overview.
5. Enter an overall profile ID, such as the standard overall profile 00000000003 for collective availability checks.
6. Consider whether production orders, planned orders, or both are to be checked for the next availability check only.
7. If necessary, temporarily change the customized overall profile by selecting View→Object selection and limiting the search to order headers and, exceptionally, individual material components.

8. Inspect the list of selected orders.

9. Mark the orders to be checked.

10. Press the function key Check availability.

11. Maintain the availability check parameters.

12. Press the function key Check availability.

If you create a background job in the individual object list, the job is started immediately. If you wish to schedule a background job for a different point in time, you must create the job in the System Administration menu and specify a variant for the job.

The following sequence will carry out availability checks on several orders in the background, immediately:

1. Select Logistics→Production.

2. Select Production control→Control.

3. Select Information systems→OrderInfoSystem.

4. Select Indiv.object lists.

5. Mark the individual object list for the Order header and press the function key Select.

6. Specify whether you want to select planned order, production orders, or both, as well as a profile.

7. Enter your criteria for order selection.

8. Maintain the availability check parameters.

9. Select Program→Exec. in background.

10. Maintain the necessary print parameters.

11. Press Enter to save the background job.

The system will generate availability logs for planned orders or when you generate collective availability checks in the background. Messages are not issued during the check in either of these circumstances.

The following sequence will display the background job status and results:

1. From the main SAP menu select Tools→Administration.

2. Select Jobs→Select jobs.

3. Your user ID is suggested by the system. Enter additional selection criteria if necessary, such as job status.

4. Press Enter to display the jobs as selected.

The following sequence will check the availability of several orders in the background at a chosen time:

1. Select Tools→Administration.

2. Select Jobs→Define jobs.

3. Enter a job name and a job class.

4. Press the function key Start date and specify when the background job should be started.

5. Press STEPS in order to create the program.

6. Press the function key ABAP.

7. Enter the program name PPIOH000 and a variant number that has been defined in the order information system for the collective order check you require.

8. Save the background job.

Checking the Availability of Production Resources and Tools

The PRT categories material, PRT master, document, and equipment store a status indicator in their master records which specifies whether the PRT is available. A material PRT also allows you to check the plant stock of this PRT in the following inventory categories:

- Unrestricted-use stock
- Inspection stock
- Unrestricted-use consignment stock
- Consignment stock in quality inspection

Whether the system will check only the status, or the status and the plant stock, are matters predefined in customizing. PRT availability can be checked manually or automatically, during order creation or at order release.

The status *PRT Shortage* becomes active in the order header if there is going to be a problem in making a necessary PRT available.

The operation of the PRT availability checking functions is directly comparable to the procedures for checking the availability of material components.

Checking the Availability of Capacities

A work center may be scheduled to process more than one production order over the same time period. When the system checks that there will be sufficient capacity for every operation in a production order, it takes into account any other work that has been scheduled for the work centers concerned.

When creating or changing a production order, the following sequence will call up the capacity availability check:

1. Select Order→Functions.

2. Select Availability check→Capacity.

3. A dialog box is displayed if a capacity shortage is detected.

The capacity availability check can also be called at operation level and at sequence level.

The function key Dispatch will dispatch, in the background, all operations at all work centers in the production order. All operations that have not already been dispatched will be dispatch if they will need capacities that have to be taken into account in finite scheduling. This type of scheduling is designed to consider any capacities that have already been assigned to other production orders.

The function key Overloaded work centers displays any overloaded work centers. Continue leads back to order processing. The production order will show the status *Missing capacity* (MCAP).

When dispatching has completed, you are shown the Operation dates dialog box where the dates are displayed of all the operations in the order that have been changed by scheduling. You can also see the number of days that production has been shifted as a result of dispatching.

At this stage you can confirm the new dates and they will be copied into the production order. The MCAP order status will not be set.

Alternatively, you can command that all the operations that were dispatched within the capacity availability check are deallocated again.

If you specify "Today" scheduling, any operation dates that are scheduled in the past will be shifted to the current date or into the future.

Determining the capacity load of a work center during an availability check will be controlled by parameters that have been set in customizing for capacity leveling in conjunction with the requirements grouping of a selection profile. If you have not set any status conditions, the system will only consider released operations when checking availability.

Releasing Orders and Operations

When you create a production order, the system automatically assigns it the status *Created*. A production order marked with the *Created* status indicator is not going to initiate any production activities, because, for example:

- Completion confirmations cannot yet be carried out for the order.
- Shop papers cannot be printed.
- Stock movements cannot be carried out for the order.

These restrictions apply until the order is released for production.

While a production order is in the creation mode or in the change mode, the following sequence will release it:

1. Select Order→Functions.
2. Select Release within production order processing.
3. Save the order to initiate the release.

Releasing a production order releases all the operations in it.

You can arrange for automatic release of created production orders. During customizing, a production scheduling profile can be defined. This profile can specify that a production order is to be released as soon as it is created.

The automatic release will not take place unless the production scheduling profile has been assigned to the production order. In the first work scheduling screen of a material master record you can assign a predefined production scheduling profile to that material. This will allow automatic release of any production order created for that material.

Another approach is to customize the production scheduler so that created orders are automatically released.

You can release an individual operation within a production order provided all preceding operations have already been released. A released order is status marked *Released*. If you do release one or more individual operations in a production order, the order will be status marked as *Partially released*.

The order will receive the status *Released* as soon as you have released all the operations in it.

If you assign trigger points to operations in the routing or in the production order, you can use these trigger points to release one or several successive operations.

The following sequence will release one or more successive operations:

1. Within production order processing, select Goto->Operation overview.
2. Mark the operation(s) you want to release.
3. Select Operation→Functions→Release.

Collective order release begins by selecting production orders by order type, plant, and MRP controller. You can apply the following search criteria to identify orders for collective release:

- Material number
- Order number (interval)
- Release date (interval)
- Selection profile
- Status

The following sequence will release several production orders at the same time:

1. In the initial menu of Production Orders, select Order→Release.
2. Select the relevant plant.
3. If required, enter further criteria for the order selection, such as MRP group, material, or status.
4. To select orders according to their release date, enter suitable dates in the fields Release and To Release. These dates may have been suggested on the basis of the entries in your user master profile.

5. Mark all the production orders you want to release. The system automatically uses the current date as the release date when suggesting production orders for release.

6. Select Collective release→Proceed. ●

CHAPTER 9

Administering a Production Line

Taking Advantage of Collective Production Orders

You can create a structure that links planned orders or production orders over several production levels. Each order in the collective has a separate order number, but stock movements are carried out only for the top order in the structure. One of the advantages of representing an integrated production process as a collective order is that you can display and manage the entire production process as a single entity. Only one stock movement needs to be maintained, rather than separate movements for each of the constituent operations. There are no movements between production levels that need to be separately maintained.

The costs of production are often calculated on the basis of the moving average price of the various materials. This is maintained in the material master of each material, and so there can be average prices for the various semifinished materials that are created in the production sequence. With a collective order, the costs of production are calculated for the material that is the finished product of the collective. This value is a more realistic estimate of the costs of production than a composite value based on moving averages of component materials that could take part in many different routings that are not related to the production line represented by the collective production order.

However, you have the option of processing the whole collective order, a subtree of the structure, or a single order within it.

If you are working with a collective production order, some business transactions can be carried out simultaneously on several orders. For example, if you release one order in a collective, the system will release all other orders in this collective that are dependent on the order you have released.

Similarly, the system will automatically update dependent orders if you make a change in a particular component. You might change the quantity of one order, for instance. The effects of this change will be automatically promulgated through the collective order. The requirement quantity will change if you alter the order quantity, and so on, throughout the dependent orders in the collective production order.

Working with a Collective Production Order

In the second MRP screen of a material master record is a field to hold a special procurement key. If this key is 52 in the standard R/3 system, this indicates that direct production of the material is allowed. You can use this material as a component in a collective production order.

To create a collective order you must specify an order type that is created with internal number assignment.

The following sequence will call up a collective production order:

- Select Logistics→Production.
- Select Production Control.
- Select Order→Display, or Order→Change.

A collective production order may be very extensive, so you have to decide which parts of it you need to access:

- To call up a single order within a collective order, enter the relevant order number and set the indicator *Order entered.*
- To call up a subtree of a collective order, enter the number of the order at the top of the subtree and set the indicator *Coll. order subtree.*
- To call up the entire collective order, enter any order number that is part of the collective order and set the indicator *Entire coll. order.*
- To call up the collective order overview, enter any order number that is part of the collective order and set the indicator *Display overview.*

Part
III

Ch
9

Display overview is the default setting.

A collective production order may well contain various links between individual orders. Therefore you have to be careful about carrying out a business transaction on a particular order, because you may not want all of the alterations to be promulgated to every one of the linked operations. For example, you may not want to release all the linked operations.

The prudent procedure is to access and display all the linked operations of a collective production order and check their relationships before you make any changes that could be widely promulgated.

The planned and the actual costs of any order within a collective order can be displayed as for a standard production order. However, all phantom assemblies are costed in collective production orders. The actual costs are determined for each individual order and then rolled up to the next higher level.

There are some restrictions that apply to the releasing of individual production orders if they are part of a collective production order:

- An order cannot be released until the operations in subordinate orders are released.
- An operation cannot be released until all the preceding operations are released.

For example, an operation in a collective production order may have a component allocated to it for which a separate subordinate production order has been created. You will not be allowed to release the main operation until all the operations of the subordinate have been released.

If you call up an individual order in a collective production order, the system will not let you release it unless it is the very last order in a subtree. The last order has no dependent subordinates.

However, if you specify that you want to call up the entire collective production order, or if you call up an entire subtree, the system will be able to check that all preceding operations have been released if you decide to release any individual operation.

Confirming the Completion of Collective Production Orders

Confirming the completion of a part of a collective production order is subject to some restrictions:

- If you confirm at the order header level or at the suboperation level, you are only allowed to confirm that particular order.

- If you confirm at the operation level, you can only confirm operations simultaneously across several orders if all these operations are identified as milestone operations.

Posting Subassemblies to Stock in a Collective Order

If assemblies are produced in a collective order, and the assemblies are designated for direct production, each assembly will be transported to the next work center as directed by the superior order.

The system will automatically record and allocate costs when a completion quantity is confirmed as a yield of acceptable quality. There will be a simulated goods receipt for the subordinate order and a simulated goods issue for the superior order. This causes a crediting of the subordinate order and a debiting of the superior order.

However, there may arise situations in which you want to post a portion of the finished subassembly to stock rather than allow it to proceed along the production sequence. For instance, you may have planned for a certain percentage of the product of a particular operation to be assigned to scrap. If the plant is working well, there may be less scrap than planned for. The confirmed yield may exceed the planned requirement for the next operation in the sequence. You could post the surplus to stock.

When the yield from the subordinate order is confirmed, there is a credit posting to this order and a debit posting to the superior order. However, if an excess is produced by the subordinate operation, you will not want the superior order to be debited by product that has gone into stock. The solution is to create an unplanned goods receipt for the excess quantity, which you attribute to the superior order.

The following sequence will handle this type of situation:

1. Confirm the actual yield of the subordinate order. The system automatically credits the superior order with the yield quantity.
2. Select Logistics→Materials management.
3. Select Inventory management→Goods movement.
4. Select Goods receipt→Other.
5. Enter goods movement type 531 (goods receipt for by-product).
6. Enter the plant and the storage location, press Enter.
7. Enter the number of the superior order in the field Order.
8. Enter the assembly of the subordinate order and the excess quantity as Item 1.
9. Save the goods movement.

Using the Production Order Information System

The production order information system provides a reporting system and a method of mass processing. The source of the data is the logical data base IOC and the original production order tables. The advantage of using this source is that the production order information system is always active and no steps need be taken to update statistical tables.

An evaluation called for by the information system can embrace any orders that have not been archived, including those with deletion indicator flags. Various list formats are available and can be customized.

Production orders can be accessed using the following selection criteria:

- Plant
- Order type
- Material
- MRP controller
- Production scheduler
- Work center
- Component
- Sales order

You can establish a selection profile to choose production orders according to their system status or user status at header level. Orders marked with deletion flags but not yet archived can be included if necessary.

You can specify whether the choice of an order that is part of a collective production order should cause a display of the rest of the orders in the collective.

If you do not want a full selection of control parameters to be offered for each inquiry, you can define selection variants and assign them to particular users.

The production order database can be very large, so you might want to exclude certain types of object when defining your search specification. For example, if you need an overview of a particular type of order, you should deselect all object types except the order header.

If you select an object type, for example, *operation*, the system will also select the object type *sequence* because this object is hierarchically superior, and so on. The following hierarchy of object types can be selected or deselected from the logical database:

- Order header
- Order item
- Sequence
- Operation
- Suboperation
- Component

- Production resource/tool
- Trigger point
- Individual capacity requirements
- Confirmation at the order header level, operation level, or suboperation level
- Automatic goods movements at the order header or operation level
- Incorrect automatic goods movements at the order header or operation level

Although a selection profile may be active, you can change the settings manually in the initial inquiry screen.

Customizing the Production Order Information System

When you access a selection of objects from the production order logical database, the object overview screen displays them in hierarchical form so that you can see the relationships. For instance, you can discern which objects are allocated to a particular operation. You can structure the object overview display using the following functions, either in the selection profile, or per information system transaction:

- Suppress irrelevant orders.
- Suppress irrelevant objects.
- Compress selected superior or subordinate objects.
- Display particular fields.
- Change the field sequence in the display.

When you have made changes in some production orders and carried out business transactions, releases, availability checks, and so on, you can refresh the information system list display to see the effect of your actions. A *complete refresh* will update all production orders in the list. A *partial refresh* will reduce the processing requirement, but you have to mark the objects that are to be refreshed.

In addition to the object overview display, any selected object can be shown in the detailed list. The objects in this detailed list can be grouped by order or by operation.

The contents of the object detail lists are as follows:

- Header detail list—Order headers
- Item detail list—Order items
- Sequence detail list—Order sequences
- Operation detail list—Order operations, Order suboperations
- Component detail list—Order components
- Confirmation detail list—Confirmations of orders, Confirmations of operations, Confirmations of suboperations
- PRT detail list—PRTs
- Trigger point detail list—Trigger points

- Capacity detail list—Operation capacities, Suboperation capacities
- Goods movements—Goods issues for backflushed components, automatic goods receipts
- Failed goods movements—Goods issues for backflushed components
- Automatic goods receipts

The content and display format of a detailed list can be altered online or specified in the user selection profile. The following aspects are amenable to adjustment:

- Which fields are to be displayed for the object
- Layout of the fields—grouping or width of columns
- Sort order in which the objects are displayed—ascending or descending
- Selection profile—makes the format dependent on the status of the object displayed

The following functions are available for the object detail lists:

- Print
- Filter
- Branch to other objects as marked by your cursor—select Environment→Display object

Part

III

Ch

9

Using Production Order Information System Profiles

The objects selected and the layout of the screen can be determined by an overall profile defined in the initial screen of the production order information system. The overall profile embodies various subordinated single profiles.

An overall profile can be assigned the following specifications:

- A variant which can be used to suppress selection criteria
- Which objects to read from the database
- Which of these objects are to be displayed in the list
- The object up to which objects are to be expanded on the object overview
- Single profiles for all objects

A single profile is made up of sets of parameters. The first set of parameters applies to both the object overview and the object detail list. The other sets of parameters are subprofiles that apply only to the object detail lists. A profile controls the following aspects of the information system display:

- Fields displayed in both object overview and object detail list
- Subprofile defining the fields to be displayed in the object detail list
- Specifications on how the list is formatted with respect to column width, field grouping, format of the values displayed
- Sort criteria
- Subprofile sort specification for the object detail list

- Grouping criteria
- Subprofile field grouping for the object detail list
- User filters
- Filter criteria to be used for selecting objects—defined as a report variant for each set of criteria
- Status filters—objects that are status controlled can be filtered according to a selection profile

Using the Production Order Information System for Collective Availability Checks

A collective availability check carries out an overall availability check for each of the constituent orders.

The orders to be checked can be any combination of production or planned orders. The checking rule is determined by consulting the order type for production orders or the MRP group and plant parameters for a planned order.

Collective availability checks are also discussed in chapter 8, "Planning and Controlling Shop Floor Production Orders."

Moving Goods for a Production Order

The goods necessary for a production order have to be physically issued from stock and accounted for by posting a goods issue document. When these goods arrived into stock, they were acknowledged and accounted for by posting a goods receipt.

As well as posting the relevant documents, these goods movements trigger the following actions:

- Stock quantities of the materials received or withdrawn are revised.
- The stock values of the materials are updated in the material master records and in the stock and consumption accounts of the general ledger.

Each operation in a production sequence may require a different set of material components. When you create a production order, the system automatically creates a reservation for the necessary material components. Each material component appears as a separate item number in the reservation. The reservation number is displayed on the general view screen of the components.

A material component mentioned in a reservation line item cannot be physically issued from stock until the operation in which it is needed is released for production. When components are withdrawn from stock, the posting of their goods issue document causes the value of the components issued to be debited to the order. These values are classified per cost element and origin as actual costs.

If you need to issue material components from stock, you refer to the order number or to the reservation number. The following sequence will issue material components from stock:

1. Select Logistics→Materials management.
2. Select Inventory management.
3. Select Goods movement→Goods issue.
4. Select Create w. reference.
5. Select either To reservation or To order.
6. Enter or select search criteria to identify the reservation or order number.
7. Press the function key Continue.
8. The system automatically proposes the movement type 261 (goods issue for order).
9. The system suggests all the material components in the order, unless they are marked as bulk material or as material to be backflushed.
10. Check the list of material components proposed for issue and save the goods issue.

If you do not refer to a reservation or a production order when posting a goods issue, the system will not cancel the reservation of the required quantity of material, even though the goods issue will have satisfied the requirement.

Making Unplanned Withdrawals of Components for an Order

It is possible to withdraw materials from the warehouse that are not listed as required components for an order. These, by definition, are unplanned withdrawals. They will affect the actual costs of the order.

The following sequence will carry out unplanned withdrawals for a production order:

1. Select Logistics→Materials management.
2. Select Inventory management.
3. Select Goods movement→Goods issue.
4. Select Movement type→Consumption.
5. Select To order→From Warehouse.
6. The system automatically proposes movement type 261 (goods issue for order).
7. Enter the storage location from which the goods are to be issued, press Enter.
8. In the screen Enter goods Issue: New Items, enter the number of the order.
9. For each material to be issued, enter the material number, the quantity, the quantity unit, and, if required, the batch number.
10. Save the goods issue.

Delivering Manufactured Material to the Warehouse

The delivery information is held in the header screen titled Goods receipt/Valuation of the order. From the order, Select Header→Goods rcpt/Valuation.

The following information is displayed in this goods receipt screen:

- Underdeliv. tol.—the underdelivery tolerance percentage. If a receipt is within the tolerance, it is accepted as a partial delivery. If the receipt does not fall within the underdelivery tolerance, the system issues a warning message.

- Overdeliv.tol.—the overdelivery tolerance percentage. If a receipt is within the tolerance, it is accepted as an overdelivery. If the receipt does not fall within the overdelivery tolerance, the system issues an error message when the goods receipt is posted.

- Unlimited—if this indicator is set, unlimited overdeliveries are accepted without warnings.

- Quality inspection—this indicator triggers the system to automatically propose the material for posting to stock in quality inspection.

- *Goods receipt* indicator (GR)—shows that a goods receipt is expected for the production order that should be handled by inventory management.

- *Delivery complete* indicator—automatically set by the system as soon as a delivery is posted within the delivery tolerances. This indicator can be set manually during a goods receipt posting.

- *Nonvaluated goods receipt* indicator (GR non-val)—automatically set by the system if the order is assigned to an account other than that of the material to be produced. Used, for example, for a sales order.

- Storage location—proposed by the system if a storage location is maintained in the material master of the material being produced.

- Batch information.

- Goods recipient.

- Unloading point.

Specifying an Automatic Goods Receipt

Only one operation in a order, usually the last, is allowed to be assigned the control key that specifies automatic goods receipt. This key directs the system to automatically post the finished material to stock when the operation is confirmed.

A warning will be issued if more than one operation in an order has been assigned the automatic goods receipt key. In these circumstances, you have to identify the correct operation manually.

In the case of collective orders, an automatic goods receipt is only possible for the leading order. Thus the key is ignored if it appears in any of the dependent orders.

Checking During a Goods Receipt

When a goods receipt is posted for a material delivered to stock after production, the system performs the following checks automatically:

- Goods receipt indicator—Is a goods receipt permitted for the order? Is the goods receipt to be valuated?
- Under- or Overdelivery tolerance—issue warning or error message.

Delivering a material to stock after production can affect the costs of the production order and the values held in the material master.

The following sequence will deliver all or part of an order to stock:

1. Select Logistics→Materials Management.
2. Select Inventory management.
3. Select Goods movement→Goods receipt→For order.
4. Select Movement type→Order to warehouse.
5. Enter the order number, plant, and storage location, and press Enter.
6. The system proposes the planned quantity of the production order as Goods Receipt for Order: New Items 0001.
7. Enter the quantity that you want to deliver to stock if not the planned quantity.
8. If the production order is finished, set the indicator *Final delivery*. If only a part of the order quantity is delivered to stock, do not set this indicator.
9. Save the goods receipt.

Arranging External Procurement and Processing of Components

A purchase requisition is an internal document that requires the purchasing department to procure a specified quantity of a material or service by a given date. The system assigns a number to each purchase requisition.

The system creates a purchase requisition for the external procurement or the external processing of any nonstock components or components that require external processing operations.

The purchase requisition number appears in the external processing screen of an operation if it is conducted externally by a vendor or contractor.

The purchase requisition number appears in the purchasing screen of a nonstock (category N) component. The purchase requisition is created automatically during order creation for any category N component. The necessary data is copied from the purchasing data screen of the component.

Similarly, a purchase requisition will be created automatically during order creation for any operation that is performed by external processing. The data is copied from the external processing screen of the operation.

Delivering Externally Processed Material

The material procured or processed externally is delivered to stock when the work on it is completed. If a goods receipt has been posted for an externally processed operation or a nonstock component, the system displays the received quantity. The external processing screen of the operation will show the quantity of processing. The purchasing screen of the component will show the quantity of material.

If you make any relevant changes in a production order that includes external procurement or processing, the system will automatically adjust the data in the purchase requisition if a purchase order has not already been posted. If the purchasing department has already generated a purchase order, the external processing screen or the purchasing data screen will indicate this, and the system will not automatically adjust the data in the purchase order to bring it up to date with any changes you have made.

Costing External Procurement

A control key assigned to an operation that is externally processed will indicate whether this operation is to be costed. An external processing operation is costed by consulting a costing variant that will refer to a valuation variant that specifies the price to be used for costing the external processing activity.

If the external procurement is of a nonstock material component, the value of this component is taken to be the value of the purchase requisition, which will be calculated using the price defined in the component.

When the goods receipt of the material is posted, the system will debit the production order with the actual costs of the external processing or procurement. At the same time, the consumption accounts will be updated in financial accounting.

When the goods or processing services purchased for an order are delivered there is no increase in the quantity and value of the warehouse stock.

Managing the Coproducts of a Production Order

A production order header refers to a material that is deemed to be the main product. The system automatically creates a separate order item for this main product. However, other products may be manufactured alongside the main product, sometimes deliberately as valuable coproducts, sometimes as inevitable by-products that are not particularly valuable.

The system automatically creates separate order items for the coproducts if the following conditions are satisfied:

- The coproduct must be listed as an item in the bill of material of the main product.
- The *Coproduct* indicator must be activated on the general data screen of the BOM item.

Thus the separate order item allows the actual costs of the coproduct to be displayed.

Assigning the Coproduct Indicator

A material that can appear in a production order as a coproduct must include an active Coproduct indicator in its first MRP screen. Furthermore, a material that will be a main product produced with a coproduct must also show the Coproduct indicator in the first MRP screen of its material master.

One of the advantages of creating several coproducts is that goods movements for all the products can be posted at the same time.

The system does not automatically create separate order items for by-products. The valuation of a by-product material is based on the price specified in the material master. A by-product must be listed as an item in the bill of material of the main product, but this item must be assigned a negative quantity to show that it is to be processed as a by-product quantity. A by-product does not carry the indicator for coproducts.

Costing Coproducts

The main and coproducts can be settled on different cost receivers. The total costs for a production order are assigned to the order header. The system then consults equivalence numbers in order to apportion these costs to the main product and the coproducts. These equivalence numbers are set up as an apportionment structure in the material master of the main product. When a production order is created, the system creates a settlement rule that distributes the total actual costs over the order items, which will represent the main product and the coproducts. The system also creates a separate settlement rule for each item to assign the actual costs of that item to stock.

For example, a main product material may be produced with a single coproduct. The origin structure of the main product and the coproduct may attribute the actual costs to the following cost element groups:

- Production costs
- Material costs
- Overhead

If you do not have a structure with different equivalence numbers for different cost element groups within the same apportionment structure, the system will assign an equal proportion of the actual costs to each cost origin. However, if you use a set of equivalence numbers, you can set up an apportionment structure such as illustrated in Table 9.1.

Table 9.1 Equivalence Numbers with Cost Origin Structure

Cost element group	Main product	Coproduct
Production cost	1	4
Material costs	2	1
Overhead	5	3

The origin structure has to be defined in customizing and the apportionment structure has to be defined in the material master of the main product.

Managing Missing Parts in Production Orders

A production order is given the *missing part* (MSPT) status indicator if one of its components is not expected to the available on the required date. This test is first performed during the overall availability check. The MSPT status remains active until a subsequent availability check confirms that all the necessary components are going to be available. A subsequent goods receipt, for example, may have supplied the missing part.

The missing parts list can be filtered and structured as follows:

- Parts missing from a specific production order
- Parts missing from a collective production order
- Parts missing from several orders selected through the missing parts information system

The missing parts overview screen offers the following functions:

- Edit missing parts data by changing the requirement quantity or the issue storage location.
- Check the availability of individual components.
- Filter or sort components.

The missing parts list always reports the results of the most recent availability check. The missing parts list offers the following functions:

- Display the missing parts of all orders that have been checked from a collective order.
- Check the availability of individual components.
- Filter or sort components.
- Print the missing parts list.
- Vary the field selection.

Using the Missing Parts Information System

The purpose of the missing parts information system is to allow you to display the missing parts list for all materials or for a selection of materials identified with a specific plant, MRP group, or particular requirements data.

Two standard profiles are available for selecting missing parts data and displaying it, as follows:

- Missing parts sorted by order number
- Missing parts sorted by material number

You can create other profiles in customizing, and you can create a profile variant by saving a specific set of missing parts selection criteria. This profile variant can then be specified when generating a missing parts list.

The missing parts list allows you to branch directly to backorder processing.

Backorder processing recalculates the available-to- promise (ATP) quantity of the material. The backorder display shows the following information:

- The stock and requirements situation of each material
- The quantities that have been committed to orders, reservations, and so on
- The cumulative ATP quantity

Sales orders may have been posted to identify individual requirements. These requirements are displayed at the end of the backorder display.

In the backorder screen, you can manually change the quantity of a material committed to an order or reservation. However, this change will not automatically update the missing parts list. You have to select List→Refresh when you are in the missing parts list.

The following sequence will generate a missing parts list:

1. Call up the initial menu of production order maintenance.
2. Select Control→Information system.
3. Select MissingPartsInfoSyst.
4. Call up the entry options of field Profile to select a profile.
5. Enter search criteria if required.
6. Press Continue.
7. Select Goto→Save as variants if you intend to use this search specification frequently.

You can select missing parts by any logical combination of the following attributes:

- Material
- Plant
- MRP group
- Requirements date or date interval

Your search can use these criteria to include or to exclude missing parts. You can also nominate a particular field to be the upper or lower alphanumeric range limit for the selection filter. You have to mark the field and select Edit→Selection options to enter your choices.

To use a variant in a search, select Edit→Get variants when you are calling for the missing parts list. Choose the variant and Execute or Execute+print.

Once you have displayed a missing parts list, you can branch directly to the following linked objects:

- Current stock/requirements list
- Stock overview
- Material master record
- Backorder processing
- Production order in the display or change mode

Covering Missing Parts by Backorder Processing

The backorder processing display shows all the goods receipts and goods issues that are relevant to the most recent availability check. You can use this display to process missing parts.

If the committed quantity is less than the required quantity of a material needed in a sales order or production order reservation, the material is considered to be a missing part. There are various reasons why a material can be in shortage, for example:

- A sales order has been confirmed, even though it cannot be delivered in its full requirement quantity on the date requested.

- A sales order has been confirmed because its requested delivery date is not within the replenishment period. The sales representative expects the stock of the material to be replenished, but the quantities needed have not been procured at the time the availability check is carried out.

- A material reservation dependent on the material apparently missing is not yet confirmed.

There are two principal strategies for backorder processing, as follows:

1. Commit open requirements—a recent goods receipt shows that sufficient suitable stock is now available to promise.

2. Redistribute, from one requirement to another, some or all of the quantities already allocated.

You may have a mail link that has been customized to automatically inform a designated MRP controller if a goods receipt has been posted for a part that has been marked as missing.

During the customizing for shop floor control, a checking rule for backorder processing will have been defined. Similarly, a checking rule will have been defined for production orders. If these rules are not the same, it may not be possible to handle missing parts by backorder processing.

Calling Backorder Processing

You have the option of entering backorder processing from the production activity control menu or from the missing parts information system.

The following sequence will call up backorder processing from the initial screen of production activity control:

1. Select Control→Backorder processing.
2. Select Material.
3. Enter the material number.
4. Enter the plant.
5. Press Enter.

The following sequence will call up backorder processing from the missing parts information system:

1. Mark the missing part entry.

2. Select Environment→Backorder handling.

The display lists the ATP quantities, the plant stock, any existing storage location stock, and any open sales orders. Any quantities of individual customer stock or stock in other locations are listed separately.

Displaying Reservations for Production Orders

A backorder processing screen can be customized to show only those missing quantities that are actually relevant to production activity control. You assign the setting *Reservations for production orders*.

The system will then show the following display elements:

- Dependent reservations that have not yet been confirmed.
- Dependent reservations for which a goods receipt has not yet been planned.
- In each element, the missing quantity is displayed.

The following sequence will automatically commit ATP quantities to the open reservations:

1. Position the cursor on the line with the reservation to which you wish to commit an ATP quantity.

2. Press the function key Change Committed Qty.

3. Select the requirement date.

The following details of the reservation on the date selected are displayed:

- Origin—number of the assembly that requires material
- Order—number of the source production order of the reservation
- Reqmts qty—total quantity required for the reservation
- Committed—quantity that has been committed in backorder processing
- ATP qty—available quantity that can be used to commit to requirements

You have to enter the quantity that you can commit to the requirement in the field Committed, and then press the function key Transfer before saving your entries.

Backorder Processing of Sales Orders

If you select Settings→Only SD requirements, the system will display missing parts from sales orders only. The requested delivery date of a sales order may be outside the replenishment lead time of the material components. If the availability check is configured to take account of the replenishment lead time, the system assumes that the material required for this sales order will be available when needed.

It may happen that a sales order can be delivered only in partial quantities on the date requested. The full quantity may have been committed to the sales order in spite of a warning from the availability check. These situations are reported as follows:

■ Line one shows the quantity missing on the requested delivery date in column Req/recpt.

■ Line two shows the committed quantity on the committed date.

You are thus given the chance to commit the full quantity on the requested delivery date, providing this quantity is available.

The following sequence will automatically commit ATP quantities to the open sales orders or customer requirements:

1. Position the cursor on the sales order or customer requirement to which you wish to commit an ATP quantity.

2. Press the function key Change committed quantity.

3. Select the sales order date.

The following details of the sales order on the date selected are displayed:

■ Open—total requirement quantity of the sales order or customer requirement.

■ Mat.av.dt.—the material availability date is the date on which the quantity must be available for the sales order item.

■ Tot.commttd—quantity that has been previously committed, for example, when creating a sales order or customer requirement.

■ Committed—quantity that has been committed in backorder processing.

■ ATP qty—available quantity that can be used for open requirements.

You then have to enter the quantity that you can commit to the requirement in the field Committed, and then press the function key Transfer before saving your entries.

Managing Inspection Lots in Production Orders

An inspection lot is a document that records a request for an inspection to take place. It may be necessary to set aside a quantity of the material for inspection, or the inspection may take place on the entire quantity, which is then consigned to stock if it passes the inspection.

Each inspection lot document is allocated one or more inspection characteristics that define what has to be inspected. A distinction is drawn between quantitative and qualitative inspection characteristics.

If an inspection is to be performed during a production process, an inspection lot is created and assigned to the production order. The individual characteristics defined in the inspection lot document are assigned to the individual operations in the production order.

The results of inspecting each of the characteristics specified for the individual operations are stored in the inspection lot document.

The examination of a specific inspection characteristic can be planned or unplanned. The planned inspection characteristics are maintained in the routing, and so they will be copied to all orders using this routing. The unplanned inspection characteristics are maintained in the production order.

A material master can have a quality management view. This is where inspection data is maintained. You can configure the system to generate an inspection lot automatically as soon as the first operation in the production order is released. Alternatively, you can create an inspection lot manually in the production order.

You are not allowed to create an inspection lot if the order is technically complete, or if it carries a deletion flag or deletion indicator in the order header.

The following sequence will create an inspection lot manually:

1. Call up the production order.
2. Select Order→Functions.
3. Select Inspection lot→Create insp. lot.

If the system has automatically generated an inspection lot for a production order when the first operation in the order was released, the header of the production order will show the system status *Inspection lot created* (*ILCR*). Otherwise, it will show *Inspection lot not created* (*ILNC*). You can use this indicator to find all orders that failed to generate inspection lots automatically so that you can create inspection lots manually for them, if necessary.

It is possible to delete an inspection lot so that no inspection activities take place. However, you are not allowed to delete an inspection lot if any of the operations in the production order contain unplanned characteristics. Again, you cannot delete an inspection lot once it has been used to record inspection results.

The following sequence will attempt to delete an inspection lot:

1. Call up the production order.
2. Select Order→Functions.
3. Select Inspection lot→Delete Insp. lot.

An unplanned inspection characteristic is defined as an inspection characteristic that has not been copied from the routing, but created in the production order. You cannot create an unplanned inspection characteristic until an inspection lot has been created and saved in the production order.

The following sequence will create unplanned inspection characteristics for the production order:

1. Call up the production order.
2. Branch to the operation overview and mark the operation to which you want to allocate an inspection characteristic.
3. Select Operation→Function.
4. Select Unplanned insp. char.

If an inspection characteristic has been allocated to an operation, it will show the system status *ICHA*. In order to delete an operation showing *ICHA*, you have to first delete the entire inspection lot for the production order, then delete the operation, then recreate the inspection lot.

This procedure will not work if the inspection characteristic is of the planned variety, because all the planned inspection characteristics will be regenerated from the routing.

If inspection results have already been recorded for the operation, it will show the quality management (QM) data status indicator *QMDA*. You cannot delete an inspection characteristic for which results have already been recorded.

When you delete an operation that has already been released for production, the system will assign it the status *DLFL*, *Deletion flag*. The operation remains visible in the operation overview.

Understanding the Restrictions on Inspection Lots

A reference operation set can be included in a routing, and it may have inspection characteristics attached to it. This reference operation set can be included, perhaps triggered by a critical condition, in a production order after an inspection set has been created for this production order. In these circumstances, the added inspection characteristics inherited with the reference operation set will be ignored.

A routing will include a standard sequence of operations. If this standard sequence contains an operation that has inspection characteristics, the system will not allow an alternative sequence to replace the standard sequence. If the standard sequence contains no inspection characteristics, replacing it with an alternative sequence that does include inspection characteristics will not necessarily add them to the order unless the routing is consulted and a fresh inspection lot created.

A routing may include some operations with inspection characteristics. If the order creation process copies this routing, the inspection characteristics of its operations will be copied also.

Arranging Rework After Faulty Processing

Rework in a production order in the form of extra operations may be needed in the following circumstances:

- Faulty processing of components
- Insufficiently precise processing of components
- Substandard quality of the finished product

Rework may be needed for only a partial quantity of the production order. There are three ways to manage rework:

1. Insert additional operations into the production order where they are needed.
2. Insert a reference operation set.
3. Create a separate production order without a material and assign it to the original production order.

Planning Rework

Rework that is anticipated at any particular point during a production process can be initiated by a trigger point that will insert a planned sequence of operations, perhaps with inspection characteristics, following a designated operation. The trigger point embodies conditions that have to be satisfied before the trigger will fire.

The trigger point can be configured to introduce a reference operation set or to create a rework order.

An operation that has been introduced for rework will be identified by its control key. Automatic goods receipts cannot be arranged for rework operations. An operation marked as a rework operation will have to have its quantity updated in completion confirmation according to the following rules:

- If a rework order is created, the confirmed rework quantity is taken over as the order quantity.
- If rework entails the insertion of a reference operation set, the confirmed rework quantity is taken over as the operation quantity of the inserted operations.
- If an individual operation is assigned for rework, you maintain the operation quantity in the production order.
- The operation quantity of a rework operation is not taken into account when scheduling calculates scrap-adjusted quantities for the operations in an order.
- Any change in the order quantity has no effect on the quantity of the rework operation.

Rework quantities and rework operations have to be confirmed. If you confirm at the order header level, the system assumes that the rework occurred in the last operation of the production order. The rework quantity is defined as the amount that required additional processing before it could be counted as yield. You can enter this quantity directly during rework confirmation.

The system will calculate the variance between the expected yield and the actual yield. Confirmed rework quantities are counted as actual yield.

The backflushing process allows goods issue for manufacturing to be based on the confirmed yield quantities, the scrap quantity, and the rework quantity.

If you arrange for automatic goods receipts, the system will automatically post the yield to stock. If some of the quantity planned for the operation has to undergo rework, this will not be automatically included in the yield quantity posted to stock. The confirmed reworked quantity has to be manually posted to stock using the inventory management functions.

Controlling the Progress of a Production Order by Status Management

A status indicator is a code. It marks a specific point in a sequence of statuses that are standard or that are defined in customizing. The status of a data object, such as a production order or an operation, is automatically changed when specified business transactions have been successfully carried out upon it.

Each status indicator can be used to control which subsequent operations are permitted on the object to which it is attached.

A system status is a status that is set by the system and that cannot be altered directly by the user. A system status indicator on an object will change only if the predefined business transactions have been successfully completed.

For example, if you release a production order, it will be marked with the system status *Released*. This indicator can be changed only by a very few business transactions, of which the obvious one is to mark the order as *Technically completed*. This control logic ensures that a released production order has to remain "on the books" until it has been executed.

Unlike a system status that can be changed only by the system, a user status is never changed by the system.

A user status in an item is a status profile that has been defined in customizing for a particular purpose or usage. A production order can be provided with an unlimited number of predefined user status indicators.

A status can be displayed in a screen or on a document in either of two forms: a 30-character text, or a 4-character identification code. Both forms are available in any of the languages supported by SAP.

To inspect the statuses activated in a production order, select Order→Functions→Status.

The kind of business transaction that is used to alter the status of a production order is any of the following:

- Releasing an order
- Releasing an operation
- Posting a goods receipt
- Entering a completion confirmation
- Printing an order

A status indicator can be used to control what happens next. A specific status can be configured to perform the following types of action in relation to a certain type of business transaction:

- Allow the business transaction.
- Issue a warning before the business transaction is carried out.
- Forbid the business transaction.

For example, the system will issue a warning if you want to mark a released production order for deletion if it has not been accorded the status of technically completed. But you can still have the order deleted.

Some statuses allow particular types of business transaction, some forbid it. The rule is that a business transaction is allowed if at least one of the active status indicators allows it, and none of the active status indicators forbids it.

A status that has been set in the object is said to be active. A status is considered to be inactive if it has never been set, or if it has been active but has since been deactivated.

Developing a User Status Profile

Each order type is assigned a status profile in customizing. The status profile defines user status ID codes and can store a long text for each to explain their functions.

You can also signify which status is to be automatically set when an instance of the object type is created, or when a specified type of business transaction is successfully completed.

The status profile can be configured to forbid certain types of business transaction if a certain status indicator is active.

The statuses in a profile can be arranged in their expected sequence by assigning a status order number to each user status. If you do not assign a status order number to a user status, there are no constraints on when this status can be assigned, apart from the restriction that only one user status can be active at a time.

However, if a status order number has been allocated, the system will expect you to specify a lowest and a highest number to define the range from which the subsequent status must be selected. This constraint can be used to narrow the variety of permitted sequences of statuses through which an object may pass.

For example, you could define a user status called *Locked during planning*. You could leave this status without a status order number so that it can be assigned without restriction.

By contrast, you could define the same user statuses in a numbered sequence and constrain the possibilities by defining the range that could follow each status in the sequence. Table 9.2 illustrates the data in the status profile.

Table 9.2 User Statuses with Status Order Numbers

Status order no.	Status name	Lowest next	Highest next
-	Locked during planning	-	-
1	Preparation	1	2
2	Execution	1	3
3	Check	2	4
4	Completion	4	4

The data in a user status profile, as illustrated in Table 9.2, is interpreted as follows:

- Only one status can be active at a time.
- The unnumbered status *Locked during planning* can be assigned at any time, and will deactivate any currently active status.
- *Preparation* (1) can be followed only by *Execution* (2).

- *Execution* (2) can be followed by further *Preparation* (1) or by *Check* (3).
- *Check* (3) can be followed by *Execution* (2) or *Completion* (4).

Any status can be followed by itself to signify that the business transaction has not been completed that will justify a change of status.

A user status has to be defined in a status profile that has already been created. The following sequence is appropriate:

1. Create a status profile.
2. Assign the corresponding object types to the status profile, such as order, operation.
3. Define the required user statuses in the status profile.
4. Assign the user statuses to the corresponding business transactions.
5. If necessary, translate the names of the status profile and the user statuses to the log-on language of the intended users.
6. Assign the status profile in customizing to the order type in which it will be used.

Developing a Selection Profile

The purpose of a selection profile is to specify the attributes of objects that will determine whether they are collated for some purpose.

The production order information system will accept a selection profile as a search specification. You can also use a selection profile when you create a trigger point.

The selection profile is a logical combination of user statuses and system statuses that will identify a particular set of records. For example, you can specify production orders or operations that meet a combination of status indicator conditions.

During customizing you can build an order selection profile that includes user statuses, but you have to identify the user status profile that defines what these user statuses signify. You cannot subsequently assign a status profile once you have created and saved a selection profile.

Activating User Statuses

The following sequence will activate a user status at order header level:

1. Select Order→Functions→Status.
2. Select Edit→Activate status.
3. Mark the status required in the list of permitted statuses.
4. Press the function key Choose.

The following sequence will activate a user status at the operation level:

1. Select Goto→Operation overview.
2. Mark the operation.
3. Select Operation→Functions→Status.
4. Select Edit→Activate status.

5. Inspect the list of permitted user statuses.

6. Mark the required user status and press the function key Choose.

Recording Status Change Documents

You can define statuses for any of the following objects in the production order:

- Order header
- Operation
- Material component
- Production resource and tool

Furthermore, you can specify that status change documents should be created for any of these objects every time their status is changed by a permitted business transaction during the processing of an order. The contents of a status change document is as follows:

- Which status was changed
- Who changed the status
- When the status was changed
- Whether the status was activated or deactivated
- During which business transaction the status change occurred

Although you can activate status change documents at the order item level, it is probably better to save processing time by activating them only at the order header level.

The following sequence will specify per order type and plant, whether status change documents are to be written:

1. Select Production→Shop Floor Control.

2. Select Master→Order.

3. Select Define Order Type Dependent Parameters.

4. Select Maintain status change documents.

5. Inspect the overview of the order types and plants.

6. Mark the line with the corresponding order type and plant.

7. Press the function key Detail.

8. Select the objects for which you wish to create change documents.

9. Save your entries.

The status change documents will be written in the order header or operation as specified, but only for production orders that have been created since the change document specification was saved.

Status change documents can be inspected at the various levels. In each case the display begins with a list of the statuses that are active, from which you can make a selection to limit the number of change documents to be inspected.

- Select Order→Functions→Status, or, in the Operation Overview screen, mark the operation and select Operation→Functions→Status.
- Display statuses at the component level by marking a component on the component overview screen and selecting Component→Status.
- Display statuses at the PRT level by marking the operation to which the PRT is allocated on the Component Overview screen and selecting Goto→Object for operation→PRT for operation. Mark the PRT and select Prod.resources/tools→Status.

Whichever level you choose, the system will lists all the statuses that are currently active in the selected object.

The next filter to apply is based on whether you wish to see the change documents for one or for several statuses. If you are interested in a single status and the status is already shown in the list, mark it and select Environment→Change documents→For status. Otherwise, select Environment→Change documents→All.

If you ask for all change documents, the system will present the change documents for all the statuses that have ever been active in the object.

You can still filter the items displayed by double-clicking a single status of interest and selecting Goto→All changes.

Selecting Goto History will present all change documents in chronological order.

The following sequence will show you which statuses changed at a specific point in time:

1. Position the cursor on the left half of the corresponding list entry (Date, Time, Last changed by).
2. Press the function key Select. The system displays all the statuses that were active and all the statuses that were deactivated at that particular time.

Position the cursor on the right half of an entry in the list (System status/User status) to display all statuses and their short texts that were active at that point in time. The function key Business Transactions will list first the allowed transactions and then the prohibited.

The function key Transaction analysis reports why a particular transaction was prohibited or allowed at the time. The system lists all statuses which influenced the transaction. A business transaction is allowed if at least one status allows the transaction and no status prohibits it.

Documenting the Completion of Operations and Capacities

The purpose of a completion confirmation is to record the significant facts about the progress of a production order. The completion confirmation reports the processing status of the following components of a production order:

- Operations
- Suboperations
- Individual capacities

Completion data for an operation includes the following information:

- How much yield was produced in the operation
- How much scrap was produced in the operation
- How much activity was used to carry out the operation
- At which work center the operation was carried out
- Who carried out the operation

Various actions can be initiated by the posting of a completion confirmation; for example:

- A reduction in the committed capacity load on the work center
- An update of costs based on the confirmed data
- An update of the order data, such as the delivery times
- Update of the order statuses
- Withdrawal postings for backflushed components
- An automatic goods receipt for one operation per order, usually the last
- Rework to be triggered
- An update of the expected yield in the order that can be used in MRP

A completion confirmation can be entered for any of the following types of object:

- An order
- An operation
- A suboperation
- An individual capacity of an operation
- An individual capacity of a suboperation

All these objects are confirmed in the same way that an operation is confirmed.

Providing Confirmation Data

Completion confirmations include fixed parameters determined in customizing and variable parameters that depend on the object being confirmed and the values entered during confirmation.

For example, an operation is confirmed by entering some or all of the following data:

- Quantities—yield and scrap (not for suboperations)
- Activity data—durations of, for example, setup and machine time
- Estimates of the remaining activity still available for use—used to update the standard activity values assigned to the operation

- Times and dates—of setup, processing, teardown
- Personnel data—confirm the personnel number of the employee, or the number of employees needed to carry out the operation
- Work center where the operation was carried out
- Posting date—defaults to the current date
- Goods movements—planned and unplanned goods movements can be posted with the completion confirmation
- Reason for variance in a confirmation—why the confirmation data does not accord with the planned values, entered as a standard reason key
- Long text—to describe the completion confirmation

You can associate a completion confirmation reason key with a user status that is able to trigger a follow-up function such as a mail message to the MRP controller or a new production order.

Understanding the Fixed Parameters in Confirmations

The fixed parameters of a completion confirmation are established in customizing to control the following types of action:

- Whether a partial or a final confirmation should always be proposed by the system.
- Whether the type of confirmation proposed should be determined automatically by the underdelivery tolerance, set to partial confirmation if the confirmed quantity comprising yield plus rework plus scrap is less than the order quantity adjusted by the underdelivery tolerance percentage. Capacities are confirmed in terms of the planned quantities of capacity splits rather than underdelivery tolerances.
- Whether all open reservations should be cleared for final confirmations.
- Whether an error log is to be displayed if errors occur during the calculation of actual costs.
- Which time unit the system should propose in completion confirmations.
- Which confirmation detail screen the system should automatically branch to after the initial screen.
- How the system should react if the operation sequence is not followed when confirming operations—information message, error message with a data locking action.
- How the system should react if the confirmed quantity entered for an operation is larger than that reported by the confirmation of the previous operation in the sequence— information message, error message with a data locking action
- Whether the underdelivery and/or overdelivery tolerances of the order are to be checked during confirmation.
- Whether to display data that was obtained from a previous confirmation.
- Whether to display planned confirmation data during confirmation.

- Whether an error log is displayed for goods movements with errors for backflushing or automatic goods receipts.

- Whether you are allowed to correct goods movement errors in the material overview before posting the confirmation.

The settings of the fixed parameters can only be maintained in Customizing. They can be inspected during confirmation by selecting Parameters→Fixed parameters.

Entering the Variable Completion Confirmation Parameters

The confirmation function allows you to specify the following variable parameters for each completion confirmation:

- Whether a partial or final confirmation is to be carried out

- Whether the underdelivery tolerance should automatically determine whether a partial or final confirmation is posted

- Whether all open reservations should be cleared with final confirmations

- Which confirmation detail screen should be displayed after the initial screen

- Whether previously confirmed operations, or only open operations, are to be displayed during a confirmation

- Whether an error log is displayed for goods movements with errors for backflushing or automatic goods receipts

- Whether you are allowed to correct goods movement errors in the material overview before posting the confirmation

- Whether an error log is to be displayed if errors occur during the calculation of actual costs

- Whether to display only operations that are expected to be confirmed

The variable parameters are maintained in the confirmation function by selecting Parameters→Var. Parameters. Each new confirmation consults the customized fixed parameters for any information that has not been maintained in the variable parameters of the confirmation function.

Entering Completion Confirmations

When you are confirming an operation, there are two possibilities, as follows:

- Confirm quantities, durations, activities, or personnel data by entering a confirmation for a time confirmation ticket.

- Confirm specific times by entering a confirmation for a time event, such as *Start setup*, or *Finish processing*. The system will calculate the duration of the activity between the time events.

The system classifies time events into record type groups as follows:

- Setup time events are assigned to record type group 1.
- Processing time events are assigned to record type group 2.
- Teardown time events are assigned to record type group 3.

These records are used to calculate the duration of the setup, processing, and teardown activities. Each work center will have been assigned a standard value key that enables it to associate each activity duration with a value that is appropriate for calculating the actual costs of the operation being performed there.

For example, records of type group 2, processing time, can be associated into time pairs to provide a duration that can be processed as machine time and as labor time using values stored in the standard value key.

The only moment when you can confirm quantities is when you confirm processing time events. There may be some activities that cannot be assigned to a particular record time group. These activities are associated with the time event *Variable activity*. You can confirm a quantity for this variable activity and it will be related to an appropriate value in the standard value key parameters and so added to the costs of the operation.

Confirming an Order at the Header Level

A completion confirmation entered at the order level causes the system to confirm all operations in the production order that carry a control key which allows them to be confirmed or requires them to be confirmed.

The quantities confirmed in the component operations will be in proportion to the quantity entered in the confirmation at header level.

You can enter a confirmation with a reference to a previous confirmation, identified by its confirmation counter number. This allows the system to use the data of the previous confirmation to generate the current confirmation.

The collective entry function can be used to create confirmations for several operations from different orders at the same time. The following data can be confirmed in a collective:

- Yield
- Scrap
- Reason for variance
- Personnel number
- Work center

You can also specify for each operation whether the entry is a final confirmation. If the *Open reservations* indicator has been set in customizing for a particular operation, the system will automatically clear any open reservations for that operation.

The following sequence will allow you to enter completion confirmations at the operation level:

1. Select Logistics→Production→Production control.
2. Select Confirmation→Enter.

3. Select For operation→Time confirmation ticket or Time event.

4. Specify the operation you want to confirm—enter the completion confirmation number or the order number, sequence number, and operation number. If you only enter the order number, select the operation from the list of the operations contained in the order.

5. Specify which data you want to confirm (for example, dates).

Entering Data for a Completion Confirmation

There are three methods for entering completion data, as follows:

- Goto a detail screen of your own choosing.
- Press Enter and work on the screen sequence that has been specified in the screen control parameters.
- Select Goto→Actual data and enter the details referring to the quantity, activity, and personnel.

If you select Goto you will have the choice of the following detail screens:

- Quantity/activity
- Dates
- Personnel data
- Qty/Activity/Forecast

Entering Final or Partial Confirmation

If the data you are confirming do not represent the full planned quantity, select the *Partial confirmation* indicator. Otherwise, select *Final confirmation*.

You can leave the decision between partial and final to the system. Select *Automatic confirmation* to instruct the system to consult the underdelivery tolerance percentage in the order header and automatically mark the confirmation as partial if the yield is insufficient.

If you mark the indicator *Clear open reservations*, the system will clear any open reservations still assigned to the operation when a final confirmation is posted.

When you are entering completion confirmation data, you may need to use the function keys or the menu to access additional screens that contain entry fields for your confirmation data.

You can post goods movements in the same transaction as your confirmation. Press the function key Material overview if you need to check or change any goods movements that are to be posted with the confirmation.

Confirming Several Operations as a Collective Entry

The following sequence will allow you to build up a collective entry for posting completion confirmations:

1. Select Confirmation→Enter.
2. Select For operation→collective entry.
3. Enter the relevant confirmation numbers and the data you want to confirm so that each line represents one confirmation. The system will assign each line a separate confirmation counter.
4. Save your collective confirmation.

The system will use the confirmed quantity and the planned standard values to calculate the activity details of each line item in a collective confirmation.

Entering Confirmations at Order Level

The following sequence will allow you to confirm individual orders:

1. Select Logistics→Production.
2. Select Production control.
3. Select Confirmation→Enter→For order.
4. Enter the order number and press Enter.
5. Enter the data that you wish to confirm.
6. Save your confirmation.

The system will accept a degree of processing as an alternative to the value for the yield.

Confirming Individual Capacities

An operation can be divided between several persons or several machines. In these circumstances, the operation is divided into individual capacities or capacity splits. A split number is assigned to each individual capacity.

If you identify the capacity category and the split number, you can manually confirm the completion of work attributed to the individual capacity. Alternatively, you can enter a summary confirmation that is applied to all the individual capacities. At the same time, you can specify a degree of processing for all the individual capacities. Thus all the planned activities are confirmed in proportion to the degree of processing

One or more of the suboperations might have already been confirmed manually. If you set the *Final confirmation* indicator in a summary confirmation, the same status indicator will be set in all the individual suboperations and their capacity requirements will be deleted.

Updating Actual Values

During customizing, the indicator *NoActValue,* No actual values, can be set in selected capacity categories. If set, this indicator directs the system to reduce the capacity requirement of only the individual capacity when this capacity is confirmed.

If the *NoActValue* indicator is not set, the system reduces the requirements of the operation as well as the requirements of the individual capacity. If you are working with standard value capacity splits and are not aware of this "double reduction of capacity requirement," it is possible to confirm and hence reduce too much capacity. If backflushing is operating, there will be a goods issue of double the necessary quantity of components. In addition, automatic goods receipt could be functioning and so post too much material to stock when the capacity is confirmed.

If you have not set the indicator *NoActValue*, the actual values of the split capacities are copied to the operation. When you confirm splits for a capacity category, the confirmed values of the individual capacity are passed on to the operation. However, not all capacities necessarily pass on actual values representing the activities they perform. You have to ensure that these activities are also confirmed so that they may be accounted for.

The reason for this kind of arrangement is that costs can be calculated by applying standard values to a quantity that is proportional to the work performed. Thus, for example, you could apply a standard rate to the machine time or to the labor time of the person in charge of the machine. If you have two different rates for machine time and labor time, then both capacities need to be confirmed. If your rate is a composite value representing the costs of the machine and its operator, then you do not need to confirm the machine time separately from the labor time.

Entering a Completion Confirmation Using a Reference

You can confirm an operation by using a previous confirmation as a reference for your current confirmation, as follows:

1. Select Logistics- ›Production.
2. Select Production control.
3. Select Confirmation→Enter→With reference.
4. Enter the confirmation number and confirmation counter to identify which confirmation you want to use as a reference. Otherwise enter the operation number and the operation number, and select a confirmation to be the reference.
5. Press Enter.
6. Edit the data copied from the reference confirmation if necessary.
7. Save your confirmation.

Posting Goods Movements in Confirmations

There are two types of planned goods movements: backflushing and automatic goods receipts.

If a component has an active backflushing indicator, the system will automatically post a goods issue document for this component when you confirm the order or operation to which it is assigned.

If an operation has a control key that specifies automatic goods receipt, the system will automatically post the material produced by this operation to stock when the operation is confirmed. Only one operation per order should be marked in this way, normally the last in the operation sequence.

Coproducts cannot be designated for automatic goods receipt and neither can materials that require serial numbers.

By definition, an unplanned goods movement is a goods movement that has to be executed because something unexpected has happened, such as a shortfall in the stock of available-to-promise components that is not detected until backflushing is attempted. Thus you may need to post an unplanned goods movement at the time you are entering a completion confirmation. For example, you may have to reduce, in another production order, the reservation of the material in shortage because the order you are working on has had to draw on part of this reserved stock.

Planned and unplanned goods movements can be directed from the material overview. During customizing, the material overview screen can be designed to show all components per operation or only those that are to be backflushed and those that have been assigned for automatic goods receipt.

If you intend to take corrective action from the confirmation screen, you can arrange that the system will react to an error by displaying an error log before saving a confirmation. This allows you to branch to the material overview where you can post goods movement to correct the error before you save the completion confirmation.

The confirmation parameter *All components* is set if you want the material overview to list all components. Otherwise, the system will display only the components designated for backflushing or automatic goods receipt.

The following sequence will allow you to process goods movements with errors:

1. Select Environment→Goods movement.
2. Select FailedGoodsMovments.

There is an indicator that can be set in customizing to temporarily store planned goods movements such as backflushing and automatic goods receipt when you post the confirmation. These planned goods movements are later posted in the background if you have set up a background job in customizing by selecting Operations→Schedule background jobs. You can periodically start a background job using Program CORUAFW0.

Using Special Types of Completion Confirmation

Three special types of completion confirmation are possible, as follows:

- Milestone confirmation
- Summary confirmation
- Standard confirmation

The confirmation of one milestone operation causes other operations or suboperations to be automatically confirmed at the same time, in particular, all operations previous to the operation designated as a milestone by its control key.

Partial completion confirmation of a milestone operation causes a partial confirmation, using the same proportions, of the preceding operations.

If an order includes more than one milestone operation, the confirmation of the milestones must be carried out in the same sequence as their processing. Automatic completion confirmation is performed from a milestone back to the preceding milestone. Operations that have been previously confirmed manually are not altered by milestone confirmations.

You can enter a scrap quantity or percentage in a milestone confirmation, in which case the scrap quantity is automatically confirmed as part of the yield in the preceding operations.

Automatic confirmation does not extend to the suboperations of a milestone operation.

Confirming a milestone operation in a collective production order can be used to confirm the corresponding operations of other orders in the collective.

Creating Summary Confirmations

A summary confirmation allows you to confirm the completion of a specified degree of processing for all suboperations belonging to an operation. The degree of processing causes all planned activities to be confirmed proportionally. However, you cannot directly confirm quantities for suboperations.

The following sequence will allow you to carry out a summary confirmation:

1. Select Confirmation→Enter.
2. Select For operation→Time ticket.
3. Enter the order number, the sequence, and the number of the operation for which you want to enter a summary confirmation.
4. Select Goto→Summary confirmation.
5. Either enter a degree of processing, **or**
6. Select one of the suboperations confirm the individual suboperation manually.
7. Save the summary confirmation.

If you set the indicator *Final confirmation* in the summary confirmation, any suboperations already manually confirmed will be updated if necessary.

Entering Standard Confirmations

If the actual values completed by an operation are to be set to the values planned for it, you can apply a standard completion confirmation. You have to apply standard confirmation one operation at a time. You cannot enter a standard confirmation for an operation that already bears the status indicator *Finally confirmed*.

If you enter a standard confirmation for a milestone operation, the system will carry on to complete the appropriate milestone confirmation.

The following sequence will enter a standard confirmation:

1. Select Confirmation→Enter.

2. Select Time ticket or Time event.

3. Enter the order number for which you want to enter completion confirmations.

4. Select the operation you want to confirm.

5. Save the completion confirmation.

The system confirms the values planned for the operation as actual values.

Canceling Completion Confirmations

Any completion confirmation entered in the system can be canceled. If the act of confirming an operation has activated any statuses, these will not be deactivated if the confirmation is canceled. If there has been more than one completion confirmation for an operation, you have to indicate which of them are to be canceled.

The following sequence will cancel a confirmation

1. Select Confirmation→Cancel.

2. Enter the completion confirmation number, **or**

3. Enter the order number, the sequence number, and the operation number, **or**

   Enter the order number alone to be shown a list of the operations and their existing confirmations from which to make a selection.

4. Press Enter.

5. Check the data to be canceled on the detail screen.

6. Save the cancellation with, optionally, a long text explanation of the reason.

To reverse the cancellation of a confirmation you have to manually reenter the confirmation.

Collecting Plant Data from Third-Party Systems

Plant data collection (PDC) is a data transfer function that is classified as one of the cross-application (CA) functions. The purpose of PDC is the collection and display of plant data. Plant data processing includes checking, processing, editing, evaluating, and transferring messages that provide information on machine utilization, order situation, quality checks, and any other user-defined data.

A plant data collection system can be used to gather information about people, such as the date and time of work start and finish. Absence for a business trip or a training course can be recorded at a data collection terminal and conveyed to the human resources (HR) module for interpretation and evaluation, perhaps as part of a performance-related remuneration scheme.

The PDC can also be set up to collect data regarding the operation of plant, setup and teardown times, quantities produced, and scrap amounts. The statistics of machine utilization and malfunction can be derived from the same kind of interface source.

The PDC can be interfaced with mechanized systems for detecting and recording significant events, provided that the equipment matches the interface specification. A PDC data transfer function can be configured to transfer the information automatically to the R/3 installation.

Collecting completion confirmations is an important task of a manufacturing PDC. The following sequence will allow you to manually trigger the transfer of PDC data for completion confirmation from a non-SAP System into R/3:

1. Select Confirmation→PDC.
2. Select Data transfer.

If errors are found in confirmation data after the transfer from the non-SAP System has taken place, the incorrect confirmation is stored in the PDC error records held in the R/3 system. The following sequence will access these error records for rework:

1. Select Confirmation→PDC→Error records.
2. Select one of the data transfer records containing errors.
3. Inspect the list of all error records in the selected data transfer.
4. Mark an error record line item.
5. Press the function key Actual data.
6. Correct the detail screen and save it, thus deleting the incorrect confirmation record.
7. Delete any error records that are no longer required.

Settling the Costs of a Production Order

The procedure of settling costs entails collating the actual costs for a production order and assigning them to one or more receiver cost-objects. For example, the costs of a sales order are settled on the sales order as the cost-object.

The costs of a production order can be settled on an account established for the material produced. If a material stock account is debited, a balancing credit has to be settled on the production order each time a quantity of the material is delivered to stock.

You can create a production order in response to a sales order. In this case, the costs for the production order are settled to another receiver, namely, the specific sales order. The production order is credited automatically at the time of settlement, and the receiver cost-objects are debited accordingly.

The debit posting remains on the sales order and can be displayed even after the costs have been settled. The settled costs are updated in the corresponding receiver cost-object and can be displayed in reporting.

Maintaining Settlement Parameters

The settlement procedure is controlled by the parameters established in customizing for each particular type of order. The settlement parameters include the following:

■ Settlement profile

■ Settlement structure

■ Settlement rule

The standard settlement settings instruct the system to assign the costs of a production order to the stock account of the material produced. The settlement share is 100%, and the settlement type is *Full settlement*. In this case the settlement rule includes a distribution rule, which is to assign all of the costs to the receiver, namely, the stock account of the material produced. If you want to set aside the standard distribution rule, you have to set the percentage rate of the settlement share to zero.

You can create a distribution rule manually. Unlike a standard settlement rule, you can change or delete any distribution rule you have created manually, provided it has not yet been used to actually settle an order.

The following sequence will display the settlement rule of a production order:

1. Call up the production order.

2. Select Header→Settlement rule.

3. Inspect the settlement rule and its distribution rules.

The following sequence will allow you to change a distribution rule:

1. Call up the settlement rule of the order.

2. Select the distribution rule using a double-click.

3. Edit the data in the Distribution Rule Detail screen.

The following sequence will allow you to delete a manually created distribution rule:

1. Call up the settlement rule of the order.

2. Position the cursor on the required line item.

3. Select Edit→Delete rule.

Creating Distribution Rules

The maximum number of distribution rules allowed per order type is defined in the settlement profile. The following sequence will create a distribution rule:

1. Select Edit→Delete rule.

2. Call up the settlement rule of the order.

3. Select the required cost receiver using the menu option Receivers.

4. Inspect the corresponding detail screen.

5. Maintain the new distribution rule.

The following sequence will allow you to check that you have not attempted to assign a total of more than 100% in your distribution rules:

1. Select Settlement rule.
2. Select Percent validation.

A warning message is issued if the total percentage rate of the settlement rule is more than 100%.

Delivering to Stock

A production order can be settled to a material account. In this case there should be one or more deliveries to stock. Each delivery to stock will credit the order and debit the stock account of the material when the goods receipt is posted.

When a goods receipt is posted, the system consults the production order customizing parameters to find out how to arrive at a value for the amount of material delivered. This value is then credited to the production order when the goods receipt is posted.

Each valuation area is provided with a valuation variant that specifies which price is to be transferred from the material master record when a production order is credited.

In the material master is a price control indicator, which specifies how stocks of a material are to be valuated. If the price control indicator is **S**, the quantity delivered is to be multiplied by the standard price for this material. If there is a difference between the value of this debit posting and the value of the credit posting to the production order, the difference is posted to a price difference account.

If the price control indicator in the material master of the material produced is **V**, the quantity delivered is multiplied by the price specified in the valuation variant. This amount represents the cost and hence value of the stock produced. It becomes a debit in the stock account for the material produced. The moving average price of this material therefore changes accordingly.

When a production order is settled to a material account, the production order cannot be settled until after the final delivery has taken place for this order.

You do not necessarily want to settle the costs of a production order on the stock account of the material produced. If the costs for a production order are to be settled to another receiver, you must set the goods receipt indicator, GR, to blank on the header screen for goods movement and valuation.

Settling the Actual Costs Incurred in a Production Order

To settle the actual costs incurred in the order:

1. In the production order menu, Select Environment→Settle.
2. Enter the number of the production order that you wish to settle.
3. Enter at least the fiscal year and the accounting period.
4. Enter the settlement type or accept the settlement type specified in the distribution rules of the order.

5. Enter the posting date so that Financial Accounting and Cost Accounting can assign the settlement to a fiscal year (default is to the last day of the current accounting period).

6. Enter the value date—used as the key date for determining the exchange rate between different currencies (default is to the posting date).

7. Enter the reference date for Asset Management—must be in the posting year, but can be different from the posting date if the reference date is to be in a posting period already closed for Financial Accounting.

8. Set the necessary indicators.

9. Select Settlement→Execute.

Controlling the Settlement

The following settlement indicators are available:

■ Process with update—do not set this indicator if you require only a simulation run of the settlement without an update of the database. It is used to check and, if necessary, correct the objects to be settled.

■ Process with list display—set if you require a detailed log of the settlement run or the settlement simulation.

There are no limits to the number of times a production order is settled.

A production order is often settled to a stock account for the material produced. In this situation, the amount settled is the difference between the actual costs incurred for the order and the costs credited to the order when the goods produced were delivered to stock. When the stock account for the material is debited with the settlement amount, the order is credited with the same settled costs. This credit posting to the production order brings the order balance to zero.

The receiver cost object for the offsetting entry is determined as follows in accord with the calculation used for the actual costs incurred for the order:

■ If the price control indicator in the material master record is **S**, a price difference account is debited.

■ If the price control indicator in the material master record is **V**, the total stock value and the moving average price change accordingly.

Thus an order will be credited with the costs of the materials when a goods issue is posted. A further offsetting entry can be credited to the order when the material produced is delivered to stock. Just how this offsetting entry is arrived at is determined by the price control indicator. For example, you could calculate the costs of the material from a standard price, or you could use a moving average price that depends on how much material is in the warehouse after the production order has made a delivery, and what costs were incurred to produce this total stock.

Suppose an order for 10 pieces incurred $110 of actual costs. Perhaps the order was credited with $100 when the material it produced was delivered to stock on the basis of a standard price of $10 per piece. When this order is settled, it has to be credited with additional costs of $10 as an offsetting entry so that the production order balance will be zero at the end of settlement.

In this example, the actual costs of the goods produced by this order are higher by $1 per piece than the amount credited to the order when it delivered to stock. Therefore the average cost of the material in stock ought to be increased in proportion.

In practice, your company may maintain a different pricing policy for different materials. The price control indicator **S** in a material master record specifies that the standard price is to be used. Price control indicator **V** specifies that the price of that material will be allowed to vary as a moving average.

Managing Settlement with Stock Undercoverage

When a production order is settled, the warehouse stock may not be sufficient to cover the order quantity. Some of the goods may have been already issued from stock.

If the price control indicator of the material is **V**, the quantity still in stock is used to calculate the corresponding proportion of the variable costs for the order. The remaining costs are automatically posted to a price difference account. This procedure allows for changes in the moving average price, so that they do not have a disproportionate effect on the costs of an order occasioned by unrelated stock issues occurring before the order is settled.

Settling Scrap

If a production process causes some product to be scrapped, the average price of the material is increased because there is a difference between the order quantity and the yield quantity. The standard settlement rule distributes all the costs of a production order to the quantity of material actually produced.

You can manually adjust the existing distribution rule so that only a percentage of the actual costs are settled on the yield. The remaining percentage of actual costs could be settled by a new distribution rule to a cost center designated as the settlement receiver for scrap.

Printing Production Order Information

Production order information is printed as shop floor papers that appear in list format of the following kinds:

- Operation-related lists—time tickets, completion confirmation slips
- Component-related lists—material provision lists, withdrawal slips
- PRT-related lists—PRT overview
- General lists—object overview, operation control ticket

Most lists generated and printed by the system refer to all the operations, suboperations, components, and production resources/tools contained in an order. Suboperations are treated the same as operations for printing purposes. The name of an individual list can be changed. The list names and SAPScript forms are available in each of the supported languages.

During customizing each order type, plant, and MRP controller can be assigned individual values of the printing parameters. These parameters control the following factors according to the user:

- Which lists a particular user is allowed to print
- Which lists may be printed from each transaction
- Which data a list is to contain
- The list layout, and, for example, inclusion of barcodes
- Spool parameters for printing and the number of days held in the spool before deletion

Identifying Printing Types

The system maintains the distinction between the follow printing types:

- Original printout—first printout of orders
- Reprint—reprint of orders that have already been completely printed, limited to display mode only
- Partial print—printout of partially released orders

The system can prints lists for operations that are released but not yet printed.

The following sequence will print from a production order

1. Select the production order.
2. Select Order→Print.

In creation mode and change mode, printing is carried out after saving the order. In display mode, printing is carried out immediately.

The following sequence will print lists for one or more production orders from the initial menu:

1. Select Order→Print.
2. Enter criteria for the selection of production orders.
3. If necessary, change the predefined print type—original printout, reprint or partial print.
4. Enter plant and, if required, MRP controller, production scheduler, and order type.
5. Enter an order number or an order number interval, or, select production orders for a particular material.
6. Press the function key Selections to enter criteria to limit the production orders selected for printing.
7. Press the function key Proceed.

Printing can be limited to production orders selected by the following criteria:

- Release date, scheduled start, scheduled finish
- System status, such as *Partially confirmed*
- User status

Select Order→Print settings.

Archiving Production Order Records

Archiving is the final step in the process of reorganizing production orders:

1. Activate the deletion flag in the order, manually or by running a background report.
2. Activate the deletion indicator in the order. Run a background report after the Retention period 1 has elapsed since the deletion flag was activated.
3. Carry out an archiving run by running a background report after Retention period 2 has elapsed.

The following sequence will call up archiving management:

1. Select the production control menu.
2. Select Tools→Archiving→Order.

Archived orders can be displayed by selecting the retrieval function. ●

Part

III

Ch

9

Implementing PP in Repetitive Manufacturing

Managing Long Period Repetitive Manufacturing

The repetitive manufacturing (PP-REM) module is designed to manage planning and control for repetitive manufacturing environments that are characterized by the following features:

- Master plans are created and processed. They specify periods and quantities of the materials to be produced. These master plans are typically released automatically for production.
- Quantities in the master plans are processed by easy-to-use backflushing functions.
- Constituent materials are dispatched to production lines.
- Planning includes both capacities and quantities.
- Information is maintained on the range of coverages expressed as the number of days for which an adequate supply of material is available for a particular production activity.
- Materials are typically procured for more than one order at a time.
- Material allocations are not usually firmed, so activities may use whatever is necessary.
- Planning and control of the manufacturing is normally period based.

PP-REM is supported by the following functional components:

- Creation of run schedule header in PP-REM-ORD
- Planning for repetitive manufacturing in PP-REM-PLN
- Planning run schedule quantities in PP-REM-PLN
- Planning planned orders in PP-REM-PLN
- Creation of master data in PP-REM-ADE
- Evaluation in PP-REM-ALY

Most repetitive environments will require all of these functions to be installed and configured, especially if production is delivered to both stock and specific orders.

Understanding the Run Schedule Header

The run schedule header function creates a run schedule (RS) header document, which is essential if a material is to be planned for repetitive manufacturing. This header is also required for settling the accounts for the finished and semifinished products as they are produced over a long period.

The RS header does not contain production quantities or any dates. The system accepts the RS quantities assigned to the RS header and creates the necessary plans with quantities and dates.

The RS header does not have to be assigned an individual production cost collector. Costs can be settled in the following ways:

- Via a production cost collector per RS header
- Via a production cost collector that is created for several RS headers
- Via production orders

Planning for Repetitive Manufacturing

The planning for repetitive manufacturing functional component works with the master plan. The PLN component displays the master plan as a periodic planning table showing all run schedule headers, materials, product groups, production lines, and groups of production lines.

The PLN planning table shows all the important information, in particular, the capacities and available quantities of necessary materials. You can access this planning table interactively and use it to control the production lines.

Planning with Run Schedule Quantities

The planning with run schedule quantities component allows you to specify the production quantities for a run schedule header that are to be produced in a certain period. When the production takes place, the actual data and cost settlement data are collected by the production cost collector.

Your company will probably conduct planning with run schedule quantities if the same routings and same work centers are deployed as production lines that continue repetitive manufacturing over a relatively long period.

Planning with Partial Orders

The planning partial orders component is designed to support planning partial orders in a run schedule header. Part of the RS header planned quantity is converted into a production order to be delivered on certain dates.

Planning a production order with partial orders is often used when producing complex, multi-level products, each with a separate routing, which are to be settled separately. Another reason to use partial orders is if each production lot is to be settled using a separate production order.

Backflushing

Goods can be released from storage and held in a dispatching point or manufacturing location until they are actually dispatched or used. Accounting normally requires that the value of these goods be posted as a goods issue when they leave the primary storage location. In repetitive manufacturing, however, it will often be more convenient to delay this accounting until the items are no longer available for use in another order, that is, when the original order is confirmed.

The components that have been authorized to be accounted in this way are referred to as backflushed components. Accounting takes place through goods issue posting of backflushed components, which is carried out during confirmation. Arrangements have to be made to keep account of the goods held in temporary storage until the backflushing procedure occurs.

The functional component responsible for controlling backflushing in repetitive manufacturing is Creation of Master Data (PP-REM-ADE). The following backflushing options are provided to post the accounts to the production cost collector:

■ Post goods receipts with automatic reduction of the open master plan.

■ Post goods issues.

■ Post actual costs to the production cost collector.

■ Update the statistics without any financial transaction.

If a production cost collector is not to be used, the following options are available to initiate backflushing in repetitive manufacturing:

■ Post goods receipts.

■ Post goods issues.

■ Post confirmations.

Evaluating Repetitive Manufacturing Progress

The purpose of the evaluations component is to provide the following progress reports:

■ Pull list

■ Reporting point overview of goods in process

■ Component reprocessing list

■ Document log

■ Controlling reports

The following statistics and analyses can be accessed from the logistics information system (LIS):

■ Goods receipt statistics

■ Reporting point statistics

■ Material consumption analysis

■ Production costs analysis

Using the Repetitive Manufacturing Component for Production Planning and Control

The purpose of using a sophisticated business data processing system in repetitive manufacturing is to reduce the amount of hands-on data entry and checking activities. The tasks that can be most demanding are:

■ Creating and revising production quantities on a period and quantity basis

■ Maximizing the benefits of backflushing without restricting its functionality

Characterizing the Repetitive Manufacturing Situation

A repetitive manufacturing plant typically produces a product material that remains essentially the same for a long time. It is not normally manufactured in lots that are individually defined, although the total quantity produced per accounting period may be manufactured at different rates over some of the part periods.

By contrast, a make-to-order job-shop environment typically involves a different variety of machines and work centers for each order. The sequence of work is controlled by a task list, such as a routing, and there may be queuing and interim storage of semifinished products during the sequence.

Repetitive manufacturing will normally require a relatively constant flow through several production lines, each responsible for producing an assembly, which later become a component in the finished product. The routing task lists of these component assemblies tend to be relatively simple and may be constant over long periods and perhaps across several variants of the finished product.

In make-to-order production, the organization, documentation, and staging of the materials are all centered on the individual production lot. Completion confirmations are used to monitor and control the progress of the job through the plant.

In repetitive manufacturing, components are typically staged at the production lines anonymously; that is, they are not individually designated for a specific order. Completion confirmations tend to be simple reports of the actual data at the various stages.

Accounting in repetitive manufacturing begins by allocating material consumption or usage to a product line on the basis of planned values rather than actual quantities used.

The storage of intermediate products is unusual in repetitive manufacturing; components pass directly to the next process.

Controlling Repetitive Manufacturing by Demand Management

Demand management is essentially an integration of the following business functions:

- Sales and distribution—processing sales orders from stock
- Requirements administration—forecasting the requirements needed

The overall requirements are generated by existing sales orders, by anticipated sales orders, and by any requirements planned independently of sales, such as production orders that have been authorized in order to take advantage of a favorable purchase price of an important component material.

The materials produced as a result of the requirements administration are then held in stock until they are consumed by actual sales orders.

The demand program produces an input to master planning that represents the overall requirements situation. The repetitive manufacturing components can accept information from the demand program and use it to maintain a master plan to control the production processes.

The repetitive manufacturing (PP-REM) functions can be used selectively. For example, you can have some assemblies managed as repetitive processes yielding anonymous assemblies that are held in stock until they are needed for specific make-to-order products.

Understanding Time Buckets

Planning and control in repetitive manufacturing are based on a framework of time buckets. For each accounting period, a specific quantity of product is planned, taking note of the overall requirements situation and the anticipated dates when these requirements are going to be needed.

The scheduling data for products and product groups is thus broken down into a series of time buckets that can be used to display the requirements for each period for checking and revision. In order to allow scheduling of production quantities to the minute, a graphic planning table is available that can be customized to suit company requirements.

Production completion confirmations normally include backflushing of components and the posting of production costs. These confirmations usually refer to the material being produced rather than to any particular production or sales order.

The production requirements organized into time buckets can be scheduled as planned orders or production orders. There are various ways of managing the production runs so the quantities produced reach an optimum between the efficiency of the plant and the costs of holding material in store or delaying delivery to customers.

Costing for repetitive manufacturing can be arranged using cost collectors for the materials produced, with variants of this procedure assigned to order types as necessary. Alternatively, you can manage repetitive manufacturing using standard production order procedures.

Building a Profile for Repetitive Manufacturing

If a material is to be managed using the repetitive manufacturing functions, it has to be associated with a repetitive manufacturing profile defined in customizing and identified in the material master record. You must also authorize the material for repetitive manufacturing in the master record.

The material master record must also identify production versions that are suitable for this material. Planning can be simplified by creating planning ID records. These IDs have to be entered in the material master record before you attempt to use them for planning the material.

Cost collection is directed after consulting the run schedule header and the order type. If you want the costs to be collected at a particular cost collector, you have to create suitable run schedule headers that identify the intended cost collector.

A repetitive manufacturing profile has various control functions, including the specification of a run schedule header. The system uses the order type defined in the run schedule header to determine whether repetitive manufacturing is used with a cost collector, or whether the costs incurred during production are assigned to a production order for settlement. For example:

- Order type SA—run schedule headers are created without cost collectors. All the costs incurred during production are allocated to production orders, which are used for settlement.

- Order type PKSA—run schedule headers are created with cost collectors. The system automatically creates suitable cost collectors when creating the run schedule header.

- Order type PKMN—run schedule headers require cost collectors but the cost collectors must be created manually by the user in the CO system.

A repetitive manufacturing profile includes control parameters that define a backflushing policy—how goods receipt postings, backflushing, and activity postings are carried out for the material to which the profile is assigned. The profile will also indicate which variant of repetitive manufacturing planning is to be used with this material.

Discriminating Production Versions

A specific material may have several bills of material that determine the components used in its production. Each of these BOMs may be amenable to more than one routing for the same product. The details of the various acceptable combinations of BOM and routing are stored in different production version records. Thus a production version specifies both the component materials and the manufacturing techniques to produce a product.

A production version may include the following kinds of data:

- Alternative BOM and BOM usage for BOM explosion
- Task list type, group, and group counter for allocation to task lists or routings
- Lot-size restrictions and area of validity
- Production line and delivery to storage location

A material can have one or more numbered production versions, but these are normally all associated with a single plant location. The usage of different production versions for the same material includes the following:

- Production using different production lines
- Production using different processes or procedures, hence different routings
- Reprocessing of qualitatively substandard products
- Assignment of individual production quantities, so that different production lines can be balanced by the allocation of production versions

Individual production quantities can be assigned by the user on an interactive basis or automatically within the framework of the planning run.

Creating Production Versions

A material must be assigned for in-house production if it is to have production versions. The material must be allocated for repetitive manufacturing and a repetitive manufacturing profile must be identified.

You can create production versions in the MRP and work scheduling sections of the material master record when creating or changing a material master record. The following sequence will allow you create a production version:

1. From the MRP or Work Scheduling data screen, select Production versions.

2. Enter a version number and a text that describes the production version.

3. Enter dates in the Valid from and Valid to fields.

4. Select the field RS to allow the creation of a run schedule header for this production version if you want to use the planning table.

5. Select Details to enter additional data.

6. Select Material→Save.

Additional data for this production version could include the following, for example:

- Alternative BOM and BOM usage
- Receiving storage location for backflushing
- Task list type, task list group, and group counter

If you create a new material master record by referencing an existing one, the system copies the reference material's production version data from the relevant plant. You can edit this data before saving it as a new master record.

The following sequence will allow you to filter from the available production versions a short list from which to choose:

1. From the repetitive manufacturing menu, select RS Header→Display or Change.

2. Select Version overview.

3. Enter the criteria you wish to use to limit the selection.

4. Execute.

Planning with Repetitive Manufacturing Planning IDs

Planning in repetitive manufacturing can be carried out using either planning IDs or production lines. A planning ID is used to group different materials according to location or time period. For example, you can assign a planning ID to all the materials that will be manufactured by a particular production line. You could group materials by time period by assigning a planning ID to a certain shift. You can combine location and time characteristics to form a composite that is identified by a planning ID. Thus the products from a particular production line on a specific shift could be assigned a planning ID. Planning IDs can be logically combined with other characteristics, such as the production line, for the purpose of classification during planning.

The following sequence will create a planning ID:

1. From the repetitive manufacturing menu, select Master data→Planning IDs.

2. Select New entries.

3. Enter the plant.

4. Enter the key code for the planning ID.

5. Enter a descriptive text for the planning ID.

6. Identify the unit of quantity measure to be used for this planning ID in the planning table.

7. Identify a planning calendar—default is to use days, weeks, months, years.

8. Save the data.

A production version can be assigned a maximum of two planning IDs in the material master when the production version is created.

Planning Repetitive Manufacturing with Production Lines

A production line can be used to group materials together on the basis of a specified location. Unlike planning with a planning ID, you can perform quantity planning based on the production line with capacity planning. You have the option of selecting records by a combination of production line and planning ID for repetitive manufacturing planning.

If you intend to assign a production line to a material, you must first use the following sequence to create a work center that corresponds to your production line:

1. Select Logistics→Production.

2. Select Master data→Work centers.

3. Select Production line as the work center type if you want the system to copy the standard values already set for Requirements, Set up, and Tear down.

If you select another work center type, you must assign it a standard value key that allows the standard values for Requirements, Set up, and Tear down. If other capacity categories are needed, you must maintain the values and formulas for calculating their capacity requirements.

Creating Rate Routings

A production line will need capacity planning. To achieve this, a routing, such as a rate routing, must have been created for the material to be produced. See chapter 8, "Planning and Controlling Shop Floor Production Orders," for the method of creating a rate routing. This rate routing for the production line has to be assigned a control key that allows capacity planning. You have to maintain standard values for the operation, such as machine time and labor time. When you create a production version for a material in the material master record, you identify the intended production line. You must also enter the routing to be used for each of the following levels at which capacity planning can take place:

■ Detailed planning—for the individual work centers on the production line

■ Rate-based planning—an aggregate for the whole production line

■ Rough-cut planning—key resource requirements identified from the master production schedule

Repetitive manufacturing is usually controlled from the planning table. This tool can display the values for detailed planning or the values of rate-based planning. Detailed planning must be specified if you intend to use reporting point backflush so that confirmation can trigger goods issue. If the system fails to find a different routing for detailed planning, it will apply the routing specified in the rate-based planning line.

Although repetitive manufacturing normally uses only one production line per material, you can have several production lines in parallel. In this circumstance you have to select just one of these lines for capacity planning. And it is prudent to choose the one most likely to suffer a bottleneck.

Understanding Run Schedule Headers

A run schedule header is a control document that is created for a specific production version in repetitive manufacturing. The validity period of the run schedule header can extend over a long period, perhaps the life cycle of the product.

No production quantities or dates are mentioned in the run schedule header. These are generated by planning as run schedule quantities for the run schedule header, but they are actually saved as planned orders. However, the planned orders resulting from a run schedule header do not have to be subsequently released and converted to production orders.

A run schedule header is uniquely identified by a run schedule header number. It always refers to just one production version of a material and has a defined period of validity.

If you need a production cost collector, you must choose a run schedule header that has been assigned a cost collector. There can be only one cost collector for each run schedule header for a given material. When the run schedule header is used to control a specific production run, the production costs are attributed to the run schedule header in use and therefore are settled on the cost collector identified in this header.

The same cost collector is used for all run schedule headers of a particular material and for all production versions. Releases of R/3 after 3.1 allow several materials to be grouped in a production line and therefore to have their costs aggregated at a common cost collector.

The repetitive manufacturing profile specifies whether the cost collector for a particular type of order is to be created automatically when the run schedule header is created or created manually by the user.

Using Reporting Points as Milestones

A run schedule header can be used to identify certain operations as reporting points. These operations will then act as milestones in the routing and they will limit the extent of backflushing in the same way. The backflushed quantity is saved as the work-in-progress quantity per reporting point. These quantities are reduced when the final backflush is released. The reporting point backflush is controlled by the repetitive manufacturing profile.

Creating a Run Schedule Header

A run schedule header is an instrument for grouping together the quantities of a material produced over a certain period to form a production run. The following sequence will create a run schedule header:

1. Select Logistics→Production→Repetitive mfg.
2. Select RS header→Create.
3. Enter the number of the plant in which the run schedule header is to be created.
4. Enter the run schedule header number or leave blank if you allow the system to assign RS header numbers.
5. Enter the number of the material.
6. Enter the material production version for which the run schedule header is to be created.
7. Press Enter.

The data screen for run schedule headers is divided into the following sections:

- Material data—copied from the material master record.
- Run schedule data—overwrite the start and end dates of the run schedule header validity period.
- Planning data—copied from the material master record. Enter the time buckets into which the run schedule is to be subdivided: buckets of days, weeks, months, or freely definable periods or planning calendar periods.

The RS description defaults to the description of the production version. Check that the *RSheader blcked* indicator has not been set if you want the RS header to be released as soon as you create it.

When you save the run schedule header data, the system will create the run schedule header and release it. If your chosen repetitive manufacturing profile has specified an order type that automatically creates a cost collector, the system issues a message confirming that a cost collector has been created in the controlling module.

If your order type does not automatically generate a cost collector, you must create one manually.

You can change data in the production version of the material after you have created the run schedule header, but you have to copy this data into the run schedule header via the menu option Copy version data.

Displaying a Run Schedule Header

The following sequence will display a run schedule header from the repetitive manufacturing menu:

1. Select RS header→Display.
2. Enter the plant and run schedule header number, **or**
3. Specify the material, the production version, and a date within the validity period of the run schedule header, **or**
4. Enter the number of the material only to list all run schedule headers for all versions of the material. Mark one.
5. Press ENTER to access the detail screen of the RS header.

Part
III

Ch
10

Managing RS Headers Collectively

You can branch between the create and change functions and then save the results collectively.

When you are creating run schedule headers, the system will locate all materials that have production versions and then show you those that do not have run schedule headers that are valid in the period you are working with. You can then choose from this selected list and save to generate valid run schedule headers.

However, when you are changing run schedule headers the system filters records according to the following logic:

- Select all materials that have run schedule headers that lie within the period specified but that do not cover the complete period. (You are allowed to activate a selection indicator to extend their validity before saving them.)
- Select all materials that have run schedule headers that cover the complete period. (You cannot change these.)

The following sequence will create or change run schedule headers collectively from the main menu of repetitive manufacturing:

1. Select RS header→Crte/chge collectv.
2. Specify a plant.
3. Enter the dates to define the period in which you want to create run schedule headers.
4. Enter an MRP controller and a product group, if necessary.
5. Select either Create or Crte/chnge to generate a list of run schedule headers.
6. Mark the materials for which you want to create run schedule headers or whose run schedule headers you want to change.
7. Branch as required by selecting Displ/chge and then Change.
8. Select Save to save the changes you made in both functions. The numbers of run schedule headers changed and created are reported.

The following sequence will allow you to view run schedule header overviews from the repetitive manufacturing menu:

1. Select RS header→Overview.
2. Enter the criteria by which you wish to limit selection.
3. Select Execute.

Using the Run Schedule Header Functions

If you select Goto→BOM/Task list from the run schedule header screen, the following data will be displayed:

- The alternative BOM and BOM usage assigned for BOM explosion in repetitive manufacturing.

■ The task list type, group, and group counter the system uses for detailed, rate-based, and rough-cut planning.

If you select Goto→Cost data from the run schedule header data screen, and if a cost collector is automatically created for a run schedule header, you can display the costing data recorded at the cost collector.

The order type and the number of the cost collector is displayed and you can change the costing data, if necessary. Select Goto→CostCollec: details to display the master record of the cost collector.

If you select Goto→Settlement rule, you will be able to check the receiver cost object that is used for settling the order costs.

Creating a Cost Estimate for Each Production Version

The backflushing procedure is conducted according to the repetitive manufacturing profile. In particular, the profile determines whether the standard cost estimate for the material will be used, or whether activities will be backflushed according to the cost estimate for the individual production version. You will be invited to create a cost estimate for the production version when the run schedule header is created.

If you are changing a run schedule header, you can initiate the creation of a cost estimate by selecting Edit→Cost estimate.

Displaying Run Schedule Headers

Production versions and run schedule headers can be displayed in a time graph by the following sequence:

1. From the Run Schedule Header screen, select Goto→Graph—RS version.
2. Enter a selection specification if necessary.
3. Press Select.

You can display reporting points if they exist for the run schedule header by selecting Goto→Reporting points from the change mode of the Order Data screen. You will be able to inspect work in progress (WIP) in the form of the quantity that has passed through each reporting point and has been backflushed but that is not yet finished. These quantities are reduced at the final backflush.

Planning the Run Schedule Quantities in Repetitive Manufacturing

The run schedule quantities are the results of planning in repetitive manufacturing. You can create these quantities manually, or you can have them created automatically in the course of a planning run. Furthermore, you can opt for production versions of the material to be assigned automatically in the planning run.

Part III

Ch 10

You might want to aggregate run schedule quantities in various ways:

- Use the RS header for a single product—process the planned production quantities of one production version for a material, but inspect others for information purposes.
- Access the run schedule quantities screen for a particular material—process all production versions for the material from an overview of the entire planned production.
- Nominate a planning ID, a production line, a group of production lines, a production group—process the planned production quantities of the selected materials.

Interpreting the Planning Table of Run Schedule Quantities

The planning table is able to generate a variety of views of the run schedule quantities, and you can scroll horizontally and vertically on the time axis within the selected period. The data elements of a planning table are time buckets. Each bucket refers to a unit of production time and contains a value representing the quantity of material planned for production in that time. Buckets normally appear as columns in the planning table, and their number on display can be controlled by the mouse. The time bucket duration can be readily changed.

If you mark any field value, the system will display further information about it and you can update the data. In particular, you can change the quantity in a time bucket and assign it to a different production version, which may control another production facility.

When you change quantities and assign them to production versions, the system automatically adjusts the orders or the run schedule quantities behind the individual quantities accordingly in the background.

Displaying the Schedule

The system assigns each run schedule quantity to a specific period in the planning table. Customizing determines whether the schedules are based on the order finish date or the production finish date. If capacity planning is active, the time of day will be considered with the production finish date.

A planning table can include planned orders in which no production dates exist. These undated planned orders could have been generated manually without capacity planning or automatically by an MRP run without capacity planning. You can activate capacity planning using the backward scheduling technique from the planning table. The system uses the factory calendar appropriate to the capacity category relevant to the production line and can take account of available capacity defined for shifts.

Accessing Run Schedule Quantities Using an RS Header

The following sequence will obtain an overview of the planned production quantities of the selected run from the repetitive manufacturing screen:

1. Select RS Quantities→Create + change, **or**
2. Select RS quantities→Display.
3. Enter a plant number.

4. Select RS header→Choose.

5. Enter a run schedule header number or choose one by a matchcode, **or**

6. Enter a material number, production version, and key date.

7. Press Continue and inspect the planning table.

8. Process the run schedule quantities and then save the data.

Interpreting the Planning Table

The time bucket used to display the planning table will default to the smallest needed for whatever RS headers are being displayed.

Layout of the planning table contains the following line items:

- Period—the selected time bucket with the individual periods. Double-click on a period to display all the planned independent requirements and the customer requirements of this period.

- Total demand—the demand of the chosen material in the corresponding period.

- Total supply—the sum of the receipts per chosen material. The total comprises the run schedule quantities that are assigned to the run schedule header, not assigned, and assigned to other run schedule headers.

- Quantity available—of the chosen material in the corresponding period.

- Firmed planned qty—the firmed run schedule quantities that are assigned to the run schedule header.

- Planned quantity—the planned run schedule quantities for the run schedule header that can still be firmed.

- RS header total—of firmed and planned run schedule quantities.

- To be assigned—the quantity that has not yet been assigned to a production version and therefore has not yet been assigned to a run schedule header.

- Other RS + ProdOrds—the quantities of the same material that are assigned to other run schedules or are production orders for the material.

Accessing Run Schedule Quantities Using a Material

From the repetitive manufacturing menu, the following sequence will obtain an overview of the total planned production volume for a certain material or product:

1. Select RS quantity→Create + change or Display.

2. Enter a plant number.

3. Select Material.

4. Press Choose to enter the material number or choose one using a matchcode.

5. The system will add a customized number of days to current date to propose an end of the period to be searched. To change the period of examination, overwrite the Start and End fields in the Period of examination section of the screen.

6. Press Continue.

7. Process the planning table.

8. Save the data.

Interpreting the Planning Table

The following sequence will branch into the graphic planning table from the planning table:

1. Select Capacity planning.

2. Select Graphic plnng table.

When the system displays the planning table, the screen is split into two halves: Overview data of RS quantities and Detailed information for RS quantities.

The overview data of RS quantities includes the following data elements:

- Total demand
- Total supply
- Available quantity of the selected material

If you double-click on one of the periods on the total demand line, the system displays all planned independent requirements and customer requirements of this period.

The detailed information for RS quantities includes the production lines on which the material is produced and the corresponding production quantities.

If there are individual customer requirements for the material, the detailed information screen displays two lines for each production line, as follows:

1. The run schedule header for the production line

2. The individual customer requirement

An assignment for a sales order would be displayed in the line for the individual customer requirement.

Some of the elements shown in the planning table might be procured externally, for example, through purchase requisitions or schedule lines. If you double-click on the element to be procured externally, the system branches to a dialog box from which you can access information on the externally procured element.

You can inspect capacity planning data from the planning table by marking a line and selecting Show capacity data. If your system is operating with planning levels, you will be invited to use a dialog box to select the planning level. For example, customizing may have specified that capacity requirements are to be created at the detailed scheduling level and at the rate-based scheduling level for the order type PE (run schedule quantities).

The middle section of the planning table displays the results of capacity planning for the chosen capacity category in a three-line format:

- Line 1—three-character capacity category key and the capacity available for the production line in each period.

- Line 2—total capacity requirements in this capacity category for the production line in each period. Double-click on any value to inspect the pegged requirements.
- Line 3—the capacity load of this production line.

Line 3 can be switched to show the capacity requirements that are not created by run schedule quantities from repetitive manufacturing. The following sequence will toggle line 3:

1. Select Capacity planning.
2. Select 3rd capacity line→Capacity load, **or**
3. Select 3rd capacity line→Capacity requirements.

The following sequence will access information for another capacity category:

1. Select Capacity planning→Capacity categories.
2. Select Overview + selection, **or**
3. Press Next capacity categ.

Planning Run Schedule Quantities Using a Production Line

You can access an overview of the total planned production volume on a certain production line in either of two ways: via a planning ID or by identifying a production line. The difference is that the planning ID allows you to plan production quantities in a simplified way, whereas calling a defined production line allows you to perform capacity planning on it.

From the repetitive manufacturing menu, the following sequence will access the run schedule quantities via a production line:

1. Select RS quantities→Create + change, **or**
2. Select RS quantities→Display.
3. Enter a plant number and select Production line.
4. Press Choose.
5. Into the dialog box, enter the desired production line.
6. Select the Capacity planning check box if you intend to carry out capacity planning.
7. Select the Extended material data check box if you want to see the availability, the range of coverage, and so on, for the material.
8. Select the proposed period of examination.
9. Press Continue. You will be invited to select the planning level at which the capacity requirements are to be displayed if detailed scheduling is in operation.
10. Process the planning table and then save the data.

In the section of the screen entitled Detailed information for RS quantities, the system displays detailed information on the production line. You can see the run schedule quantities of the individual materials that are produced on this production line. If there is more than one production line for a material, the run schedule quantities of the various production versions are listed below the material. Individual customer requirements and material assigned to a sales order appear as a second line for each material.

Accessing Run Schedule Quantities Using a Shift

Shifts are defined in the work centers. If you access the planning table by nominating a shift, you will see a detailed view of the capacity loads and the run schedule quantities assigned to the individual shifts. Capacity planning is activated automatically. The system only takes into account planned orders that have been dispatched in the graphic planning table.

Changes to a shift can be made from the planning table.

Accessing Run Schedule Quantities Using a Group of Production Lines

A group of production lines can be identified by nominating a work center hierarchy and a node work center. Starting from the node work center, the hierarchy can be exploded level by level for display purposes.

The system displays the available capacity, capacity requirements, and the capacity load as percentages. Any work centers that are also defined as production lines in the production version will be included in the hierarchy.

If you need to change the run schedule quantities, you branch into the individual production lines. The capacity requirements are automatically adjusted.

From the repetitive manufacturing menu, the following sequence will access the run schedule quantities for a group of production lines:

1. Select RS quantities→Create + change, **or**
2. Select RS quantities→Display.
3. Enter a plant number, select Production line group.
4. Press Choose.
5. Enter the appropriate hierarchy or select one using a matchcode.
6. Overwrite the Start and End fields to change the period of examination.
7. Press Continue.
8. Process the planning table and save the data.

A similar procedure is used for accessing run schedule quantities using a product group.

Processing Run Schedule Quantities in the Planning Table

The following sequences are used to maintain the selection criteria used to access each view of the planning table:

1. Select View→Settings→Save.
2. Select View→Settings→Delete.

Arrow keys scroll the planning table horizontally on the time axis within the selected period of examination. If the planning table is larger that a page, you can scroll vertically using the standard scroll buttons. Alternatively, you can overwrite a line number with a target line number.

Changing the Time Bucket of a Planning Table

The run schedule header specifies a time bucket. If there are several run schedule headers included in the planning table, the system always displays the planning table using the smallest bucket. Select View→Time bucket→Day or Week or Month or Planning calendar, if you need to change the bucket in the display. If the planning table is in the production line view, you can select View→Time bucket→Shift.

If you mark blocks in the planning table and press F2, or double-click, you will obtain detailed information on individual lines, as follows:

- Text blocks—see the individual lines that make up the totals and the detailed data that is available for a run schedule header.
- Number blocks—see the scheduling quantities that are hidden behind the relevant figures.
- Period descriptions (column headings)—see the first and last day of the relevant period.

Part
III

Ch
10

Changing and Assigning Quantities

You can enter new quantity specifications for planned quantities and quantities that have not yet been assigned to production versions. There is a choice of the following methods:

- Change quantities directly in the planning table—overwrite any number block that can be changed, reset if necessary, and terminate the simulation mode by saving the data.
- Change quantities in the details screen—select the planned orders that you wish to change and save the data to terminate the simulation.
- Change quantities in the planned order—select Accept changes to terminate the simulation and save the data.

Several run schedule quantities (planned orders) can make up one production quantity. In these cases, the first planned order is always adjusted if you change the production quantity. If you reduce the production quantity, then as many planned orders are reduced until the target quantity is reached.

Backflushing with Production Orders

When you carry out a backflush in repetitive manufacturing with production orders, you effectively update the progress of the production order. The backflush updates the following data objects:

- Goods receipts
- Goods issues
- Completion confirmations

When goods receipts and completion confirmations are posted, the system can consult pre-defined strategies that determine which actions are to be automatically triggered. For example, when you confirm the completed production of a quantity of a product at a certain time, the following postings can be automatically triggered:

■ Backflush the components used as planned.

■ Post the goods receipt of the semifinished product.

■ Post the goods issue for the manufacture of higher-level assemblies if there is an open requirement in this connection.

None of these strategies can be defined unless you have set up version links in the system. And before a component can be backflushed, the backflushing indicator must be set in its material master record.

Maintaining Version Links

A material component needed for a higher-level material assembly can itself be an assembly that requires components of a still lower level, and so on through a hierarchical structure.

A version link is a document that specifies that there is a connection between a material and an assembly. Thus the manufacture of a quantity of a component material that has a version link with other materials can be a very significant event if some of these higher-level material assemblies are awaiting delivery of their reservations of this component.

When the quantity of the lowest-level material is completely manufactured, you post the completion confirmation. If you have set up backflushing, this completion confirmation can automatically post a goods receipt to stock and goods issues to whatever higher-level assemblies have been defined by version links in the lowest-level material. The defined backflushing strategy may include rules to control what should happen if there is a shortfall in the component material. Are some higher-level assemblies to be given priority? Should the yield be shared out proportionally?

From the repetitive manufacturing menu screen, the following sequence will maintain version links:

1. Select Master data→For discrete RS.

2. Select Linking versions→Maintain.

3. Specify the plant, material, and production version for which a version link is to be created or changed.

4. Press Continue and inspect an overview of all version links previously created for the material.

5. To change an existing version link, overwrite the data with the new values.

6. To create a new version link, press New entries.

7. Enter or accept Counter, a consecutive number used for internal numbering.

8. Enter or accept Plant, the number of the plant of the higher-level material.

9. Enter or accept Material, the number of the higher-level material in the production of which the lower-level material is to be used.

10. Enter or accept Version, production version of the higher-level material.

11. Enter or accept StLoc, the number of the storage location at which the higher-level material is stored.

12. Enter or accept PlHor, the number of workdays taken into account as the planning horizon during version linking.

13. Save your entries.

If reservations exist in the production order for the higher-level material when receipts of the lower-level material are posted inside the planning horizon, the issue of the lower-level material for the relevant production order is posted at the same time.

Creating Goods Receipts

The following are examples of goods receipt strategies:

- No version links are taken into account when entering goods receipts for assemblies—only the goods receipts for the finished assemblies are posted.

- Goods receipts for assemblies take account of version links by automatically posting goods issues for the same assemblies if reservations for them exist for the production orders of the higher-level materials.

If there is going to be automatic posting of goods issues, there are two possibilities:

1. No online control. The system allocates the goods issues to cover the first reservations it finds.

2. Goods issues are posted with online user control. The system uses the goods issues to cover the first reservations it finds; however, the user can change the allocation.

The following sequence will create goods receipts for finished assemblies:

1. From the repetitive manufacturing main menu, select Backflush.

2. Select For discrete RS→Goods receipts.

3. Enter a plant and the number of the run schedule header for which you wish to enter goods receipts, **or**

4. Enter the material number, the production version, and a date to identify the run schedule header.

5. If necessary, specify the relevant dates in the Start and End fields of the period of examination section of the Run Schedule Header screen.

6. Press Continue.

7. Enter the goods receipts.

8. Save your data.

The goods receipts data entry screen comprises an upper section describing the run schedule header. The lower section is a planning table that includes the following information:

- Period
- The chosen time bucket with the individual periods
- Released quantity—the quantities expected as receipts from production orders
- Planned quantity—the quantities expected as receipts from planned orders
- Actuals—the quantities already entered as goods receipts in previous user sessions
- Total—the figures in this line are the totals of the quantities shown in the lines above
- Total supply—the quantities entered as goods receipts (supply) during the current user session

The following options are provided for entering goods receipts:

- Create goods receipt quantities directly in the planning table.
- Create goods receipts in a dialog box.
- Make an individual goods receipt posting.

The following sequence will create goods receipt quantities directly in the planning table:

1. In the data screen for entering goods receipts, specify the quantity to be entered as a goods receipt in the field Goods receipt quantity.
2. Press F2 on this field to work on the details screen if there is only one production order involved. If there are two or more production orders, or production orders with a distribution key, use the dialog box to manage the entries.
3. If only one production order exists, the entire quantity is allocated to it.
4. If several production orders exist, the quantity is always allocated to the first one. If the goods receipt quantity exceeds the quantity of the first production order, the remaining quantity is allocated to the next production order, and so on.
5. To display and change the details, double-click on the relevant production orders.
6. Press Copy.
7. Press Save.

Goods receipts are always created for assemblies, but no goods issues are posted for assemblies. When the completion confirmation for an assembly is posted, the goods issues for the backflushed components are automatically posted.

Goods issues are created with reference to component withdrawals, but only if the components are not backflushed.

Evaluation Reporting in Repetitive Manufacturing

The *Interactive pull list* is a display created by the system in response to the commands Evaluations→Pull list. This list shows the quantities of each of the material components required by the run schedules of a production line.

From the Pull List screen you can carry out an availability check for the material components.

If you find that there is a shortage of any material, you can work on the pull list to create a replenishment delivery for the production line. The system creates a stock transfer in inventory management or a transfer requirement in the warehouse management system.

If you select Evaluations→Reporting points from the main menu of repetitive manufacturing, you will access the reporting point overview. This provides a statistical overview of all run schedule headers of a production line.

The system displays the quantities that have passed through each reporting point, but that have not yet been backflushed. No goods receipt has yet been posted for these quantities.

There is a display of this information for every run schedule header for which reporting points exist.

Select Evaluations→Displ.document logs if you want to list and print the backflushed documents.

Reporting from the Controlling Module

The controlling (CO) module provides extensive facilities for managing cost objects. From repetitive manufacturing, you can create various CO reports for analyzing production costs.

Consulting LIS Statistics in Repetitive Manufacturing

The following information is available from the logistics information system (LIS):

■ Goods receipt statistics—actual production and scrap quantities if you have previously updated the planned quantities.

■ Reporting point statistics—the recorded backflush quantity per reporting point.

■ Material consumption statistics—the recorded component requirements and the actual component consumption.

■ Production cost statistics—evaluated from the recorded product costs.

If you trigger the planned quantity update, the planned quantities are also included in the goods receipt statistics. As a background job, planned quantity updates can be customized to occur at specified intervals.

As a one-off background job, you can update planned quantities as follows:

1. From the repetitive manufacturing main menu, select Evaluations→LIS statistics.
2. Select GR statistics→Update planned qties.
3. Specify the plant and the production line, if necessary the planning ID.
4. Press Execute.

The system issues a message when it has completed the transaction update.

Exchanging Information with the Plant Data Collection Interface

The plant data collection (PDC) interface is used in repetitive manufacturing for downloading and uploading between the R/3 and whatever external or third-party systems you have for communicating with your production and warehousing facilities.

RM_RS_DOWNLOAD is the function module for run schedule download. It provides PDC systems with run schedule data. The selected RS data has to be assembled in tabular form and the download module is accessed using the remote function call (RFC) technology.

RM_RS_UPLOAD is the function module for run schedule upload. It receives and posts the data from the PDC that will be used to perform the backflush for the run schedules. This upload function module is also accessed from PDC systems via using RFC.

RM_SO_DOWNLOAD is a function module that is specialized for downloading sales order records.

These PDC functions are called from the ABAP/4 Workbench Function Library. They can be configured to transfer data additional to the run schedule information. For example, the transfer to the plant can include reporting point information, the revision levels of the material to be manufactured, and the assigned planned orders for it.

The following standard run schedule selection criteria illustrate the way in which the PDC is controlled:

■ I_WERKS—mandatory selection criterion for run schedule headers; selects all RS headers in the specified plant; defaults to RM61B-WERKS.

■ I_MATNR—selects all RS headers for this material in this plant; defaults to RM61B-MATNR 'Blank'.

■ I_VERID—selects all RS headers for this production version in this plant; defaults to RM61B-VERID 'Blank'.

■ I_MDV01—selects all RS headers for this planning ID in this plant; defaults to RM61B-MDV01 'Blank'.

■ I_MDV02—selects all RS headers for planning ID2 in this plant; defaults to RM61B-MDV02 'Blank'.

A further selection key can be assembled using combinations of the following criteria:

■ RS headers with/without reporting points

■ Selection includes planned orders

■ Selection includes all planned orders or only the assigned planned orders

■ Selection of the RS headers with or without revision levels ●

Assembly Processing in Make-to-Order Production

Making to Order

Assembly processing is a method of providing a make-to-order service to the customer. It has the particular advantage of offering reliable delivery dates because the finished product is managed as an assembly of components. And each component is automatically checked for availability to promise at the time the sales order is being considered. Automobiles and personal computers are examples of products that are beneficially managed by assembly processing.

The logistics system cooperates with the assembly processing (PP-ATO) module to automatically create a procurement element, such as a planned order, when creating the sales order. Furthermore, should any changes arise in either delivery dates or quantities, the alterations are immediately apparent in the sales order document. By the same mechanism, if the customer requires any alterations in the sales order, the changes are automatically submitted to the production system.

Production by lots and projects are supported in the context of repetitive manufacturing.

Assembly Processing in Repetitive Manufacturing

The repetitive manufacturing (PP-ATO-REM) component allows you to use the planning and control tools from the repetitive manufacturing module. When you create a sales order, the system automatically creates a planned order. This means you can take materials from a repetitive manufacturing run that is under control of a run schedule header, and use them to meet a make-to-order sales order. When the order is delivered, the backflushing process of the RS header will post the outcomes directly to the sales order.

Assembly processing in repetitive manufacturing is a technique that is most effective under the following conditions:

- The production process of the finished product is simple with clear production processes.
- The production of the assemblies is carried out in a constant flow through the production lines.
- Simple routings are used, or the assembly can be carried out without routings.
- The components are anonymous—any example will suffice.
- The components are procured using KANBAN production techniques, consumption-based planning, or assembly planning.
- The production control effort is to be kept to a minimum and backflushing is to be simplified.

Assembly Processing in Production by Lots

The production by lots (PP-ATO-LOT) component is able to use production orders to control the production. When a sales order is posted, the system automatically creates a production order. Alternatively, a planned order can be created that will later be converted to a production order when the manufacturing capacities have been confirmed.

Complex production procedures are beneficially controlled by the PP-ATO-LOT component. The advantages of using production orders include the option of adopting the following control techniques:

- Collective orders
- Status management of the production order
- Use of various business operations at operation level

Using assembly processing with production orders for individual lots is typically associated with the following situations:

- Process flow production
- Manufacture of coproducts
- Production with parallel production lines

Working with Assembly Orders

When a sales order is posted, there can be an automatic creation of a network or an assembly order in the background. Which of these alternatives is set in motion depends on the strategy group specified in the material master records of the material that is the focus of the sales order.

A network is a structure of processes that are executed according to the specifications in the order. The network can satisfy many different customer requirements by executing a particular subset or sequence of the operations that comprise it.

An assembly order is a planned or production order to cover the independent requirement. The requirement is referred to as independent because the production order may be for a quantity that exceeds the exact requirements of the order. If the production order matched the sales order, you would expect the production to be managed as a make-to-order event.

A posted sales order causes the transfer of the following information to an associated assembly order:

- The material staging date
- The order quantity
- The costs of the goods to be manufactured
- The available quantity, if an availability check was carried out
- The confirmed delivery date

There are some preliminary actions that have to be completed before you can work with an assembly order, as follows:

- The field Strategy group in the material master record (MRP 1) of the finished product must contain a strategy that allows assembly orders.
- The finished product must have a BOM.
- The field Indiv./collec.reqmts in the material master (MRP 2) of the components should contain the indicator *Only collective requirements*.

Scheduling an Assembly Order

A sales order will normally have an agreed or requested delivery date. The purpose of scheduling is to ensure that the work is finished in time to meet the delivery, allowing for the work calendar, with its planned holidays and perhaps machine shutdown for maintenance.

The transportation services will be subject to delivery scheduling, so the requested delivery date may have to be replaced by a staging date as a result of the constraints of delivery scheduling.

The staging date is when the goods have to be available for transportation to the delivery destination. Processing the goods receipt document can take some time, so the goods receipt processing time is subtracted from the staging date. The result is the basic finish date of the production order.

Thus the basic finish date makes allowances for goods receipt processing, queuing for transportation, and the time taken to deliver to the customer. The same calculations have to be performed if the customer is actually another stage in the production order processing.

The start of the production order has to be determined by backwards scheduling from the basic finish date. This calculation of basic start date can yield various kinds of results, as follows:

- If the basic start date of the production order is not in the past, then the requested delivery date of the sales order is confirmed because there will be time to complete the necessary processing.
- If the basic start date of the production order is in the past, the order has to be rescheduled.

When the basic start date of a sales order turns out to be in the past, the system has to determine a new basic finish date using the Today scheduling procedure that works out what can be achieved if the order processing begins immediately.

The system adds the goods receipt processing time to the basic finish date to arrive at a staging date. A second delivery scheduling run is carried out to find out the best delivery date that can be confirmed.

Improving Delivery Date Reliability

It would be useful to be able to check resources and the availability situation for make-to-order production when creating the sales order. You could then be sure when the order could be delivered partially, or in full. The method is to check the stock of the components needed for the assembly that is the subject of the sales order or inquiry.

It may make sense for the sales department to be constantly aware of the stock and production situation in detail. If there have to be changes in the dates or quantities, or in the procurement of externally sourced components, then this information should be added to any relevant sales orders that are still open. The sales department may have standing arrangements for confirmation that should be updated to reflect any changes in the predicted delivery situation.

Assembly processing is an R/3 planning strategy that has been provided with the software functions necessary to perform component availability checks in response to a customer quotation or an inquiry.

The system determines a committed order quantity for each sales order. This committed quantity is based on the component with the smallest available quantity. The quantity of an assembly has to be limited by the quantity available of each of its components.

Furthermore, the assembly processing function calculates the confirmed delivery date for the sales order. The confirmed delivery date is based on the availability date of the component that is latest on the time axis to be available. You cannot begin the final assembly until the last of the components has arrived.

As you would expect, if you change the date or quantities in a sales order, there may have to be changes in production and procurement. As a result, there could be changes that alter the confirmed delivery date and the committed quantity.

Creating a Sales Order with Assembly Processing

Assembly processing can be used on a customer quotation or an inquiry. The system automatically creates a procurement element—the *assembly order*. Any of the following procurement elements can be chosen for the assembly order:

Part
III

Ch
11

- Planned order
- Production order
- Network (project)

Scheduling is carried out automatically for the assembly order. You can also plan capacity when creating the sales order for assembly processing.

The bill of material is usually exploded for the assembly order to determine the corresponding components and the system automatically conducts an availability check for the components. The availability check can apply the ATP logic or refer to planned requirements at the assembly level that are independent of any particular order.

As a result of these assembly processing activities, the system determines the committed quantity for the desired delivery date.

It may happen that the system can commit no quantity at all for the desired delivery date. Failure to discover a quantity of the product that can be committed is handled as a missing parts situation. The system determines which are the missing parts and displays the details.

If you are working with available-to-promise logic, the system will determine a partial quantity and a total confirmation date when the full requirements can be delivered.

Instead of defining the product by a BOM, the material can be configured in the sales order. In this situation, the results of the configuration are copied to the assembly order and the system carries out availability checking of the necessary components.

If your customer requires a change of date or quantity in a sales order, the details are immediately reflected in the assembly order. The same applies if the sales order is being executed by a planned order. However, if you are meeting a sales order with a production order, you can make changes in the dates or quantities only up until the production order is released for production.

It is possible to arrange for an assembly order to be changed without having the alterations reflected back into the sales order from which it was created.

The assembly processing function supports the following procedures:

- Static procedure—one procurement element exists for each sales order item
- Dynamic procedure—sales order items can be split for dates and quantities between procurement elements

Assembly Processing with Production Orders

You can assign a production order to assembly processing if you need to monitor and control the production process with the status management functions. In this context, status management could be used to implement the following logic, for example:

- Document the current processing status of an object
- Allow or forbid certain business transactions
- Group or select objects by status, such as *missing part*
- Trigger rework functions automatically using trigger points

If you conducted assembly processing using a production order, you would also be able to manage individual operations, for example:

- Release operations individually or in groups
- Print shop papers
- Enter completion confirmations
- Keep track of the costs during the production process because each confirmation or goods movement causes an update of the actual order costs

The collective order management functions are available for production orders. This offers a number of advantages, for example, in continuous flow production, production using parallel production lines, and make-to-order production:

- Any changes to dates or quantities have an immediate effect on any dependent orders within the collective order.
- No goods movements are required for subassemblies.
- You can carry out an availability check across all production levels.
- Each production order is automatically settled to the superior production order. The top production order is then automatically settled to the sales order.

■ You can use the rework functionality to compensate for malfunctions or errors. If the malfunctions or errors have been anticipated, you can initiate planned rework using trigger points. If the malfunctions or errors are unplanned, you can insert rework operations or reference operation sets or create rework orders.

If you wish to produce coproducts using assembly processing, then you have to use assembly processing with production orders.

Creating a Planned Order from a Sales Order

If you create a production order directly in response to a sales order, you will have all the facilities of production orders immediately on call. However, you can create a planned order that is later converted to a production order.

There are two advantages in working with planned orders:

1. You can implement preplanned decisions regarding external procurement of some or all of the order.

2. You can call on in-house production that has been already planned.

For example, you may want to wait until a batch of sales orders has been assigned as planned orders so that a single production order can be created to deal with them all after suitable adjustments to the planning.

However, you cannot convert planned orders into production orders within assembly processing unless you have previously defined a suitable strategy group or requirements class that is associated with a dynamic assembly type.

When to Use Assembly Processing with Repetitive Manufacturing

The following conditions favor the use of assembly processing in the context of repetitive manufacturing:

■ Production of the finished product is carried out in clear and simple steps.

■ The assembly is produced in a constant flow over the production lines.

■ Simple routings are used, or no routings at all.

■ Components can be staged anonymously at the production lines, as with consumption-based planning, subassembly planning, or KANBAN.

■ You want to reduce the effort required for production control and backflushing.

If you can treat the product as an assembly of only a small number of components, although perhaps combined in various ways to generate a large number of different products, then repetitive manufacturing techniques would seem to make sense. The production process should be relatively simple and not involve many production levels.

It is best if the components can be gathered in batches of stock at various stages where they are anonymous, that is, they have not yet been assigned to a specific sales order. You can still apply availability checking to determine whether the necessary components for an order are

Part

III

Ch

11

going to be ready when and where they are needed. This check would normally exclude components that are almost always available at the appropriate work center.

Assembly Processing with Projects

If you are considering a product as a complex assembly, you could process it using a network or as a project. For example, you may design and manufacture all your products to order. In which case it may be difficult to determine a delivery date because you are not sure what will have to be achieved to execute the sales order.

In these circumstances, networks and projects should be considered. The network allows you to plan in the midterm or long-term sense, even if you are unable to enter precise dates for short-term planning. The network offers a rough-cut planning framework that can begin developing when the sales order is entered. Refinement follows and eventually production orders are created to execute the work. A network is particularly helpful if there are component processes that necessarily lock together in temporal relationships that must be planned for.

The R/3 project system (PS) is a specialized functional module that supports the development of a work breakdown structure (WBS) when a sales order is created. The WBS becomes the principal planning and control instrument for the project.

If you implement assembly processing with projects, you can choose where the costs are collected. For example, in a WBS element, in the sales order, or in the network.

Assembly Processing with Variant Configuration

A configurable product can be manufactured using assembly processing. The strategy group assigned to the material determines whether the system will automatically create one of the following when the sales order is entered:

- A planned order
- A production order
- A network

The characteristic values that are to control the configuration are passed on to the planned order, production order, or network. The components that include subordinate items that are themselves configurable have to be checked manually for availability.

Alternatively, you can define a subordinate configurable assembly as a phantom assembly that will have the job of gathering together a particular set of parts ready for use in the main assembly. You may need to define a different phantom for each variant of your main material. You cannot create a separate production order for a phantom assembly.

Setting for Assembly Processing

Planning is controlled by standard strategies that have been assigned to the three procurement elements:

■ Production order

■ Planned order

■ Network

If you intend to use assembly processing, your planning strategy must allow it. Strategies are assigned as groups to individual material master records. A planning strategy includes the following data:

■ Assembly type—sets which procurement type is created and whether the link is static 1:1 or dynamic with date and quantity splitting

■ Order type—required for production orders, process orders, networks, and projects

■ Availability check at component level or only for the finished product

■ Type of component availability check—ATP logic or against planned independent requirements

■ Dialog assembly—displays missing parts overview with information on calculated quantities and dates for quantities not fully available; allows interactive processing in the sales order

■ Capacity available—selects lead time scheduling or capacity planning when creating the sales order

■ No update—controls whether changes in the procurement element are allowed to influence the committed quantities or dates in the sales order

These indicators are available in all standard requirements classes. You can establish other settings by copying the existing requirements class and editing the data before saving the copy as a new requirements class. This requirements class has to be assigned to a requirements type, which in turn has to be assigned to a new strategy created for it. A new strategy group has to be created to which the new strategy has to be assigned.

You may find it convenient to direct the availability check to one or more critical components of an assembly. You have to mark the components to be checked by assigning them to a checking group indicated in the MRP 2 availability check field. The MRP 2 screen also allows you to switch off the availability checking for the noncritical components.

The indicator *indiv./collective* in the MRP 2 screen has to be set to *Collective requirements* to prevent the system from generating separate stock segments for each component when the higher-level assembly is undergoing requirements planning.

Setting for Assembly Processing with Production Orders

The finished material to be manufactured under control of the assembly processing with production orders functions must have a valid bill of materials.

Strategy group, requirements class, and order type are predefined for assembly processing with production orders. Strategy group 82 (assembly processing with production orders) specifies a 1:1 link between production order and sales order. The requirements type is KMFA and the requirements class 201. Order type PP04 is assigned for a production order with assembly processing.

Setting for Assembly Processing with Repetitive Manufacturing

The strategy group and requirements type or class parameters for repetitive manufacturing are the same as are used for planned orders. The special goods receipt posting with reference to the sales order is available whether you work with or without the planning table.

However, there are some additional settings that have to be made if you intend to use the planning table for make-to-order repetitive manufacture. The advantages of using the planning table include being able to assign the production quantities to production lines and to carry out capacity planning. You have the following options:

- Plan the run schedule quantities.
- Use the current stock/requirements list from MRP to gain an overview of the run schedule quantities.
- Use the capacity leveling functions from the stock/requirements list or from capacity planning to adjust the master plan.

The following arrangements must be made if you want to use the planning table:

- Allow repetitive manufacturing for the material in the material master record.
- Identify a repetitive manufacturing profile.

The repetitive manufacturing profile specifies the movement types in backflushing and for posting costs. A cost collector is not required for make-to-order production, so it is best to choose a repetitive manufacturing profile that does not automatically create cost collectors.

In your choice of profile there are options to control whether the costs of the order are to be posted automatically with activities, such as machine costs and labor costs, on the final backflush. The alternative is to post the costs without these activities.

A production version of the material has to be created for Assembly Processing with Repetitive Manufacturing. This production version must specify at least the appropriate bill of material and the production line where the work will take place. The production version record can also specify an alternative BOM, a strategy group, and a group counter.

This production version must be identified as a reference in the run schedule header created in the Repetitive Manufacturing menu.

If you do not intend to work with the planning table, you have to enter a repetitive manufacturing profile in the material master record.

Setting for Projects and Networks in Assembly Processing

Strategy group, requirements class, network type, and condition type are all predefined settings, as follows:

- Strategy group 83—assembly processing with networks with requirements class 202
- Strategy group 85—assembly processing with network/project with requirements class 212

In order to create a network from a sales order, you have to assign an appropriate MRP controller or strategy group to the material that is to be manufactured.

Requirements classes are predefined for networks, as follows:

- Requirements class 202—a network with network type PS05 (header account assignment) and account assignment category E (assignment to the sales order).
- Requirements class 212—a network with network type PS04 (activity account assignment) and account assignment category D (assignment to project or WBS element).

Network types PS04 and PS05 are predefined to adopt the scheduling type Backwards. You can assign other network types by specifying a key and activating the indicator *Adjust basic dates*. The system updates the network basic dates with the scheduled dates and then writes them into the sales order as confirmed dates.

A network can be created from a sales order if the material master record specifies a strategy group that allows a network to be created from the sales order. This strategy group record must include an appropriate requirements class indicator to ensure that the following parameters are available:

- Assembly type
- Network type
- Configuration
- Account assignment category

Using a Standard Network for Production or Assembly Processing

When a network is created from a sales order, the system consults the material master to determine a suitable standard network from which to make a copy. If the sales order is to be settled to a project, the standard network is assigned to a standard work breakdown structure element.

A standard network record can be used to store links between the material, the network to be created for assembly processing, and the account assignment. If you do not set this linking data in the material master, you have to enter it online each time the material appears in a sales order for assembly processing.

The following sequence will allow you to make the settings from the Basic data menu:

1. Select Standard structures.
2. Select Alloc mat→std.ntwk.
3. Consult the screen titled Network Parameters—From Sales Order.
4. Allocate the material to a standard network.
5. Allocate the material to a standard WBS element for account assignment. ●

Part

III

Ch

11

Managing Materials

Defining a Material

It is standard throughout the SAP R/3 system to define *material* to include whatever is used in the production process. The following are examples of material in the SAP R/3 system:

- Finished products
- Intermediate assemblies
- Unfinished products
- Raw materials
- Part-processed materials
- Resources such as energy, air, and water
- Packaging
- Services

Storing Information as a Material Data Structure

Two principles apply to the storage of data in the SAP R/3 system:

- Information that is expected to remain constant for a long time is entered in one place only, and any changes to it are logged.
- Local information is stored at the level encompassing all the operational units for which it is pertinent but can be made available elsewhere.

You have the following range of options:

- At the level of the client or the company code, maintain general data valid for the whole organization—for example, material code numbers, multilingual text concerning each material code, and classification rules applicable to material.
- At the plant level, maintain the data for material requirements planning and production planning and control, and also valid bills of material and routings.
- Maintain inventories at the level of the individual storage location, of which a plant may have more than one.
- Maintain the sales data at the level of each purchasing organization and distribution channel.

You can define individual access authorizations as create, change, or display only. These can be specific to each user and each organizational level. If you are authorized to create transaction data, you can obviously display and change it unless the item is reserved as read-only. At the intermediate level of authorization comes the permission to alter a record but not generate a new one. For example, a sales representative might be allowed to change the address of a supplier, but not to create new suppliers or delete existing addresses.

Confining Materials to User Departments

Sections of the information on a material master can be allocated to different user departments, such as the MRP department, the work scheduling department, and so on. By doing this, you can give each department access to just the information it needs about a specific material.

Establishing Material Types

Material data is maintained centrally. Different views of the master records can be called for by making reference to the material type. For example, you could maintain data for work scheduling in the case of a material of the type "semifinished goods," but you cannot schedule raw materials.

The material type determines certain other control parameters:

- Which user departments can maintain the data for a material of this type
- Procurement type—which indicates how this material is procured: in-house manufacturing or external procurement
- Type of inventory control to be used—for example, whether by quantity, value, or both

You may create and configure material types to suit your business.

Recognizing Industry Sectors

If a material is used in more than one industry, you may decide to create industry sectors in which the material type is configured in a special way for each sector.

Managing Batches and Special Stock

Batches of a material are managed at the storage location level, but you may want to differentiate between, for example, special stock and batches:

- A batch is a full or partial quantity of material. The material in the batch is managed separately on the inventory. It may be a production lot or a delivery lot, for example.
- Special stock may be designated vendor special stock, for example, because it is a consignment from a particular vendor.
- Customer special stock might be the designation of, for example, packaging materials returnable by the customer.
- Activity-related special stock may be identified because it is going to a particular customer on a make-to-order product, for example.

Using Departmental Profiles for Materials

An existing material master record can be used as a reference when creating a new material master. The data necessary on the user departments of your company can be maintained in the form of user department profiles, which contain no reference to any specific material, but you can reference them when creating a new material master. Each user department can set individual options to control how this data is applied.

Part
III

Ch
12

Creating Bills of Material

The bill of material (BOM) is an instrument for describing the structure of a product for any of the following production types:

- Repetitive manufacturing
- Manufacturing products with variants
- Process manufacturing
- Make-to-order production

You can also maintain bills of materials for sales orders, projects, equipment, and documents.

The BOM is used in central planning functions, such as materials requirements planning and product costing. Five forms of the basic BOM are supported in Production Planning and Control (PP). They may be created at any time by extending a simple BOM:

- Simple BOM—one rigidly defined bill of material is associated with one material.
- Variant BOM—several similar materials are associated with one bill of material.
- Multiple BOM—a set of bills of materials describing each of several different production processes, constituents, or relative quantities of components, all of which produce the same material. There are several ways of making the same thing.
- One-time BOM—a bill of material for a specific sales order that is used in make-to-order production.
- Configurable BOM—a bill of material that is configured automatically on the basis of logical links. It is used for complex variant structures or process-dependent BOM configuration in continuous flow production.

Exploring the BOM Data Structure

The BOM has a header and one or more items. The header indicates that the BOM is assigned to one or more plants and specifies its validity period. The header also carries its status indicator, which determines whether the BOM is released for production in its current form.

The BOM items each describe a component of the assembly in terms of the following categories, which you can subdivide as the need arises:

- Stock items are components kept in stock.
- Nonstock items may have purchasing data that you have maintained and that can be used to link with Materials Management Purchasing.
- Variable-size items must have the quantity to be used calculated automatically from the sizes entered.
- Document items include drawings or safety instructions integrated into the BOM.
- Text items are available for you to store all types of text in association with the BOM.

By-products and scrap can be represented on the BOM by negative quantities that will be processed in Material Requirements Planning (PP-MRP) and Product Costing (CO-PC).

Parts of a BOM can be marked for the attention of a particular department, or a separate BOM can be used for each department.

Maintaining a BOM

You can update a BOM from the CAD system or directly in Production Planning and Control (PP). Copying and editing functions are available. The standard SAP R/3 classification system can search for suitable materials quickly.

Engineering change management is facilitated by mass changes to bills of material. The integrated engineering change management functions allow you to track the complete history of changes to a BOM.

Using BOM Explosion Numbers

A BOM explosion is the process of identifying each item in a bill of material. Each item in turn is then examined to determine its constituent parts, and each part is examined for its constituents, and so on, until the lowest-level units are those managed in the inventory. A *BOM explosion number* is a method of making particular subsets of this extra information available to the users of a BOM in a controlled manner. The BOM is given a master record that indicates whether it applies specifically to one product or to many. The BOM explosion number may go through several revision levels, each of which will carry the *fixed key date* (the date on which that particular version of a BOM explosion should come into force). From that date, the content of the BOM explosion number has to be taken into account by the production scheduling and routing functions.

The BOM explosion number is a reference to a technical document that can serve a range of functions—for example:

- Notifying the details of product liability obligations
- Referencing ISO standards for quality assurance
- Documenting an engineering change made during the production process
- Referencing the relevant technical drawings and pointing out the salient features
- Documenting the technical status according to which a product is manufactured for all BOM levels
- Ensuring that the correct BOM and the corresponding routing are used in orders for spare parts

Directing the Materials

The BOM can be used to control production in several different plants, if they have the necessary resources. The R/3 system documents production resources in terms of work centers through which the materials are routed. Thus different plants may employ different work centers and therefore need individual routing instructions.

Defining Work Centers

A work center is both a place where a process is carried on by means of activities and a technical concept in the production planning and control system. The real work center has people, machines, production lines, assembly lines, and all the paraphernalia of industry. The work center in SAP R/3 is a data object.

In the data object of the type "work center" you can specify the data for the scheduling, costing, and capacity planning of operations. Formulas held there can compute execution times, costs, capacity requirements, and so on.

The SAP customizing module allows you to specify the data at your work centers so as to serve your company's needs. The system will supply default values for a work center to simplify and speed up work scheduling, or you can copy or reference from one source to another. The work center will have standard texts to assist you in maintaining the correct operation descriptions in routings. Any parameter unit held at a work center can be given up to six standard values to speed up complex costing or duration calculations, for example. You just specify by a key the value to be used on each occasion.

Work centers are assigned to a cost center during work center data maintenance. This provides the link to the controlling system (CO).

Every aspect of activity at a work center can be assigned a capacity value, which will then take part in capacity planning, production control, and the scheduling of routings. Not only can you define capacities for machines and labor, you can set up capacity parameters to define virtually any resource that you might need to improve the value added by each work center. Here are some examples:

- Energy consumption
- Emissions
- Reserve capacities for rush orders

Planning Material Requirements

The purpose of material requirements planning (MRP) is to ensure that the materials needed for the planned or anticipated production will be available when they are needed at the relevant work centers. Material requirements planning (PP-MRP) is the SAP R/3 functional module used in the context of the production planning and control (PP) application. PP-MRP includes the following components:

- Basic data (PP-MRP-BD)
- Planning execution (PP-MRP-PR)
- Procurement proposal (PP-MRP-PP)
- Planning evaluation (PP-MRP-PE)

MRP can be tasked to procure or produce the quantities required on time for both internal purposes and sales. Stocks have to be monitored and order proposals generated for in-house production and procurement elsewhere.

The aim of MRP is to optimize the levels of service to the customer while minimizing costs and capital lockup. The aim of the MRP modules is to minimize the effort required to plan and generate the relevant documents.

A procedural distinction can be made between consumption-based planning and materials requirements planning. And the system can support planning across several production plants.

One or more MRP controllers, perhaps divided into MRP groups, are allocated responsibility for the following activities:

- Specify the type, quantity, and time of the material requirements.
- Calculate when and for what quantity an order proposal has to be created to cover these requirements.

The MRP controller needs the following information:

- Stocks
- Stock reservations
- Stock on order
- Lead times
- Procurement times
- MRP procedure per material
- Lot-sizing procedure per material

The logistics chain tends to include the following elements, although not always in this operational sequence:

- Sales and distribution—sales orders containing specific customer requirements and dates received directly from the market.
- Demand management—sales planned ahead using a sales forecast based on make-to-order or make-to-stock strategies.
- Planned independent requirements—the demand for the finished product, assemblies, tradable goods, and replacement parts generated during demand management.
- Material requirements planning—to calculate reorder and procurement quantities and dates.
- Dependent requirements—BOM explosion to calculate quantities of components needed for in-house production of the finished products or assemblies.
- Procurement elements—planned orders and purchase requisitions in a planned schedule.
- Planned orders to cover the in-house dependent requirements.
- Purchase requisitions to cover the dependent requirements produced or procured externally.

- Production orders for in-house production including scheduling, capacity planning, cost accounting and status management.
- Purchase orders for external requirements including vendor selection and outline agreement management.
- Materials produced or procured placed in stock under inventory management.

The central functions of MRP are executed in the MRP planning run in which the system attempts to automate the planning and procurement of the material requirements. Critical parts and exceptional situations are notified to the MRP controller.

The following functions are provided for material requirements planning:

- Total planning and single-item planning
- Net change planning and regenerative planning
- Materials planning procedures (MRP and consumption-based planning)
- Lot-sizing procedures
- Easy-to-use functions for processing order proposals
- Assembly processing
- Ranges of coverage (days' supply)
- Discontinued parts
- Using alternative and substitute parts
- Direct procurement and direct production (collective order)
- Easy-to-use functions for evaluating the planning result
- Exception messages and rescheduling check
- Capacity planning
- Availability check and backorder processing
- Single- and multi-level pegging
- Single-item planning for sales orders
- Planning configurable products
- Event-based MRP
- Multiplant/site planning

These MRP functions are discussed in the sections that follow.

Choosing the Scope of Planning

Total planning considers all the materials in one plant that are relevant for planning. Single-item planning concentrates on one particular material.

Single-level planning considers only the BOM level of the selected material. Multilevel planning plans the level of the selected material plus all the lower BOM levels.

Net change planning is a method of conserving computer system resources without compromising the accuracy of the planning results. The system plans only those materials that have encountered a change in requirements. A new sales order could be the cause of this change, or an excessive amount of scrap created by a production order.

A planning file is maintained to control the planning run. The planning file lists all the materials relevant for planning and their respective MRP types. If a pertinent change occurs, the relevant items in the planning file are marked with a net change indicator that will ensure that it is included in the next net change planning run.

The planning horizon is identified by a date that has been selected by the user to limit the period to be used in the net change planning run. The planning horizon can be set to regular intervals, such as weekly or monthly.

A regenerative planning run is a particular planning run that plans all materials that have been marked as relevant for planning. This type of run is conducted during system implementation or after a major change in the materials inventory.

Material requirements planning (MRP) is a procedure that works from the future sales quantities. These anticipated quantities are cumulated after consulting the planned independent requirements, sales orders, material reservations, and so on.

The MRP material forecast can be used to plan the total requirements or as an aid for calculating unplanned additional requirements or the safety stock. The MRP normally focuses on finished products, important assemblies, and selected key components.

For materials that are produced in-house, the system calculates dependent requirements for assemblies and components during BOM explosion using the requirements for the finished product.

Master Production Scheduling

Master production scheduling (MPS) is a form of MRP that concentrates planning on the parts or products that have the greatest influence on company profits or which take up critical resources. These items are marked as **A** parts.

Items marked as master schedule items may be finished products, assemblies, or raw materials. These items are selected for a separate MPS run that takes place before the MRP planning run. The master production planning run is conducted without a BOM explosion so that the MRP controller can ensure that the master schedule items are correctly planned before the detailed MRP run takes place.

Consumption-Based Planning

The idea behind consumption-based planning is to use historical data as the starting values on which to build a forecast of the future consumption quantities and hence to set targets.

Consumption-based planning is often used in plants where there is no in-house production. Another use is to plan the **B** and **C** parts when the **A** parts have been planned by a master production run.

Part
III

Ch
12

Planning the Size of the Production Lot

Standard procedures are provided for managing the common lot-sizing strategies, and user-specific formulas can be implemented during customizing.

Static lot-sizing procedures depend on consulting the quantity specifications recorded in the material master record of the material being planned. Three static lot-size procedures are available:

- Lot for lot order quantity
- Fixed lot size
- Replenishment up to maximum stock level

Period lot-sizing procedures group together the requirement quantities for a material from one or more periods. These periods can be defined as follows:

- Daily lot size
- Weekly lot size
- Monthly lot size
- Lot size according to flexible period lengths based on accounting periods
- Lot size according to freely definable periods based on a planning calendar

Optimizing the Lot Size

An optimum lot-sizing procedure depends on grouping the requirement quantities for several periods to form a lot. How large the optimum lot size will be has to be calculated by applying a ratio. This ratio connects the independent costs and the storage costs. A large lot may be cheaper to produce but entail higher storage costs before all the lot quantity is needed.

The following optimizing strategies are available as standard functions:

- Part period balancing
- Least unit cost procedure
- Dynamic lot size creation
- Groff reorder procedure

Restricting the Lot Size

A material master record can specify that the material is to be produced in lot sizes that fall between stated minimum and maximum quantities. A lot size that is being optimized will be rounded up to the minimum size if necessary. Alternatively, requirement quantities will not be grouped together if the total goes beyond the maximum allowed.

Yet another restriction that can be applied is known as a rounding value. For example, you can specify that a calculated lot size must be adjusted to accord with the rounding value, which may be the number of units that can be conveniently packed or shipped together.

It may make sense to apply a different lot-sizing procedure for short-term and long-term requirements. Provision is made for you to enter a long-term lot size that differs from the short-term size.

Processing Order Proposals

The planning run generates output in the form of easy-to-use order proposals that you can adjust or accept as they stand. These order proposals can be classified as follows:

- Planned orders
- Purchase requisitions
- Delivery schedules

You can change or reschedule order proposals and you can create new ones.

You can create planned orders manually and subject them to the following functions:

- Capacity planning
- Component processing
- Availability check

Assembly Processing

Assembly processing is an organizing technique that allows you to carry out the availability check at component level and not just at finished-product level.

If you create a sales order for a material that has been marked for assembly processing, the system will automatically create a run schedule quantity as part of a planned order or of a production order.

The repetitive manufacturing functions are available for the planned orders, such as capacity planning and lead time scheduling. The planned order can be converted into a production order.

The system can also create a production order directly. This allows you to use the full range of production order functions.

Ranges of Coverage (Days' Supply)

Safety stock requirements are defined in terms of the current requirements by using the average daily requirements quantity. You can establish a range of coverage profile that can be assigned to a material to direct how the safety stock shall be calculated.

A useful statistic is the range of supply of a particular material. The following formats are standard:

- Stock range of coverage—displays the number of days that a material can cover requirements from the current plant stock.
- Receipt range of coverage—selects receipt elements for inclusion in the range of coverage calculation.

Part
III

Ch
12

Planning with Discontinued Parts

The engineering and design departments may decide to replace one material with another on a certain date. The replaced material is known as a discontinued part. In planning, the stock of discontinued material may have to be used up before the system switches to the follow-up material.

In the planning run, the system reassigns the dependent requirements quantity of the material to be discontinued to the follow-up material.

Using Alternative and Substitute Parts

It may be possible to group some materials because they can all be used in an assembly as alternative items in the same BOM. The members of such a group are marked as alternative items.

One use of alternatives is to allow the people in the work center to install an alternative if there should be any part missing. You can plan for this eventuality by assigning a usage probability to the alternative in the planning run.

Direct Procurement and Direct Production by Collective Orders

Direct procurement and direct production are procedures in which materials are not placed in stock. When the materials have been procured or produced in-house, they are directly assigned to the specific sales order or production order account for which they are destined. Direct procurement and direct production can both be initiated by the planning run.

In the case of direct procurement, no dependent requirements are created for the material to be procured directly. What the system does instead is to create a purchase requisition, which is then converted to a purchase order. When the goods arrive, they are consumed immediately and are not placed in stock.

If the dependent requirements of the material components are to be produced in-house, the dependent requirements can be created by a collective order. A special indicator is assigned to these components and a planned order is created for assigning to the account. The planned order for the finished product will be converted to a production order to begin the manufacturing. At this stage, all the dependent requirements planned will be automatically converted to production orders so that they too will be produced in time.

No goods issues or goods receipts are needed in direct production because no goods are placed into stock.

The dependent parts are manufactured as a result of production orders, so these production orders are assigned to the account of the higher-level production order. This gives rise to a collective order in which the costs and dates are interpreted as a single order.

Evaluating the Planning Result

MRP and its associated MPS are regarded as easy-to-use functions because they offer clear presentations of the MRP results and immediate access to any exceptional situations and the relevant information. The MRP controller has the following options for evaluating the MRP results:

- Planning result of single-item planning—check and correct the result before saving
- Interactive single-item planning—check and correct or reschedule through simulated planning runs before saving
- MRP list per material—future stock and requirement development according to the most recent planning run, with exception messages displayed in the list
- Stock/requirements overview per material—automatically updated MRP list showing changes to the stock and requirements

Interpreting Exception and Rescheduling Messages

Exception messages show the MRP controller what requires manual intervention; for example, a planned order that has missed its start date or a stock level below the safety stock level.

Among the most important exception messages are those that point to accounting objects that cannot be automatically changed by the system, in particular, production orders and purchase orders. The system can only make suggestions for remedial actions. For example, if the requirements situation has changed, it may be necessary to schedule new dates for firmed order proposals. This has to be a manual operation.

Capacity Planning for Planned Orders in the Planning Run

Before you pass a master plan to production, it may be wise to check that the work centers will have the necessary capacities available when they are needed. The system can carry out capacity planning for planned orders using the information from lead time scheduling and the formulas for capacity requirements calculation.

The collation of this information is presented to the MRP controller in terms of possible bottlenecks and overloads anticipated from discrepancies between the capacity requirements and the available capacities. There is still time to replan the schedule of planned orders by another planning run before production is initiated.

Availability Checking and Backorder Processing

The material availability check compares the planned requirements with the stock and the planned goods receipts. When the system is checking the availability on behalf of a planned order, it checks all the requirements that are dependent on this order. Every time the availability check is performed, the system collates the relevant stocks, goods issues, and goods receipts.

If the planning result shows that a certain material will have stock that is still available to promise (ATP), this material is said to have goods receipts still open for new issues such as sales orders. The MRP controller can decide if the master plan needs to be altered.

The backorder processing function generates a list of goods receipts and goods issues for a particular material that are relevant for the availability check. You can process missing parts from this list. The missing parts identify the materials for which the committed quantity is less than the requirement.

Single- and Multi-level Pegging

The Pegging function has the job of identifying which dependent requirements gave rise to which order proposals. The dependent requirements are each listed with a source material and a planned order number for this source. Single-level pegging is displayed in the planning result, in the MRP list, and in the stock/requirements list.

Pegging also shows which independent requirements, such as sales orders, would be set at risk if the controller were to delete or change any order proposal arising from a lower BOM level. Thus pegging can be used to trace materials dependencies across the BOM structure.

Single-Item Planning for Sales Orders

Individual sales orders can be assigned a special planning run. There is also a special evaluation function that starts from the sales order and builds an overview of the progress of production of the complete BOM structure.

Planning Configurable Products

A configurable product is one that can be produced in a range of variants of a standard product. A maximum BOM is defined with all the nonvariable parts plus all the possible variants.

When the sales order is created, configuration functions are called, which allow you to define a particular model or variant of the standard product. The configuration data identifies the particular components required for the assembly of the finished product as required by the customer.

Event-Based MRP

A sales order that is sensitive to the customer's requirements may have to be able to pass on changes to the MRP without delay. You can configure a single-item planning run to run automatically every time a sales order is changed.

Multiplant/Multisite Planning

You can plan materials across more than one plant or across a multisite plant by using a combination of the following procedures:

- Stock transfer
- Withdrawal from an alternative plant
- Production in an alternative plant ●

Planning and Integrating

Master Planning

In this chapter

Introducing the PP Master Planning Components

The master planning (PP-MP) module comprises the following components:

- Material forecast (PP-MP-MFC)—uses material consumption history to calculate forecast values that can be transferred to demand management or consumption-based MRP. The forecast values are used as the basis for creating the demand program and for automatically calculating the reorder point and safety stock levels.

- Demand management (PP-MP-DEM)—defines the future requirement quantities and dates for selected finished products and important assemblies. PP-MP-DEM also determines the strategy to be used for planning and producing/procuring particular finished products.

- Master production scheduling (PP-MP-MPS)—marks critical parts, products, or materials as master schedule items for precise planning and scheduling.

- Long-term planning or simulation (PP-MP-LTP)—simulates the effects of various versions of the demand program and calculates the capacity and activity requirements for the cost centers and the number of purchased parts needed. PP-MP-LTP consults the bills of material, routings, and work center data.

Building a Demand Program

The demand program is represented as a set of production quantities and their associated dates. Two sources of logic and information are needed to develop the demand program:

- Production planning strategies that create sales orders and sales forecast values for the demand program

- Consumption logic that controls how the component assemblies and materials shall be stocked, replenished, and used in production

The flexibility of the system allows you to specify a wide range of strategies. Individual components of the BOM can be subjected to particular planning strategies.

Each material master record specifies a strategy group that signifies the planning strategies allowed for that material. Up to seven strategies can be allowed for each material. Each strategy nominates one or more requirements types, such as the requirements types for demand management and for sales and distribution.

A requirements type is a text that represents the planning strategy. The requirements type text includes a key that nominates a requirements class. The requirements class contains all the control parameters required for demand management and for sales and distribution. The requirements type master record can also contain an explanatory text.

R/3 provides the following standard planning strategies:

- Make-to-stock production
- Production by lot size for sales and stock orders
- Planning with final assembly

- Planning without final assembly
- Planning with planning material
- Planning at assembly level
- Planning at phantom assembly level
- Make-to-order production
- Make-to-order production with configuration
- Make-to-order production for material variants (3.0C: stockable types)
- Planning material variants (3.0C: stockable types) without final assembly
- Planning material variants using planning materials
- Characteristics planning
- Planning variants

When a planning strategy is applied, the result is expressed in the form of a demand program of planned independent requirement quantities and dates. These quantities of materials are then consumed according to a logical consumption strategy.

Assigning Consumption Strategies and Logic

The role of a consumption strategy is to specify how planned independent requirement quantities and dates shall be compared with actual customer requirements. During customizing, every planning strategy is assigned a consumption procedure which is made up of a combination of a requirements type from demand management with a requirements type from sales order management.

Consumption logic decrees how a customer requirement shall "consume" a planned independent requirement quantity. There are two consumption modes: backward consumption and forward consumption. The direction refers to whether a customer requirement shall consume the planned independent requirement quantity that comes before or after it in a date-sorted list as follows:

- Backward consumption—the system looks for the planned independent requirement quantity that lies directly before the sales order.
- Forward consumption—the system looks for the planned independent requirement quantity that lies directly after the sales order.

The planned independent requirement that lies directly before the customer's requirement may not cover the customer's requirement, in which case the system looks for the next closest planned independent requirement either in the future or the past.

The future and the past in this context are defined in terms of consumption periods that limit intervals within which the customer requirements are allowed to consume planned independent requirements. If you fail to define consumption periods, the default period is the current day.

This process of allocating customer requirements to planned independent requirements is carried out dynamically. During the rescheduling of sales orders or planning, the allocation is automatically deleted and redefined.

Part
IV
Ch
13

Another way of assigning the strategy group is to define it in the MRP group, which is then assigned to the material master record.

If the strategy group contains more than one planning strategy, the system proposes the requirements type of the main strategy. You can overwrite this proposal using one of the requirements types from the alternative strategies.

Using Functions in Demand Management

A planned independent requirement identified in demand management contains one date and one planned quantity. Alternatively it contains a set of planned independent requirements schedule lines that record that one planned quantity has been split between particular dates within a specific interval.

Functions are available to apply the following methods for creating planned independent requirements:

- Manually enter quantities and dates.
- Automatically copy the material forecast.
- Automatically copy the results of sales and operations planning.
- Automatically copy the original plan.
- Automatically copy the planned independent requirements of another material.
- Automatically copy another planned independent requirements version of the same material.

Maintaining Demand Program Change Histories

You will be likely to make several changes to a demand program during its lifetime. A standard change history will be maintained automatically if you activate the *History* indicator field in the initial screen when creating planned independent requirements.

The following sequence will display the change history for one or more schedule lines:

1. Select the schedule line for which you want to see the changes.
2. Select Goto→Sched.line history.

The basic data of the selected schedule line appears in the header of the display screen. The lower part shows the date, the old and the new quantity, the name of the person who made the changes, and the date of the change.

The following sequence will display the complete change history for the planned independent requirements item:

1. Select the item.
2. Select Goto→Item history.

If you mark an item and select Display values, you will see the values of the planned independent requirements with respect to the price maintained in the material master record.

The upper half of the screen displays the basic data of the selected material and the total value of the planned independent requirement item. The lower part of the screen displays the corresponding period value for every schedule line. The period value is the price maintained for the material in the accounting screen of the material master multiplied by the quantity in the schedule line.

To display the cumulated values select Edit→Change period. Then choose the period in which you are interested.

The display settings made in customizing can be overruled by the user-specific settings in the requirements parameters.

Long-Term Planning

A long-term production plan typically extends to annual planning or a rolling quarterly plan. The long-term plan depends on information on the future stock and requirements situation. Can the capacities available meet the requirements identified from the sales plan? Will it be necessary to bring on other work centers or additional machinery to cope with bottlenecks?

The long-term plan is also used by the purchasing department to estimate future orders, from which they can negotiate delivery schedules and contracts with vendors.

In order to build a useful long-term plan, various versions of the master plan are created and tested in simulation. In simulated planning runs and in capacity planning, the system calculates the capacity requirements, the activity category requirements of the cost centers, and the purchased parts requirements.

Valid information for the long-term plan is available in the BOMs, routings, and work centers used by the production facilities. The demand program can be accepted or replaced by the most acceptable simulated program.

Releasing the Planning Scenario

A planning scenario is a specification of the settings to be used for a long-term plan, including the following characteristics:

- Short, medium, or long-term period.
- Plants in which long-term planning is to be carried out.
- Versions of the demand program to be simulated in long-term planning—already existing operative versions, or versions created specially for long-term planning.
- Version of the available capacity to be used in long-term planning.
- Whether firmed receipts (production orders, purchase orders) are included in long-term planning. If so, any firmed receipts that were already planned in the short-term period are included in the net requirements calculation.
- Whether dependent requirements are also created for materials planned using one of the consumption-based planning procedures as used for bulk material or for materials planned using KANBAN techniques.

A planning scenario is not processed until you release it for long-term planning. Upon release, the planning scenario is used to build a planning file in the background for all materials and plants as specified. This long-term planning file has no effect on the operative planning activities and the operative planning file. You can generate various long-term planning files for comparison purposes if you have created the necessary planning scenarios.

However, the long-term planning file does include all the materials that appear in the operative planning file.

The procedure is to select and adjust if necessary the most promising simulated planning result and then activate the independent requirements version in the chosen planning scenario. Once you have activated this version, it is valid for operative planning.

Performing MRP for Long-Term Planning

MRP is carried out per plant, including any storage locations that were planned separately or excluded from the planning run.

MRP for long-term planning creates only planned orders, using the order types designated for internal and external procurement. Planning proceeds down to the lowest level, using net change planning and regenerative planning. Purchase requisitions or delivery schedules cannot be created in long-term planning.

Once you have released a planning scenario, the planning file is set up automatically. Every change relevant to MRP then triggers an entry in the planning file as in operative planning.

Linking to the Purchasing Information System

A special report is available to transfer the data for external procurement to the purchasing information system. This system offers graphical presentation and manipulation of a wide range of standard analysis procedures for evaluating materials, material groups, and vendors.

Linking to Inventory Controlling

If the system has access to existing requirements and planned future receipts, it can calculate future stock levels.

The calculations from long-term planning concerning the stock and requirements situation can be transferred to inventory controlling. Here it can be evaluated using the standard analysis functions.

Evaluating Long-Term Planning

Long-term planning generates the following results:

- Simulative planned orders at finished product level for the long-term planning version of the demand program
- Simulative dependent requirements and receipts for the components
- Simulative capacity requirements for materials that are produced in-house

- Separate MRP lists for long-term planning
- The stock/requirements list
- The planning situation displayed in a user-specific layout
- Comparisons of long-term planning with the operative planning for all standard evaluations
- Comparison of long-term planning with the operative planning for a particular material per planning scenario

Limiting the Scope of Long-Term Planning

The following controls are available to restrict the scope and hence the processing demands of a long-term planning run:

- Exclude materials using the material status.
- Exclude materials for individual BOMs.
- Exclude capacities in the work center from capacity planning checks.

Linking to Cost Center Accounting

Activity requirements, calculated in long-term planning, are transferred to cost center accounting as planned figures. These figures are transferred by a separate report program executed after the long-term planning run. The system calculates the production costs for each cost center and for each product.

Using Computer Aided Production Planning

Computer aided production planning (PP-BD-CAP) is a component that uses the computer aided process planning (CAPP) functionality to derive standard values for work scheduling. Tables and formulas are provided in the work center records that can be used to calculate the standard values for a routing.

Standard values and quantities are used in the formulas that are consulted as follows:

- In scheduling—to determine the dates for executing the operations
- In capacity planning—to determine the capacity requirements for executing operations in relation to the capacities available
- In costing—to calculate the costs incurred when a material is produced in-house

The costing results are used in the following activities:

- Pricing and developing pricing policy
- Evaluation
- Cost control
- Profitability analysis

Planning Sales and Operations

The sales and operations planning (PP-SOP) component is used to forecast and plan sales and the production operations needed to meet the planned targets. SOP can also be used to set up targets for any link in the supply chain. You can carry out rough-cut planning to arrive at a reasonable prediction of the amounts of resources and the capacities you will need at the various work centers included in the plan.

The data for these plans can be developed from historical records, or you can begin from the existing production data. Alternatively, you can work on estimated future production and create a plan to achieve it.

The PP-SOP component can produce plans that address each level of a complex planning hierarchy through the supply chains to the production resources, including staff. The component can also produce detailed plans based on the targets of finished products.

You can use the bottom-up method to find out what is needed to produce your targets; or you can see what could be produced given your existing or planned financial, plant, and energy resources—the top-down method.

The system can be configured to accept target key figures at any organizational level. These targets will then be distributed automatically and consistently to all the other organizational levels up and down the hierarchy.

Standard Sales and Operations Planning is delivered as a preconfigured procedure that is customized only so as to fit your company. Standard planning is based on product group hierarchies and is always carried out level by level.

Flexible SOP can be freely configured. For example any hierarchies containing any chosen organizational levels can be targeted by a single plan. Thus you could develop a plan for a particular sales organization, distribution channel, material, and plant.

In the flexible planning option, you are able to specify the content and layout of the planning screens to suit your users. If your planning hierarchies stretch across a distributed environment, your customizing must also configure application link enabling (ALE).

The PP-SOP component comprises four subcomponents, all of which are essential for standard sales and operation planning:

- Basic data (PP-SOP-BD)—contains the administrative and technical functions.
- Sales plan (PP-SOP-SP)—allows you to set sales targets for product groups or finished products and submits planned sales quantities to demand management.
- Production plan (PP-SOP-PP)—allows you to set the production quantities required to meet your sales targets and submits planned production quantities to demand management.
- Distribution requirements planning (PP-SOP-DRP)—allows you to optimize inventory replenishment in a network of warehouses.

Master Planning the Production Quantities

The role of the master planning (PP-MP) component is to define the production quantities for a stated interval. Four subcomponents are needed for this kind of master planning:

- Material forecast (PP-MP-MFC)—uses known rates of consumption to forecast what should be available for production. The forecast values are submitted to demand management or to consumption-based material requirements planning components, where they can be used to calculate the reorder point and the safety stock levels automatically.

- Demand management (PP-MP-DEM)—defines future requirement quantities and dates for finished products and the important assemblies, including items procured elsewhere. The demand program can be created automatically from preceding sales planning, SOP, and material forecasts. A demand program can also be created under manual control.

- Master production scheduling (PP-MP-MPS)—allows you to mark certain parts or products as master schedule items for special attention because they take up critical resources or dominate profits. Includes functions for separate planning, planning time fence and fixing logic, interactive planning, and a special evaluation layout for master schedule items.

- Long-term planning or simulation (PP-MP-LTP)—uses current operations data to anticipate the detailed consequences of the master plan. The module calculates capacity requirements, activity requirements for the cost centers, and the number of purchased parts required.

The long-term planning functions allow you to generate both annual plans and a rolling quarterly plan that previews the future stock and requirements. The system can automatically use future requirements for materials to suggest production details such as reorder point materials, bulk material, or KANBAN materials.

The purchasing departments will also use long-term planning results when negotiating delivery schedules and contracts with vendors.

Capacity Planning

The capacity planning (PP-CRP) component (formerly known as capacity requirements planning), has the role of determining available capacities in relation to the capacity requirements, and, if necessary, leveling the assignments between work centers.

Capacity planning differentiates between the following time frames:

- Long-term rough-cut planning
- Medium-term planning
- Short-term detailed planning

The following applications can use the capacity planning functions:

- Sales and distribution (SD)
- Production planning and control (PP)
- Plant maintenance (PM)

Part

IV

Ch

13

- Project system (PS)
- Personnel planning and development (PD)

The CRP component comprises the following subcomponents:

- Scheduling (PP-CRP-SCH)—uses standard times from task lists and may operate lead-time scheduling disregarding capacity loads and finite scheduling which does take account of capacity loads. Used with production orders, for example.
- Capacity loads (PP-CRP-LD)—calculate as a percentage the ratio between requirement and availability of each capacity.
- Capacity Evaluations (PP-CRP-ALY)—prepare the data for capacity leveling by comparing available and required capacities.
- Capacity Leveling (PP-CRP-LVL)—distribute the capacity underloads and overloads to work centers. Also suggests the optimum commitment of machines and production lines and selects appropriate resources.

The ALY and LVL subcomponents are not needed if capacity leveling is a manual task that uses the capacity load outputs of the LD function.

Ensuring that Materials Are Available by MRP

The material requirements planning (PP-MRP) component has to guarantee material availability for sales and distribution and for internal purposes. In particular, stocks have to be monitored and replenished by timely purchasing and production, preferably by automatically creating order proposals for purchasing and production.

Materials planning can be seen from two aspects: the amounts of materials and other resources consumed over recent similar periods, and the planned production levels for the future. The module is able to support planning across more than one production or storage plant.

Overall, materials planning entails finding optimum levels for two interacting factors:

- Level of service to the internal or external customers
- Profitability, by minimizing costs and capital lockup

MRP can take place for all the relevant materials that are planned for a particular plant—*total planning*—or for a single material or product group—*single-item planning*.

The MRP component uses the following subcomponents:

- Basic data (PP-MRP-BD—maintains the data used in MRP controlling, lot-sizing, and special procurement types
- Planning execution (PP-MRP-PR)—executes MRP for all materials or assemblies whose requirement or stock situation has changed since the last MRP run
- Procurement proposal (PP-MRP-PP)—takes manual entries from the MRP controller or the quantities and dates suggested automatically by the MRP component and compiles proposals for in-house (internal) procurement and external procurement
- Planning evaluation (PP-MRP-PE)—provides checks on the planning results

Checks on the MRP results are provided by the PE subcomponent in the following formats:

- MRP list
- Current stock/requirements list
- Comparison of the MRP list and the stock/requirements list
- Planning situation, in a format that can be configured to provide the most useful evaluation
- Planning result, also configurable
- Comparison of the planning situation and the planning result
- Pegged requirements that are limited by requirements defined higher up the BOM
- Order report on relevant orders still open

Defining Basic Data for Production in the PP-BD Component

The objects of interest to production planning are obviously the products and the methods by which they are produced and managed. The SAP R/3 system is designed for medium-sized and large organizations. The same products and production processes might appear in different divisions, so the organizational structure must be defined and then referenced in the basic data records for production and production planning.

Assigning Data to Organizational Units

The SAP R/3 general organizational units relevant to production planning are taken from the SAP R/3 Enterprise Data Model:

- *Author Instance* is the highest level in R/3 and is identified by code sysid. It is at this level that some data is managed because it can be set up for all lower levels. Currencies and units of measure are examples.

- *Client* is the second highest level. Clients 000, 001, and 066 are updated only by SAP. A copy of 000 is created as client 100, and this may be customized. As the system is developed, further client numbers may be used so as to distinguish the data generated by successive developmental implementations. Client 450 is reserved for use as a test environment. Client 800 is reserved to signify the production environment upon which no developmental work may take place and which will contain no experimental or test data.

  The data of one client may not interact with another client. There is often a training client in addition to the client 800 that represents your group or corporate identity and under which the SAP system runs normal business. Some data is managed at the client level because everyone in the corporate group of companies will want to refer to exactly the same information and be certain that it has been maintained as up to date and correct. Vendor addresses would be an example of data managed at the client level.

- *Company Code* signifies a legal unit under the client that produces its own financial documents, including the balance sheet and the profit-and-loss statement, and may well continuously reconcile them.

■ *Plant* is an organizational unit that is seen as central to the production planning concept. A plant can be a production site or a group of storage locations that share materials. Plant is the unit for which MRP prepares plans and maintains the inventory. It is the focus of materials management (MM). Each plant will have been given planning and control elements such as material, inventory, operations, work centers, and so on.

Planning can take place across plants. For example, products manufactured in different plants can be combined for planning purposes into a product group. Manufacturing can also take place and be controlled on a cross-plant basis.

The stocks held in individual storage locations within a plant can also be managed separately with respect to inventory and planned using MRP.

You may have defined other organizational units to suit your own planning and production needs. These user-defined organizational units can be used to focus materials requirements planning:

■ *Planning Plant* is the one plant chosen as the central unit when you are engaging in cross-plant material requirements planning.

■ *Work Center* is the central planning element to use when you are applying shop floor control and capacity planning. The system will allow you to build work center hierarchies and use them for MRP.

■ *Planner Group* is a definition of people who are chosen, not by name necessarily, but by their personnel group, which is assigned by the human resources functions. This way, the members of a planning group can be selected from those who are available on the day they are needed and who have the necessary experience and qualifications. You can define other planning groups. Three planner groups are commonly assigned materials, resources, and production tools.

■ *MRP Controller Group* is an identification for those who are experienced at materials requirements planning.

■ *Work Scheduler Group* is an identification of those with experience of the scheduling of work resources including people.

■ *Shop Floor Controller Group* is an identification of those with experience in the detailed management of shop floor personnel and the places where they work.

Using the Planning Table for Sales and Operations Planning

Sales and operations planning (SOP) is a generic planning and forecasting tool that allows you to compare your operational capacities with the market demand. The aim is to anticipate and prepare for the demand rather than react to it when it occurs.

SOP can be used for high-level or detail-level planning of any logistical data. This tool is flexible because it works with user-defined planning hierarchies that control how the data is collated and presented.

Aggregate planning through the SOP planning table supports long- and medium-term planning of sales, production, purchasing, inventory management, and so on. Previous planning and operational data can be accessed, and there is a wide range of analytical and simulation facilities.

The sales and operations planning application component belongs to the Logistics Information System. This allows it to plan in the Sales Information System, the Purchasing Information System, Inventory Controlling, and any other logistics information systems.

Planning with Information Structures

An information structure is a statistics file containing planned or historical operational data. The format is common throughout the logistics information systems. The following kinds of information are held in an information structure:

- Characteristics—attributes of the data that can be used to form aggregates, such as plant of origin
- Key figures—important ratios and calculations, such as Sales per employee
- Period unit—standard unit of time, such as week

The following sequence suggests the method of using a planning table:

1. Choose the planning method.
2. Create the master data framework for the planning and forecasting activities.
3. Create the planning data that relates to your master data.

The standard planning table layout is based on the spreadsheet format, and it can be freely customized and saved to create a user version. Mass processing functions automate the planning of large volumes of data.

Finalized planning data is passed through the following functions in turn;

1. Demand management
2. Master production scheduling
3. Material requirements planning
4. Cost center accounting
5. Application link enabling (ALE) linkages to the different operating units

Standard SOP offers planning limited to the product group hierarchy, with predefined key figures and a set planning table layout. Standard information structure S076 is mandatory.

Flexible SOP accepts any information structure so that you can plan any combination of organizational units and any key figures. You can define a planning type, which will control the display of a customized planning table layout.

The following sequences will access SOP:

1. Select Logistics→Production→Standard SOP.
2. Select Logistics→Logistics controlling→Flexible planning.

Part

IV

Ch

13

Differentiating Planning Methods in SOP

Three planning methods are available:

- Consistent planning—data stored at the most detailed level, all changes promulgated throughout the structure by automatic aggregation and disaggregation
- Level-by-level planning—changes confined to levels, but top-down and bottom-up planning possible using proportional factors
- Delta planning—changes aggregated to higher levels but not disaggregated to lower

Table 13.1 Summary of SOP Planning Methods

	Consistent	Level-by-level	Delta
Automatic aggregation	Yes	No	Yes
Automatic disaggregation based on factors saved in database; automatic time-dependent	Yes	No	No
Disaggregation based on previous planning data	Yes	No	No
Create planning hierarchy	Yes	Yes	No (not necessary)
Planning types/macros	Yes	Yes	Yes
Set opening stock automatically in background	Yes	Yes	No
Forecast	Yes	Yes	Yes (but not possible to save different forecast versions)
Events	Yes	Yes	No
Resource leveling	Yes	Yes	No
Background processing	Yes	Yes	No
Fix key figure values in the planning table	Yes	No	No
Long texts for versions and periods in the planning table	Yes	Yes	No
Standard analysis for info structure	Yes	No	No
Transfer to Demand Management	Yes	Yes	No

Running the Master Data Generator in Flexible Planning

The Master Data Generator creates planning objects for an information structure on the basis of existing or planned data. These objects form a planning hierarchy.

The following sequence will run the Master Data Generator in flexible planning:

1. Master data→Generate master data.

2. If necessary, change the results manually by selecting Planning hierarchy→Change.

If you run the generator with an active *Simulation* indicator, the system will report the number of records that would be generated. You may decide to restrict the items in the planning structure.

Planning with Mass Characteristics

Mass characteristics is the name of a virtual container to which you can assign the less important materials for planning. You have to create a product group containing all these materials and transfer to it the planning data that has been generated for the mass characteristics container. You can then transfer the product group planning data to demand management.

You can add mass characteristics directly to the information structure by selecting Master data→Mass characteristics→Create.

Using Planning Types and Macros in the Planning Table

A planning type is a master record that sets up a customized view on the planning table. Thus the sales planner would probably use a different planning type than the production planner. Planning types provide a flexible tool for the planning, storage, and analysis of any logistics data.

A planning type has to be based on a standard information structure or on one defined by the user. You can have many planning types that act as templates or filters on the same information structure because the planning data is saved in the information structure, not in the planning type.

A line in a planning type master record contains one of the following:

- Planned key figure
- Actual key figure from the current year
- Actual key figure from the previous year
- Cumulative events for a key figure
- Proportional events for a key figure
- Corrected key figure as the result of the events
- User exit data
- Freely defined text or numbers

Only the planned and actual key figures are saved in the information structure. The information on the other lines is calculated or read from the planning type record into the planning table at runtime.

The function of a line in a planning type is described by the text or numbers from one of the following sources:

- A key figure from the information structure is quoted as a reference.
- The description of the line is supplied by the user.
- The line description is the text of the currently planned characteristic.

A planning type defines a planning horizon. You enter the number of historical periods and future periods to be shown in the planning table. You can arrange for historical periods to be updated or have them locked.

Using Self-Defined Macros

A macro is a sequence of instructions for performing mathematical operations. You execute a macro with a single keystroke or mouse-click. SOP macros are used to perform operations that involve several lines in a planning type.

Therefore a planning type can act as a macro. The following standard planning types are executed automatically when supporting the planning table in standard SOP:

- SOPKAPA—used for the planning of individual product groups
- SOPKAPAM—used for the planning of individual materials
- SOPDIS—used for the dual-level planning of product group hierarchies

Using Events in SOP

One of the problems with an automatic forecast based on historical data is that is does not, and cannot, predict the unexpected—unless, of course, you tell the system that an unusual event is on its way.

SOP can handle the unexpected if you record some events. What counts as an event could be something like:

- A change in price such as a promotion
- A special deal with a major customer (do you have any minor customers?)
- A special deal with a vendor
- Management overrides for whatever reason
- Delivery problems of a competitor
- Market intelligence

You could perhaps sketch a sales curve that took cognizance of these untypical events. Your curve might well be a better guess at the future than a fabrication by R/3 based on historical data. However R/3 has a way of dealing with events. You create an event and store it as an event master record.

SOP can use events you have created as follows:

1. Assign the event to a planning type.
2. View the impact of the event in the planning table.
3. You, the master planner, decide whether the planning table needs further fine-tuning.

When it comes to being specific about an event, you have to decide whether it will affect the data as a cumulative event in which a whole number or set of numbers will be added to or subtracted from specified key figures. Alternatively, you may decide that it would be better to model the disturbing event by making a percentage adjustment, plus or minus, to one or more key figures.

Once you have created an event and set out its arithmetic, you can make it happen by controlling its *Event* status. An inactive event has no influence on planning. But you can change its status to active at any time by editing the list of assignments.

Events do not last forever. You can define how long. If you specify the period in terms of the posting period, then you must also indicate which fiscal year variant you have in mind. When you are defining an event, a screen is offered on which you can enter the cumulative or proportional values for as many time periods as you think will be affected by the event.

You have to link an event with a specific information structure. The second definition screen requires you to specify the characteristic value(s), the key figure(s), and the planning version(s) of the information structure that you expect to be affected by the event. The planning version you enter must already exist in the system, and it cannot be a delta planning version.

Naturally you have to enter the starting date for your event. If you do not, the system will default to the current date. You can enter several dates, in which case the system will assume that the event is going to influence all the planning versions that are valid on these various dates.

If you want to see the event in the planning table, your planning type must include lines for the event that will display the values for the key figure around which the event is designed. These event lines represent cumulative events, proportional events, and the corrected key figure values. If the event creates a corrected key figure that you wish to have saved on the database, you have to write a macro that copies the corrected line into the line of a key figure that is going to be saved.

The following sequence will create an event in SOP:

1. From flexible planning or standard SOP, select Tools→Event→Create.
2. Either enter an event number in the field of that name or leave the field blank to receive a system-assigned event number.
3. Select Enter.
4. Enter a description.
5. Define the event type and event status.
6. Specify the length of an event period.
7. Choose Continue.

8. Enter values for the event in the desired periods.

9. Choose Goto→Assignment.

10. Enter the name of the information structure to which you want to assign the event.

11. Choose Continue.

12. Specify the characteristic value(s) that will be affected by the event.

13. Select the key figure that will be affected by the event.

14. Select the version(s) of the information structure to which you want the event to apply.

15. For each version that you select, enter next to it an assignment date. Entry of a description is optional.

16. If you want to create another assignment, choose Event→Flag assignment and then choose Goto→Other info structure.

17. Enter the same or a different information structure.

18. To save the event master record, choose Event→Save.

Navigating the Planning Table

The sales and operations planning table comprises two areas:

- Header area—shows which master data you are planning, the planning version, and whether active.

- Input matrix—rows and columns depicting the key figures and their units of measurement. The key figure view can be selected to show the characteristic values.

The columns represent the time buckets for the time periods displayed in the column headers. You can use the scroll buttons to inspect the planning table.

If you use the split planning screen, the aggregate data will appear in the top half and detailed data in the bottom half. This arrangement is used when planning has more than one level.

The standard planning table for SOP comprises six lines containing the following key figures:

- Sales—plan sales quantities here

- Production—plan production quantities here

- Stock level—derived by the system from your sales and production figures

- Target stock level—can be controlled by entering the target stock level strategy key alongside the values

- Days' supply—cannot be edited

- Target days' supply—can be controlled by entering the target days' supply strategy key alongside the values

The following sequence will access the planning table in standard SOP:

1. Choose Planning→For product group Create/Change/Display, **or**

2. Choose Planning→For material Create/Change/Display.

2. Enter the product group or material that you want to plan, together with its plant.

3. If you are in Change or Display mode, use the Active version or Inactive version pushbuttons to select an active version or one of the inactive versions.

4. Choose Enter.

5. If you are in Create or Change mode, maintain your data.

6. Save your data.

Planning in Finer Detail

The storage periodicity defined in customizing for the standard SOP information structure (S076) is the posting period. The start of the planning horizon and the number of periods open to planning are defined in the planning type.

Depending on customizing you may be able to change the period unit of either the entire planning horizon or a preselected part of it provided you are working with standard SOP or flexible planning because these use the level-by-level planning method.

You can select a number of columns of the planning table for further processing in detail, such as the splitting of periods.

Standard SOP offers the following display format controls:

- Goto→Owner, for an aggregate view
- Goto→Member, for a detailed view
- Goto→Next member
- Goto→Previous member

Flexible planning offers the following display format controls:

- Goto→Total—If the planning method is *Consistent planning*, you see the total key figure values for all selected characteristic value combinations. If the planning method is *Level-by-level planning*, you see the total key figure values at owner level. If the planning method is *Delta planning*, you see the total key figure values at the level above the detailed level.
- Goto→Details.
- Goto→Next detail.
- Goto→Previous detail.
- Mark a key figure and select Goto→Key figure format.

Calculating Row Totals in the Planning Table

Six procedures are available to display the sum of a key figure's values on a chosen line of the planning table:

1. To calculate the sum of a key figure's values in the visible section of the planning horizon, choose Extras→Line totals→Current columns.

2. To calculate the sum of a key figure's values throughout the planning horizon, choose Extras→Line totals→All columns.

3. To calculate the sum of a key figure's values in a selected section of the planning horizon, choose Extras→Line totals→Selected periods.

4. To calculate the sum of a key figure's values in all historical periods (not ready for input), choose Extras→Line totals→Historical periods.

5. To calculate the sum of a key figure's values in all future periods, choose Extras→Line totals→Future periods.

6. To hide the line totals, choose Extras→Line totals→Hide.

Using Standard SOP Macros in Planning Table Maintenance

Macros are processing sequences that can be rapidly activated. Standard SOP provides pre-defined macros for the following functional sequences used in dual-level planning of product groups and materials in the split-screen planning table:

■ Aggregate production—from the detailed information level to the aggregated production display line and overwrite the existing production quantities.

■ Aggregate sales—from the detailed information level to the aggregated sales line and overwrite the existing sales quantities.

■ Disaggregate production—distribute the aggregate production data to the production lines of the product group members using the proportional factors maintained in the product group master record. Overwrite existing production quantities at the detailed level.

■ Disaggregate sales—distribute the aggregate sales data to the sales lines of the product group members using the proportional factors maintained in the product group master record. Overwrite existing sales quantities at the detailed level.

■ Disaggregate target days' supply—copy the aggregate target days' supply to the target days' supply lines of the product group members. Overwrite existing target days' supplies at the detailed level.

■ Disaggregate target stock level—distribute the aggregate target stock level to the target stock level lines of the product group members, using the proportional factors maintained in the product group master record. Overwrite existing target stock levels at the detailed level.

■ Production synchronous to sales—bring the production quantities at the detailed information level into accord with the sales quantities maintained at that level. Production quantities at the aggregated information level are not affected.

The following sequence will execute a macro in the planning table:

1. Choose Edit→Macro.

2. Select a macro.

3. Choose Continue.

Interacting with Graphics in the Planning Table

Planning table data can be automatically presented in graphical form using characteristic graphics and key figure graphics. Each graphic is available as either a business graphic in two- or three-dimensional formats or as a statistics graphic that gives an overall view of the entire planning horizon.

All the graphics can be marked and then used interactively.

Creating and Modifying Sales Plans in Standard SOP

The following methods are available for working with sales plans in standard SOP:

- Manual data entry
- Arithmetic distribution functions
- Copying data from the sales information system (SIS)
- Copying data from controlling-profitability analysis (CO-PA)
- Forecasting sales quantities on the basis of past usage
- Transferring product group proportions
- Interactive graphics

SOP is part of the logistics information system (LIS). This allows SOP to call upon existing information structures, planning versions, and key figures in order to generate a copy. If necessary, a frequently used combination of these structures can be specified in your user-defined values records. The information structure selected from SIS must include material as one of its characteristics.

The values of any quantity key figures can be copied—for example, planned order quantities, planned invoiced quantities, or planned delivery quantities.

The following sequence will copy data from the sales information system in standard SOP:

1. Choose Edit→Create sales plan→Transfer plan from SIS.
2. Specify the name of the information structure in which the planning data was created, the number of the desired planning version, and the start and finish dates of the planning horizon for which you want to copy the data.
3. To open the Key Figure dialog box, choose Enter.
4. Select one of the quantity key figures in the list.
5. Choose Enter.

The key figure values from the SIS now appear in the sales line of the planning table.

Using the Automatic Forecast Functions in the Planning Table

If your system analyzes a series of consumption values it may be possible to match the resulting pattern with one of the following forecast models:

- Constant consumption flow
- Trend
- Seasonal—periodically recurring peak or low values which differ significantly from a stable mean value
- Seasonal trend
- Copy actual data—no forecast is attempted

A selection of smoothing parameters are open to user modification to improve the fit of a forecast model with the available data.

The following possibilities exist for deciding which forecast model to adopt:

- Manual model selection—following analysis of historical data
- Automatic model selection
- Manual model selection with the system also testing for a pattern

Forecast profiles are records that store the profile strategy and the settings for forecasting so that you can apply more than one profile to the same key figure.

Resource Leveling in SOP

The aim of resource leveling is to make best use of the available resources by planning the resource load for work center groups or product families. The focal points are usually the superior work center in the hierarchy, perhaps the root, a bottleneck work center, or a product grouping.

Resource leveling depends on being able to consult a PP task list, such as a routing, a rate routing, or a rough-cut planning profile for the material, product group, or characteristic value combination whose resources you intend to plan.

Standard SOP allows resource leveling for the production quantities of a product group or material in a single-level planning screen. The following resources are recorded in a rough-cut planning profile:

- Work center capacities—also available from a routing or rate routing
- Materials
- Production resources/tools
- Costs

The system generates resource requirements from the quantities that have been entered in the production line of the standard planning table.

Planning and Leveling Work Center Capacities

The SOP split screen uses the lower section to display the available capacity, the capacity requirements, and the capacity load. These values are displayed for each work center used in production and for each capacity category.

You can enter and change production quantities or key figure values in the upper section of the split screen. Available capacity is compared to capacity requirements on a period-by-period basis.

Capacity load is the ratio of required capacity to available capacity at a particular work center. SOP consults the capacity requirements of all materials, product groups, or characteristic value combinations for the same capacities. The capacity requirements and capacity load lines report total requirements for a particular capacity.

The system creates an internal SOP order to record the production requirements in each period in the planning table. Capacity requirements are saved in the planned information structure when you save the planning version.

The resource load for materials, production resources/tools, or costs is displayed in the form of a standard analysis based on the information structures S093 for materials and PRTs and S092 for costs. Any item can be subjected to the drill-down function to reveal further levels of detail.

You can save the results of a standard resource analysis as a version of the corresponding information structure.

Rough-cut planning profiles are used in resource leveling to plan the requirements of one or more resource hierarchies within a plant in the medium and long term, that is, work days rather than hours or minutes. The results are shown as a planned resources table along a time line.

Transferring SOP Data to Demand Management

Data generated by SOP can be transferred to demand management for further processing. A transfer profile has the task of specifying one of the following transfer strategies:

- Transfer the planning data of a material directly from the sales plan created in the standard planning table.
- Transfer the planning data of a material from the sales plan, created in the standard planning table, as a proportion of the product group of which it is a member.
- Transfer the planning data of a material directly from the production plan created in the standard planning table.
- Transfer the planning data of a material from the production plan, created in the standard planning table, as a proportion of the product group of which it is a member.
- Transfer the planning data of a material from either a planned information structure or a planning type based on an information structure.

Mass processing in the background transfers the SOP data up to the planning horizon specified. You have to create a planning activity in order to perform mass processing for any of the following tasks:

- Forecasting
- Copying key figures from one information structure to another
- Executing macros
- Transferring data to demand management

Part
IV

Ch
13

The only occasions when you do not need a planning activity is when you intend a high-level copy with distribution subsequently or when consistent planning is nominated for both the source and the target information structures.

An activity can include several actions that are each performed completely in the sequence determined by their numbers. Planning activities can be created online or during customizing.

Planning for Preliminary Costing

The system automatically calculates the planned order costs when you create a production order and after each subsequent change of data in the order. These planned costs are allocated to primary and secondary cost elements.

The following types of costs are examples of primary cost elements:

- Material costs
- Costs for external procurement or external processing

This type of primary cost appears in the production order in the form of material issues or purchases of externally processed parts.

The following costs are examples of secondary cost elements:

- Production costs
- Material overhead costs
- Production overhead costs

These secondary costs are allocated to the order by means of internal cost allocations.

Understanding Cost Segments

Each fiscal year is managed using cost segments that cumulate the different types of cost per financial accounting period. When you create a production order, the system consults the latest start date of the operation or the requirement date of the material. This date is used to assign the planned costs of the production order to a particular period of the fiscal year. For accounting purposes, the planned costs of an order are said to be incurred in this fiscal period.

In customizing, you can arrange to use either the latest start date of the operation or the requirement date of the processed material as the key date for preliminary costing.

Recording Planned and Actual Cost Data

Cost segments collate both planned costs and actual costs. You can therefore compare planned with actual costs at any stage of order processing.

The materials needed for an order are identified as stock and nonstock components. Costs are planned for both. Actual costs become available when material issues or completion confirmations are posted for the order. If a material component is procured externally, the actual costs are updated when the goods receipt is posted.

Each material component in an order is assigned a costing relevancy indicator if it is fully relevant to costing. The indicator will appear in the Component Overview screen of the production order.

The system can automatically allocate a material component to the relevant cost element because it has access to the MM consumption account assignment, which is part of the standard chart of accounts. The following are examples of standard consumption accounts:

- 400000—Consumption raw materials
- 410000—Consumption trading goods
- 890000—Change in stock of unfinished products

For a material component of a production order that is manufactured in-house, the system calculates the planned costs by using the valuation variant and price stored in the material master record.

At the customizing stage, a costing variant is defined per order type and plant. The costing variant identifies a valuation variant that is to be used for that order type processed in that plant.

The choice of valuation variant determines which price from the material master record is used to calculate the planned costs of a material. Thus you can apply a standard price for the material or calculate the moving average price and use that to calculate the planned costs of the material component of the production order.

For a material component of a production order that is procured externally, the system makes a distinction between stock components and nonstock components. If a material component of a production order is manufactured externally but kept in stock, the planned costs are calculated in the same way as for a material component manufactured in-house.

If an externally manufactured component is not a stock item, it will have to be procured through a purchase requisition. The value of this requisition is used as the planned cost of this component. The value of the purchase requisition is calculated from the valuation price per price unit of the requisitioned material.

Planning Manufacturing Costs

It is customary to divide the activity required to complete a production order into internal and external activities. Planned costs are calculated for each of these.

A costing variant of a valuation variant is identified for each operation or suboperation by reference to the order type and the details of the operation. Each activity at a work center is defined in the accounting records of the cost center to which the work center is assigned. The cost center attributes a value to each unit of each activity.

For costing purposes, a suboperation is treated in the same way as an operation. When planning the costs of production for a production order, the system consults the control key of each operation to determine whether the operation is to be included in the costing. If an operation is marked as relevant for costing, the costing relevancy indicator of each activity in the operation has to be set in the General Data screen.

The costing calculation for an internal activity entails applying a price to a quantity structure for the activity.

At the work center level, each activity is allocated to an activity type. A formula is identified for each activity type so that the standard times for an operation can be converted to quantities of the activity types needed in the operation. Given the amount of each activity type, the system can apply the standard price of each activity and so calculate a cost of each activity and hence the cost of the operation, divided between the various activity types.

Calculating the planned costs for an external processing operation requires the system to consult a cost element maintained for this operation. For example, you may have a purchasing info record number for an externally processed operation. The system will use this info record when calculating the planned costs of an externally processed operation. If there is no appropriate info record, you have to enter a price manually.

The costing variant defined in customizing refers to a valuation variant which in turn specifies the price with which the external activity is to be valuated. This variant can determine whether a price is to be taken from the purchasing info record or from the operation master record. Your company may wish to associate a value with a purchased activity that is not the same as the price paid for it.

A production order can be assigned some overhead costs in the form of surcharges. For example, surcharges can be defined for the cost of electricity and perhaps general storage. These overhead costs are updated in the production order in the fields set out in the costing sheet.

A costing variant is defined in customizing per order type and plant. This costing variant refers to a costing sheet that controls the calculation of overhead surcharges that are to be assigned to the production order. The scope of the costing sheet includes the following:

- Which direct costs shall attract surcharges
- The conditions that will trigger the calculation of an overhead surcharge
- The surcharge percentage for each critical condition
- Which costing object, such as a cost center, is to be reduced under which cost element during actual postings

The costing sheet can refer to an overhead group key. This indicates that the material is a member of a particular overhead group for which specific overhead conditions and calculations have been predefined. The material master record must include an indicator that confirms membership of the overhead group.

Displaying the Costs of a Production Order

The costs of a production order can be displayed according to cost element or itemized according to cost element and origin. You can also call for a cost stratification breakdown.

The following sequence will display the order costs per cost element:

1. Call up the production order.
2. Select Goto→Costs→Analysis.

The following sequence will display the cost itemization broken down into cost elements and their origins, provided these origins have been maintained according to origin in the production order:

1. Call up the production order.
2. Select Goto→Costs→Cost itemization.

Grouping Planned Cost Elements into Cost Components

You may find it helpful to be able to identify the total planned costs in a production order split into cost components that cumulate similar activities.

During customizing, you can define up to forty different cost components per order type. And each cost component can be divided into fixed and variable costs. The following sequence will display a planned cost component split in the production order per cost element:

1. Call up the production order.
2. Select Goto→Costs→Cost comp.structure. ●

CHAPTER 14

Managing Resources for the Process Industries

Production Planning for the Process Industries

Some industries are obliged to manage and document their products in batches because conditions and raw materials may change during a production run to such an extent that the characteristics of different batches may vary considerably. The application module Production Planning for Process Industries (PP-PI) is designed to apply the PP techniques of planning, control, and execution management under the particular circumstances of batch-oriented process manufacturing.

Four examples illustrate the scope of PP-PI:

- Chemicals
- Pharmaceuticals
- Food and beverages
- Process-oriented electronics

The functions that are particularly emphasized in PP-PI are as follows:

- Integrated planning of production, waste disposal, and transportation within a plant
- Integration of plants vertically within the company by continuous information flow management
- Integration of plants horizontally within the company by coordinating planning between production plants, recycling, waste disposal facilities, and production laboratories

The following higher-level planning components are usually integrated with PP-PI:

- Sales and operations planning
- Master planning
- Material requirements planning

PP-PI may need data and services provided by other functional modules, such as the following:

- Material master (logistics—general, basic data) and materials management (MM), for the planning of input materials required and products to be manufactured
- Batches (logistics—general) for batch-oriented manufacturing
- Classification system (cross-application functions), to search or select classified data more easily
- Engineering change management (ECM) (logistics—general), to create a change history as well as to implement a release procedure
- Variant configuration (VC) (logistics—general) enabling you to create different production variants using material master formulas (recipes)
- Quality management (QM), to carry out in-process inspections
- Controlling (CO), to carry out order settlement

Storing Master Data in PP-PI

The basic data component in PP-PI-MD controls the storage of the PI data that is unlikely to change over time and is used in the same form in many places. Some of the master data items in PP-PI correspond to similar items in the discrete manufacturing data stored in Basic Data (PP-BD). This correspondence is illustrated in table 14.1.

Table 14.1 Corresponding Master Data in PP-PI and PP-BD	
PP-PI process manufacturing data	**PP-BD discrete manufacturing data**
Resource	Work center
Master recipe with material list	Routing and bill of material (BOM)

Defining PI Resources

A resource is an object or person involved in the production process with specific allocated capacities. Because the resources identify units of capacity, they are allocated to operations and phases in the master recipe and process order. As a result of collected data or shrewd experience, the assumption is that the resources assigned to the master recipe and process order will be just sufficient to ensure that the product successfully meets the delivery deadline and the quality standards.

The resources component of PP-PI-MD allows you to define resources and then assign them to master recipes and process orders. This resource data is used as the basis for the calculation of costs, capacity requirements, and dates.

The work center is equivalent to a PI resource. However, the PI module will allow you to create a resource network that specifies the sequence in which the various resources are to be used. A work center in discrete manufacturing is not able to represent a network, although it can be an element in a network.

Storing Master Recipes

A master recipe is a scheme that details how a company's various manufacturing processes are to be deployed in order to produce the intended product. The master recipe does not depend on the requirements of any particular production order or customer order. It is intended to define the most efficient way of manufacturing one of the company's standard products.

A master recipe can also be used to specify what has to be done to clean out a production facility and prepare it for another batch of product or to effect a changeover in preparation for using the facility for another product.

Each company will have its own master recipes that may differ because they produce different materials and because they may use different resources, even to manufacture the same product. Indeed, parallel production lines in the same plant may use different master recipes for the same reasons.

The master recipe component in PP-PI-MD enables you to maintain and assign master recipes.

The scope of the data held in a master recipe in the R/3 system is defined in accordance with the following standards authorities:

- The International Standards of the European Batch Forum (EBF)
- The Norms Working Committee for Measuring and Control Techniques in the Chemical Industry (NAMUR)
- Standard S88 of the Instrument Society of America (ISA)

In summary, the master recipe data will normally include the following information:

- The individual steps in the production process defined as operations and phases.
- The sequence in which the steps are to be carried out.
- The planned durations as standard values.
- Other activities associated with the production process such as plant cleaning, defined with standard values.
- The resources required for the individual steps in the production process.
- The ingredients required for production, specific in a material list.
- Instructions for in-process quality inspections, such as the characteristics that are to be monitored and the scheduling of inspections.
- Parameters relevant to the control of the production process defined as process instructions. These parameters are specified during process planning and have to be communicated to process control for each run.

The master recipe is used as the main source of information when creating a process order.

Planning and Executing a Process Order

The process order (PP-PI-POR) function takes the information from the master recipe and creates a process order for a production run or for the output of a service. The process order is the principal document used in the detailed planning and execution of process manufacturing.

The process order becomes the repository of the following kinds of information:

- Planned quantities
- Planned dates
- Planned resources
- Control data for the process order execution
- Rules for the account assignment and settlement of the costs incurred

Specifying the Steps of Process Order Execution

The order execution function in PP-PI-POR manages the central processing steps entailed in process order execution. These steps are as follows:

1. Process planning—process order creation using a master recipe, creating reservations or copying them from planned orders, calculating planned costs, creating capacity requirements for the resources needed

2. Scheduling from the basic order dates, with the option of subsequent automatic or manual rescheduling

3. Release of process order to begin process order execution and process management

4. Creating and downloading control recipes (optional)

5. Printing shop floor documents

6. Carrying out material withdrawals under control of goods issues from the warehouse

7. Recording confirmations

8. Carrying out in-process quality inspections (optional)

9. Posting goods receipts—initiating delivery of the manufactured product to the warehouse by posting a goods receipt

Control recipes have to be created during process order execution if you use process instruction sheets and/or process control systems. In this case, you must also install the corresponding components from the process management component.

If you intend to carry out in-process quality inspections for your orders, you must install the relevant components from quality management.

Closing a Process Order

The order close function in PP-PI-POR manages the following steps that are needed to close a process order after it has been executed:

- Process order settlement
- Archive process orders

To be able to settle a process order, you must install the special functions for process manufacturing within product cost controlling.

Manipulating Process Capacities

The capacity planning component in PP-PI-CAP is able to determine the available capacity and carry out capacity leveling to meet capacity requirements. Three levels of capacity planning are available:

- Long-term planning
- Medium-term planning
- Detailed planning

Part
IV

Ch
14

Integrating PP-PI with Other R/3 Applications

PP-PI is part of the R/3 logistics system, and therefore it can utilize the functions and databases belonging to the related application modules.

Integrated interfaces to the following applications are provided:

- Production planning (PP)
- Sales and distribution (SD)
- Materials management (MM)
- Controlling (CO)
- Project system (PS) and
- Personnel planning and development system (PD)
- Interface with process control systems (PI-PCS)
- Interface with external plant data collection systems (PDC)

The focal concept of the PP-PI application is the recipe. Process orders are generated on the basis of recipes, and the operations of recipes and process orders use specific resources.

An extensive suite of functions is devoted to processing resources. For example, you can specify the following details for each operation and phase of a recipe:

- Which processing units, persons, or other resources are to be used
- How costing, capacity planning, and scheduling are to be carried out

A resource is what you need to carry out an operation within a production run. The resource tells you where the work is to be done.

There are two types of resources: statistical and production. The statistics that summarize data are held in statistical resource records. By contrast, production resources represent the actual objects and activities as they are needed in a production network.

A production network can include any of the following operations that are the consumers of resources:

- Recipes
- Routings
- Reference operation sets
- Maintenance task lists
- Inspection plans
- Work orders
- Activities in networks

Resources are represented by records that contain data used by production processes such as:

- Costing
- Scheduling
- Capacity requirements planning

Relating Resources to Routings and Capacities

A routing is an example of a standard task list because it nominates a series of worksteps. Each of these steps has to take place in a particular location and it will entail the consumption of some kind of resource, perhaps many different kinds.

Therefore the system requires that you specify a resource for every operation or activity. You can store default values for these operations in the resource records so that the values can be transferred into the operation when the resource is allocated.

Capacity is defined as the ability to perform a task. Processing units and people have capacities to do things. These capacities are expressible in terms of the amount of work or product that can be processed in a given time. One resource, a person or a work center, for example, can have several potential capacities, not all of which need be used in a particular manufacturing operation.

Thus a named resource can have different capacity categories associated with it; for example:

- Processing unit capacity
- Labor capacity
- Emissions
- Energy

The resource master records store the resource data that is used by the following business functions:

- Costing—internal labor costs calculated per unit of finished product and allocated to the resource as a cost object. Charge rates are planned for each activity type in product costing. The activity type controls how the standard values are calculated in costing.
- Scheduling—operation dates determined through scheduling formulas maintained in the resource records, using processing times dependent on the resource used.
- Capacity requirements planning—capacity requirements for operations are calculated from the orders using formulas maintained in the resource. Capacity requirements are compared with the available capacity defined in the resource.
- Resource hierarchies—used to summarize available capacity and capacity requirements from subordinate to higher-level resources.

Using Standard Values

The planned values for an operation are specified in the form of standard values. A standard value key can be used to signify which standard values are mandatory for an operation and which are optional.

Costs, processing times, and capacity requirements are calculated from these standard values using formulas. The processing time of an operation is an example of a standard value.

Assigning Resources to Other Objects

A resource assignment is a record that signifies that a resource is linked to another R/3 object, such as the assignment of resource activity types to a cost center.

Additional resource assignments of the following kinds are permitted if you have the human resources (HR) management system installed and configured:

- Assignment of a certain qualification to a resource to define the minimum education or skill level required of an employee who is to work at this resource.
- Assignment of a position to a resource. A position is an established and approved post.
- Assignment of a person to a resource.

Default values that are maintained in the resource are automatically copied into the operations to be processed at that resource. These default values may be changed in the operations from the recipe screen.

By contrast, if you use the defaults maintained in the resource by entering the resource as a reference, the default values cannot be changed in the recipe.

Calculating Capacity Requirements

A formula can be assigned to every resource capacity to calculate capacity requirements for every operation.

If you do not specify a formula, the system will not calculate capacity requirements.

Using Formulas

Every resource capacity can be associated with a specific formula that is used to calculate the capacity requirements for each operation. If you do not enter a formula, the system will assume that this capacity is not to be calculated as a requirement.

Each formula is identified by entering its formula key. Within each formula, the parameters are identified by their parameter ID. The parameter ID determines the following:

- The definition and key word assigned to a parameter
- The parameter's dimension
- The parameter's name in a formula

Parameters are differentiated by their origins. For example, the following origins for a parameter are set up in customizing:

- Standard value—a standard value is assigned to the parameter used in the formula via a standard value key.

- Formula constants in the resource—a fixed value is assigned to the parameter in the resource, and this value is used in the formula.

- General operation value—a field is directly assigned to the parameter from the general operation data. Examples are lot size, base quantity, number of employees. The value in this field when the calculation is performed is used in the formula.

- User-defined field from the operation—a user-defined field will be assigned to the data field in the operation. The value in this field is entered into the formula at runtime.

Using Resource Hierarchies

A resource hierarchy is a structure created by establishing superior and subordinate resources. A particular resource can be mentioned in more than one resource hierarchy.

For example, resource hierarchies can be used as follows:

- To locate resources.
- To cumulate available capacity during capacity requirements planning.

Thus the capacity available in a number of subordinate resources can be cumulated and stored at a superior resource level. You can record that certain work centers are located in a particular section, and this section can be used as a superior resource level for cumulating available capacity. And there can be several such sections in a department, and so on.

The same resource hierarchy structure can be used in capacity requirements planning to cumulate capacity requirements or in a recipe to identify particular resources.

The resource hierarchies can be displayed graphically and maintained in the graphic screens.

Defining a Resource Network

The processing units of a production line are resources that necessarily have to be physically linked in a particular sequence. The batch of material being processed may have to pass from unit to unit.

The sequence of the material flow is defined as a network of resources in which the relationship is always finish-start (FS). The operation in the predecessor resource has to finish completely before the start of the operation in the successor resource.

Resource networks can be displayed and maintained graphically in the master recipe and the process order screens.

Assigning Resources to Cost Centers

A cost center is a unit of the company defined according to responsibility, location, or billing areas. A cost center is itself assigned to a single controlling area under which it is managed for financial accounting.

Several resources can be assigned to a cost center, and they can each be assigned for a limited period of time. A resource cannot be assigned to more than one cost center at a time.

The values used with an activity type for costing are stored in the cost center record. Thus the same operation performed in different work centers can be valuated differently if these work centers are assigned to different cost centers.

Activity types are valuated using a charge rate that includes a fixed portion and a variable work-related portion. Either of these portions may be nil.

The primary resource is defined as that part of a line or processing unit at which an operation is carried out and which is committed for the duration of the operation. One or more secondary resources may have to be allocated to an operation or a phase of it. These secondary resources may not be needed for the whole processing time of the primary resource.

Maintaining Capacity Data

A capacity record can be maintained for a particular resource or independent of any resource. The following capacities are differentiated:

- Resource capacities
- Pooled capacities
- Reference capacities
- Default capacities

Each resource can have several resource capacities, each of which may be defined with parameters unique to that resource. The resource-specific capacities are divided into categories including:

- Capacity of a line or processing unit over time
- Labor capacity
- Emission capacity
- Energy consumption

Each capacity category can be assigned only once to each resource and it will normally be maintained in the resource master records.

One pooled capacity can be assigned to several resources. Pooled capacities are set up in capacity maintenance. For example, a group of employees can be defined as a pooled capacity if they are able to work in any resource at a particular level in a resource hierarchy.

A reference available capacity is an available capacity that is used as a model when creating new capacities. The reference capacity can be maintained for several resources or allocated to one specific resource. The system is delivered with a standard available capacity in several versions. The appropriate version can be copied and marked as active in a particular resource.

A capacity has to be associated with a specific plant. A default capacity is a reference model comprising a capacity category and a plant ID. The system will propose this default capacity category and plant when you are creating a new capacity.

Using Available Capacity

A resource has an operating time and a daily available capacity. You can define the available capacity for individual resources or for all resources.

Each resource has a defined available capacity in each of the capacity categories available to it. However, you can reference the available capacity of another category when you are maintaining available capacity. For example, you may wish to specify that the operator, as a resource, shall be in attendance for exactly the operating time of the machine resource. Alternatively, you could specify that a particular work center is going to be available for exactly the working hours as defined by the works calendar, and the daily start and finish times.

In practice, the following factors reduce working hours:

- Break times
- Technical malfunctions
- Organizational problems

The operating time is defined as the productive working hours. This quantity is the available working hours less the technical and organizational downtimes. Each capacity can be assigned a percentage to be used to estimate the proportion of the available working hours that will be available as productive working time, allowing for technical and organizational downtimes.

These calculations can be performed separately for each resource, or similar resources can be valuated as a group per capacity category. You can also customize various versions of the available capacity calculations per capacity category so that an appropriate version may be activated according to the occasion.

A *reference available capacity* is a model used as a model for copying. This model can be used to set up calculations for several similar resources by first assigning each of them an identical reference available capacity, and then editing each one as necessary to take account of their differences.

Using the Standard Available Capacity

It is very useful to specify work start and finish times, break times, and the capacity utilization in the standard available capacity. The standard available capacity is unrelated to orders. It is used to calculate overall lead time for routings.

The standard available capacity has an unlimited validity period. It is valid every workday as long as no interval of available capacity has been defined. This interval refers to a period of time over which the standard available capacity is not valid. It is recurring over a specified cycle length so that the interval recurs.

Calculating Shift Values

If you need to calculate the total available capacity in a shift when an interval of available capacity has temporarily replaced the standard available capacity, you have to define shift values, as follows:

Part
IV

Ch
14

- Capacity utilization—the percentage of capacity actually used in relation to the theoretically available capacity. Used to compile the average capacity utilization of all individual capacities in one shift for each capacity category.
- Number of the individual capacities in a shift.
- Operating times.

Defining a Shift

A shift definition is a record in which you define the start, finish, and break times in a shift for all resources. Once you have a shift definition for a shop floor area, you can alter it and so promulgate the alteration to all available capacities that refer to it.

A shift sequence is a data record in which the shift sequence is predefined for all resources that refer to it.

Managing Resources

The following sequence will display the initial resource screen:

1. Select Logistics.
2. Select Production→Process.
3. Select Master data→Resources.

The following options are available in the initial resource screen so that you can change a resource in all the recipes in which it appears:

- Resource—create, change, or display a resource, assign a resource to a hierarchy.
- Capacity—create, change, or display capacities. Pooled capacities can be maintained only by using this menu option.
- Hierarchy—create, change, or display hierarchies. This is the only place to maintain the position of a resource in a hierarchy.
- Resource network—create, change, or display resource networks.
- Evaluations—standard SAP reports, where-used lists for the resource in recipes, where-used lists of capacities.
- Extras—create standard texts that are included in the recipe.

The PD module, personnel planning and development, has access to any resource records that you create in logistics. PD holds the details of all employees that have a personnel reference number. This number can be used to reference these details, subject to authorization control. Alternatively, you can specify qualifications by assigning them to resources so that the PD system can be asked to locate suitable employees who would be available on the dates when the resource is needed.

It is also possible to create a resource in the personnel planning and development system that you signify as being relevant to logistics (PP-PI). In particular, you will be invited to specify the plant and the usage of this resource.

Creating Resources

The following sequence will create a resource:

1. Select Logistics→Production—process.
2. Select Master data→Resources.
3. Select Resource→Create.
4. Enter the plant ID.
5. Enter a resource key that clearly identifies the resource within the plant.
6. Enter a resource category.
7. If necessary, enter a resource to be copied.
8. Press Enter to reach the Basic Data screen.

The following detail screens can be selected via Goto:

- Basic data
- Assignments—further screens
- Capacity—further screens
- Scheduling
- Default values
- Hierarchy—further screens
- Network

If your system is integrated with PD, personnel planning and development, you can enter a text term to locate all PD resources that include the search term in their short text entries.

Finding a Resource

The following search criteria are available to locate a resource using a matchcode:

- Resource category
- Class
- Resource name
- Technical data
- Person responsible

Click on the arrow or select the function key F4 to use matchcodes. Mark the entry and select Choose.

Alternatively, you can search for resources by entering a generic search criterion comprising the first few letters followed by the symbol *.

The class of a resource is predefined in the R/3 classification system. If you assign specific characteristics to a class, these characteristics will be applied to all existing and subsequent members of that class.

The following sequence will create a class:

1. Select Logistics→Central functions.
2. Select Classification→Class→Create.

The following sequence will assign a resource to a class in resource maintenance:

1. When creating or changing a resource, go to the Basic Data screen.
2. Select Extras→Classification.
3. Enter the class to which you want to assign the resource.
4. Accept or change the class type suggested by the system.
5. If necessary, maintain the characteristic value by selecting Values.

Assigning a Resource to a Subsystem

You may wish to have resource data transferred to one or more external subsystems, such as plant data collection (PDC) systems. You can nominate the subsystem or subsystems within resource maintenance by accessing the Extras function, which will invite you to enter the subsystems group where the resource data should be sent.

Checking a Resource for Data Completeness

Normally the procedure for creating a resource will take you through the necessary screens so that you may select or enter the necessary parameter data. However, you may be interrupted and have to save the entry screens before they have all been completed.

The Check function can be called from any of the resource maintenance screens. If the system finds that any information needed to operate with the resource category is not going to be available, it displays the screens where entries are still needed.

If you are not going to need a resource immediately, you can lock it against further changes. If it called in a recipe, for example, the user will see a warning message. From the Basic Data screen, select Extras→Status→Lock/Unlock. The system reports the outcome immediately.

Deleting a Resource

If a resource is no longer needed in a recipe or process order, you can delete it by the following sequence:

1. Select Resource→Change.
2. Select Resource→Delete on the Basic Data screen if the resource is not being used. This resource can no longer be used or archived.
3. If the resource is being used, mark it for deletion on the Basic Data screen by selecting Extras→Status→Deletion indicator.

Creating a Resource Hierarchy

Resource hierarchies have to be created before any resources can be assigned to them. The following sequence will create a hierarchy:

1. Select Logistics→Production—process.
2. Select Master data→Resources.
3. Select Hierarchy→Create.
4. Enter the name of the hierarchy and the plant.
5. Press Enter to reach the Header Data screen.
6. Enter a short description of the hierarchy.
7. Select Hierarchy→Save.

Assigning Resources to a Hierarchy

The following sequence will allocate a resource to a hierarchy within hierarchy maintenance:

1. From the Header Data screen of hierarchy maintenance, select Goto→Resource allocation or press the function key Resource allocation.
2. Identify the resource by plant and resource name, or select from a list of resources compiled by a search specification. Those already allocated to this hierarchy will be indicated in the display.
3. Select the menu options Goto→Back.
4. Place the resource in the correct position in the hierarchy.
5. Press the function key Graphic.

You can also allocate a resource to a hierarchy in resource maintenance using the create and change options.

1. From one of the resource maintenance screens like Basic Data, select Goto→Hierarchy→Relationships.
2. Inspect the existing resource allocations to the hierarchy.
3. Select Edit→New entries.
4. Enter the plant and the key for the hierarchy to which you want to allocate the resource.
5. Select the function key Continue.

If the hierarchy does not already have a root, you can set the root indicator on one of the resources, which will then be placed at the highest level of the hierarchy. If you do not either identify the resource as the root or nominate a superior resource, there will be no resource assignments in the hierarchy.

If necessary, maintain the stop explosion indicator on the Hierarchy Detail screen. This is used to prevent the cumulation of available capacity in the branch from subordinate resources below the *stop explosion* indicator.

Part
IV

Ch
14

Connecting Resources

You can assign resources to individual hierarchy levels in hierarchy maintenance in the display area of the hierarchy graphic:

1. Select the function Connect. A dashed line appears in the graphic when you move the mouse pointer or the cursor.

2. Move the cursor to the superior resource and click on the left mouse key.

3. Connect the resource by holding down the left mouse key and drawing a line to the subordinate resource.

You will not be allowed to subordinate a resource if it has previously been assigned a superior position in the hierarchy. However, you can delete the existing connection by marking the subordinate resource and selecting the function Split.

The graphical display functions are controlled by the user. The display options have no effect on the underlying data processing functions.

Creating a Resource Network

You can assign resources to a network that has been created previously:

1. Select Logistics→Production—process.

2. Select Master data→Resources.

3. Select Resource network→Create.

4. Enter the plant and the name of the resource network to be created. Press Enter.

5. Enter the short text for the resource network.

6. Press the function key Resource allocation.

7. Mark the resources to be allocated to the network.

8. Press the function key Graphic.

9. In the graphic, use the key Link to join the individual resources with one another.

10. Save the graphic.

Navigating a Resource Relationship Network

The following sequence will allow you to inspect the resource relationships:

1. Choose Logistics→Production—process→Master data→Resources.

2. Select Resource→Change, or Resource→Display.

3. Enter the plant and the name of the resource you created.

4. Choose Goto→Resource network→Relationships.

5. Inspect the Position within Network screen

6. Choose Goto→Resource network →Relationship detail, to display the predecessor and successor resources of the resource you selected.

7. If you want to display the network graphics from within this screen, choose the menu options Goto→Resource network→Graphics.

If you are in change mode, you can also change the position of the resources on the Graphic screen and save them. ●

Managing Master Recipes

Understanding a Master Recipe

A master recipe is a stored document that describes the company-specific application of manu-facturing procedures without reference to a specific order. In the R/3 system, the master recipe is a type of task list. Recipes are used for the manufacturing of products and for the specification of complex procedures such as the clean-out or changeover of a processing unit.

The data held in a master recipe is specified in accordance with international standards as defined by the following authorities:

- The European Batch Forum (EBF)
- The Norms Working Committee for Measuring and Control Techniques in the Chemical Industry (NAMUR)
- Standard S88 of the Instrument Society of America (ISA)

When the records of a master recipe are considered from the planning view, the data contains the following information or recipe objects:

- The individual steps in the production process (operations and phases) in the sequence in which they are to be carried out as well as planned durations and other activities (standard values)
- The resources required for the individual steps in the production process
- The ingredients required for production (material list)
- Specifications for in-process quality inspections (for example, inspection characteristics)

The master recipe also contains planned parameters relevant to the control of the production process. These parameters are expressed as process instructions so that they may be commu-nicated to process control.

The master recipe is used as the basis for the process order.

The task list structure of the master recipe in the R/3 system is identical to that of the follow-ing objects:

- Routings
- Inspection plans
- Maintenance task lists
- Standard networks

The master recipe has task list type 2. You can also use routings (type N) and inspection plans (type Q) as copy templates for master recipes.

Maintaining Master Recipes

You need suitable authorization to maintain a master recipe, because you may need to create, change, delete, and archive records.

A master recipe belongs to a specific plant, and it must use only those resources that belong to that plant. It can be assigned to a recipe group within that plant. Any changes to a master recipe can be documented using the engineering change management (ECM) procedures.

The following procedures are designed to minimize the maintenance effort required:

- Use existing recipes as templates from which to copy and edit to create a new recipe.
- Define a recipe profile that will suggest frequently used values as defaults.
- Use the mass changes function to replace resources and process instructions and materials in several master recipes simultaneously.
- Mark recipes for deletion and therefore lock them against further use.

Using Recipe Groups

Recipe groups are used to associate recipes according to the following principles:

- Similar production processes for different materials
- Different production processes for the same material such as for different lot size ranges

Recipe groups also help you locate a specific recipe. When you are maintaining a recipe, the system will load all the members of the group. Therefore you should not allow recipe groups to become too large.

If you fail to allocate a newly created recipe to an existing recipe group, the system will automatically create a new group for it. If you do not allocate an alphanumeric key to the recipe group, the system will assign a number from the range determined in customizing. Each recipe within a recipe group must also be assigned an alphanumeric key.

Navigating the Recipe Levels of Detail

The recipe header data is valid for the entire master recipe; for example:

- General data, such as recipe status, recipe usage, and charge quantity
- Materials you want to produce with this recipe
- The resource network of the plant to be used
- General parameters for an in-process quality inspection
- Information on the validity of the recipe
- A long text providing a detailed recipe description

The operation overview is the main maintenance screen of master recipes. The overview contains, for example:

- The operations and phases describing the processing steps of a master recipe
- The resources at which the steps are to be executed
- The control system or line operator that is to carry out the steps
- A short description of the individual processing steps

Detail screens and further overview screens are provided to allow maintenance of all other operation and phase details, such as standard values and other information relevant to scheduling.

Every operation and every phase has further detail screens for the following data:

- Material components
- Secondary resources
- Inspection characteristics
- Process instructions allocated to the respective processing step

Copying from a Recipe Profile

Master recipes will tend to have the same values in many of the fields. These values can be entered once during customizing into a recipe profile from which the system will automatically copy them when a new recipe is created. You may have several recipe profiles to choose from.

A recipe profile can contain any of the following types of information:

- Operations and phases—for example, control keys, intervals of operation, and phase numbers
- Relationships—for example, the layout type of the graphic
- Process instructions—interval of process instruction numbers and their characteristics
- Inspection specifications—for example, interval of inspection characteristics and base sample quantity

If you need to change a profile during recipe maintenance, the changes will remain valid only until you exit the recipe. If you make changes in the recipe itself, your alterations will be permanent.

Meeting Recipe Documentation Requirements

Engineering change management (ECM) is automatically applied to recipes in many industries. In some cases, recipes have to be formally checked and approved before they are released for production.

Differences in the regulations are accommodated in R/3 by a system of recipe maintenance types controlled by change rules.

Applying Change Rules to Recipe Maintenance

Master recipes can be changed under the following logical rules:

- Without a change number
- With a change master record
- With an engineering change order

To change a master recipe without a change number, you need the authorization to change the specific recipe. Changes are valid for the entire validity period of the selected change status.

The status before the change is recorded in change documents. However, it is not saved as a separate change status.

If you change a master recipe with a change master record, you effectively plan and execute simultaneous changes to related objects, such as recipes, materials, and bills of material. The validity date is specified in the change master record. The system creates a new change status for all changed recipe objects such as operations or relationships. The status before the change is saved.

If your circumstances demand a formal approval procedure, you have to initiate changing a master recipe with an engineering change order. You can then create process orders that will only accept recipes that have been approved by an engineering change order.

You can specify how a recipe is to be maintained by nominating a change rule on the General View screen of the recipe header. The change rule designates the following restrictions for recipe maintenance:

- No restrictions
- Change master record required
- Engineering change order required
- Engineering change order required that stipulates a specific change type for the relevant recipe and thus a specific approval procedure in the object management record

Once you assign a change rule to a recipe, this particular recipe is locked against any changes that are less restrictive. Thus any changes you make have to be under the same change rule or one that is more stringent.

Change master records are identified by a unique change number and can include the following information:

- Detailed documentation of the planned changes
- The date from which the changes are to be valid
- The types of objects and, if required, object management records for the individual objects to be changed
- A special authorization that you need in order to work with the change master record
- For change numbers related to a material, a revision level that marks a particular processing status of a material

Maintaining a Master Recipe with Reference to a Change Master Record

If you enter either the change number or the material with the desired revision level on the initial master recipe maintenance screen, the valid-from date in the change master record is then used as the key date. The effect of using a reference in this way is as follows:

- When you create a recipe, the new recipe is valid from this date.

■ When you display or change a recipe, the system displays the change status that is valid on this date.

■ Unlike recipe maintenance without a change number, the system creates a new change status for all changed recipe objects. This change status is valid from the valid-from date of the change number.

This procedure allows you to plan changes in advance and allow the system to release them automatically on their valid-from date. The status before the change is saved.

Documentation of Changes

If you have changed a master recipe with reference to a change master record, you can change it again afterwards without using a change number, but your alterations will not be fully documented. You can define a change rule in the recipe header that will ensure that all recipe changes are under ECM conditions, including documentation.

If you activate a date check when customizing for engineering change management, you can have the system make sure that no additional changes are made to a change status specification once the validity period has started.

Managing Change Approvals

Engineering change orders have the same functions as change master records, with the following additions:

■ An unapproved engineering change request can be converted and released as an approved engineering change order.

■ You can restrict the authorization to change to only those objects for which you have created an object management record in the change master record. Thus, recipes and bills of materials, for example, can be traced throughout their life cycles.

■ You can arrange to trigger a workflow task such as sending a message to the person responsible at a particular processing stage.

Engineering change requests are created within engineering change management and identified via a change number.

Tracing the Approval Procedure for Engineering Change Requests or Orders

The procedure for approving and releasing engineering change requests and engineering change orders is controlled via links between statuses and business transactions.

The statuses mark particular processing stages during the approval procedure. Approval cannot progress from one stage to the next without carrying out a specified business transaction.

The status situation in a particular plant can comprise a fixed network of system statuses provided by R/3 plus a set of company-specific user statuses than may be used in addition to, or instead of, parts of the standard status network.

Exploring the R/3 Standard System Status Network

The R/3 standard approval procedure has been implemented via a network of system statuses. The route through the network taken by an engineering change that is approved at every stage is as follows:

1. An engineering change request is created that describes planned changes to various objects, including a master recipe.

2. The planned changes to the individual objects are checked and marked as possible or unnecessary.

3. After the check has been concluded, the engineering change request is approved and converted into an engineering change order. The system status *Engineering change order to be processed (ECOP)* is assigned to the change order.

4. You execute the planned changes by maintaining the master recipe with reference to the engineering change order.

5. After the changes to all objects have been made, the entire engineering change order is completed.

6. Finally, the engineering change order is released and assigned system status *Engineering change order released (ECOR)*.

The recipe has now been approved and it can be used to create orders requiring an approved recipe.

Adding User Statuses

You can attach an additional *User* status to the standard approval system by defining the extra approval procedure and assigning it at the change order header or to a particular change object.

Your additional user status has to be introduced in customizing for engineering change management as a status profile. This profile is associated with a new change type that you assign either to the engineering change request at header level or to specific change objects.

The status profile links the user statuses to the business transactions defined in the standard status system. This joins the user statuses to the existing network of system statuses.

You will probably specify that a special authorization is required to set or delete a user-defined status.

Controlling the Validity of Master Recipes

Every recipe is represented by a data object that has its own validity period. The start of the validity period is determined by a key date entered on the initial screen when creating or changing master recipes. If you are operating with change numbers, the valid-from date in the change number is used as the key date.

When you display or change a master recipe, the system consults the key date and considers the change status that is valid on the key date for each recipe object.

If you are creating a recipe object with a change number, the validity of this object will begin on the date of the change number and be of unlimited duration.

If you are changing a recipe object with a change number, you will create a new change number. The valid-from date of this change number will be used as the key date of the object you are changing. Subsequent changes without a change number are possible, but they will not affect the validity period.

It is possible to call a recipe that has different validity periods for some of its operations or phases. When you identify a key date, or accept the current date as the key date the system will only display the recipe objects that are valid on that date. You will not see any changes that have been planned for a subsequent period.

Checking Master Recipe Consistency

The following errors illustrate the need for running a checking procedure after creating or changing a master recipe:

- You have created a phase and entered a number for it that has already been assigned to a phase that will become valid at a later date.
- The control key for an operation or phase signifies that inspection characteristics are required, yet you have not yet created any inspection characteristics for it.

Some errors cannot be corrected until a later stage in the production planning process. You may have to delay some of the consistency checks.

The following checks will be automatically performed when you create an order, if they have not already been carried out in the master recipe:

- Operation and phase number are unique.
- Secondary resource numbers are unique within an operation or phase.
- Process instruction numbers are unique within a phase.
- Characteristic numbers are unique within a process instruction.
- Inspection characteristics required by the control key are defined.

The consistency check is always carried out for the entire recipe group and for the whole of the validity period of the change status called for the recipe. During the check, the system creates a consistency log where system messages on errors are collected.

If a master recipe has been checked and found to be without errors, the header is marked so that no further consistency checking is performed when an order is created. However, the following situations will reinstate checking:

- If you change the recipe again without repeating the consistency check
- If you change the valid-from date of a change number used in the recipe

- If an order is released but the transferred recipe is internally marked as inconsistent
- If an order is released with a consistent recipe that includes a configurable material at header level

Creating a Master Recipe

The following sequence will create a master recipe:

1. In the R/3 main menu, choose Logistics→Production—process→Master data→Master recipe.
2. Choose Master recipe→Create.
3. Maintain the data on the initial screen.
4. Choose Enter to reach the Header General View if your recipe group contains only one member, or the Recipe Overview screen if there are several members.
5. Choose Edit→New entries.
6. Maintain the General Data for Recipe Header.
7. Choose Goto→Operation overview.
8. Create the operations and phases for your master recipe.

If you can identify a suitable master recipe to act as a template, choose Recipe→Copy from… and continue after you have selected the task list type of your model. You then have to enter a search specification in the dialog box and select the recipe to copy from.

The following data is not copied:

- The production version of the template recipe
- The model's material lists
- The material components

When the copying is finished, you will see the Create Master Recipe: Check Header screen for the new recipe. Here you can add or change data before selecting Continue to have the system check all your changes and offer you the relevant screens to make any corrections necessary.

When the header is free of inconsistencies, the operation overview appears so that you can change the copied operations and phases or, if necessary, add new ones.

Checking Recipe Data Consistency

One of the options in the Extras menu of the operation overview of a recipe is the function Recipe check in which you can elect to display the log of the error messages generated during the most recent consistency check. You can filter these messages by message type, and you can call for a long text to explain any particular message.

The consistency log is available until you exit the master recipe. You can call the log from within the recipe at any time.

Understanding the Header Data of Master Recipes

The master recipe header carries the information that is applicable to the entire recipe:

- General information such as usage, status, and change rule of the recipe
- Data on the material to be produced and its bill of material (BOM)
- General instructions for in-process quality inspections

Classifying Master Recipes

If you want to classify master recipes, you must use classes that you create with class type 018, which is designated for task lists. What you have to do is to build a framework of recipe features that will define recipe classes to suit the work of your company. Then you can assign matchcodes that will locate a subset of recipes; for instance:

- All recipes of a class
- All recipes of a class with a specific characteristic value

Maintaining Header Data

Before you come to the point where you are maintaining recipe header data, the following data elements will exist in the system:

- The resource network of the production line at which you want to carry out the manufacturing process
- The master record of the material you want to produce
- The dynamic modification rule you want to use in in-process inspections for this recipe
- The classes with which you want to classify the master recipe

What you have to do is to maintain the general data of the master recipe in the recipe header before you can create the operations and phases of your recipe.

If the recipe is to be used for production, you must allocate to the recipe the material you want to produce. If you define a production version for this material, you effectively specify which alternative BOM and BOM usage is to be used in conjunction with the recipe to manufacture the material.

You must enter the quality data for in-process quality inspections and you should enter a long text with explanations and notes on the master recipe to make clear the quality management constraints and processes applicable to this recipe.

The following sequence will allow you to maintain general data for a recipe header:

1. On the recipe overview, select the recipe for which you want to maintain general data.
2. Choose Recipe header→General view.
3. Maintain the general recipe header data.

The following sequence will maintain a long text for a master recipe:

1. On the recipe overview, select the recipe for which you want to maintain a long text.
2. Choose Recipe header→Long text.
2. In the long text editor, enter the text as desired.
3. Save your text.
4. Choose Back to exit the text editor.

The following sequence will allow you to classify a master recipe:

1. On the Header: General View screen choose Extras→Classify header.
2. Enter the class of class type 018 (task list) to which you want to assign the recipe.
3. Choose Edit→Values.
4. On the list of the class characteristics assigned to the task list class you have chosen, assign the values valid for the recipe you are working with.

Allocating a Resource Network to a Recipe

A resource network is a way of representing the possible pathways that a production line can take through the available resources. Obviously, only some resources are physically linked together with pathways that allow the transfer of the material being manufactured.

You allocate a resource network to a recipe by entering it at the header level. You can inspect the network at any time from the recipe. When you create an order, the system automatically transfers the resource network to the order. When this order is released, the system checks whether the primary resources you have planned are actually contained in the network. And when an operation needed in the order is dispatched in the planning table, the system again checks the following conditions:

- Whether the resource network of the order contains the primary resource allocated to the operation
- Whether the preceding operation is allocated to a preceding resource
- Whether the succeeding operation is allocated to a succeeding resource of the resource network
- Whether the resource network has been maintained for the same plant as the master recipe and the process order

Understanding Primary Resources

A primary resource is defined as that part of the production line at which a production step is carried out. Every internally processed operation and every internally processed phase of a master recipe or process order has exactly one primary resource allocated to it.

The primary resource is committed for the entire duration of the operation or phase. Thus you could define the primary resource as what is committed for the duration of the operation or phase.

A phase is defined as a partial step of an operation. Therefore a phase has to be allocated the same primary resource as the operation of which it is a part. When you create a phase, the system automatically transfers the resource of the superior operation to the phase.

Primary resources are subject to some constraints:

- The resource must have been maintained for the same plant as the master recipe or process order.
- The resource must be released for master recipes via its task list usage.

If you have allocated a resource network in the recipe header, the system will check, when you release an order, whether the resources you used are contained in this network. Therefore you should not use a primary resource unless it is part of the resource network indicated in the recipe header.

Selecting Resources Automatically

You can select the resource you want to use in the process order instead of the master recipe, for instance, if there are several resources that could be used for an order.

You have to select which production resource you intend to use by the time you release the order. If you have made the corresponding settings, the system can propose suitable resources from which you can choose the one you want. However, there may be some data held in the various resources that will affect how operations and phases are executed.

For instance, there may be a standard value key with rules for maintenance that specifies which standard values you can or must maintain in the recipe and order. Formulas may be assigned to an operation or phase that calculate the dates and costs of the phases in scheduling, capacity requirements planning, and costing. Default values may be in place.

Naming a Person

The capacity planning table can specify which person is to carry out a processing step by referring to a personnel number. Taking resource and operation data into account, the system can propose suitable persons. However, the system will not recognize personnel numbers unless it has been integrated with the human resources (HR) system or at least the personnel planning and development (PD) module of HR.

Using Secondary Resources in Operations or Phases

A primary resource may well need a secondary resource—a line operator, for instance, or a set of test equipment for in-process quality inspections. You can allocate a secondary resource to an operation or phase.

If you are using external contractors to carry out a processing step, you can show this as a secondary resource. You define a secondary resource in the master recipe but do not allocate a resource master record to it because it is supplied from external sources.

A secondary resource does not have to be maintained for the same plant as the master recipe, nor does it have to be contained in the resource network of the recipe or order header.

A secondary resource is not automatically committed for the entire duration of an operation or phase. You normally have to maintain different standard values and dates relative to the start and finish of the operation or phase.

Secondary resources may be separately processed for the following functions, provided you have defined a control key to specify which functions are allowed for the secondary resource:

- Scheduling
- Capacity requirements planning
- Confirmation
- Costing

Secondary resources cannot be chosen by automatic resource selection in the process order.

Working with Planning Resources

A planning resource can be used to mark an operation that has to be assigned a valid production resource before the production order is released. By this technique you can wait until the last moment before you commit a particular resource. The system can help you choose which resource to assign by considering the following factors:

- Whether the resource appears in the resource network of the order header
- Whether you have specified some user-defined resource characteristics that you have attached to the resource records for use as selection conditions

The system will also perform these checks when you release an order for production.

For example, you can set up task list usage constraints, such as a time period or type of customer. These restrictions can be assigned to a resource so as to ensure that this resource can only be committed elsewhere up to the moment when it is converted from a planned resource to a production resource, which will be when the order is released. You can group several resources by assigning them the same planning resource identification so that they will all be converted together.

Once you have allocated a planning resource to operations in a master recipe, you can use the planning resource in the normal business operations as follows:

- Scheduling
- Capacity requirements planning
- Costing

It is only when you want to release the order that you have to decide which actual production resources are to take the place of the planning resource.

Classifying Resources for System-Aided Resource Selection

The system can select resources using the R/3 classification system, but only if you have previously classified these resources. You have to create user-specific classes using the class type 019, work center class, to store information on important resource characteristics that will be suitable for choosing resources during release of the process order.

You have to enter or select class characteristics to specify the following conditions:

- The characteristics of a resource that have been stored in its resource master record
- The requirements the primary resource must meet in the resource selection condition of an operation—that is, what the resource has to be capable of.

Planning Resources—Persons

You can allocate personnel resources or resources with personnel capacities to your operations, phases, and secondary resources. However, you must also decide which person is to carry out a processing step before you can start production.

If your system has been integrated with the personnel planning components, you will be offered a list of suitable and available persons when you are releasing the order. If you have defined required capacity in terms of personnel qualifications, you can choose from suitably qualified employees during resource planning in the capacity planning table.

In personnel planning, you assign a qualification profile to a person. Then you can assign this person to a resource directly in the resource master record. Alternatively, you can specify a position for the resource, in which case the suitable persons are defined as the available current holders of this position.

This assignment of persons can be directed at the entire resource or only at specific capacities categories that are available at the resource. A requirements profile can be defined to set up a complex selection specification, which can then be assigned to operations and secondary resources in the master recipe.

When selecting individual capacities in the capacity planning table, the system locates the persons with all or some of the qualifications specified in the resource and operation.

Using Default Values from the Resource

You can enter field values for operations, phases, and secondary resources in the resource master record. This allows you to mark these values as defaults or references. If a field value is marked as a reference, it will be copied to the recipe and then to the production order, but you will not be allowed to change it. If you mark a field value as a default, it will be suggested for you to accept or edit, provided there is no value in this field already. You can still change the existing value to the default.

Designing Operations and Phases

A phase is the main focus of production planning because it is a more detailed representation of a particular detailed step within an operation. An operation is an independent workstep or stage carried out at a primary resource, which is a processing unit.

Operations and their phases are stored in the master recipe.

The planning of the general production process and the setting up of production lines is carried out at the level of operations. When it comes to business transactions, such as scheduling, capacity requirements planning, and costing, the system automatically aggregates all the data from the individual phases and allocates it to the relevant operation. The primary resource for the operation is automatically identified in its phase data.

You can apply the following settings for individual phases:

- A control key—signifies processed in-house or externally; whether the system will determine dates, capacity requirements, and costs for the phase; whether confirmation is to be sent during order execution.
- Standard values—planned values for activities, used for scheduling, capacity requirements planning, and costing.
- A control recipe destination—indicates the process control system or the line operator who is in charge of carrying out the phase.
- Relationships between phases—determines the time sequence of processing steps.
- Specific allocations—materials per phase, checks and inspections, process instructions to be sent to process control during order execution

The relationship graphic of the master recipe displays the time sequence of operations and phases, and you can maintain the details in the graphic. The operation overview table allows you to enter operation and phase data because you can call up any detail screen and all the operation and phase allocations.

Interpreting a Control Key for Operations, Phases, and Secondary Resources

A control key has to be allocated to each operation, phase, or secondary resource when it is created. The control key determines how the respective object is treated in order execution and product costing.

An operation can be assigned settings that control the following business functions:

- Inspection characteristics
- Time ticket printing
- Printing (general)

A phase can be assigned settings that control the following business functions:

- Scheduling
- Capacity planning
- Costing
- Automatic goods receipt
- Inspection characteristics
- Confirmation printing
- Time ticket printing
- Printing (general)
- External processing
- Confirmation

A secondary resource can be assigned settings that control the following business functions:

- Scheduling
- Capacity planning
- Costing
- Confirmation printing
- Printing (general)
- External processing
- Confirmation

Ordering External Processing

When you create a process order, the recipe data is copied to the order. When you save the order, the system automatically creates a purchase requisition for any externally processed phase or secondary resource.

The purchasing department then creates a purchase order from the requisition. After the vendor has rendered the service you ordered, you create a goods receipt for the purchase order.

You can make changes to dates and quantities in the order, and they will be automatically transferred to the purchase requisition. But there may be an existing purchase order. This will not be updated by your subsequent changes.

You can track the situation in the General Data Phase detail screen of the process order. This screen shows the following information on the ordering status:

- Number of the purchase requisition
- Indicator that specifies whether a purchase order has been created
- The quantity received from a goods receipt posted for the purchase order

Maintaining Data for External Processing

A phase or a secondary resource can be externally processed by a contractor. The General Data detail screen for the phase or secondary resource displays the fields that require entries.

If there exists a purchasing info record for the specific vendor and there is a purchasing organization designated for dealing with this contractor, then the vendor, material group, purchasing group, planned delivery time, sort string, and data for purchase order price processing are transferred from the info record. This info record is treated as a reference, which means that the data transferred is not amenable to alteration.

However, if you obliterate by overtyping blanks the reference to the info record and purchasing organization, you can then make alterations to the rest of the transferred data. The info record type should be type 0, which signifies normal info records without material master records. Such records can be selected using matchcode P, which identifies info records for external processing.

Alternatively, you can enter a sort string, a material group, and the planned delivery time. In this instance, the purchasing department will select a vendor and supply the corresponding data during order processing.

The control key of the phase may specify that the phase or secondary resource is to be costed, in which case you must also enter a cost element for order settlement.

Planning Standard Values for Operations, Phases, and Secondary Resources

For planning purposes, standard values are assigned to the activity to be performed in a processing step. Thus you may use a standard value for the processing time required or the energy needed.

Standard values are maintained in the master recipe and in the process order. Such values are needed for each activity type involved in internally processed operations, phases, and secondary resources. These standard values are used in scheduling, capacity requirements planning, and costing.

Much of the data needed for planning can best be stored in the individual resource you use to carry out a processing step. Thus the following settings for the planned standard values have to be made in the individual resource master records:

■ Assign a standard value key to the resource—determines that up to six standard values can be maintained. The specific parameters are assigned to the key in customizing.

■ Define a rule for maintenance for each standard value—determines whether you may, should, or must maintain the value. This rule is consulted when checking phases and secondary resources.

If required, you must maintain default values for the units of measure of the standard values as well as the texts about the corresponding activity types.

Although you can also create standard values for operations, these will be for information purposes only because the system performs scheduling, capacity requirements planning, and costing using the data at phase and secondary resource level only.

The system does not check any standard values you may have entered at operations level.

Formatting Standard Values

When you enter a standard value, you must use a quantity that will be multiplied by the base quantity of the material you intend to produce. The base quantity will normally be suggested by default.

You can use a different unit of measure for the base quantity than for the charge quantity in the recipe or order header. However, you must enter a corresponding conversion rule in these cases.

If they are marked as relevant to costing, you have to enter the activity types for phases and secondary resources.

You can also maintain formulas in the resource. A formula can refer to standard values by using the parameters allocated in the standard value key. The system uses the appropriate formula to calculate the processing time, capacity requirements, and costs for phases and secondary resources.

It may be useful for you to define some user-specific fields for which you define the usage and document the meaning at the customizing stage. Such user-defined fields can be associated with a field key, which is then entered in the operations, phases, and secondary resources as necessary. This key will then establish which user-defined fields are available for maintenance and show the names used for them.

User-defined fields are not checked by the system.

Exploring User-Defined Fields

Every field key can nominate up to twelve data fields. They can be of different formats, as follows:

- Up to four general text fields, for such information as the person in charge, names of deputies, internal telephone numbers.
- Up to two quantity fields, which may have formula parameters allocated to them so that they can be used in calculating processing times, capacity requirements, and costs. These quantity fields retain the old values if you later change the field key.
- Up to two value fields and their units of measure.
- Up to two date fields to store internal start dates, for example.
- Up to two check boxes for user-defined functions.

Linking by Relationships Between Phases

The phases of a master recipe or process order can be linked by the following kinds of time-based relationship:

- Sequential
- Parallel
- Overlapping

A relationship must not create a loop to a phase that has already taken place.

You can create a relationship between phases that belong to different recipes—for example, a clean-out recipe with a production recipe. When you link two master recipes, they have to be of different recipe groups.

Interpreting the Types of Relationship

Relationships link the start or end of a preceding phase with the start and end of a succeeding phase. There are four relationships:

- FS relationship—from the finish of a phase to the start of the next phase
- SS relationship—from the start of a phase to the start of the next phase
- FF relationship—from the finish of a phase to the finish of the next phase
- SF relationship—from the start of a phase to the finish of the next phase (a logical possibility but of virtually no practical significance because you can simply interchange the phases in their sequence and use FS)

Using Time Intervals in Relationships

A relationship can have a positive time value so that the reference date and time of the successor phase is delayed by the specified interval after the reference date and time of the preceding phase. The reference date could be the start or the finish, depending on the type of the relationship.

If a relationship is maintained with a negative time value, this specifies that the successor reference date and time is earlier than the preceding phase reference date and time.

Allocating Materials to the Master Recipe

You specify which materials are to be processed and manufactured by allocating them to the master recipe. The material to be produced is allocated to the master recipe header. The other material components, whether input materials, output materials, or temporary intermediate products, are defined as material components in the bill of material (BOM). The items of the BOM include the materials and their quantities.

Although several alternative BOMs can exist for one material, you designate one as the production version by allocating it to the master recipe. The alternative BOM that you have designated then forms a material list for the master recipe.

In the material list, you allocate the material components to the operations and phases that require them during production. Once you have made these allocations, the system can check on their availability on the dates required or make a material reservation in the order. The allocations of materials also contribute data to product costing.

From the material list, you can define formulas for material quantity calculation. These formulas calculate the quantities used or produced in the production process. A formula may have to take account of the potency or concentration of an active ingredient as well as the quantities of other ingredients of the master recipe. These formulas also yield results that are needed for the calculation of material quantities in the order and in costing.

Some manufacturing processes are best represented as a set of coproducts. However, in the master recipe you have to designate just one of these coproducts as the leading material and enter it at header level. The other coproducts are entered as material components of the BOM.

Master recipes are also conveniently used to describe nonmanufacturing activities, such as cleaning or changeover activities in a plant line. You can create a process order from the master recipe for the work that needs to be done and for the materials needed. You may also have to specify in a clean-out master recipe how the scrap or waste materials are to be dispatched.

Using the Flexibility of the Master Recipe Concept

Material to be produced is entered in the header level of a master recipe, but there is considerable flexibility in the way the rest of the master recipe data is deployed:

- The master recipe can belong to a planning plant for materials management that is not the same as the production plant.
- A master recipe can be configured to manufacture different materials or variants.
- Different master recipes can exist to produce the same material, possibly in different plants or production lines.

During customizing, only some material types will have been designated for assignment to master recipes. The base or alternative unit of measure in a material master record must correspond to the charge quantity in the recipe.

Managing Coproducts

At recipe header level, you assign a "leading" product that in general initiates production. The process of material requirements planning will automatically create planned orders for this product. If you need to work with coproducts of the leading product, you have to manually create a process order.

Materials that are to be managed as coproducts have to have this fact indicated in the material master records.

Some production plants are paced by the availability of input materials and production capacities, rather than by the demand for the finished product. Oil refineries are perhaps an example, depending on the market. In these circumstances, the master recipe header material can be an important process material rather than the finished product.

In the BOM, you must allocate materials according to the following conditions:

■ Allocate input materials with positive quantities.

■ Allocate output materials, such as by-products and remaining materials with negative quantities.

■ Allocate catalysts and intramaterials with two items—material entering and material leaving the process.

Although a BOM is part of the master data of production planning and is used in discrete manufacturing, the following usage is normal in continuous process manufacturing:

■ The BOM is created and maintained directly from within the master recipe for which it is required.

■ By maintaining production versions, you can uniquely combine a master recipe with one or more alternative BOMs.

■ You can allocate an apportionment structure of the header material to the production version. The apportionment structure determines how the production costs are distributed to the individual products during order settlement.

Allocating Material Components to Operations and Phases

When you allocate a BOM version to a master recipe, the system generates a material list. You then allocate these material components to the operations and phases of the master recipe. This will allow the system to work out what is required for each phase. By consulting standard values, the system can also develop a timetable into which these material components must be scheduled.

The item category of the component you have allocated determines how it will be processed. For example, some components can be backflushed as stock items. Thus the allocations have to be taken into account during availability checking or material reservation, and probably for product costing.

The material allocations are copied from the master recipe to the process order when you create it. Any material components not explicitly allocated to an operation or phase are automatically staged for the first operation.

Although you can still change material allocations in the process order, it is recommended that you allocate material components to phases instead of operations because backflushing of material components can only be carried out if they are allocated to phases. Furthermore, all material components allocated to an operation will be staged as if they are all required at the beginning of the first phase, which may not be true.

Backflushing

It is a requirement of financial accounting and good inventory management that a goods issue must be posted for all materials withdrawn for the order. Goods issue posting can be carried out as soon as the material is withdrawn. Alternatively, the goods can be withdrawn when they are needed, but the posting of a goods issue document can be delayed until the successful completion of the phase in which the material is used. The posting of a confirmation for the phase is the trigger for this delayed posting of a goods issue. This procedure is called backflushing.

Backflushing can take place only at the level of the phase. You cannot backflush a material component that has been allocated to an operation.

There are various places where you can establish the settings that specify whether a material is to be backflushed, as follows:

- In the material master record (MRP view)
- In the resource (Basic Data screen)
- In the master recipe (General Data screen for component allocation)
- In the process order (General Data screen for the material component)

The backflush settings in the master recipe are copied to the process order, where they may be changed if necessary. If you set the backflushing indicator in the process order, the material will be backflushed, even if the material master record is set otherwise.

If you do not set the backflush indicator in the process order, the system will consult the setting in the material master. This setting can determine that the material is always backflushed or that the setting in the resource is to take precedence.

Calculating Material Quantities in the Material List

The bill of material stores the amounts of the various material components needed to manufacture a reference quantity of the material to be produced. This reference quantity is referred to as the base quantity.

If you are maintaining several production versions of the master recipe, you can maintain formulas for each version. For example, these formulas can calculate the component quantities of the corresponding material list as well as the quantities that should be staged for the various operations and phases. These calculations will all refer to the base quantity of the material to be produced, that is, the header material.

The values used or calculated by the formulas include the following:

- In the master recipe screen—enter the base quantity of the header material in the BOM header
- In the process order and product costing screens—enter the order quantity or the material quantity you want to produce
- Operation and phase quantities for material requirements planning

- Quantities of material components for material reservations or direct cost statements
- Material attributes for which a numeric value can be recorded; for example, the potency of the active ingredient or concentration

You can save the formulas in the master recipe and also copy the results to the material list or BOM if required. The correct formulas are accessed automatically when you enter the production version, because this will identify a master recipe and its BOM. The formulas are copied from the master recipe to the order when you create a process order. They are used to calculate order-specific quantities.

In the process order, you may wish to change or define formulas and restart calculation. For example, if the batch determination has changed to suit the customer or the production plant, you may have to select or define a different formula.

You need not maintain formulas for material quantity calculation if you are content to let the system assume that the order quantity and the operation and phase quantities are identical. The calculation will then arrive at the quantities of the individual material components in proportion to the order quantity.

Consulting Material Attributes in Calculation Formulas

A material attribute is a value stored in a field of the material master record. In particular, material attributes are used in managing batches of material that can differ significantly in one or more of their attributes because of the variability of the ingredients or the production process.

If you intend to use a material attribute in a calculation formula, the following requirements must be met:

- Classify the material master record and/or the BOM item with a class of class type Batch.
- Define the material attribute as a characteristic of this class.
- Assign a value to the material attribute in the material master record, the BOM item, or material list.

You then have a value of one of the classification characteristics for this batch class which is a material attribute. This value is copied to material quantity calculation.

The value of a material attribute that has been specifically assigned to a BOM item will overwrite the default value taken from the material classification. If multiple values or value ranges have been defined, the system uses the lowest value.

When a specific batch has been selected in the process order, the system will update the value assigned to the classification characteristic after consulting the batch specification.

Maintaining Material Data

Your system will have access to the master records of all materials involved in a process. The operations and phases of the master recipe will have been defined, but you have to carry out the following data maintenance before production can begin:

1. Allocate the material you want to produce to the master recipe.
2. Define a production version—specify which alternative BOM and BOM usage is to be used in conjunction with this recipe to produce the material.
3. Create the BOM or alternative BOM for the recipe.
4. Maintain the material components required for production together with the quantities.
5. Allocate the material components of your alternative BOM to the operations and phases of the recipe that require them for production.
6. Check and correct the cost apportionment structures for any coproducts maintained for the header material.
7. Define the formulas for calculating input materials and operation and phase quantities.
8. Calculate the values of the material quantities and copy them to the BOM or material list if required.

The main procedures for these data maintenance operations are outlined in the sections that follow.

Maintaining a Production Version

In the screen for creating or changing a production version you can enter data for certain attributes only unless you are creating a new production version. You will be allowed to change the following attributes of the production version:

- Lot size
- Charge quantity range
- Validity range
- Apportionment structure for coproducts

The system will suggest the selected master recipe for detailed planning of process orders and planned orders. However, if you are working on a repetitive manufacturing plant, you may wish to initiate rough-cut planning, in which case you could overwrite the master recipe by entering a different task list or task list type.

If you are creating a new production version, you will be allowed to maintain the production version key and the corresponding alternative BOM and BOM usage.

Maintaining Bills of Material

If you want to maintain a BOM that has been changed with a change number, you must enter the change number on the initial screen for recipe maintenance.

Go to the Material List or the Material Components for Operation screens. If you have not already created the alternative BOM for the selected production version, you will be shown the initial screen for creating a BOM. When you press Enter, the item overview of the existing BOM appears.

If an alternative BOM already exists, the component overview of the material list appears. You call the item overview of this BOM by choosing Change components.

You then enter the BOM data and choose Back to return to the master recipe. The BOM is automatically saved when you save the master recipe.

Allocating a Material Component to an Operation or Phase

The following sequence will allow you to allocate materials to operations or phases:

1. Go to the Material List screen.
2. Mark the material components you want to allocate.
3. Choose Edit→New allocation.
4. Enter, or select from the Operation list (pushbutton) the number of the operation or phase to which you want to allocate the material components.
5. Choose Continue to allocate the component to the operation or phase.
6. Mark the component allocation.
7. Choose Op./Comp. allocation→General data.
8. Make the required settings for the component.
9. Choose Back to return to the component allocation overview.

A similar procedure allows you to reallocate a material component from one operation or phase to another in the same recipe. You can also delete an allocation of a component and thus make it available for reallocation elsewhere.

Inspecting for Quality During Manufacturing

Just like any other activity, carrying out inspections has to be planned. The master recipe is an ideal instrument to use as an inspection plan for inspections during production. In particular, the quality management department can create a set of inspection specifications that can be applied to the master recipe.

You have the option of recording inspection results for an individual operation or phase within an operation. Or you can record several individual inspection points within the operation or phase. An inspection point is a reference object that defines what has to be inspected and stores the result; for example, a quantity, a time, or an inspection basis defined by the user.

Dynamic modification of the inspection scope is a procedure that can be directed to adjust the scope of the inspection according to the quality level expected. There are various ways of sampling and combining the inspection results.

The master recipe header contains the following inspection information:

- Whether inspection points are used
- The field combination used to define inspection points, such as one container per shift
- Whether to combine the manufactured quantities into partial lots or batches—defaults to the settings made for the plant in customizing for quality management

Each processing step in the operations and phases of a master recipe can be assigned the following inspection data:

- The time factor for the interval between the inspection points—for example, 10 minutes or three containers, whichever occurs first
- How the quantity is to be recorded for time-related intervals
- Whether the last partial lot assignment for goods receipt is to take place when the inspection results are being recorded for this operation/phase—ensures that the inspection results are up to date

The final partial lot inspected in process manufacturing may not complete the quantity required to trigger order confirmation. In these circumstances, inspection result recording cannot be initiated by goods receipt.

Dynamic Modification

Adjusting the scope of inspections according to the quality expected can take place at the inspection lot or inspection characteristic level.

The adaptation is controlled by the current quality level as indicated by a specified sampling procedure and processed by dynamic modification rules. The dynamic modification rule tightens or reduces inspection stringency.

The master recipe header contains the following information regarding dynamic modification:

- Whether the inspection scope is modified dynamically
- The level (lot or characteristic) at which dynamic modification takes place
- The dynamic modification rule used

A sampling procedure is always assigned to a specific characteristic. The dynamic modification level you have chosen will determine whether the dynamic modification rule either is binding or only represents a proposal for the rule to be maintained in the characteristic. ●

CHAPTER 16

Optimizing the Continuous Production Processes

Interfacing PP-PI with Process Control

The process management (PP-PI-PMA) component provides a flexible interface between the PP-PI and the process control facilities. The component can link to manually operated production lines, to automated lines, and to partially automated lines.

The process management (PMA) interface performs the following tasks:

- Receives control recipes with process instructions from released process orders
- Transfers control recipes to the corresponding line operators or process control systems
- Edits process instructions in natural language in PI sheet format so that they can be displayed and maintained on the screen by the line operator
- Receives, checks, and transfers process messages with actual process data
- Accepts manual entry of process messages

Sending Process Messages from Process Control

Process Message in PP-PI-PMA is a functional component that maintains a message structure that can be dispatched to one or more of the following types of destination:

- R/3 function module or component, such as inventory management (MM-IM)
- User-defined ABAP/4 tables such as are used for process evaluation purposes
- Users of the SAPoffice mail system, particularly the shift leader
- External functions, such as a third-party process control system

A process message can update an existing data record, as well as contribute to batch and production records. The content of each process message can be determined individually by assigning predefined characteristics and characteristic values. Thus the potential content as well as the destinations of process messages are customized specifically for a particular plant.

A process message can arrive via the PI-PCS interface from an external system, or it can be created when an R/3 PI sheet is maintained. Process management then consults its records to identify the destinations for this message.

Directing Control Information to the Operator

The control recipe function in PP-PI-PMA prepares a control recipe that contains all the information needed by a particular process control system or line operator. In particular, the control recipe includes the following items taken from the process instruction (PI) sheet:

- Information on the processing steps to be carried out during process control
- Information on the actual data to be reported

After a process order or a phase of one has been released, the relevant process instructions are repackaged into control recipes and transferred to the control system or line operator destinations as specified in the process order.

Reading the Process Instruction Sheet

The PI sheet function in PP-PI-PMA allows the process instructions contained in a control recipe to be formatted as a PI sheet for display and maintenance from the screen. This facilitates communication between supervisors, the PP-PI module, and line operators where the lines are not fully automated.

The content of a PI sheet will depend on the process instructions contained in the control recipe. The following possibilities are supported:

- Displaying control information in natural language
- Recording actual process data
- Calculating values
- Reporting entered and calculated values using process messages
- Recording inspection results by jumping directly to QM
- Calling R/3 function modules to access, for example, order confirmation, document management, or material quantity calculation

Archiving Process Data

The process data documentation (PP-PI-PDO) component is responsible for listing and optically archiving order-related and batch-related process data. The key factor is that these records cannot be manipulated. Thus an electronic batch record (EBR) can be produced for any product batch should the need arise after delivery.

The content and format of these archived lists are based on international standards such as those defined in the guidelines on good manufacturing practices (GMP). Customer-specific enhancements to the GMP standards are possible.

Evaluating Process Data

Process Data Evaluation (PP-PI-PEV) is a component that can be configured to evaluate collected process data using standard evaluation procedures and user-defined calculations.

The following data can be analyzed from the shop floor information system:

- Resources
- Business transactions
- Materials
- Process orders
- Materials consumption
- Product costs
- Process message evaluation—displays message data using SAP Business Graphics or transfers it to Microsoft EXCEL for further processing

If you have installed the ODBC software interface, process data may be extracted from the database for evaluation by third-party analysis tools.

Integrating PP-PI with Higher-Level Systems

When PP-PI is part of a decentralized production planning configuration, it can use the integration with higher-level systems (PP-PI-LHL) component to exchange data with higher-level or central planning systems in the following matters:

■ ID number of the material to be produced

■ Delivery date

■ Requirement quantity

These requirement specifications may be accepted from an R/2 system or from a third-party system.

Through the data exchange facility, the process data may take part in cross-application cost processing and efficiency studies, for example.

Linking to Other Systems

The mainframe SAP system R/2 may be used for central planning and financial management. The link to R/2 (PP-PI-LHL) component can be installed to exchange order information with one or more R/3 installations using PP-PI.

Links to third-party systems are enabled by Link to External Host Systems (PP-PI-LHL).

Collecting and Displaying Plant Data

Plant data includes messages related to the work of the line operators and the automated or partially automated machinery. Collecting plant data provides up-to-date information on machine utilization, order situation, and quality. The collected data also contributes to the stored statistics.

If you have installed external or third-party systems, the collection and display of their plant data is controlled by the plant data collection component (PP-PDC), which is able to provide functions under the following headings:

■ Check

■ Processing

■ Editing

■ Evaluation

■ Transfer

Recording Time Worked on Production Orders

A production order will have been planned on the basis of standard times. If you can record the actual times of the process phases you can make comparisons and arrive at an estimate of the effectiveness of the process in relation to the time planned for it.

The work order time recording (PP-PDC-WOT) component collects and evaluates all the time-related messages arriving as a result of work done on the particular order. The component has to be integrated with an external subsystem, such as a time recording system, which has been configured to communicate via a standard SAP interface.

PP-PDC-MOT is a work order time recording component for PM orders that manages work order time recording and evaluation against standard times for a plant maintenance (PM) order.

Personnel Time Recording (PP-PDC-LTR) has the task of recording all labor-related messages that are associated with particular production orders. The time messages signal when a line operator arrives and leaves or takes a break. The evaluated time data may be used in performance-related or time-related payment systems. The time management component is extensively covered in the QUE book *Administering SAP R/3: HR—Human Resources Module*.

PP-PDC-LTR has to be linked to a time recording system through an SAP standard interface.

PP-PDC-PTR is a project time recording component that collates collected time data in relation to a specific project.

Consulting the PP Information System

The information system (PP-IS) component provides a shop floor information system for monitoring, controlling, and planning your business operations relating to production. The particular features of the PP-IS are that it provides a choice of points of view on the data and you can control the level of detail displayed. The system is also referred to as Shop Floor Information System (SFIS).

The display of production information is based on key figures. A standard key figure is provided for many of the measurements that can be derived from collected plant data. The PP-IS looks after the collation of records and the calculations for the following types of key figures, for example:

- Lead times
- On-time delivery performance
- Capacity load utilization
- Costs
- KANBAN evaluations of just-in-time manufacturing

You can accept the standard evaluation procedures or specify flexible analysis in which you can modify the evaluation logic and parameters online or in customizing.

The shop floor information system (PP-IS) contributes to flexible planning systems, the early warning system (EWS), and the LIS logistics information library. LIS also integrates with the purchasing information system (PURCHIS) and inventory controlling (MM-IM). All information systems in LIS use similar techniques of analyzing data and they are all controlled in the same way by the user.

PP-IS can be linked to external data from third-party systems.

Reporting (PP-IS-REP) is the component that provides reports from the PP-IS information system. Analysis options take the following forms:

- Standard analyses—allow targeting of specific key figures for analysis, graphical display, and selective levels of detail
- Flexible analyses—allow grouping and aggregation of key figures to your specification followed by standard analysis and display

The R/3 standard analysis and display functions include the following:

- ABC analysis of important, less important, and relatively unimportant result sources
- Cumulative frequency curve
- Correlation curve
- Previous year comparison
- Planned/actual comparison

Linking PP with Sales and Operations Planning

The role of the planning component (PP-IS-PLN) is to link with the planning functionality of the logistics information system (LIS). LIS is integrated into the central component Sales and Operations Planning (SOP).

The SOP system is a flexible forecasting and planning tool with the following areas of applicability:

- Sales
- Production
- Supply chain

You can use the SOP to set targets on the basis of historical, existing, and estimated future data. Rough-cut planning forecasts the amounts of the capacities and other resources required to meet these SOP targets. You can conduct high-level planning of complex planning hierarchies and the detailed planning of finished products. Standard SOP is configured to use product group hierarchies planned level by level. Flexible SOP allows you to determine the structure of the planning hierarchies.

By configuration, you can arrange for target key figures set at one level of the organization to be distributed automatically and consistently to all the other organizational levels in the hierarchy. Alternatively, you can arrange that each level is planned separately.

Linking PP to the Logistics Information Library

PP-IS-LIS is the interface to the logistics information library (LIL) component that allows a PP user to create, classify, and find key figures in the area of logistics and the information systems connected with it.

A simple search will elicit all the key figures that are available in the LIL with their associated calculation procedures. You can arrange your own structured catalog of any key figures of interest. From the LIL, you can also build integrations of the reports, transactions, information systems, and tables from different areas of Logistics, such as purchasing, sales and production.

Building a Logistics Data Warehouse

Data Collection (PP-IS-DC) is an essential component of the logistics information system (LIS). You can use the PP-IS-DC component to define your own logistics data warehouse.

The technique of allowing a client to define information structures is used to ensure that any local data structure can be used without explicit modification by other user groups who can assign specific data to them. Update groups and update rules are used to help standardize the data warehouses across user groups.

Setting Up Early Warning Systems

The early warning system (PP-IS-EWS) component is integrated in the shop floor information system so that you can use it to select weak points in the production processes and have them monitored. The results are expressed in terms of selected key figures. You can also define exceptions that will initiate follow-up actions, such as a mail or fax message accompanied by a display of the critical data. ●

Part
IV
Ch
16

CHAPTER 17

Continuous Manufacturing with Process Orders

Manufacturing Batches

A process order is the main data object used for the detailed planning and execution of continuous process manufacturing. The batches in a production run or the output of a service can be represented by a process order generated from the appropriate master recipe. Necessarily, the process order contains all the information specified during process planning—the quantities, dates, and resources needed to manufacture the product or deliver the service.

The process order also specifies the rules for the account assignment and settlement of the costs incurred. Thus the process order in the PP-PI module performs the same business function as the production order in the PP application.

Managing Process Orders

Process order management entails the following activities:

- Process planning
- Process order execution and process management
- Order completion

Process planning entails the following steps:

- Order creation
- Scheduling
- Capacity requirements planning
- Material availability check
- Order release

When the process order is released, the process order and process management functions begin.

Process instructions are maintained in the process order. The process management converts these process instructions into control recipes.

Control recipes can be transferred to a process control system via a specific third-party interface. Alternatively, or in addition, they can be displayed in natural language in the form of a process instruction (PI) sheet. The PI sheet can be maintained by the line operator.

The following activities comprise process order execution:

1. Withdraw the required material components from the warehouse.
2. Record confirmations on the order processing statuses.
3. Perform in-process quality inspections for the inspection lot.
4. Post the goods receipt from production.
5. Send actual process data to different destinations using process messages.

Process messages are used for batch documentation and process evaluation.

The following activities comprise order close:

1. Process order settlement
2. Process data documentation
3. Reorganize process order documents by archiving and deleting

Creating a Process Order

Process order creation requires the following activities:

1. Select a master recipe.
2. Create reservations or copy them from planned orders.
3. Calculate planned costs.
4. Create capacity requirements for the resources.

When you create a process order you have to accept the current date as a basis or enter the basic order dates. The system then automatically schedules the process order. If circumstances change before the process order is started you can have it rescheduled automatically or enter the changes manually.

When a process order is released for production, your system may be configured to create or download control recipes, followed by the printing of shop floor documents, and the withdrawal of the materials needed for production. In this context, a withdrawal is the posting of a goods issue document that will allow the materials to be issued from the warehouse and trigger the necessary inventory control and accounting processes. When the process order has been executed, the delivery of the manufactured product to the warehouse is recorded by posting a goods receipt, which again triggers inventory control and accounting.

The process management component provides the data objects needed for using control recipes to generate PI sheets and data transfers to process control systems.

The quality management component provides the data objects needed to manage in-process quality inspections for process orders.

The product cost controlling component provides special functions for settling a process order.

In most respects, the sequence of control activities in process order execution is very similar to the sequence for production orders in discrete manufacturing. For example, you can create a process order with or without a reference to a material and with or without a master recipe. You can reference a planned order.

The following sequence illustrates a typical procedure:

1. Choose Logistics→Production—process →Process order.
2. Choose Process order→Create→With material.
3. Enter the material, the plant, and the process order type.
4. Enter the header data, such as the total quantity, the lot size, and the order start or finish date, or both.

Process orders are generally scheduled backwards although you can specify the SchedType and the margin key to control whether the floats will be assigned before or after production, together with the release period if some time has to elapse before the manufactured product is released for delivery.

If your system has more than one production version, you will be required to select one before the master recipe is copied. The operation overview is then displayed for you to make any necessary changes to the operations or their phases.

Scheduling a Process Order

The scheduling function in order processing is responsible for calculating the production dates and capacity requirements for all operations within a process order. If you are creating a process order manually, when you choose a scheduling type, the system will prompt you to enter the basic order dates. If your process order is converted from a planned order created in MRP, the basic dates of the order will be already determined.

The scheduling function uses the basic or "required" dates to calculate a scheduled start date and a scheduled finish date during the next scheduling run. Customizing establishes whether an order is to be rescheduled automatically every time you save a change that would be relevant to scheduling.

The following scheduling types can be entered in the process order main header:

- Forward scheduling—from the order start date, with a calculation of the scheduled start and finish dates.
- Backward scheduling—from the order finish date, with a calculation of the scheduled start and finish dates.
- Scheduling to current date—adopts current date as the order start date and schedules forward. You enter the order finish date and the system calculates the scheduled start and finish dates.
- Only capacity requirements—from entered start and finish dates from which the system calculates scheduled start and finish dates, which it assigns to all the individual operations.

Customizing the Scheduling Parameters

Each order type, plant, and planner group is associated with a set of process order scheduling parameters as follows:

- Scheduling type—for example, forwards, backwards. Proposed in the order header screen. Can be overwritten for individual process orders.
- Current date scheduling—the process order is forwards rescheduled automatically if the order start date has been passed by more than a specified number of days.

To change the scheduled start and finish of the order manually, select Header→Change in Dates→Scheduled dates. You can also change the scheduling type at the same screen. To reschedule, call the function Process order→Functions→Schedule.

Allowing Order Floats

Malfunctions and interruptions are allowed for by consulting float data taken from the scheduling margin key, which is set in customizing and assigned to the material master record of each material that is manufactured.

The float before production can be used for capacity leveling if a resource bottleneck is anticipated. The float before production also provides a margin against delays in the provision of the material components.

The float after production provides a buffer against unexpected malfunctions in the production process. The hope is that the magnitude of this buffer will allow the process to finish on or before the scheduled finish of the order.

The scheduled start of the order is calculated by adding the float before production to the required order start date. The scheduled finish date of the order is calculated by subtracting the float after production from the required order finish date.

Part IV
Ch
17

The system calculates the release date of the order by subtracting the release period defined in the scheduling margin from the scheduled start of the order. Thus the order is released early enough for the production planner to make use of the floats if necessary.

If an operation is not scheduled, the system assumes that it has a duration of zero. If the assigned control key marks an operation for scheduling, the duration of the operation is calculated by cumulating the duration of each of its phases under control of a phase network from which the phase order dates are copied to the operation. Thus the start time of the first phase becomes the start time of the operation, and the finish time of the last phase becomes the finish time of the operation.

The system will operate with default values for the phases taken from the master recipe if they have been maintained there. A single phase can be marked as relevant for scheduling, in which case the whole operation is considered relevant for scheduling. Conversely, if an operation is marked as relevant for scheduling, then at least one of its phases must be relevant for scheduling.

Phases can be overlapped in time by defining relationships between them. You can also link the scheduling of two or more process orders by maintaining relationships between particular phases of the different process orders. Chapter 7, "Scheduling Routings," describes the basic operations for arranging the timetable of production activities. The simplest relationship between two phases is for one to begin as soon as the other finishes.

Interpreting Working/Operating Time

The working or operating time establishes when work can be performed. This will normally have to take account of the plant calendar or some other calendar defined so as to identify which days and shifts may be counted as working time. You can specify working time by defining the start and end of shifts or by defining the breaks in a standard working day.

The following rules are used by default to calculate the duration of a process phase:

- If the unit of the phase duration is smaller than the unit day, the working/operating time per working day applies.
- If the unit of the individual phase is greater than or equal to the working day, the phases are scheduled to the day on the basis of the calendar used for scheduling.

Scheduling Secondary Resources

A secondary resource may be needed for only some of the duration of a phase or operation. These secondary resources are scheduled in relation to reference dates in the operation or phase in which they are needed. This information is displayed in the Secondary Resources screen, which is reached from the Operation Overview screen.

In addition to the reference date, which is the start or finish date of the operation or phase, the system needs to know a time period to use as an offset for calculating the usage of the secondary resource. A positive offset is added to the reference date, a negative offset is subtracted from the reference date.

If you fail to maintain scheduling data for a secondary resource, the system will default to the setup start date and the execution finish date of the respective operation. It is assumed that the secondary resource is needed throughout the operation. These values can be entered using a predefined key, which can have the following entries:

- Reference date for start
- Offset
- Reference date for finish
- Offset

Scheduling Capacity Requirements

In capacity scheduling, the system takes work breaks into account. Thus secondary resources can also be scheduled to allow for work breaks when assessing capacity availability.

An operation is always deemed to have a capacity requirement value of zero. However, the individual phases of this operation do have capacity requirements that are subject to availability checking and hence to scheduling. The results appear as dates of calculated capacity requirements, and they will correspond to the dates of the operation.

Interpreting the Scheduling Log and Results

After each scheduling run, a process order will contain a scheduling log that contains any messages generated during the most recent run. You can decide how such messages should be sorted and grouped. You can also decide at the customizing stage whether the scheduling log is automatically displayed after each scheduling run or only on demand from the menu.

Monitoring the Dates and Quantities of Process Orders

The header screen titled Date/Quantity Overview displays the release, start, and finish dates of the currently released process orders. Any planned order you may have converted will also be shown.

If you want to inspect the dates and times of the individual operations and phases, you must go to the Operation Overview screen. There you must flag the operation or phase you are interested in and select Operation→Overview of dates to access the Detail screen of Operation Dates.

Scheduling Material List Components

The components in the Material list are those required for production. The necessary information may be already stored in master data as a material list, and it can be automatically transferred to the process order.

The following data is needed for each material component taken from the material list:

- Item category, for example,

    L: item kept in stock

    R: variable-sized item that is kept in stock

    N: item not kept in stock that requires a requisition

    T: text item, of various types

    D: document item, of various types

- Costing relevancy Indicator (CR)
- Bulk material indicator (BM)—provided at the resource and not issued from stock or costed
- Backflushing (BF)—withdrawal of the material is not posted until the corresponding operation is confirmed
- Coproduct (CO)—entered in the material list with a negative quantity; item type is **L**

If you have a master recipe for the material to be produced, you can allocate each component to specific operations or phases in the recipe. You can also change any component.

If you have neither material list or master recipe for a material you intend to produce, the system will remind you when you attempt to create a process order for it. However, there may exist a material that has a similar material list that you can select for copying. Whether or not you identify a material list at this stage, the system will allow you to create a process order.

You will be shown the Material List screen, even if it is empty. Here you can enter, delete, or change material components, provided the system status for the process order is either *Created* or *Released*. You must work within the following restrictions:

1. You cannot change the item category of a component once it has been created in the order.

2. If you delete a component that is allocated to a released operation, the system will still display the component in the order, but with the status *Deletion* indicator active, which will prevent you from entering data for this operation.

The following detail screens for components can be maintained:

- General data
- Coproduct
- Purchasing data
- Text item

The following sequence will change component allocation to operations or phases:

1. Select the component whose allocation you want to change.

2. Select the menu options Edit→Reallocate.

3. Using the Reallocate pop-up, change the allocation of the component from one operation or phase to another.

Click on Operation list to display all the operations and phases in your process order.

Exploring the General Data Screen

The General Data screen for process order components contains the following component data:

- Material—name of the material component you have selected.
- Item—item number of the component in your material list.
- Item category—such as stock item or nonstock item.
- Status—component status, such as *Released*.
- Storage location—storage location of the material.
- Batch—batch number if relevant.
- Plant—plant in which the material component is stored.
- Requirement date—by which the requested quantity of material is needed.
- Sort string—string that can be defined for sorting components in the display.
- Revision level—indicates the change status of an object. You can assign the revision level to a change with reference to a change number.

The General Data screen includes the following quantity data:

- Requirements quantity—the amount you require of the individual component in order to produce the order quantity
- Unit of measure—the unit of measure in which stock of this material is managed in this plant

- Committed quantity—the quantity confirmed in the availability check
- Issue quantity—the component quantity already issued from stock for the order
- Final issue—indicator set automatically for a goods movement when the total reserved quantity has been withdrawn or delivered
- Coproduct—indicator showing that this material component is a coproduct

Exploring the Coproduct Item Data

The coproduct procedure is used to represent the manufacture of different materials within the same process order. An order for several coproducts specifies the common materials needed and describes the shared production processes.

A coproduct can be allocated to an operation or to a phase according to where it is processed. Each coproduct is assigned an equivalence number or percentage, which is used when distributing the costs of the operation to the various coproducts.

The starting point for a master recipe that involves coproducts, and for a consequent process order, will be one or more materials of the process material type. No updating of inventory quantities or costs is required for a process material.

If a material is marked as a coproduct in the material master record, and in the material lists, you will be able to access the coproduct screens that display the general data plus the following information:

- Order item data
- Tolerance data
- Control data
- Goods receipt data
- Delivery data

Order item data includes the following:

- Quantity—of a coproduct produced using this order.
- Valuation type key—uniquely identifies stocks of a material subject to split valuation. The valuation category determines which valuation types are permissible for a material.
- GR quantity—the quantity of goods received for the order item.

The tolerance data comprises the Underdelivery/overdelivery tolerance, which can be flagged as Unlimited.

Control data includes the following:

- Quality inspection—indicates that the component is subject to quality inspection and that the goods receipt is posted to quality management (QM) stock.
- Delivery completed—indicates that no further goods receipts are expected for this order item.
- GR processing time—indicates the goods receipt processing time in days.

The goods receipt data comprises the following:

- Storage location—location to which the component is posted
- Batch—enter existing batch number or create a batch master record
- Distribution—the distribution key for MRP

The delivery data includes the following:

- Goods recipient—for whom the material is destined
- Unloading point—the point, such as a dock, where the material is unloaded

Exploring the Coproduct Settlement Rule

The coproduct settlement rule is maintained in a screen of that name. The actual costs incurred for the order are settled to one or more receiver cost-objects. An account may exist for the material produced or the sales order may be the receiver cost-object. Your company may post coproduct costs to a particular cost center. The system posts offsetting entries automatically to credit the process order.

If you are using more than one receiver, the system will accept either a percentage or an equivalence number assigned to each receiver. The costs of the order are then distributed proportionately to the settlement receivers.

The Purchasing Data screen allows you to maintain data for the external procurement of material components of category **N**, which is for nonstock items.

A component of the item category **T** will be a text item. It can be maintained in the Text Item screen as general data plus a descriptive text about the item.

Checking the Availability of Material

You can initiate an availability check manually, or preconfigure the system to check automatically during order creation and order release. The only stocks that will be checked will be of materials that are marked for inventory management and have the stock component item category **L**. The checking is customized for each plant and for each order type; but you can always start a check manually.

The checking scope is defined by a combination of the check group and the valid check rule. The result is a definition of the following form:

- Which MRP elements are taken into account in the check
- Which inventory categories are taken into account
- Whether the replenishment lead time is taken into account

A material component is allocated to a check group by activating the Availability check field in the Sale/Plant Data or *MRP2* screens of the material master record. Materials in a check group are checked at the same time.

The following entries are accepted in the Availability check field:

■ Check group 01—materials produced in-house. The system need not check purchase orders or purchase requisitions, since they are irrelevant to materials produced in-house.

■ Check group 02—materials produced externally. In this checking scope, you specify that the system need not check sales or production orders, since they are irrelevant to materials produced externally.

If you fail to allocate a material component to a check group, a message will appear in the availability log after the checking run.

Check rules are maintained in customizing for each application. A different rule may be defined for the same material in each application.

Checking Availability to Promise

The ATP method determines the quantity of a material that is available to promise. In particular, the method checks the following:

■ Whether the material requirements can be covered on the requirements date

■ When the requirements can be covered, if a full coverage of the requirements is not possible on the requirements date

The availability check can be carried out at plant or warehouse level, storage location level or batch level. You have to designate the level per component in the Material List screen. If a check at warehouse or batch level finds that the components are not available, the system automatically carries out an additional check at plant level.

If you call for a check at process order header level, either automatically or manually, you will find out about all the material components. Otherwise, you can manually check on the availability of particular components. There is a log of material availability that you can consult to find the details of any material shortfalls that have been flagged MSPT in the order header.

At the customizing stage, you can arrange that process orders with material shortfall are blocked for release.

Calculating the Quantity of Material Required

The calculation sheet is a tool to assist in the use of the material quantity calculation function.

The following sequence will call up the calculation sheet:

1. Select Material→Material quantity calculation in the material list.
2. The system branches to the calculation sheet. The top row is available for entering a formula definition. The data table below the formula lists your components, the requirements quantities, and various columns for the characteristics you have assigned to your components in the classification function, if any.
3. Row 1 is locked and contains the material number and requirements quantity of the material you want to produce.

4. Mark the cell you want to formulate and then click on Formula definition. The requirements quantity of this component or a formula, if one exists, will appear in the Formula definition row at the top of the sheet.

5. Use the mathematical functions in the sheet to enter a formula to calculate the amount required for each component. The row you are working on remains highlighted.

6. Press Enter to have the system calculate the quantity you need of the respective component.

7. Using the characteristics of the component, identify further factors for your calculation, if necessary. For example, calculate concentrated quantities from effective quantities.

8. Select Transfer results to return to the Material List screen.

The system will have entered the quantity calculated in the calculation sheet as the requirements quantity for the component you are working with.

Preliminary Costing

The system automatically calculates the planned order cost when you create a process order and after each subsequent change of data in the order. The planned costs are then allocated to cost elements.

Primary cost elements include:

- Material costs
- Costs for external procurement

These costs reach the process order via goods issues, for example.

Secondary cost elements include:

- Production costs
- Material overhead costs
- Production overhead costs

These costs are allocated to the order via internal cost allocations derived from phases and secondary resources.

Using Fiscal Year Cost Segments

The system cumulates cost elements into cost segments. These segments are separately managed for each fiscal year.

The planned costs are incurred in an accounting period that includes the latest start date of the phase or the requirement date of the material.

Actual costs for material produced in-house are updated when material issues or completion confirmations are carried out for the order. For an externally procured material component the actual costs are updated when the goods receipt is posted.

Both planned costs and actual costs are recorded in cost segments so that you can compare planned with actual costs at any stage of order processing.

Planning Costs for Components

The costing relevancy indicator of the component determines whether a material component is to be considered when costing. This indicator may be edited in the General Data screen for the process order.

The assignment of a material component to the relevant cost element is performed automatically by the materials management consumption account assignment function.

In customizing, each order type for each plant can have a costing variant defined for it. The costing variant consults a valuation variant which determines which price from the material master record is to be used. For example the moving average price or the standard price can be selected by the valuation variant to calculate the planned costs of a material component.

The planned cost of a material manufactured in-house is calculated using the valuation variant and a price stored in the material master record. For materials procured externally, the system distinguishes between stock components and nonstock components.

The planned costs for a stock component are calculated as for a material manufactured in-house. By contrast, the planned costs for a component that is not kept in stock are assumed to equal the value of the requisition created for that component. This value reflects the valuation price and the price unit of the requisition.

The manufacturing activity used in the order can be divided into internal activity and external activity. Planned costs are needed for both.

Operations are not directly costed; only their individual phases are. And a phase is not costed unless the control key assigned to the phase indicates that the phase is relevant to costing. If the phase is relevant, then the costing relevancy indicator is used to specify a factor, which may be zero, that is used to calculate the services performed in a phase.

The system has to develop a quantity structure to represent the activities that are planned for the phase. Then the quantity structure can be valuated by applying a price.

The resource that provides the activities, such as a work center, has a master record that stores the data needed to set up a quantity structure for the activities produced in or by the resource. Each of these activities is allocated to a specific activity type. Each activity type is allocated to a formula that can be specific to that particular resource.

This resource-specific formula for an activity type will process the standard times in the phase to calculate how much activity of the particular activity type would be needed if the phase, in fact, took exactly the standard time to process the standard quantity of material. Once the system knows how much of each type of activity is needed, it can consult the price for each activity type and arrive at the preliminary costs for each activity and hence for the phase.

Part

IV

Ch

17

Assigning Overhead Costs as Surcharges

Some costs cannot be assigned directly to a process order in the way that material and activity costs can. For instance, energy costs and general storage costs may have to be assigned indirectly as overhead surcharges, which are updated in the order under the cost elements as defined in the costing sheet. A costing sheet determines which overhead surcharges are assigned to an order. The costing sheet is chosen by a costing variant that is defined in customizing for each order type and for each plant.

The costing sheet specifies the following conditions:

- Which direct costs shall have surcharges applied
- Under which conditions an overhead is calculated
- The surcharge percentage for each set of conditions
- Which cost object, such as a cost center, is reduced under which cost element headings when actual costs are posted

It can be convenient to have a different overhead percentage calculation for different materials to be produced. You assign the products to overhead groups and consult this group via an overhead key when applying the costing sheet formulas.

Releasing a Process Order

CRTD is shown under *System status* in the main header when you create a process order. There are some constraints on a process order that has been created but not yet released.

- You cannot carry out completion confirmations for the order.
- You cannot generate a control recipe.
- You cannot carry out goods movements for the order; that is, you cannot withdraw any components.

Releasing the process order removes these restrictions and changes the status to *REL*. If you are working on a process order in the creation or change mode, select Process order→Functions→Release.

You can customize a production scheduling profile that releases a process order as soon as it is created. You have to assign the profile to the process order in the material master record (Work Scheduling 1) of the material to be produced, or via the order type in customizing.

If you release an individual operation, then all the constituent phases will also be released. The process order will have a system status of partially released, *PREL*. When you release the last operation of the process order, the system status of the order will be set to *REL*.

If you have released all the phases of an operation, then the operation will be released. Similarly, if you delete the last phase of an operation without releasing it, the operation is released.

The following sequence will release an individual operation or phase:

1. In the Main Header screen, select the functions Goto→2-line operation overview in order to see the status of the operations.

2. Select the operations/phases you want to release.

3. Select Operation→Functions→For operation/phase→Release.

If you carry out the same functions on the 1-line operation overview, you can also release the marked operations or phases.

Releasing Process Orders Collectively

You can select process orders according to the following criteria, in any logical combination:

- Order type
- Plant
- MRP controller
- Material
- Process order number (interval)
- Release date (interval)
- Status profile

The following sequence will release the selected process orders:

1. Select Logistics→Production—process →Process order.

2. Select Process order→Release.

3. Select the relevant plant.

4. Enter further selection criteria if necessary.

5. To select process orders according to their release date, enter the interval desired in the fields Release and To release.

6. If a release period is already proposed in your user master record, the corresponding values are automatically taken over into the fields Release and To release.

7. Select all the process orders you want to release.

8. Select Release.

If you select Release+Control recipe, the system will also create control recipes after the release of the selected process orders.

Interpreting Actual and Planned Data After Order Release

A process order is planned in terms of resource classes. However, when the order is released for production, each instance of the planned resource class is replaced by a particular resource of the appropriate class. The actual characteristics of the reserved ingredients replace the values copied from the master recipe. Thus the active ingredient potency, for instance, is taken from the records of each warehouse batch that has been assigned to the individual resource.

Part
IV

Ch
17

Furthermore, if scheduling and capacity requirements calculations have been carried out in the rough-cut planning phase for the planned order, these results can be automatically taken over into the process order.

Notifying Schedule Deviations

A periodic background job can be run to determine whether there are going to be any schedule deviations for any operation or phase in any of the currently released process orders.

If the schedule deviation alerting system is to be successful, each critical operation must have a deviation recording variant defined in customizing. This deviation recording variant must include the following data:

- Selection criteria—when to be used
- Tolerances—in each of the values to be recorded
- ID of the user to be informed if any tolerance is exceeded

Using Inspection Lots to Plan and Control Quality

An inspection may need to be carried out on a sample of the product that has been set aside for the purpose and identified as an inspection lot. An inspection lot document can also be created to document a request for an inspection that does not require a sample to be set aside.

An inspection lot document stores inspection characteristics that have been allocated to the lot in order to particularize the request for an inspection.

Characteristics that are to be inspected can be qualitative or quantitative.

For a within-process inspection, an inspection lot is created for the process order. Characteristics are assigned to individual operations in the master recipe, and the inspection results are assembled in the inspection lot document.

An operation that has been assigned an inspection on at least one phase will have the system status *ICHA*.

Differentiating Planned and Unplanned Inspection Lot Characteristics

Planned inspection characteristics are maintained in the master recipe. Unplanned inspection characteristics are maintained in Quality Management (QM) results recording. The QM module is normally integrated with R/3 and you can branch to QM from the operation/phase overview of the process order.

Inspection data is maintained in the quality management view of the material master of the material being produced. The inspection data has to be activated before it will be consulted by the system.

If the system finds activated inspection data in the material master, it will automatically create an inspection lot when the first operation of the process order is released for production. It is also possible to create an inspection lot manually from the process order.

Under the QM system, a process will be inspected if you generate an inspection lot, in which case the inspection is referred to as a *process-accompanying inspection*. You cannot initiate an inspection of a process that has reached the status of *Technically complete*. Nor can you inspect a process if the process order has been flagged for deletion.

The material master of the material to be produced must contain the relevant inspection data. The following sequence will allow you to maintain this data from the QM view of the process order:

1. Mark the field Quality inspection.
2. Call the function Inspection data.
3. On the detail screen QM Inspection Data, enter an Inspection type such as 03 for inspection in production.
4. Enter a Quality score procedure.
5. Enter an **x** in field Act to activate the QM inspection for this inspection type and this material.

In the master recipe that you have used to create the process order, there must be entries for the QM data at the operation or phase level that specify the inspection characteristics. At the recipe header level, you must have activated the indicator for inspection point processing.

The following sequence will manually create an inspection lot:

1. In the Operation overview of the master recipe, mark the operations during which you want an inspection to take place.
2. Select Operation→Quality data.
3. In the section Check points in production, click on Offset change to change the type of check point. You must have Time-related flagged here to manually create an inspection lot.
4. Enter the Time factor and the Time unit.
5. At the operation level of the Operation overview, set up at least one inspection characteristic for at least one operation or phase.

In the process order, you select Process order→Functions→Generate inspection lot. The system status *ILC* in the header of the process order signifies that an inspection lot has been created. *ILNC* indicates that an inspection could not be created. This status indicator can be a useful adjunct to a search profile when reviewing many process orders.

Deleting an Inspection Lot

You will not be allowed to delete an inspection lot if any of the operations in the process order contain an unplanned inspection characteristic. You can delete an inspection lot that does not contain any inspection results.

Part

IV

Ch

17

The following sequence will delete an inspection lot:

1. Call up the process order.
2. Select Process order→Functions.
3. Select inspection lot→Delete insp. lot.

Creating Unplanned Inspection Characteristics

By definition, an inspection characteristic is unplanned if it does not appear in the master recipe. The unplanned inspection characteristic is created in QM results recording.

The following sequence will create an inspection characteristic:

1. Call up the process order.
2. In the operation overview, mark the operation to which you want to allocate an inspection characteristic.
3. Select Operation→Functions.
4. Select Unplanned insp. char.

The process order you are working on must have been released, and it must already have an inspection lot.

Deleting an Operation with Inspection Characteristics

You can delete an operation from a process order provided that no QM results have yet been recorded, and provided no unplanned inspection characteristic has been assigned to the operation.

System status *ICHA* indicates that an operation has been allocated an inspection characteristic. System status *QMDA* indicates that QM results have been recorded for this operation.

Thus an operation with status *ICHA* can be deleted if you first delete the inspection lot allocated to the order, then delete the operation. Finally, you must regenerate the inspection lot for the process order so as to retain the inspection characteristics that are needed for the operations that remain.

If an operation has been released and you delete it, the system status *DLFL* will be activated to allow the operation to be flagged for deletion, yet its details will remain visible in the operation overview.

Inspecting Partial Lots

A partial lot can arise if you are manufacturing using different resources, or if you use the same resource at different times. If the material is managed as documented batches, you assign individual batch numbers to the partial lots when recording the inspection results in QM.

Inspection characteristics have to be assigned to the operations in the master recipe or in the process order so that the partial lots generated by these operations will be inspected. You can simplify this assignment operation by creating a general characteristic that includes all the inspection characteristics. Then you can classify the material you are producing with this general characteristic.

Printing Shop Floor Papers

The traditional term *shop floor papers* is used to refer to such items as a complete printout of a material provision list, or a printout of time tickets.

Any of the following shop floor papers can be reprinted at any time after a process order has been scheduled and released, provided your print profile allows it:

- The operations of a process order
- The operation control ticket
- The goods issue slip
- The job ticket
- The pick list
- The completion confirmation slip
- The wage slip

The lists of shop floor papers allowed by your profile can be inspected by selecting Process order→Print→List control.

Part
IV
Ch
17

Printing Completion Confirmations

The progress of a process order is monitored by inspecting the completion confirmations, because they document the processing status of orders, operations, phases, and individual capacities.

The following information is recorded in a completion confirmation:

- The quantity processed in a phase
- How much activity is used to carry out a phase
- The actual dates of a phase
- The resource at which the phase is carried out
- Who carried out the phase

The following actions can be triggered by a completion confirmation:

- A reduction in the capacity load on the resource
- An update of the costs because the actual or confirmed data is available
- An update of the order administrative data, such as times or order statistics
- Withdrawal postings for backflushed components
- An automatic goods receipt for one designated phase per order
- An update of the expected yield in the order, as used in MRP

A completion confirmation can be posted for orders, phases, or individual capacities of phases. You cannot confirm an operation because costing, scheduling, and capacity planning are based solely on the confirmation data of the phases.

Therefore you have to ensure that material components for which backflushing has been defined have been assigned only to phases. The system automatically posts the goods issue for a material component when the phase in which it is used is confirmed. Individual capacities of secondary resources are generally confirmed in the same way as phases.

Any of the following data elements can be confirmed for a particular phase:

- Quantity processed.
- Amount of activity used to carry out the phase, such as the duration of the processing time.
- Estimated amount of activity remaining unused after the phase is completed, which can be consulted in scheduling and capacity planning to adjust the standard values assigned for the phase.
- Time and date when the processing of the phase started or finished.
- Personnel data, such as the number of employees needed for the phase or the personnel number of the employee who carried out the phase.
- The particular resource at which the phase was actually carried out.
- A long text may be entered for each completion confirmation.
- The posting date is mandatory for every completion confirmation. The system proposes the current date.

In the Material Overview screen you can post planned and unplanned goods movements with every confirmation.

Using Fixed and Variable Parameters in Completion Confirmations

Completion confirmation can be accelerated by entering settings. Fixed parameters are established in customizing and the variable parameters are entered with each completion confirmation, where they may interact with the fixed parameters previously assigned.

Phase completion confirmations can be customized in the following respects:

- Whether partial or final confirmation should be suggested by the system
- Whether a costing log should be displayed if errors occur during the calculation of costs
- The default time unit for completion confirmations
- Whether the underdelivery and/or overdelivery tolerances of the order should be checked during confirmation
- Whether the system should react if there are any deviations from the specified phase or operation sequence
- Whether previously confirmed data, or data which is planned to be confirmed, should be displayed during confirmation

- Whether an error log is displayed for erroneous goods movements for backflushing or automatic goods receipts, and whether you can correct the errors in the material overview before posting the confirmation
- Whether the system should check that the date is not in the future

To display these settings in the process order confirmation screen, select Parameters→Fixed parameters.

When you are about to enter the actual data in the confirmation function, you can select Parameters →Variable parameters to specify the following variable parameters for each completion confirmation:

- Whether a partial or final confirmation should be carried out
- The confirmation detail screen to which the system should automatically branch after the initial screen
- Whether previously confirmed phases should be displayed during a confirmation, or only open phases
- Whether an error log should be displayed for goods movements with errors
- Whether an error log should be displayed if errors occur during the calculation of actual costs
- Whether only phases which require confirmation should be displayed, as specified by the phase control key

Entering Completion Confirmations

If you enter a completion confirmation for a time confirmation ticket for a phase, you can confirm quantities, durations, activities, or personnel data. If you enter a completion confirmation for a time event, you can confirm just specific times such as the start or finish of processing.

Managing Process Order Statuses

A status is an indication of the stage reached in the processing of a data object. The status of an object changes when a business transaction is carried out on it. The current status of an object controls which business transactions are allowed on this object.

A system status is set by the system and cannot be influenced by the user except by performing one of the permitted business transactions. A user status is never activated except by the user. Each user needs a customized status profile for each order type in order to be able to activate or deactivate the user statuses nominated in the profile. Any number of user statuses can be defined.

The status menu is viewable from the process order header. It shows the various statuses that will be assigned or the order during the course of processing. The currently active statuses are shown as indicators in the process order header.

The following system status indicators are predefined:

Part

IV

Ch

17

- *CRTD*—Order created
- *REL*—Order released
- *MSPT*—Material shortage
- *PRC*—Order precosted
- *CSER*—Error in cost calculation
- *EBRR*—Process data documentation required
- *SETC*—Settlement rule created
- *CRSR*—Control recipe created
- *APG*—Approved
- *APRC*—Based on approved recipe
- *APGS*—Single order approved
- *APNG*—Approval not granted
- *APRS*—Approval withdrawn

A particular status can control the following types of action:

- Allow a specific business transaction
- Issue a warning before the business transaction is carried out
- Forbid a specific business transaction

Any business transaction can be carried out only if both the following conditions are satisfied:

- At least one active status allows the transaction
- No active status forbids the transaction

A status is active if it is set in the object. However, a status can be inactive, either because it has never been activated, or because it was active before but has since been deactivated.

Each order type has to be assigned a customized status profile. This status profile can perform the following functions:

- Define user statuses and document their function in long texts
- Define a numbered sequence of user statuses in the order they are expected to occur
- Specify the user status that will be automatically set when the object is first created
- Establish rules that automatically deactivate a user status if a particular business transaction is carried out
- Establish rules that allow or forbid certain transactions when a particular user status is active

The following sequence will access a series of status management screens:

1. Select Process order→Functions→Status.
2. In the Change Status screen, you can inspect the statuses active in the process order.

3. Mark any status listed and select the button Business transactions to view the business transactions that are allowed, or prohibited, and any business transactions for which the system has issued a warning in this process order.

The Status Overview screen shows the statuses active or currently inactive in the process order, together with their status numbers showing their expected position in the sequence of user statuses. The status profile can be changed by selecting Details→Status object.

Managing Goods Movements for Process Orders

Goods movement documents have to be posted in the form of goods issues from stock with consequences for inventory management. After manufacturing, the processed material is delivered to stock. This goods movement is documented as a goods receipt.

Part

IV

Ch

17

Both goods issues from stock and goods receipts to stock have the following consequences:

1. A material document is created to record the goods movement.
2. The stock quantities of the material are updated.
3. The stock values are updated in the material master record.
4. The stock/consumption accounts are updated.

Planning the Withdrawal of Material Components

The act of creating a process order causes the system to automatically create a reservation, which has an item number for each material component. However the materials reserved in this way cannot be issued from stock until the phase or operation where they will be used is released for production.

You can manually post a goods movement from inventory management, or you can transfer a material consumption message. This message is one of a large number of standard process messages available to process control.

Although you can confirm an operation, it is usual in PP-PI to confirm only the specific phases. If the backflush indicator is set for a component contained in the material list, the goods issue is posted automatically when you create the confirmation for the respective phase or operation. The system automatically debits the process order for the value of the components as they are withdrawn from stock. This value represents the actual costs and is divided according to cost element and origin.

The system will recognize either the order number or the reservation number when you are identifying which material components to issue from stock.

The following sequence will issue material components from stock:

1. Select Logistics→Materials management.
2. Select Inventory management.
3. Select Goods movement→Goods issue.

4. Select Goods issue→Create with reference.

5. Select either To reservation or To order.

When you have entered or confirmed the details of the reservation or process order, press *Continue*. The system proposes the movement type 261, goods issue for order. All the material components in the order that are not marked as bulk material, or as material to be backflushed, will be offered for you to check and save as a goods issue.

If you have not referred to a reservation or to a process order, the reservations remain open and the required quantity is still reserved, even though the requirement no longer physically exists because you have posted a goods issue.

Moving Goods as Unplanned Withdrawals

You might have to withdraw some materials for an order even though these materials were not originally listed as components in the order. In these circumstances the system has to update the actual costs of the order by posting unplanned withdrawals.

The following sequence will post unplanned withdrawals for a process order:

1. In the initial screen, select Logistics →Materials management→Inventory management.

2. Enter movement type 261 (goods issue for order).

3. Enter the storage location and the plant from which the goods are to be issued.

4. Press Enter. The system automatically branches to the screen Enter Goods Issue: New Items.

5. Enter the number of your process order.

6. For each material you want to be issued, enter the material number, the quantity, the quantity unit.

The material you require for an unplanned withdrawal may be managed in batches, in which case you have to enter the batch number or perform the batch determination procedure by entering a batch search specification or calling for a generic search using the asterisk * as the entry in the Batch field.

When you have completed the list of unplanned withdrawals, save it as the goods issue.

Delivering Manufactured Material to the Warehouse

The process order header screen Goods Receipt/Valuation contains the information needed to deliver the manufactured material to the warehouse. The following fields and indicators are available:

■ *Underdeliv. tol.*—percentage tolerance of underdelivery quantity.

■ *Overdeliv. tol.*—percentage tolerance of overdelivery quantity.

■ *Unlimited*—indicates that unlimited overdelivery quantities are permitted.

■ *Quality inspection*—indicates that the system will automatically propose the material to be posted to stock in quality inspection when the receipt posting is attempted.

■ *Goods receipt indicator* (GR)—indicates that a goods receipt is expected for the process order because the process order is relevant for inventory management.

■ *Delivery complete indicator* (Del. compl)—set automatically by the system as soon as a delivery is posted within the delivery tolerances. Can be set manually during a goods receipt posting.

■ *Non-valuated goods receipt indicator* (GR non-val)—set automatically by the system if the order is assigned to an account other than that of the material to be produced, for example, to a sales order.

■ *Storage location*—a field in which a storage location will be suggested, if one has been maintained in the material master of the material being produced.

In the same way as a storage location can be suggested from the material master, Batch, Goods recipient, and Unloading point can be suggested for the goods receipt.

Posting Goods to Stock Automatically

If you require the finished material to be posted automatically to stock when the operation or phase is confirmed, this must be specified in the control key of the relevant operation or phase. Automatic goods receipt posting can only be assigned to one operation or phase per order. This would normally be the last phase.

The system will issue a warning and oblige you to post a finished material to stock by a manual posting if you have assigned automatic goods receipt posting to more than one operation or phase.

It is not good practice to specify automatic goods receipt posting in continuous process manufacturing because it is very seldom the case that the quantity of finished product yielded by a process is equal to the quantity of material delivered as input. The automatic goods posting will therefore tend to be an inaccurate estimate of the quantity of finished material actually delivered to stock. In PP-PI, it is more usual to have the value of the yield sent as a process message from process control when the completion of the operation is confirmed.

Checking During a Goods Receipt to Stock

The act of posting a goods receipt to document the delivery of a material to stock causes the system to perform the following checks:

■ Goods receipt indicator—does this indicator GR allow a goods receipt for this order?

■ GR non-val—is the goods receipt to be valuated?

■ Under- or overdelivery tolerance conditions satisfied?

Costing a Delivery to Stock

There are two possible ways of working out the costs of producing the material delivered to stock by a goods receipt posting. The material to be produced has a price control indicator stored in the material master, as follows:

- **S**—multiply the delivered quantity by the standard price in the material master record of the material produced.
- **V**—multiply the delivered quantity by the price defined by the valuation variant.

Updating the Material Master by a Delivery to Stock

The Accounting view of the material master record includes the following fields, which are updated automatically when you post a goods receipt for the material:

- Total stock quantity—the total valuated stock of the material.
- Total value—the value of all the valuated stock of the material.
- Moving average price—price calculated from the goods movements and invoices created for the material. The average price is calculated as the material value as recorded in the stock account of the material, divided by the total quantity of warehouse stock held in the plant. The average is recalculated at each relevant posting.

Updating the Order After a Delivery to Stock

In the main header of the order, the Date/Quantity Overview screen includes the following fields, which are updated when you post a goods receipt for the material produced:

- Confirmed quantity—total delivered to stock from this order
- Confirmed finish date—date of the most recent goods receipt for the material
- Order status—remains set to *Partially delivered* until the total quantity delivered to stock reaches the order quantity minus the underdelivery tolerance

Final delivery is the status that is activated in the process order as soon as the total quantity delivered to stock for the order is within the tolerance limits of the order. You can manually activate the *Del. compl* indicator during a goods receipt, which will also set *Final delivery* as the process order status.

Although the status *Final delivery* specifies that no further goods receipt is expected for the order, it is still possible to post goods receipts for any remaining quantities.

The following sequence will post a goods receipt for a delivery to stock:

1. From the initial screen, select Logistics→Materials management→Inventory management.
2. Select Goods movement→Goods receipt→For order.
3. Select Movement type→Order to warehouse (101).
4. Check the entry, add the order number, the plant, and the storage location.
5. Press Enter to reach the screen Goods Receipt for Order: New Items 0001.
6. The system proposes the planned quantity from the order unless inspections are involved.
7. Enter the quantity you intend to deliver to stock.

8. Set the *Final delivery* indicator if this quantity will complete the order.

9. Save the goods receipt.

If you are using inspection points, the system proposes those quantities recorded during *Results recording for the operation* that are marked by the indicator *Last partial lot allocation*. If the material is subject to handling in batches, the material quantity per batch is proposed.

Manufacturing Coproducts by Process Orders

Two or more products manufactured together under control of one process order can be separately settled. The main product and the one or more coproducts can be settled to the same or to different receivers. Their goods movements can be posted simultaneously.

A material that is to be manufactured as a coproduct in a process order must meet the following conditions:

■ The Coproduct indicator must be activated in the MRP 1 screen of the material master of the coproduct.

■ The coproduct must appear as a component of item type **L** in the material list of the main product, where it will be assigned a negative quantity.

■ The material component of the process order must show an activated Coproduct indicator in the General Data screen.

Costing Coproducts

When a process order has been costed, the manufacturing costs are assigned to the order header. If the process order includes coproducts, the process order costs are distributed to the individual coproducts according to equivalence numbers.

These equivalence numbers are specified as an apportionment structure in the material master of the main product. The apportionment structure controls how the total costs are distributed over the main product and the coproducts.

The apportionment structure is consulted by the system when a process order is created. A settlement rule is created that will distribute the total order costs over the main product and the coproducts as they appear as the individual order items.

Furthermore, the system creates a settlement rule per item that will assign the actual costs to stock, when the processing is confirmed and the goods receipt posted to effect the delivery to stock.

Using an Origin Structure with Coproducts

The costs of manufacturing usually comprise elements from different cost element groups. You can specify different equivalence numbers for different cost element groups so as to create an origin structure. When the actual costs are known, the apportionment structure will distribute different percentages to the cost receivers according to the origin structure.

For example, you could classify costs according to the following set of origins:

- Production costs
- Material costs
- Overhead

If you do not identify an origin structure, the system treats each cost origin as equivalent. You perhaps have an apportionment rule that settles costs between a main product and a single coproduct in the proportion 2:1. In this example, the system will distribute one-third of each type of cost to the coproduct and two-thirds to the main product.

Table 17.1 illustrates a more complicated settlement rule system that assigns quite different equivalence numbers so as to distribute the different types of cost between the main product and the coproduct.

Table 17.1   Apportioning Costs with an Origin Structure

Cost element group	Main product	Coproduct
Production	1	4
Material	2	1
Overhead	5	3

The origin structure that relates your cost element groups has to be defined in customizing. An apportionment structure is defined in the material master of the main product. You have to branch to the MRP 1 screen where there is a function key to access the Coproduct Manufacture dialog box. Here you can define an apportionment structure for any component material that has been predefined as suitable for manufacture as a coproduct. ●

Controlling Self-Regulating Production by KANBANs

Triggering Replenishment with KANBAN

The aim of the KANBAN method is to create a self-regulating production control system that entails the absolute minimum of manual administrative effort. The name *KANBAN* is derived from the Japanese word for the printed cards that were used in the earliest implementations of the method.

Operations defined at various levels are treated as separate modular entities, even though they all contribute to the production process. The modules are linked by the so-called backward link principle in which a lower-level production or replenishment unit does not become active unless and until it is triggered by a demand from a higher-level production module. For example, a work center that requires a material component sends a KANBAN card to the work center that is responsible for manufacturing this component. The card includes a specification of which material is required, the quantity needed, and the destination to which it is to be delivered.

If the KANBAN strategy can be made to work successfully, the benefits can include shorter lead times and virtually zero inventories.

The creation of a KANBAN card can be automated by providing a standard bar code that can be scanned at the production location. The bar code specifies all the data needed by the intended recipient of the KANBAN card. There are ways of sending the KANBAN information electronically without actually printing a card.

The accounting requirements are satisfied when a bar code is scanned because a corresponding goods receipt is automatically posted when the material is delivered.

Replenishing with the KANBAN Pull Principle

It is characteristic of the KANBAN method that material flows through a production process according to the pull principle. A work center does not receive material from the preceding work center unless and until it *pulls* the requirement.

In formal terms, the *demand source* has to pull the material requirement from the *supply source*.

Comparing KANBAN Pull with MRP Push

Material requirements planning (MRP) calculates production quantities and dates according to the actual customer requirements plus any planned requirements that are independent of specific sales orders. The required total quantity and dates of the components are calculated by exploding a bill of material for each product.

By means of the MRP functions, production quantities for various requirements can be grouped together into production lots. The size of these various lots will depend on the lot-sizing procedure stored in the material master records of each material to be produced. The lot size adopted in the production plant will have been designed to produce the material most economically and to accommodate any quality control inspection requirements.

A complex end product can have several production levels in which the material components of lower levels are assembled or subject to further processing. At each production level, the lots are usually produced completely before being passed on for further processing.

The MRP plans according to the *push* principle because the dates are calculated from the results of a detailed planning run. Each production level can be the subject of a separate planning run that need not take account of when the material will be required for the subsequent production level. The material is then *pushed* through the production process so as to comply with the dates as planned.

Separate production lots or deliveries created without reference to the dates needed at their subsequent destinations can build up into queues waiting for processing. Of course, you can estimate queue times and plan for them as increased lead times or floats before production.

In practice, the floats allowed for by MRP push principle planning are usually accepted and the subsequent processing is seldom brought forward to undercut the allowed lead time and reduce the queue. Overall, this tends to give rise to lead times in production that are longer than strictly necessary. Furthermore, the material components waiting in queues represent inventory items that are being warehoused unnecessarily.

Reducing Production Lead Times and Inventory by the KANBAN Pull Mechanism

A KANBAN is an index card, a punched card, or an electronic equivalent. Between each supply source in a production plant and the various demand sources that need the material supplies, a number of KANBANs are defined. There is a fixed number of KANBANs defined between each pair of supply and demand sources.

Each KANBAN documents a specific material quantity.

When the material quantity of a KANBAN has been consumed by the demand source, the KANBAN is given the status *empty*. An empty KANBAN is sent immediately to its supply source. The empty card is sent to pull down a fresh supply of material.

When a supply source receives a KANBAN with the status *empty*, the supply source recognizes this event as the signal to go ahead and produce the quantity of material recorded on the KANBAN.

As soon as the supply source has finished producing the quantity of material pulled by the KANBAN, the actual material is delivered to the demand source, along with the KANBAN document, which still has the status *empty*. The demand source confirms the receipt of the material by setting the status of the particular KANBAN back to *full*. Only the demand source can reset the status of a KANBAN between *full* and *empty*.

From the point of view of a supply source, the quantity demanded by a KANBAN is equivalent to a lot size. If more material is required by a demand source, more empty KANBANs will be sent to the supply source. And so the supply source will be forced to increase the replenishment frequency. If there is sufficient material at a demand source, no empty KANBANs will be dispatched and so the replenishment frequency will fall.

A fixed number of KANBANs is allowed in the control cycle between each demand source and its supply source. Thus there is a limit to the amount of material in circulation in each control cycle.

If a work center is operating as a KANBAN demand source, it will always be in a position to commence processing, because it is obliged to dispatch an empty KANBAN to its source of supply as soon as its local stock of material falls below the defined limit.

Choosing When to Use KANBAN Production Control

MRP is very widely used because it can be more flexible than production control by the KANBAN method. In particular, the KANBAN technique tends to be at its best in the following circumstances:

- The consumption of the KANBAN parts or component materials should be relatively constant. If there is an erratic demand, many KANBANs are needed for the peaks, so that high inventory levels tend to be held, even over the periods of low demand.
- The period over which a demand source tends to maintain a constant rate of consumption should be longer than the replenishment lead time of its KANBAN.
- Every supply source has to be able to produce many lots within a short interval in order to keep up with the peak demands from the KANBANs. Minimal setup times and high production reliability are essential.
- A supply source should not have to collect several empty KANBANs for one material in order to justify an efficient production run.

Controlling KANBAN Supply Areas

A delivery of KANBAN material is always to a defined supply area, which may be a designated storage or shelving area. A supply area may serve more than one work center, but a supply area is reserved exclusively for the local holding of KANBAN materials.

For inventory management purposes, a supply area is assigned to a particular storage location. This storage location may include several supply areas, plus other storage areas not operating under the KANBAN system.

A responsible person is defined for KANBAN management. The scope of the responsibility may include more than one supply area. The responsible person is normally on the shop floor and may also be responsible for monitoring the production of the materials in a particular supply source.

Combining KANBAN and MRP

Two options exist for replenishment:

- Replenishment through KANBAN
- Replenishment through MRP

Under the KANBAN procedure, the system creates a document, referred to as a replenishment element, for the container quantity when the demand source submits an empty KANBAN. The replenishment element will include the run schedule quantity, production order, purchase order, and other administrative information.

The replenishment element is used for replenishing the material and for backflushing. When the material is delivered, the system posts the goods receipt to the replenishment element.

A material that has had replenishment elements created for it will be excluded from MRP in the storage location that includes the dedicated KANBAN supply area. Otherwise, planned orders or purchase requisitions could be created for the same material requirement at the next MRP planning run. The material can still take part in MRP for storage locations that do not include KANBAN supply areas.

The material components replenished through KANBAN may themselves comprise subassemblies and components. In these circumstances, the supply source will have to be replenished, either by KANBAN or by one of the consumption-based planning procedures.

If replenishment of KANBAN sources is to take place under control of MRP, the replenishment elements are created in the MRP planning run.

In-house production can be planned using either the repetitive manufacturing or the production orders functions. The replenishment requirements will then be converted to production quantities per period.

Replenishment from external sources can be planned using purchase requisitions, which are then converted to purchase orders as required. When the replenishment elements are created in the MRP planning run, they do not automatically trigger production or replenishment directly. The production controller of the supply source has to initiate the production or procurement, using the information provided by the replenishment elements.

Thus, under MPR replenishment, setting the container to *full* or *empty* controls the material flow and triggers actual production. But the change of KANBAN status does not directly influence the planning of the total production quantity or the replenishment quantity in a certain period. However, the KANBAN supply areas are included in MRP and the material components for these areas can be planned by MRP techniques.

Backflushes and goods receipts are posted with no reference to the KANBAN. You could, for example, post daily quantities without considering the KANBAN statuses.

Obviously, you have to ensure that no production facility is activated until the relevant KANBAN is posted, even if the requirement has been planned or even scheduled.

Controlling Production Using the KANBAN Board

The KANBAN board, or its electronic equivalent, is a display of the current status of each KANBAN, normally either *empty* or *full*. If you set the status of a KANBAN to *full*, the goods receipt is posted for the material represented by the KANBAN. On the shop floor, the change of status can be entered by scanning a bar code, which triggers the system to send all the important information from the demand source to the supply source.

The KANBAN board will also accept other predefined statuses, such as *wait*. This confirms that the material in the KANBAN has been consumed, but the supply source is not to deliver another replenishment quantity immediately, which would be the case if the status had been set to *empty*.

If you decide to introduce an additional KANBAN to circulate in the control cycle, it will be assigned the status *wait* in the KANBAN board until the controller decides to release it and so add to the quantity of material that is likely to be queuing for production.

The supply source can activate the status *in process* in a particular KANBAN to indicate on the control board that the requested material is currently being produced by the supply source, but that it is not yet ready for delivery.

There may be a significant time delay while a KANBAN quantity is being transported to the demand source. For these circumstances, a KANBAN can be assigned the status *in transit*.

A KANBAN showing the status indicator *in use* is one that is currently occupied because the demand source is withdrawing material from it.

If the KANBAN board shows the status *error* against a KANBAN, it indicates that the system has rejected the most recent attempt to change the status of this KANBAN.

By the use of these various KANBAN status indicators, the KANBAN board is able to display an accurate picture of the production processes taking part in the KANBAN scheme. Both supply sources and demand sources can access the KANBAN board and update the status of any KANBAN displayed on it. The following functions are facilitated by the KANBAN board for every supply area in the plant:

- Evaluation of process information
- Overview of work progress
- Review of material consumption
- Notification of missing parts
- Anticipation of bottlenecks

The KANBAN board can be accessed from the supply source and from the demand source; each view will selectively display the relevant information. Colors are used to differentiate container statuses and the various types of error situation.

Establishing Master Data for KANBAN

KANBAN data includes the control parameters needed to automate the production processes. In particular, data has to be maintained for the following purposes:

- To indicate which materials are to be managed by the KANBAN production control procedure
- To enable the automatic creation of purchase orders and production orders
- To direct goods movements

A material has to be assigned a control cycle, which may have already identified the material and the supply area. In the material master record, the following conditions must be established:

- The MRP type must not be set to no planning (NP) if replenishment is to use the MRP planning run, or planned orders, or run schedule quantities. ND must not be set if capacity requirements are to be created or if the material is to take part in long-term planning.

- The storage location assignment for MRP that is used for inventory postings for the supply source must be excluded from the planning run for replenishment strategies where the replenishment element is created by KANBAN, but not if replenishment elements are created in MRP.

- A repetitive manufacturing profile must be identified with a cost collector for in-house production with run schedule quantities and for manual KANBAN.

Using Replenishment Strategies

A replenishment strategy documents the rules that are to be followed when a KANBAN becomes empty. These rules govern whether in-house production is to be used rather than external procurement, and exactly how stock is to be transferred between storage locations.

The in-house production replenishment strategies have the following names:

- Replenishment Using Run Schedule Quantities
- Replenishment Using Production Orders
- Replenishment Using Manual KANBAN
- Container Control: In-House Production

The external procurement replenishment strategies have the following names:

- Replenishment Using Standard Purchase Orders
- Replenishment Using Scheduling Agreement
- Replenishment Using Stock Transport Orders (Plant to Plant)
- Replenishment Using Source List
- Container Control: External Procurement

If replenishment is a matter of moving stock from one storage location to another, the following procedures are available:

- Replenishment Using Reservation
- Replenishment Using Direct Transfer Posting
- Replenishment Using Direct Transfer Posting for Storage Locations Managed by WM System
- Transfer Posting Using Replenishment Elements from MRP

Replenishing Using Run Schedule Quantities

Run schedule quantities are determined by consulting a repetitive manufacturing profile maintained in the material master record. This profile is set to the repetitive manufacturing profile 0005 in the SAP standard system.

The repetitive manufacturing profile for a material determines the cost collector and it contains the parameters for the appropriate replenishment strategy.

When a demand source sets a KANBAN container to *empty*, the system creates a run schedule quantity with forward scheduling. The container, or the relevant information in the form of a KANBAN card or its equivalent, is transferred from the demand source to the supply source. A card can be printed and attached to the empty container at the supply source.

The supply source thus accumulates information on all the empty containers in the form of the cards or via the KANBAN board. The supply source can set the KANBAN board to show which containers are in process or in transit.

When the supply source has filled a container, its status has to be set to *full*. There are several possible ways of arranging this:

- The supply source backflushes the replenished quantity. In the KANBAN backflush, goods receipt for the replenished material and goods issue for the components are linked. The run schedule quantity is deleted automatically. You can change component materials or quantities. When you save the backflush, the system automatically sets the status to *full*.

- The demand source sets the container to *full*. Then the system automatically backflushes the current data of the run schedule quantity. A backflush includes the goods receipt for the replenished material, the goods issue for the components. The run schedule quantity is also deleted.

- You change the run schedule quantity manually, perhaps in order to change component quantities. By setting the container to *full*, the system automatically carries out the backflush using the data you changed, including the goods receipt for the replenished material, the goods issue for the components. The run schedule quantity is deleted.

It is one of the aims of self-regulating production to minimize administrative work. Therefore, the system will automatically explode the currently valid BOM when a *full* KANBAN container is identified or when a backflush is posted without component processing. If you want to intervene, for example, to change components, then you must use backflushing with component processing. Alternatively, you can manually change the run schedule quantity, which will allow you to access the component screen and make any alterations.

Replenishing using run schedule quantities causes the production costs to be posted to the specified cost collector for KANBAN.

Using an Independently Triggered Supply Source

You can arrange for the supply source to simply receive the KANBAN status information without any run schedule quantities being specified. Under this procedure, the containers are assigned the status *wait* rather than *empty* when their contents have been consumed.

The idea is that the supply source can then assess the demand situation from the number of empty containers that are waiting for material. The supply source sets a date on the KANBAN board when production is to start in order to replenish all the waiting containers.

Detaching Goods Receipt and Goods Issue Posting from KANBAN Status

You may need to uncouple the automatic connection between production and a container status of *full*. You can arrange for replenishment to take place only when a backflush is executed, regardless of the container status.

The order status indicator *separate GR* is used to cause the system to post a goods receipt for the finished material as well as a goods issue for the components needed to manufacture it. These postings occur when the backflush is initiated at the supply source. However, the system does not automatically set the container status to *full*. Similarly, if you set the status of a container to *full*, the system will not automatically perform a backflush, nor will it post any goods issues or goods receipts. You cannot reset the status to *empty* before the backflush has been carried out.

The KANBAN board will append the symbol + to the container status if the separate goods receipt procedure is in operation.

Replenishing by Production Orders

Under the standard procedure of Replenishment by Production Orders, the demand source can set a container to *empty*, and the system will create a production order for the container quantity. This production order is addressed to the supply source.

You can control through customizing whether this production order is released automatically and printed in the form of shop floor papers. Alternatively, or in addition, a KANBAN board signal or a KANBAN card can be specified to signal the demand.

During production, the supply source can set the container status to *in process*.

The backflush can be customized to be linked to the goods receipt posting.

If backflush and goods receipt are not linked, there are the following separate transaction possibilities:

- Backflush—separate transaction.
- Goods receipt posting—container status set automatically to *full* in the background.
- KANBAN container status change—if set to *full*, then the goods receipt is automatically posted in the background.

Replenishing Using Direct Transfer Posting

In this standard procedure, the status change *empty* triggers a transfer posting. The warehouse manager will receive a transfer requirement which has to be converted into a transfer order by the warehouse management (WM) module.

When the transfer order is delivered, it has to be confirmed, perhaps by scanning a bar code. And with this confirmation, the container status is automatically set to *full*. If you set the container status to *full*, there will not be a corresponding confirmation of the transfer order delivery. You can set the *separate GR* indicator to prevent a transfer order from changing a container status back to *full*.

The KANBAN data can be carried through to each document in this sequence.

Running KANBAN Procedural Evaluations

The error display function allows you to selectively inspect various existing errors and delete the corresponding error messages.

The following sequence will access the error display from the main KANBAN menu:

1. Select Evaluations→Error display.
2. Indicate the selection criteria to filter the error messages.
3. Press Execute.

The selection criteria are presented as *Demand source limitations*, which are classified as follows:

- Storage location
- Supply area
- Person responsible

Further error selection criteria include *Replenishment strategies limitations*, classified as follows:

- In-house production
- External procurement
- Stock transfer

Exercising Display Options

When the selected errors have been collated, the error display screen offers the following options for the line indicated by your cursor:

- *Err.mssge:long text*—to read the error message
- *Container info.*—to view information on the container
- *Displ. control cycle*—to view information on the control cycle

Processing Error Messages from the Display

To delete all error messages of one or more error types, select the appropriate error display lines. Choose Edit→Delete messages→All selected entries.

If you select Delete messages→All until the…, you will be offered a dialog box in which to enter a date before pressing Continue.

Deleting an error message does not remove the reason for the error. To access the container correction functions mark the error line and select Goto→Container correction.

Consulting the Plant Overview

The plant overview function can be configured to focus on one plant, or offer an overview of each plant, or obey selection conditions when collating the display. For example, you can call for Evaluations→Plant overview and then identify the plant of interest. The system will then allow you to select control cycles according to the following criteria:

- Supply area
- Supply areas of an identified responsible person
- Supply areas in an identified storage location

The display of the control cycle information can be structured as follows:

- Sort list according to material number—alphabetically or numerically ordered.
- Sort list according to supply areas—alphabetically or numerically ordered.
- Sort according to priority without using the maximum empty limit—priority is the proportion of the number of empty containers to the number in the control cycle.
- Sort list according to urgency using the maximum empty limit.

In this context, *urgency* is calculated as the proportion of the number of empty containers to the maximum number of empty containers allowed in the control cycle. For this calculation, containers that have the statuses *wait, in transit,* or *in process* are also deemed to be empty. An incorrect container is disregarded.

When you have entered your display requirements, the system displays the plant overview as the number of containers, colored per status, for each control cycle you have asked for. The KANBAN board has a Legend function which will identify the status represented by each color.

Accessing Additional Control Cycle Information

Double-clicking the mouse when the cursor has marked one or more control cycle lines will allow you to inspect the control cycle data and to access information from other application modules, as follows:

- To display the current stock/requirements list, select Goto→Stock/reqmts list.
- To display the stock overview, select Goto→Stock overview.

- To display the current stock/requirements list from Material Requirements Planning, select Evaluations→Stock/reqmts list.
- To display the inventory overview in Inventory Management, select Evaluations→Stock overview.
- To access the Logistics Information System, select Evaluations→Information system. ●

CHAPTER 19

Controlling Manufacture with Process Instructions

Preparing Process Instructions

A *process instruction* is a message used to control a manual or automated process. The form of this message is determined by the communication structure predefined in customizing.

The origin of process instructions is the process management. The destination is the process control system.

Particular process instructions are assigned to the phases of the master recipe and so they appear in the process order as part of the process control data.

When a process order is released for production to begin, the process instructions contained in the order are combined into control recipes. These control recipes form part of the messages that are then transferred to process control. Thus the control recipes made up from process instructions contain information on the individual processing steps to be carried out. They also carry any process data needed for further processing by other R/3 components. The process instructions will also carry the information needed by any third-party or external process control systems installed in the plant.

Process instructions have to be defined by the user company because they pertain to the operation of the specific manufacturing and data processing equipment installed in the user's plant. However, the R/3 system requires that a user designs process instructions according to various standards that ensure that they will be correctly interpreted by the system.

Defining Process Instruction Categories

Every process instruction (PI), has to belong to a predefined process instruction category. These categories are defined per plant. Assignment to a PI category will determine at least the following conditions:

- Whether the PI sends information to process control or requests that process control provides information
- The type of information conveyed or requested

Once the PI categories have been defined in customizing, the users do not need to know the details of how any instances of a PI category actually controls the equipment. These details have to be settled only once per plant. In particular, users who are creating process instructions during the planning of a process can refer to the predefined PI categories.

Differentiating Process Instruction Types

When a control recipe is being assembled for an automated control system, the following types of process instructions can be used:

- Process parameter
- Process data request
- Process message subscription

If the control recipe is designed to create a PI sheet for a manually controlled process, the following types of process instructions can be used:

- Process parameter
- Process data request
- Process data calculation formula
- Inspection results request—R/3 PI sheet only
- Dynamic function call—R/3 PI sheet only
- Sequence definition

PI sheets for third-party control systems normally require process instructions customized to suit the particular equipment and the line operators who will use it.

Using Sequence Definitions in the PI Sheet

If you associate the start of a phase with a sequence definition, you effectively determine that this phase cannot be processed except in its assigned place in the sequence. Thus a sequence definition replicates in the PI sheet the phase relationships that were specified in the process order.

In the R/3 system, the PI sheet is a document maintained in the system. The process instructions that it contains are grouped according to the phases of the operations. If any phase contains a sequence definition, none of the process instructions of this phase will become active until all the messages have been created for the process instructions of its predecessor.

Thus the sequence definition makes sure that process instructions are created in an orderly sequence that corresponds to the phase sequence of the master recipe and the process order.

Designing Process Instructions for the R/3 PI Sheet

Part
IV
Ch
19

The materials and the material quantities to be charged into a process plant have to be provided in the form of process parameters. These can be defined in the control system or downloaded to process control as required. The process order includes material information in the material list, and this data can be transferred to the process parameters by automatic assignment of characteristic values.

As the processing passes through the various stages, the actual materials consumed have to be reported to process management. The request for this data can take the form of a process data request for each material. Alternatively, reports on all the materials can be requested by a single process message subscription.

The PP-PI module will contain some of the information needed by the process instructions. For example, the process order number and the control recipe number are generated by the system independently of the material being produced. These characteristic values can be downloaded as part of the message subscription and will then be transferred to the actual messages.

Other characteristic values such as the operation number, phase number, or reservation number, will probably be different for each material. This kind of information cannot be predefined into a message subscription. However, you may have a process control system that allows you to obtain this data from the process parameter. If not, you will have to create a process data request with the appropriate details for each individual material.

Creating Process Instructions

The guiding principle is to have as much information as possible predefined, so that there will be very little manual processing to do when it comes to creating control recipes. You may be able to set up automatic process instruction generation in the process order or during control recipe creation. This procedure is often possible if work centers tend to specialize in a particular process that does not vary so that all control recipes for a destination contain virtually the same information.

You can call for automatic creation of process instructions by a manual transaction in the master recipe and the process order. This enables you to adapt the set of process instructions for specific circumstances, such as for an individual production run. The following types of modification are accepted:

- Delete characteristics
- Add characteristics
- Assign characteristic values
- Change characteristic values

A process instruction is defined with a set of characteristics: but the instruction is not ready for use until a value has been assigned to each of these characteristics. It is possible to define a function module and assign it to a characteristic so that the value can be computed and assigned automatically when the process order is created, or when a control recipe is generated.

Customizing can arrange for virtually any programmable function to be executed in order to minimize the amount of manual input required to generate appropriate process instructions for the master recipe that will be followed to execute a process order.

Interpreting Process Instruction Sheets

The PI sheet can perform any of the following functions:

- Display control information in natural language
- Record actual process data
- Calculate values
- Report the entered and calculated values using process messages
- Record inspection results by branching directly to QM
- Call user-defined function modules in order to start a dialog or retrieve data from internal or external applications

A PI sheet, in its electronic form, comprises a header and a number of elements. These elements are constructed through the process instructions in the control recipe or by the line operator when he or she maintains the PI sheet.

The PI sheet elements include the following information:

- Control information and notes with additional information for the line operator
- Comments by the line operator
- Entry fields for the actual process data to be reported
- Fields for values to be calculated by the system
- Pushbuttons which enable the operator to call up user-defined function modules or the QM function for recording inspection results

The PI sheet is presented as an overview screen from which various detail screens can be accessed to work on the individual elements.

The PI sheet header contains the following information:

- Status of the PI sheet
- Process order for which the PI sheet was created
- Material to be produced
- Operator or operating group responsible for maintaining the PI sheet

The PI sheet overview displays control information for the line operator. The number of the process instruction and the number of the phase of the process order to which it applies are displayed, together with the relevant control information. This information is provided as a process instruction of the type *process parameter*.

The PI sheet can also give access to an Additional Information screen for each processing step. The additional information appears as a note, and this note has to be defined as a process instruction of the type *process parameter*.

If a line operator wishes to record comments on an individual processing step within the PI sheet, the comments can be stored on a special comment sheet within the PI sheet. The existence of a comment is signaled by the document symbol and the first few letters of the comment appearing on the PI sheet alongside the control information for the processing step. Alternatively, the line operator can send a process message directly to process management.

Requested values are defined in process instructions of the type *process data request*. They request the line operator to report actual values by entries in single entry fields or tables, depending on the number of values needed.

A *signature* is a special type of requested value. It signals the end of a processing step. If you enter a signature, you confirm and report the data entered or calculated in the processing step. You may need a special authorization and a password to enter a signature.

If a value is to be calculated in the PI sheet by a process data calculation formula, the field for this value will contain a question mark until a value has been calculated.

The pushbutton *Record inspection results* is displayed on the PI sheet alongside the control instruction if you are required to access the quality management (QM) function to record the inspection results.

If a PI sheet requires the line operator to initiate a dynamic function call, a pushbutton is displayed which will access the assigned function from another application.

Using Predefined Function Calls

Standard R/3 has predefined calls for the following functions:

- Order confirmation for operations and phases
- Display of material quantity calculation from order
- Display of documents created in the R/3 document management system

Processing PI Sheets

The following methods are available for accessing a PI sheet:

- Access a specific PI sheet via its number
- Create a work list of PI sheets using search criteria such as material, resource, and operating group

Given suitable authorization, you can display and maintain the PI sheets you have accessed.

The display mode offers the following facilities:

- Printing a PI sheet
- Scrolling within a PI sheet
- Displaying a note
- Displaying data to be reported
- Displaying inspection results
- Displaying comments

The maintenance mode offers the following line operator functions which are additional to those available to the in the display mode:

- Recording actual process data
- Calculating values
- Reporting data
- Recording inspection results
- Calling a function
- Maintaining comments
- Displaying the logs
- Locating a process instruction in the PI sheet

- Saving the PI sheet
- Setting the PI sheet status to *Complete*

The following functions may also be needed to manage errors and unplanned events:

- Changing control information in the PI sheet
- Canceling order confirmations
- Canceling material documents
- Activating/deactivating process instructions in the PI sheet
- Setting the PI sheet status to *Technically complete*

The following sequence will access a PI sheet:

1. From the process management menu, select the menu options PI sheet→Display, or PI sheet→Maintain.
2. Enter the number of the PI sheet you want to display or maintain. The control recipe from which it is created has the same number.
3. To access the PI sheet, press the pushbutton *Continue*.

Evaluating Process Message Data

The logistics information system (LIS) comprises a number of components that access information from the various application modules that have been integrated in your system. The shop floor information system (SFIS) is a component of the LIS. The shop floor information is collected from the production orders and work centers belonging to the production planning and control (PP) module and also from the related module, production planning and control for the process industry (PP-PI).

The PP-PI module refers to process orders and resources, whereas the PP module deals with production orders and work centers. The shop floor information system will access and analyze data from both the PP and the PP-PI applications. The relevant order type has to have been customized to yield the LIS statistics before the data can be accessed in the shop floor information system.

The information system offers standard analysis of the following data elements in the order types for which statistics have been customized:

- Resources
- Business operations
- Materials
- Process orders
- Material consumption
- Production costs

Part

IV

Ch

19

The shop floor information system can only analyze actual process data taken from process messages if this information has been posted to the order or to inventory management in the form of a goods receipt or goods issue.

Evaluating Process Messages

Process message evaluation is carried out at the plant level. Records of process messages can be selected according to any combination of their characteristic values.

The data to be displayed can be defined by the user at the time of the evaluation run, or pre-defined as evaluation versions for each of the standard analyses. The display options include the SAP business graphics component and the SAP XXL list viewer component to display and process message data in Microsoft Excel. The display option can be predetermined along with the message record selection criteria as an evaluation version at plant level.

One way to create an evaluation version is to copy and edit an existing version before saving it under a new ID. If you do not save the changes, they will revert to the original after the next evaluation run. You can delete an evaluation version online.

Setting Up the SAP Business Graphic for Process Message Evaluation

Setting up entails defining which messages should be accessed and which data elements should be extracted. You also have to decide how the information is to be displayed using the graphical facilities.

The value of an individual message characteristic cannot be displayed or used in an evaluation unless the following conditions are satisfied:

- The process message must have been sent to the process message record.
- The message characteristic must have been released for use in process messages.

The SAP business graphic function offers the following standard display options:

- Two-dimensional chart
- Three-dimensional chart
- A statistics graphic presented in the form of a line graph with two numeric axes
- A statistics graphic with time reference

The parameters that govern the display are not saved as part of an evaluation version. They are valid only for the next evaluation run.

Setting Up Message Evaluation Using SAP XXL List Viewer

The SAP XXL list viewer configures Microsoft Excel to display and process data from R/3 applications. In particular, XXL prepares the Excel display according to a data structure defined in R/3.

The XXL list viewer also supplements the functions provided by Microsoft Excel and constrains some of the Excel functions so as to ensure that the data received from R/3 is always handled consistently.

As with SAP Business Graphic, the SAP XXL list viewer will accept only data derived from message characteristics that have been released for use in evaluations. The source messages must have been sent to the process message record.

When you are operating the process message evaluation function for the next evaluation run, you have to define which messages and which message data should be displayed via the XXL list viewer. You must also specify the layout.

The results of an evaluation run can be directed as follows:

- Display and process in the SAP XXL list viewer.
- Download to and process in Excel as a Pivot table.
- Download to a PC in ASCII format for further processing via other evaluation tools, such as analytical programs developed for particular purposes.
- Transfer to the SAPoffice mail system and, if required, display and process in Excel.

If you alter any data in the XXL list viewer, you will not be allowed to upload it back into R/3.

Arranging the Layout for the SAP XXL List Viewer

The XXL list viewer offers a spreadsheet layout. You can assign the message characteristics you are evaluating to one of the following aspects of the display:

- Column characteristic—values displayed in the data columns of the spreadsheet
- Line characteristic—controls which values of the column characteristic are to be assembled as a line of the display
- Column group characteristic—controls how columns are to be grouped

You can assign several message characteristics to each of the display characteristics. You may need to define sort numbers for characteristics that belong to the same category so that they always appear in the same order.

Selecting Process Messages for Evaluations

The selection rules for identifying which messages shall be allowed to contribute data to an evaluation have to be based on the values of the characteristics of these messages. You can impose further limitations by the definition of your business graphic or spreadsheet layout. The period to be considered for the evaluation will also be used to limit the selection of process messages.

Each process message characteristic can be scrutinized by a selection rule defined for this particular characteristic so as to include or exclude the individual process message record from the evaluation. These selection rules can be assembled from arithmetic expressions, relations, and logical operations.

A process message will be rejected for evaluation via XXL unless it contains the following characteristics:

- At least one of the column characteristics defined in the layout
- All of the line characteristics defined in the layout
- All of the column group characteristics defined in the layout

If you are using the SAP business graphic function, a process message will be rejected for evaluation unless it contains all the characteristics selected for the evaluation run.

Messages can always be selected or excluded from an evaluation run on the basis of their message category and the evaluation period that you define for the run. A message that was created outside the evaluation period will be ignored.

There is a quick listing facility to generate a preview that will show whether the evaluation run is going to have any data to work upon.

Evaluating Process Message Data Using External Tools

R/3 data is saved in database tables in accordance with the specifications defined in the ABAP/4 Data Dictionary.

Master data and planning data concerning materials, resources, and orders is organized in data structures defined by SAP. When you save an object in R/3, or when the system saves an object automatically, the corresponding data structure is updated and the details of the change are logged.

Similarly, actual process data reported via process messages has to be organized in database tables. Because each plant will record different data, the process message database tables have to be defined per plant by the user, but in accord with the ABAP/4 Data Dictionary. When process management sends a process message, the corresponding message database table is updated.

Open database connectivity (ODBC) is a database interface software component that allows external data processing tools to access R/3 database structures. SQL*NET is the generic name of a family of network interface software used in the client-server environment.

Using the database interface technique allows you to develop evaluations that embrace any available data, even if it did not originate from an R/3 application.

Integrating Supply Chain Management

Material requirements planning begins from a master plan. This plan can be expressed as a structured list of the operations to be carried out by the company or by a plant within a company.

The operations in the master plan can be developed from sales targets or from confirmed sales orders—usually from a judicious combination of both. The master plan can also include research projects or projects to develop new production capabilities.

However they may arise, the elements of the master plan can be subjected to MRP techniques to arrive at a more detailed scheme of planned activities and the methods to control them. Accounting and quality management obviously figure prominently in this scheme.

One of the purposes of business data processing is to accelerate the speed of business transactions without losing accuracy. As a rule, software is designed to preprocess all relevant data and suggest sensible solutions to the operators where the automatic procedures cannot arrive at an optimum resolution. One example of a sensible improvement is to link sales with production management by electronic means, providing the necessary planning activities can be accommodated in the link.

The phrase "online management" has come to include the relatively rapid communication between sales and production departments and their decision makers. The following processing scheme can be assembled from standard R/3 modules:

1. Customer order details are passed automatically to the sales information system (SD-IS) and to the profitability analysis (CO-PA) component.

2. The sales and operations planning (PP-SOP) system selects the necessary information from the sales information system (SD-IS) and the profitability analysis (CO-PA) component.

3. The sales and operations plan is passed to the demand management functions. From here the material requirements planning (PP-MRP) component can initiate the MRP planning chain that ends with the generation of the necessary production order proposals.

4. New customer orders are offset with the orders previously planned.

5. The next cycle of the optimized planning run begins.

The integrated quality control provided by the SAP R/3 quality management (QM) system can be applied to all the operations of the production planning and control (PP) module and to its related PP-PI component for the process industries. ●

Relating Production to the Environment

Tracking Substances with the EH&S Component

Companies need to minimize the environmental risks stemming from their products as well as the risks arising during production and storage activities. An additional requirement is to document the production processes for all industries and to maintain batch history data in those industries where the finer details of production and storage may be required for product management and as a legal requirement.

SAP has developed an environment data management system to support the tracking of substances by linking all the logistics processes by efficient functions designed to maximize environmental production, industrial safety, and the safety of the product. The data management system has been enhanced to become the Environment, Health, and Safety system (EH&S). The concept includes functions that take into account requirements that are specific to an individual country, including the language of any mandatory documentation.

The following industries illustrate the situations where the Environment, Health, and Safety system is applicable:

- Producers, processors, transporters, and traders of environmentally hazardous products
- Chemical industries
- Pharmaceutical industries
- Automotive industries
- High-technology and electrical industries
- Consumer packaged goods industries
- Public utilities

The EH&S environment data component uses the cross-application modules Classification System and Document Management System. Select Logistics→Materials management→Environment data.

Building a Substance Database

You can define in the SAP EH&S component any of the following as an entity of type *substance*:

- A chemical substance
- A group of chemical substances
- An element
- A chemical compound
- A mixture of elements and compounds

A substance defined for the EH&S database may be characterized by its chemical properties or its physical properties, or by a particular combination of both. The substance may be a natural material or a substance created during manufacture. You can even define a substance as an idealized material that may never actually exist.

A mixture, preparation, or solution containing several constituent substances may itself be defined as a separate substance in the database. A substance may be pure. It may contain impurities. Both forms may exist and be classified separately.

A substance may be assigned as the identification of a *substance group* that includes members that have several characteristics in common.

You can assign substances to a *substance category*; for example:

- Real substances
- Listed substances
- Real substance group
- Listed substance group
- Reference substances

Linking to the R/3 Classification System

A *substance characteristic category* is a device for classifying substances in the EH&S database so that they can be accessed by the R/3 classification functions. A value with its units of measurement can be assigned to each category to represent significant data about the substance. A key can be defined to access extensive data if necessary. A category may be assigned a rating on a predefined scale that divides the possible values into, for example, high, medium, low.

For example, the substance characteristic type *substance properties* can have assigned to it the following *substance characteristic categories:*

- Boiling point
- Flashpoint
- Storage regulations

Similarly, substance compositions can be classified using the following substance characteristic categories:

- Precise chemical composition
- EINECS composition

Substance listings may use the following substance characteristic categories:

- Substances subject to exposure limits
- Products of decomposition processes

Interpreting Standard Substance Characteristic Types

The following standard *substance characteristic types* are provided to differentiate the functions that the characteristics normally perform:

Part
IV

Ch
20

- Substance property
- Substance listing
- Substance composition

A *substance property* is the data element that stores the details in the form of numeric values and their units of measurement, or else the textual information that identifies the property. You can link these details with their source or the method of analysis.

The following are examples of substance properties that can be conveniently grouped:

- Physical properties
- Chemical properties
- Toxicological properties
- Ecological properties
- First aid measures
- Safety measures
- Hazard avoidance training classes

A *substance listing* is a standard substance characteristic type that is used to identify a substance with an external list. The listings are normally based on a particular set of regulatory requirements, such as the following:

- EINECS—European Inventory of Existing Chemical Substances
- TSCA—Toxic Substances Control Act
- MAK-List (TRGS 900)—a German list that details the maximum work center concentrations and biological tolerance limits of each substance

The *substance composition* is a standard substance characteristic type used for substances that have several components that need to be documented. A substance component is defined as a substance that is found in a manufactured substance at the completion of the manufacturing process. The substance composition is a listing of all components including their concentration found in the manufactured substance.

Identifying a Particular Substance

A *substance identifier* is a data element that identifies a substance by referring to its substance characteristic category and substance characteristic type.

A *substance identification* is a unique description of a substance. The identification normally requires the combination of several identifiers to render it unique.

A *substance identification type* is a general description that serves to point out how the substance identification has been constructed.

The standard substance identification types are:

- Number
- Name
- Formula

A *substance identification category* classifies the data elements that can be used to build a substance identification. For example, the following standard substance identification categories are provided for the substance identification type *Name*:

- IUPAC name
- Synonym
- Trivial name
- Trade name

A *reference substance* is used as a model for other substances. If you wish to directly maintain a substance characteristic category, the reference properties are deleted for that category and you can assign private characteristics.

Defining Substance Characteristic Usage

The usage of a substance characteristic can be defined by allocating one or more combinations of validity area and substance characteristic rating. This usage will be assigned a key which can then be used to simplify data entry.

Reporting with a Substance Report Generation Variant

A *substance report template* defines the layout of a document into which substance data and information from other R/3 applications can be formatted. The template contains symbols that are replaced by the actual R/3 application data when the report is generated.

You can control the scope of a report template by predefining a *substance report generation variant* that links a substance report template with a validity area and one or more characteristic ratings.

Customizing a Substance Database

Central control parameters have to be defined to generate a general record number for each substance data record and a general record counter that will index each change made to that record.

Various precustomized substance database structures are available to set up a comprehensive substance database. Phrases that are likely to be needed in a database, such as chemical and trade names, are assigned to phrase keys that simplify building and interpreting the database.

Phrase libraries can be obtained on license, to which you can add your own phrases. You can arrange for the system to number new phrases, or you can assign numbers yourself, provided you remain within the allowed number ranges.

The languages that will be used for outputs of phrases from the substance database are defined by allocating language keys. For example, the standard settings provide for all the languages required for the European Union material safety data sheets. You can customize the sequence in which languages are displayed during translations.

The substance database can be controlled by the standard R/3 authorization management functions. An authorization specific to the EH&S database can be defined.

Documenting Process Data

The industries that are likely to benefit from the EH&S component will be those that are accustomed to keeping track of each batch of material—how and where it was manufactured, the constituents, their sources, and the inspections at the various stages of processing.

Process data documentation is a software component that exports the process data available in the R/3 system to optical archives for long-term storage. Electronic batch records (EBR) are created to combine all relevant order-related data in the form of print lists. These lists are then downloaded to the archiving database via the SAP ArchiveLink.

International standards have been defined for keeping records of manufactured batches. The good manufacturing practices (GMP) are standards that ensure that there can be no manipulation of the data once it reaches the optical archive. Therefore, the data can be used to trace the origin of any anomaly in any particular batch, if necessary, long after it has left the production facility. The optical data can be rapidly retrieved into the R/3 system for examination and analysis.

The basis of the GMP standard is that a secure record should be kept for each batch processed. This standard originated in the Food and Drug Administration (FDA) of the United States, where it is a legal requirement for the pharmaceutical industry. The World Health Organization (WHO) has revised the GMP standard and added a certification scheme. The ASEAN good manufacturing practices guidelines (1988), the good manufacturing practice for medicinal products in the European Community (1992), and the Pharmaceutical Inspection Convention are other guidelines that have confirmed the GMP standards.

It is a particular requirement of GMP that a batch record should constitute a full documentation of the production phases as planned and as actually carried out. R/3 process data documentation meets these requirements because a batch record corresponds to the documentation of a completed process order. You can also append a user list if your company requires data additional to the R/3 process documentation.

The main elements of the process order documentation are as follows:

- Process order
- Material list
- Inspection lot
- Process messages
- PI sheet

An inspection lot is a document that contains the following information:

■ The inspection specifications defined in the corresponding master recipe such as inspection method, sampling procedures, and inspection characteristics that are to be examined

■ The inspection results, inspector, dates of inspection, and the quantity checked which have been reported during the inspection process either by directly accessing the corresponding function of the QM module or by using process messages

■ The usage or destination decision and the batch number of the material produced

The inspection lot document is archived with the process order.

Process messages are sent, received, and recorded during processing. They can call for data to be entered and can direct the processing so as to meet all the process documentation requirements.

■ GMP requires that your batch record contain the product name and the number of the batch processed. Use predefined characteristics in the process message: PPPI_PRODUCT and PPPI_PROCESS_ORDER_NUMBER.

■ GMP requires that your batch record contain the start and finish dates and times of production as well as of significant intermediate stages. Use predefined messages PI_CRST (control recipe status), PI_OPST (operation status), PI_PHST (phase status), and use predefined characteristics PPPI_EVENT_DATE and PPPI_EVENT_TIME for every process message.

■ GMP requires that your batch record contain the batch number as well as the actual quantity of each starting material. Use predefined message category PI_CONS.

■ GMP requires that your batch record contain the amount of product obtained at different stages together with explanations for significant deviations. Record the material quantity produced using predefined message category PI_PROD.

■ Report any problems or deviations in a process message using the predefined comment message category PI_COMM.

Archiving

If a process message is sent to the destination PI01, it will be stored in the Process message record. This will transfer the order number to the destination field PROCESS_ORDER. When this process order is archived via process data documentation, the system will also archive all order-related messages stored in the process message record.

Archiving stores the following data for each process message:

■ The plant and category, creation date, and sender

■ The characteristics

■ The message log entries

Meeting GMP Requirements for the PI Sheet

The production line operator uses and maintains the PI sheet because it is the source of all the information on a production process that is needed at the production line. The following specification of the contents of a PI sheet is compliant with GMP standards:

- The control information defined in the process instructions of the process order
- Any changes made to these instructions after the creation of the control recipe
- The actual process data including comments and signatures maintained in the PI sheet

The PI sheet header and contents are archived when the process order is archived. Notes and comments are automatically numbered so that they appear below the overview if the archive record is recalled for examination.

Process data documentation can perform optical archiving through the SAP ArchiveLink provided the order and its related objects carry the status indicator *Process data documentation required*. This status will normally be assigned automatically if specified for the order type.

ABAP/4 programming can be used to develop a user list. This facility allows the user company to archive data additional to the GMP specification.

Archiving a process order cannot take place unless it carries the order status *Technically completed*. You can assign this status manually if the process order is carrying the status indicator *Control recipe finished*.

Even if all processing phases have been confirmed as completed, you may wish to check the process message logs in the message monitor to review the inspection situation before you initiate an archiving run for the process order and its process messages. You would expect to find the following inspection lot statuses:

- Usage decision has been made
- Inspection close completed

Executing Process Data Documentation

You can preselect process orders for archiving by entering any of the following criteria:

- The plant, number, and type of the order
- The production scheduler, MRP controller, and the person in charge of an order
- A status selection profile

For each order that meets both the conditions for archiving and your search specification, the archiving data is compiled in the form of print lists per order, as follows:

- The process order header details
- The material list
- All PI sheets for the process order
- The inspection lot assigned to the process order

- All order-related process messages
- The data selected via a user-defined user list program set up in customizing

You can display and print these print lists before archiving them. All existing lists for a process order are archived together.

After successful archiving, the system automatically sets the following status indicators:

- Order status—*Process data archived*
- Inspection lot status—*Inspection lot contained in process data documentation*
- PI sheet status—*Archived*

The statuses prevent any further changes being made to the objects so marked.

Simulating Process Data Documentation

Most of the archiving activities can be performed in the simulation mode, which will allow you to inspect print lists and any error messages without making any additions to the optical archive database.

After leaving the simulation mode, the archiving status indicators revert to their "unarchived" condition.

Inspecting Archived Process Data

The standard function Display Process Data from Archive allows you to call up the archived lists from the archiving database and display them within R/3. This function can also provide information on the program version used to create the original archiving list, the archive ID, and the object type of the archived list.

If a process order has been flagged for deletion, but not yet archived and therefore deleted from R/3, you can regenerate the archiving lists and display them. These lists will be exact replicas of the intended archive because no changes are permitted once a process order has been flagged for deletion. ●

Part

IV

Ch

20

Glossary of Terms and Concepts

ABAP   Advanced Business Application Programming, a fourth-generation language in which SAP R/3 application software is written. It has been developed by SAP.

ABAP/4 Repository   Store for all objects managed by the ABAP/4 Development Workbench.

ABAP/4 Repository Information System   Navigation aid for the ABAP/4 Repository.

ABAP/4 Workbench   Development environment that contains all the necessary tools for creating and maintaining business applications within the R/3 system.

ABAP/4 Workbench Organizer   A software development project management tool, which is an integral component of the ABAP/4 Development Workbench.

ABAP Data Dictionary   Store of metadata that contains descriptions of tables, data elements, domains, and views.

ABAP Native SQL   A method for accessing a specific database by using its proprietary commands to implement Structured Query Language.

ABAP Objects   An object-oriented language for developing business applications compatible with R/3 and ABAP/4.

ABAP Open SQL   A portable method for accessing all supported databases by Structured Query Language commands.

ABAP Query   A user tool for generating special report programs. Basic query reporting does not require any knowledge of ABAP, although more elaborate reports may be designed by utilizing ABAP code components.

ABC analysis   Analysis of materials (for example) may be conducted according to several criteria, such as importance or consumption value:

- Important part or a material with high consumption value
- Less important part or material with medium consumption value
- Relatively unimportant part or material with low consumption value

account assignment element   Work breakdown structure element to which actual or commitment postings can be made.

active R/3 repository   The directory now in operational use that contains descriptions of all of an enterprise's application data and its interrelationships, including how the data is used in programs and screen forms. During ABAP/4 program development, a separate development repository directory is maintained for versions of the program components undergoing development or modification.

activity (controlling)   Internal or external physical measure of the activity output of a cost center according to activity type.

activity (project system)   An instruction to perform a task within a network in a set period of time. Work, general costs, or external processing can be associated with it.

activity input   Transaction to plan the secondary cost quantities on a receiver cost center that uses activity from a sender cost center.

activity logs   Records of all activities in the SAP R/3 system for each transaction and each user.

activity type   Classification of an activity and the data structure—for example, number of units produced, hours, machine times, and production times.

actual costs   All the costs accruing to an object in a period.

ALE   See Application Link Enabling (ALE).

allocation group   Defines which orders within one controlling area are to be settled together:

- By settlement timing—monthly, weekly, and so on
- By order types—repair, capital spending, and so on
- By settlement receivers—cost center, GL account

allocation receiver   Object to which the costs of a cost center or order are allocated.

API   See application programming interface (API).

Application Link Enabling (ALE)   An SAP method for using documents to carry messages that control distributed applications while maintaining integration and consistency of business data and processes across many systems.

application programming interface (API)   Interface to support communication between applications of different systems.

ASCII   Acronym for American Standard Code for Information Interchange.

assembly order   Request to assemble premanufactured parts and assemblies to create finished products according to an existing sales order.

asset class   A grouping of fixed assets that are depreciated in a specified manner.

asset under construction   An asset that's still being produced when the balance sheet is prepared.

asynchronous database updating   A method of updating a database separately from the management of the dialog part of the transaction.

availability check   Stock or inventory check that's automatically carried out after every goods movement. This check should prevent the book of available inventory balance of the physical inventory from becoming negative.

background process   Noninteractive execution of programs, sometimes using prepared file data to replicate the user dialog so as to utilize the same standard functions.

backward scheduling   Scheduling a network where the latest start and finish dates for the activities are calculated backward from the basic finish date.

batch (lot) A subset of the total quantity of a material held in inventory. This subset is managed separately from other subsets of the same material. A batch of material may have to be identified by its date and place of origin. Delivery lots and lots comprising particular quality grades can be differentiated.

bill of material (BOM) A complete, formally structured list of all subassemblies, parts, and materials that go into an assembly or product. It includes a description, quantity, and unit of measure for each constituent part.

billing document A generic term for invoices, credit memos, debit memos, and cancellation documents. A billing document comprises a header of data that applies to the whole document plus any number of items.

billing element In a work breakdown structure, a data object to which you can post invoices and revenues.

bill-to party A person or company that receives the invoice for a delivery or service. The bill-to party receives the bill but isn't necessarily the payer who settles the bill.

block A mechanism that enables credit-controlling personnel to stop a customer from taking part in any transaction.

budget Prescribed and binding approved version of the cost plan for a project or other task over a given period.

business area A legally independent organizational unit within a client, for which internal reporting balance sheets can be created. The boundaries of a business area normally are determined on the basis of the responsible sales organization or division, or the delivering plant.

business segment Intersection of criteria to suit the relevant operating concern—for example:

- Country, U.S.
- Industry, farming
- Product range, animal feeds
- Customer group, wholesale

business segment criterion Chosen from an SAP proposal list or existing tables, or created manually. Comprises a field name and a field value.

business segment value field Holds a number, code, or string.

business transaction A recorded data processing step representing a movement of value in a business system, such as cost planning, invoice posting, or movement of goods.

calculated costs An order's progress toward completion represented in value terms. There are two methods for determining the calculated costs: calculation on a revenue base and calculation using quantity produced as a base. If, for an order, planned revenue is more than planned costs, there are two corresponding methods for calculating the (interim) profit realization.

calculated revenue The revenue that corresponds to the actual costs incurred for an order, determined from results analysis as

Actual costs * planned revenue / planned costs

capacity (cost accounting) Output of a cost center and activity that's technically possible during a specific period—differentiated by category and arranged hierarchically under a work center.

capacity (production planning) Ability of a work center to perform a specific task.

capacity planning Includes long-term rough-cut capacity planning (RCCP), medium-term planning, and short-term detailed planning (CRP).

capital investment measure A project or order that's too large or contains too much internal activity to be posted to fixed assets as direct capitalization. The master record of a capital investment measure stores both the actual cost data and the planned values.

capitalized costs Difference between the actual costs and the calculated costs of an order, calculated by results analysis. With deficit orders, this figure is reduced to allow for the loss realized.

capitalized profit Calculated in results analysis by subtracting the capitalized costs from the value of the inventory from which revenue can be generated.

cardinality The number of lines in a dependent table to which the table under consideration, in principle, can or must relate. A line in a table may be related to another dependent line in a cardinality of one-to-one correspondence. The relationship may be one-to-many if there can be several dependent lines for any referenced line.

CCMS Computing Center Management System.

characteristic A property of an object, such as length, color, or weight, used to describe and distinguish the object. Characteristics are also used to differentiate data objects in a database.

CIM Computer Integrated Manufacturing.

classification When an object is assigned to a class, values for the object are assigned to characteristics belonging to the class.

client The highest level in SAP R/3. The data explicitly reserved to one client may not be accessed by another client. There are often a training client and a testing client, in addition to the client code that represents your group or corporate identity and under which the SAP system runs normal business. Some data is managed at the client level, because everyone in the corporate group of companies will want to refer to exactly the same information and be certain that it has been maintained as up to date and correct. Vendor addresses would be an example of data managed at the client level.

client caches Work areas set up in the database application servers for data frequently accessed by the client's applications.

collective invoice   A billing document for several deliveries to one customer that's initiated by the vendor at the end of a billing period.

company code   A unit within a client that maintains accounting balances independently and creates the legally required balance sheet and the profit-and-loss statement.

compiler   A tool that translates source code statements written in a general programming language into statements written in a machine-oriented programming language.

condition   A data element, term, or rule that defines price, taxes, and output according to user-defined criteria.

condition record   A data record that stores a condition and perhaps refers to condition supplements. Condition records can include prices, discounts and surcharges, taxes, and output.

consignment stock   A particular inventory made available by the vendor that's stored on the purchaser's premises but remains the vendor's property until withdrawn from stores for use or transferred to the purchaser's own valuated stock.

contact person   A person at the customer location who deals with the vendor's sales or marketing department.

contingency order   A results analysis object on which the costs of complaints are collected. Reserves are created by results analysis for the expected cost of complaints and are drawn from as costs are incurred.

contract   A long-term agreement with a vendor that's fulfilled by individual release orders, which are initiated according to customer requirements.

control indicator   Determines, in cost accounting, which application components are active, how certain data is stored, and what types of validation are to take place.

control key   Determines how an activity or activity element is to be processed in such operations as orders, costings, and capacity planning.

controlling area   An area within an organization that shares a cost accounting configuration (normally the same as company code). For cross-company cost accounting, one controlling area may be assigned to multiple company codes of one organization.

controlling area currency   Default currency in cost accounting objects, cost centers, orders, and so on.

controlling functions   Financial, investment, cost, and profitability controlling.

controlling tasks   Planning, monitoring, reporting, advising, and informing.

conversion   Translation from one data format to another—for example, from decimal to binary code.

cost center   Place in which costs are incurred. A unit within a company distinguished by area of responsibility, location, or accounting method.

cost component   A group of cost origins.

cost component layout (product cost accounting and cost center accounting)   A technical term that indicates how results of a product cost estimate are saved. Assigns cost elements to cost components and determines the following:

- How the costs for raw materials and finished and semifinished products are rolled up in a multilevel assembly structure
- Which portion of the costs is treated as fixed costs
- Which costs are treated as the cost of goods manufactured
- Which are sales and administration costs
- Which are the cost of goods sold

cost element   Mandatory criterion for classifying costs arising in a company code, as follows:

- Direct cost elements for goods and services procured externally
- Indirect (internal activity) cost elements

Direct cost elements are maintained in the general ledger master records. Indirect cost elements have no counterpart in the financial accounts and are maintained exclusively in cost accounting.

cost element group   A conjunction of cost elements used to select records and to define lines and columns in reports. They can be used for planning purposes.

cost element planning   Planning primary and secondary costs on a cost center, order, or project.

cost element type   Classification of cost elements by uses or origin—for example, material cost element, settlement cost elements for orders, or cost elements for internal cost allocations.

cost object   An account assignment term for individual cost objects to which actual data—such as costs, budgets, and sales revenues—can be assigned. It can consist of individual products, such as product groups, or local situations based on classification criteria, such as shop floor areas.

cost object hierarchy   Structure of cost objects as nodes to which actual data can be assigned.

cost origin   A logical category to which costs may be assigned. Activity types and cost elements are cost origins.

cost planning   Planning the costs to be incurred during a transaction.

Apx

cost planning type   A technical term that indicates the purpose of a cost planning method. For example:

- Rough planning—estimating costs to be incurred for an order or for an element in a work breakdown structure
- Cost element planning
- Unit costing

costing   Calculating total production costs of individual product units, which may be a piece, a batch, a lot, or an order, for example. Costing may also take place on the provision of services.

costing type   Technical term used to control unit costing and product costing. The costing type determines the following:

- For which reference object a costing may be used
- Which costing object will be updated
- How the key of the costing file is made up
- Which costing application can use this costing type

costing variant   Technical term to determine criteria for a cost estimate. Comprises mainly the following:

- Costing type
- Valuation variant
- Organizational level
- Quantity structure determination, which will include the date control parameter

costing version   Technical term that determines the quantity structure when cost estimates are created. When production alternatives exit, there can be more than one product cost estimate for a material. Cost estimates with different production alternatives are given different version numbers.

cost-of-sales accounting   A form of results analysis; sales deductions and unit costs are assigned to the sales transaction.

CPI-C   Common Programming Interface-Communications. A set of standardized definitions for communications between programs.

credit memo request   Reference document for creating a credit memo. If a customer applies for a credit memo, the sales department initiates a credit memo request, which is blocked until it's checked. The credit memo block is removed if the request is approved.

customer billing document   Statement of payment due as a result of the business transaction referred to in the document.

customer credit group   A group of customers defined by industry sector, by country, or by any characteristic that is useful for credit management. Credit representatives can generate reports for statistical analysis and retrieve information such as credit holds for processing using customer credit groups.

customer delivery   A collection of sales products delivered together.

customer group   A set of customers nominated or specified in any way for the purpose of statistical reporting or other management tasks.

customer hierarchy   A method of representing complex customer structures such as a buying group. Pricing and other information that's valid for all members of a customer hierarchy can be stored in the master record.

customer inquiry   Request from a customer to a sales organization for a price and availability check of in-hand inventory.

customer quotation   An offer submitted by a sales organization to a customer for the delivery of goods or the provision of services according to fixed terms.

customer-material information record   A collection of information and references to be used in specifying material for a particular customer.

Customizing   An SAP tool, provided as part of the R/3 system, comprising two components: implementation guides, and customizing menus and the associated functions. It doesn't change the program coding. This tool provides support for all activities necessary for the following:

- Initial configuration of the SAP system before going into production
- Adjustment of the system during production
- Implementation of additional SAP applications

data element of a field   A description of the contents of a record or field in terms of their business significance.

database interface   A work area to receive data from ABAP/4 Data Dictionary tables and from which any changed data may be passed to the database.

date of next credit review   This date can be entered manually and be used to trigger an automatic credit review that will issue a warning or a block if anyone attempts to process a sales order after that date.

DBMS   Database management system, a software system used to set up and maintain a database. It will include SQL facilities.

DDL   Data Definition Language, which is used to define database objects under the DBMS.

debit memo request   A document created because of a discrepancy in the price or quantity, or as a result of a customer complaint. The debit memo request has to be approved before a debit memo can be created.

decentralized shipping   Round-the-clock shipment processing that's independent of the host computer. The following functions can be included:

- Copying data from the central sales and distribution system
- Shipping processing in the decentralized shipping system
- Confirmation of goods issued on the goods issue date to the central sales and distribution system

delivering plant   Storage plant from which customer goods are to be delivered.

delivery   A sales and distribution (SD) document for processing a delivery of goods that stores information needed for the following tasks: planning material requirements, picking, creating shipping documents, creating shipping units, transporting, and billing.

delivery due list   A work list that serves as the basis for creating deliveries. This list comprises all sales orders and scheduling agreements that are due for delivery within a specified period.

delivery scheduling   The result of determining all dates relevant for shipping the goods referred to in a goods issue note. The system determines when the delivery plant must start picking and packing activities to ensure meeting the requested loading date.

delta management   System of transferring only data that has changed when using Remote Function Calls (RFCs).

dialog module   A group of dialog steps in a program.

direct costs   Costs directly and fully identifiable with a reference object according to the costs-by-cause principle.

distribution (controlling)   A business transaction used to allocate primary costs. The original cost element is retained on the receiver cost center. Information on the sender and the receiver is documented in the cost accounting document.

distribution channel   An organizational unit that determines how a product reaches customers. This channel indicates how a company generates business and which organizations are involved in distribution activities.

distribution key   Contains rules on how the costs are to be distributed. It is used for the following:

- Planning to spread costs over the planning period
- Assessment
- Distribution of direct costs in order to divide the costs of a sender cost center among the receivers

division   An organizational unit set up to supervise distribution and to monitor the profitability of a particular product. Customer-specific arrangements such as partial deliveries, prices, or terms of payment can be defined for each division.

DLL   Dynamic link library, which is integral to the runtime functioning of the Windows architecture.

DMS Document Management System, which supports the management of documents across and within applications. Status and version can be controlled. Documents can be linked to objects such as material master records. DMS documents can be retrieved by the classification system and archived optically.

document A printable record of a business transaction in sales and distribution processing. There are three kinds of printed documents in SD: sales documents, shipping documents, and billing documents.

document date Date on which the sales document becomes valid for sales and distribution processing. The document date is different for each document in a sales sequence. In the quotation, the document date is the date from which the quotation is valid; in the order, it is the date from which the agreement becomes binding. For example, the order creation date can vary from the date on which the agreement stipulated in the order becomes binding. In such a case, the agreement date would be taken as the document date.

document flow A stored representation of the sequence of documents necessary for one particular business transaction. For example, a particular document flow could be defined as a quotation, a sales order, a delivery, and an invoice.

domain A description of the technical attributes of a table field, such as the type, format, length, and value range. Several fields with the same technical attributes can refer to the same domain.

dynamic credit limit check with credit horizon The credit exposure of a customer is split into a static part and a dynamic part. The static part comprises open items, open billing, and delivery values; the dynamic part is the open order value, which includes all orders that aren't yet delivered or are only partially delivered. The value is calculated on the shipping date and stored in an information structure using a time period that you specify (days, weeks, or months). When you define a credit check, you can specify a particular horizon date in the future by nominating a number of these time periods. When evaluating credit, the system has to ignore all open orders that are due for delivery after the horizon date. The sum of the static and dynamic parts of the credit check may not exceed the credit limit you've set for the credit horizon time period.

dynpro A dynamic program that controls the screen and its associated validation and processing logic to control exactly one dialog step.

EBCDIC Extended Binary-Coded Decimal Interchange Code.

EDI Electronic data interchange, a standardized scheme for exchanging business data between different systems via defined business documents such as invoices and orders.

enqueue service An R/3 system mechanism for the management of locks on business objects throughout client/server environments. The enqueue service can withhold the updating of a business object master until all related messages between different application servers have been processed.

entity   The smallest possible collection of data that makes sense from a business viewpoint and is represented in the R/3 system.

entity relationship model   Entities may be linked by logical relationships with business significance. Entities and their interrelations can be used to build static models of the enterprise, which in turn are portrayed in the respective computer application with its tables.

Environment Analyzer   A help program that lists the development objects that belong together and the boundaries between development classes.

EPC   See event-driven process chain (EPC).

equivalence number   A specification of how any given value is to be distributed to the different receiving objects.

event (reference model)   A status that has business relevance. It can trigger an SAP system function or can be the result of such a function.

event (workflow management)   A collection of attributes of objects that describes the change in an object's state.

event-driven process chain (EPC)   Describes the chronological and logical relationship of functions of the R/3 system and business system statuses that initialize the functions or are generated as a result of function execution.

external activities   Nonstock components and/or activities in a production order that are produced or performed outside the company.

external credit data   Credit data about a customer from external sources, such as the Dun and Bradstreet data that's standard for SAP R/3. You refer to the D&B credit information number (DUNs number) that identifies the customer and append the D&B indicator and rating. You can also enter the date when you last acquired this data.

float   Period of time that allows you to start a network or activity at a later date without incurring a scheduling delay.

follow-up costs   Incurred after the actual manufacturing process has been completed—for example, costs of rework and warranties.

forecasting   An estimate of future values based on historical data. A sales and distribution forecast is carried out using a model that you can select or allow the system to select automatically after conducting a "best-fit" analysis.

foreign key   Defines a relationship between two tables by assigning fields of one table (the foreign key table) to the primary key fields of another table (the check table).

forward scheduling   Way of scheduling a network, starting from the basic start date and adding durations to determine the earliest start and finish dates for successive activities.

free float   Time in which an activity can be shifted into the future without affecting the earliest start date of the following activity or the end date of the project. Must not be less than zero or greater than the total float.

function module   A program module that has a clearly defined interface and can be used in several programs. The function module library manages all function modules and provides search facilities in the development environment.

function-oriented cost accounting   Assigning costs to a business function for the purpose of analysis.

general costs activity   General costs incurred during the lifetime of a project are planned via this type of activity in a network. Examples of such planned costs are insurance, travel, consulting fees, and royalties.

goods issue   The decrease of warehouse inventory resulting from a withdrawal of material or a delivery to a customer.

goods issue document   A statement that verifies goods movement and contains information for follow-up tasks. A corresponding material document is initiated for the subsequent outflow of material with the goods issue document in the delivery. The material document contains one or more items and can be printed as a goods issue slip for the actual physical movement of goods.

GUI   Acronym for graphical user interface. The SAP-GUI gives users an ergonomic and attractive means of controlling and using business software.

hypertext   Online documentation set up like a network, with active references pointing to additional text and graphics.

IDoc   Intermediate document. The SAP R/3 system EDI interface and the ALE program link enabling both use standardized intermediate documents to communicate.

IMG   Implementation management guide, a component of the SAP R/3 system that provides detailed steps for configuring and setting the applications.

imputed costs   These costs don't represent operational expenditures or correspond to expenditures in either content or timing (for example, depreciation and interest).

incompletion log   A list that indicates what information is missing in a sales document. You can set up conditions to specify the information that has to be included in a document.

indirect costs   Costs for which one single receiving object can't be directly and fully identified according to the cost-by-cause principle—for example, indirect expenses such as building insurance, indirect labor costs such as supervisor wages, or indirect materials costs such as coolant cleaning materials.

initial cost split   Cost component split for raw materials procurement showing such details as purchase price, freight charges, insurance contributions, and administration costs.

inquiry   A request from a customer to a sales organization for a price and on-hand availability.

inventory from which revenue can be generated   The revenue expected in view of costs already incurred can be divided into capitalized costs and capitalized profits. It's calculated as calculated revenue minus actual revenue. Results analysis calculates the inventory for profit orders.

invoice   Sales and distribution document used to charge a customer for a delivery of goods or for services rendered.

invoice date   Date on which a delivery is due for settlement. In some firms, invoices are processed periodically. All deliveries that become due at the same time can be combined and settled in a collective invoice. As soon as the next billing date determined by the calendar is reached, the orders and deliveries are included in the billing due list and can be billed.

invoice list   Method of billing by combining all billing documents for a specific period for a particular payer. Additional discounts, such as factoring discounts, can be granted based on the total value of an invoice list. The list may include individual and collective documents.

invoice split   Creation of several billing documents from one reference document such as an order or delivery. The split may be based on materials, for example.

item   Element of a document that carries information on the goods to be delivered or the services to be rendered.

item category   An indicator that defines the characteristics of a document item. The categories for items kept in inventory, value items, and text items are predefined. The item category controls the following tasks: pricing, billing, delivery processing, stock posting, and transfer of requirements.

job order cost accounting   Instrument for the detailed planning and controlling of costs. Serves for the following: collecting, analyzing, and allocating the costs incurred for the internal production of noncapitalized goods.

joint products   Made in the same manufacturing process.

Kerberos   A technique for checking user authorizations across open distributed systems.

library network   A generic network structure that many projects can use. Used in project system for repetitive processes or for process planning.

line item   Display of posting according to activity and document number.

loading date   Date by which goods must be ready to be loaded and the vehicles required to transport them must be available.

loading group   A key that identifies the equipment needed to load the goods. For example, "crane or fork lift truck" could be defined as a loading group.

loading point   Place within a shipping point where goods are loaded.

logical database   A set of predefined paths for accessing the tables in a specific database system. Once defined and coded, they can be used by any report program.

logical system   A system on which applications integrated on a common data basis run. In SAP terms, this is a client in a database.

loop   Circular path through activities and their relationships.

lot-size variance   Variances between the fixed planned costs and the fixed allocated actual costs that occur because part of the total cost for an order or a cost object doesn't change with output quantity changes. For example, setup costs that don't change no matter how often the operation is carried out.

LU6.2   IBM networking protocol used by the SAP R/3 system to communicate with mainframe computers.

LUW   Logical unit of work, an elementary processing step that's part of an SAP transaction. An LUW is either executed entirely or not at all. In particular, database access is always accomplished by separate LUWs, each of which is terminated when the database is updated or when the COMMIT WORK command is entered.

make-to-order production   Type of production in which a product is generally manufactured only once and to a customer order.

MAPI   Messaging Application Programming Interface, which is part of the Microsoft Windows Open Service Architecture (WOSA).

master data   Data relating to individual objects; remains unchanged for a long time.

matchcode   An index key code attached to the original data that can be used to perform quick interactive searches for this data.

material   A product, substance, or commodity that's bought or sold commercially or is used, consumed, or created in production. A material master record can also represent a service.

material availability date   The date on which a material has to be available. On the material availability date, the vendor has to start the activities relevant for delivery, such as picking and packing the goods. The material availability date should allow time for the goods to be completely prepared by the loading date.

material determination   The process of conducting an automatic search for a material master record during the creation of sales and distribution documents using a key instead of the actual material number. The key can be a customer-specific material number or the European Article Number (EAN) number of the material.

material exclusion   A restriction that automatically prevents the sale of specific materials to a particular customer.

material listing   A restriction that controls the sale of specific materials to a customer. Customers can buy only materials included in the material listing assigned to them. The system doesn't allow you to enter a sales document for particular customer materials that aren't included in the material listing.

material requirements planning   Generic term for activities involved in creating a production schedule or procurement plan for the materials in a plant, company, or company group. A set of techniques that use BOMs, inventory data, and the master production schedule to calculate requirements for materials.

material substitution   Automatic replacement by another material for technical reasons or during a sales promotion.

material type   An indicator that subdivides materials into groups (such as raw materials, semifinished materials, and operating supplies) and determines the user screen sequence, the numbering in the material master records, the type of inventory management, and the account determination.

maximum document value   A specific value that the sales order or delivery may not exceed. The value is defined in the credit check and is stored in the currency of the credit control area. Checking is initiated by a risk category defined specifically for new customers if a credit limit hasn't yet been specified.

maximum number of dunning levels allowed   The customer's dunning level may not exceed this specified maximum.

measuring point   Physical or logical place at which a status is described—for example, the temperature inside a reactor or the speed of revolution of a windspeed measuring wheel

menu painter   An R/3 system tool for developing standardized menus, function keys, and pushbuttons in accord with the SAP Style Guide.

metadata   Information about data structures used in a program. Examples of metadata are table and field definitions, domains, and descriptions of relationships between tables.

milestone   An operation or task that also confirms the completion of processing of previous tasks. When you confirm a milestone, the system traces back through its component operations to confirm their completion also.

mode   A user interface window in which an activity can be conducted in parallel with other open modes.

modified standard cost estimate   A costing type. Uses the quantity structure that changed during the planning period to calculate the cost of goods manufactured for a product.

moving average price   Value of the material divided by the quantity in stock. Changes automatically after each goods movement or invoice entry.

network   In SAP R/3, an activity-on-node structure containing instructions on how specifically to carry out activities, in a specific order, and in a specific time period. Made from activities and relationships.

network type   Distinguishes networks by their usage. The network type controls costing variants for plan, target, and actual costs; order type; number ranges; open items; status profile; and authorizations.

object currency   The currency of the controlling area is the default currency of a cost accounting object, such as cost center, order, and so on.

object dependency   Product variants may entail certain combinations of parts and exclude other combinations. If the customer chooses one variant, certain options may not be available for technical or commercial reasons. These reciprocal relationships are represented in the system by object dependency. A special editor is provided in the classification system to maintain the object dependency for characteristics and the characteristic values. You can also store object dependency in a bill of material (BOM); the system uses this information during BOM explosion. Object dependency controls whether all possible components are taken into account in materials planning.

object master data   Information stored in order to produce variants for a standard product. Bills of material list the parts needed, and routings store instructions for combining the individual parts.

object master data and object dependency   Master records for the manufacture of products with many variants. Information on the objects involved and their interrelationships is stored as object master data and object dependency.

object overview   Customized list of data and line display layout—for example, routings, inspection plans, maintenance tasks, and networks.

ODBC   Open Database Connectivity, a Microsoft standard based on SQL Access Group definitions for table-oriented data access.

oldest open item   The oldest open item may not be more than a specified number of days overdue.

OLE   Object Linking and Embedding, a Microsoft technology to enable the connection and incorporation of objects across many programs or files.

one-time customer   A collective customer master record used to process transactions involving any customer who's not a regular customer. If a transaction is entered for a one-time customer, the customer data must be entered manually.

open item   Contractual or scheduled commitment that's not yet reflected in financial accounting but will lead to actual expenditures in the future. Open item management provides for early recording and analyzing for cost and financial effects.

operating concern   An organizational unit to which one or more controlling areas and company codes can be assigned. Certain criteria and value fields are valid for a specific operating concern. The criteria define business segments, and the value fields are then updated for these objects.

operating level   The planned or actual performance of a cost center for a period—for example, output quantity, production time, and machine hours.

operating rate   Ratio of actual and planned operating level. Measures the effective utilization of a cost center or activity.

operating resources   Personnel and material necessary to carry out a project; can be used once or many times. Defined in value or quantity units. Planned for a period or a point in time. Includes, for example, materials, machines, labor, tools, jigs, fixtures, external services, and work centers.

operational area   A technical term used to signify a logical subdivision of a company for accounting or operational reasons and therefore indicated in the enterprise data model (EDM). An operation area is an organizational unit within logistics that subdivides a maintenance site plant according to the responsibility for maintenance.

operations layout   List, sorted by operations, of costing results from product costing and final costing.

order   Instrument for planning and controlling costs. Describes the work to be done in a company in terms of which task is to be carried out and when, what is needed to carry out this task, and how the costs are to be settled.

order category   The SAP application to which the order belongs—SD, for example.

order combination   A combination of complete sales orders, of individual order items from different sales orders, or of partial deliveries of individual order items in a delivery. Order combination in a delivery is possible only when you authorize it for customers in the customer master record or when you manually authorize it for individual sales orders in the sales order document header.

order group   Technical term for grouping orders into hierarchies. Used to create reports on several orders, to combine orders, and to create order hierarchy.

order hierarchy   Grouping of orders for processing at the same time as in order planning and order reporting.

order phase   System control instrument for the order master data. Allows and prohibits operations on orders depending on the phase or stage: opened, released, completed, or closed.

order settlement   Complete or partial crediting of an order. The costs accrued to an order are debited to one or more receivers belonging to financial or cost accounting.

order status   Instrument to control whether an order may be planned or posted to. Reflects the operational progress, the order phase. Determines whether planning documents are created during cost element planning; the transactions allowed at the moment (phase) such as planning, posting actual costs, and so on; and when an order may be flagged for deletion.

order summarization   Allows you to summarize data by putting orders into hierarchies. Also lets you analyze order costs at a higher level.

order type   Differentiates orders according to their purpose, such as repair, maintenance, marketing, or capital expenditure.

order/project results analysis   Periodic valuation of long-term orders and projects. The o/p results analysis evaluates the ratio between costs and a measure of an order's progress toward completion, such as revenue or the quantity produced. The results analysis data include cost of sales, capitalized costs or work in progress, capitalized profits, reserves for unrealized costs, reserves for the cost of complaints and commissions, and reserves for imminent loss.

outline agreement   Generic term for contracts and scheduling agreements. The outline agreement is a long-term agreement with the vendor involving delivery of products or rendering of services according to specified requirements. These requirements are valid for a limited time period, a defined total purchase quantity, or a specified total purchase value. A further transaction determines when deliveries and services take place.

output   Information sent to the customer by various media such as mail, EDI, or fax. Examples of output are printed quotation or order confirmations, order confirmations sent by EDI, and shipping notifications sent by fax.

overall network   Network resulting from the relationships between all existing networks.

overdue open items   The relationship between the total value of open items that are more than a specified time overdue and the customer balance may not exceed a nominated percentage.

overhead   Total cost of indirect expenses, indirect labor, and indirect materials (indirect costs). Allocated to cost objects by means of overhead rates.

overhead cost management   The entirety of cost accounting activities for planning and controlling the indirect costs, as follows: responsibility-oriented overhead cost management by cost centers, and decision-oriented overhead cost management by action-oriented objects, which are orders and projects.

overhead costing   Most common method in product cost accounting, as follows: assign the direct costs to the cost object and apply the indirect (overhead) costs to the cost object in proportion to the direct costs, expressed as a percentage rate.

overhead group   Key that groups materials to which the same overheads are applied.

PA settlement structure   To settle costs incurred on a sender to various business segments depending on the cost element. The profitability analysis settlement structure is a combination of assignments of cost element groups to profitability segments.

partial delivery   A quantity of goods received that's smaller than the quantity ordered after making allowance for the underdelivery tolerance.

partial payment   Payment that only partially settles the outstanding invoice amount.

partial quantity   Quantity of a product that deviates from the standard packaging quantity. In the warehouse management system, bin quantities containing less than the standard pallet load defined in the material master are regarded as partial pallet quantities.

partner   An individual within or outside your organization who is of commercial interest and who can be contacted in the course of a business transaction. A partner can be a person or a legal entity.

payer   Person or company that settles the bill for a delivery of goods or for services rendered. The payer is not necessarily the bill-to party.

period accounting   One basis for profitability analysis. Costs are identified in the period in which they occur, irrespective of the period in which the corresponding revenue occurs.

Apx

picking   The process of issuing and grouping certain products from the warehouse on the basis of goods requirements from the sales or production department. Picking can take place with transfer orders or picking lists. The procedure distinguishes between picking from fixed storage bins and random picking.

pick/pack time   Time needed to assign goods to a delivery and to pick and pack them. The pick/pack time depends on the loading point, the route, and the weight group of the sales order.

plan version   Control parameters for comparative analyses in planning in cost accounting. The plan version determines, as follows, whether planning changes are documented, a beginning balance is to be generated, and the planning data of another version can be copied or referenced.

planned activity   The planned cost center activity required to meet the demand, measured in the corresponding physical or technical units.

planned delivery time   Number of days required to procure the material via external procurement.

planning   Assigning estimates of the costs of all activities required to carry out the business of an organizational unit over the planning period.

planning document   Line item for documenting planning changes.

planning element   Work breakdown structure (WBS) element on which cost planning can be carried out.

plant   The main organizational entity for production planning and control. Materials requirement planning and inventory maintenance are often conducted at the plant level.

pooled table   A database table used to store control data, such as program parameters, or temporary data. Several pooled tables can be combined to form a table pool, which corresponds to a physical table on the database.

price difference account   To record price differences for materials managed under standard prices, or differences between purchase order and billing prices.

price group   Grouping of customers for pricing purposes.

price variance   Occurs if planned costs are evaluated in one way and the actual costs in another. The planned standard rates for activities might change in the meantime, for example. Can also be the result of exchange rate fluctuations.

pricing element   A factor that contributes to pricing. Any or all of the following can be identified as pricing elements: price, discount, surcharge, freight, and tax.

pricing procedure   Definition of the conditions permitted for a particular document and the sequence in which the system takes these conditions into account during pricing.

pricing scale   Scale within a condition record where prices, discounts, or surcharges are defined for different customer order quantities or values.

pricing type   Controls whether prices are copied from a reference document to a new document or are recalculated in the new document.

primary cost planning   By values and as quantities.

primary costs   Incurred due to the consumption of goods and services supplied to the company from outside. Costs for input factors and resources procured externally—for example, bought-in parts, raw materials, supplies, and services.

process manufacturing   A production type; continuous manufacturing process from raw materials to finished product.

product costing   A tool for planning costs and setting prices. It calculates the cost of goods manufactured and of goods sold for each product unit, using the data in the production planning (PP) module. Product costing based on bills of material and routings is used for calculating production costs of an assembly, with alternatives for showing the costs of semifinished products, and for detailed estimates of the cost components down to their lowest production level.

product proposal   Product groupings, combinations, and quantities frequently ordered. You can save time by referring to and copying from product proposals. You can also define a product proposal for a particular customer. The system automatically enters the customer-specific product proposal when you create an order for this particular customer.

production costs, total   The costs of finished products bought for resale, or the costs of goods manufactured, plus sales overhead, special direct costs of sales, and administration overhead.

production cycle   A manufacturing process in which the output of the final manufacturing level (or part of it) becomes input for lower manufacturing levels of the same process (recycle).

production order   For the production department to produce a material. It contains operations, material components, production resources and tools, and costing data.

production resources and tools (PRT)   Needed for carrying out operations at work centers and assigned to activities for whose execution they are necessary. Stored as material master, equipment master, and document master data. PRTs include job instructions, tools, test equipment, numerically controlled programs, drawings, and machinery and fixtures.

profit center   Area of responsibility for which an independent operating profit is calculated; responsible for its own profitability. Separate divisional result is calculated.

profit order   Order whose planned revenue is greater than the planned costs. Results analysis uses the profit percentage rate of a profit order to calculate the inventory from which revenue can be generated, and to calculate the cost of sales.

profit percentage rate   Planned revenue divided by planned costs of an order.

profitability analysis   In SAP R/3, analysis by cost-of-sales approach or period accounting.

project definition   Framework laid down for all objects created within a project. The data, such as dates and organizational data, are binding for the entire project.

project management   An organizational structure created just for the life of the project, to be responsible for planning, controlling, and monitoring of the project.

project structure   All significant relationships between the elements in a project.

project type   Capital spending or customer project, for example.

PRT   See production resources and tools (PRT).

Q-API   Queue-Application Program Interface. Supports asynchronous communication between applications of different systems by using managed queues or waiting lines.

quantity structure   The quantity-related basis for calculating costs. The bill of material and routing form the quantity structure for product costing and the preliminary costing of a production order.

quantity variance   Difference between target costs and actual costs, which results from the difference between planned and actual quantities of goods or activity used—for example, more raw materials from stock for a production order, or fewer activities from a cost center than were planned for.

rate of capacity utilization   Ratio of output to capacity. Fixed costs can be divided into used capacity costs and idle time costs.

realized loss   Usage of reserves for imminent loss by results analysis. Loss can be realized when actual costs are incurred or when revenue is received. Results analysis realizes loss as the difference between the actual costs and the calculated revenue, or between the calculated costs and the actual revenue, as follows:

- Actual costs minus calculated revenue
- Calculated costs minus actual revenue

rebate   Price discount that a vendor pays to a customer after the sale. The amount of the rebate usually depends on the total invoiced sales that the customer achieves within a specified time period.

rebate agreement   Agreement between a vendor and a customer regarding the granting of rebates. A rebate agreement contains relevant information such as the rebate basis, rebate amount, rebate recipient, and the validity period.

reference date   By using the reference dates and the offsets, the start and finish dates of the suboperation or the production resource/tool usage are determined. A point of time within an activity—for example, the start date. Reference dates are used to determine the start and finish dates of suboperations as well as usage dates for production resources/tools. You can enter time intervals for reference dates.

reference document   Document from which data is copied into another document.

Apx

relationship (project system)   Link between start and finish points of two activities in a network or library network. In R/3, the relationship types are the following:

- SS→start-start
- FF→finish-finish
- SF→start-finish
- FS→finish-start

Remote Function Call (RFC)   a protocol, written in ABAP/4, for accessing function modules in other computers. RFC-SDK is a kit for integrating PC applications so that they can access SAP R/3 functions.

Remote Procedure Call (RPC)   A protocol for accessing procedures residing in other computers from C programming environments. Corresponds to Remote Function Call (RFC).

repetitive manufacturing   A production type. Many similar products are manufactured together or one after another. In R/3, bills of materials and routings are created for each product.

reserves for costs of complaints and sales deductions   Inventory can't be created for certain costs—for example, costs arising under warranties or because of sales deductions. For such costs, results analysis creates reserves equal to the planned costs. These reserves are then used when (and if) actual costs are incurred.

reserves for imminent loss   Results analysis creates reserves equal to the planned loss. These reserves are reduced as (and if) this loss is realized.

reserves for unrealized costs   Calculated in results analysis by subtracting the actual costs from the cost of sales.

resource-usage variance   Occurs if the used resource is different from the planned one—for example, the actual raw material used is different from the planned raw material.

results analysis   Periodic valuation of long-term orders. Results analysis compares the calculated and actual costs of an order as it progresses toward completion. It calculates inventory (if actual costs are greater than calculated costs) or reserves (if actual costs are less than calculated costs). The data calculated during results analysis is stored in the form of cost of sales, capitalized costs, capitalized profit, reserves for unrealized costs, reserves for costs of complaints and commissions, and reserves for imminent loss.

results analysis account   A general ledger account that records the figures calculated during results analysis.

results analysis data   Analysis of work in progress and capitalized costs, reserves, and cost of sales.

results analysis key   Determines for results analysis whether revenue-based, quantity-based, or manual; the basis on which it is carried out (planned or actual results); how profits are to be realized; and whether to split inventory, reserves, and cost of sales.

results analysis version   Describes the business purpose for which results analysis was carried out. Determines, for example:

- Whether in accordance with German and American law
- For financial accounting purposes
- For profitability analysis
- To which results analysis accounts to post the results
- How the life cycle of an object is to be broken down into open and closed periods

returnable packaging   Packaging material or transportation device used to store or to transport goods. The returnable packaging is delivered to the customer along with the goods, and it has to be returned to the vendor afterward to avoid incurring a charge.

returns   Return of goods by customers. Returns are planned by means of a returns order. A receipt of returns records the arrival of goods, which are then posted to inventory.

revenue   The operational output valued at market price in the corresponding currency and sales quantity unit:

Quantity * Revenue = Sales

revenue account determination   Notifies the revenue accounts to which prices, discounts, and surcharges are to be posted. The system uses predefined conditions to determine the appropriate accounts.

RFC   See Remote Function Call (RFC).

risk category   Enables the credit manager to classify customers according to commercial risk. Along with the document type, the risk category helps to determine which kind of credit check the system automatically carries out. For example, you may decide to carry out stringent checks at order receipt for high-risk customers but waive a credit check for customers with an acceptable payment history.

RPC   See Remote Procedure Call (RPC).

sales activity   A data record that contains information on customer interaction, including sales calls, telephone calls, conferences, or presentations.

sales and distribution document   A document that represents a business transaction in the SD module. SD documents include sales documents, shipping documents, and billing documents.

sales and operations planning (SOP)   The creation and maintenance of a meaningful sales plan and corresponding operations plan that includes a forecast of future customer demand.

sales area   An organizational unit that's responsible for three facets: sales-related aspect (sales organization), customer-related aspect (distribution channel), and product-related aspect (division).

sales document   A document that represents a business transaction in the sales department. Sales documents include inquiry, quotation, sales order, outline agreements such as contracts and scheduling agreements, returns, and credit and debit requests.

sales document type   Indicators used to control processing of various sales and distribution documents by allowing the system to process different kinds of business transactions, such as standard orders and credit memo requests, in different ways.

sales order   Contractual arrangement between a sales organization and a sold-to party concerning goods to be delivered or services to be rendered. Also, an SAP document that contains information about prices, quantities, and dates.

sales organization   The division or other organizational unit responsible for negotiating sales and distributing products and services. Sales organizations may be assigned to market subdivisions by geographical or industrial criteria. Each sales transaction is carried out by one sales organization.

sales plan   The overall level of sales, usually stated as the monthly rate of sales per product group or product family. The plan is expressed in units identical to the operations plan for planning purposes and represents a commitment by sales and marketing management to take all reasonable steps necessary to achieve actual customer orders that add up to the sales forecast.

sales unit   Unit of measure in which a product is sold. If several alternative sales units of measure have been defined for one product, conversion factors are applied by the system to convert them to the base unit of measurement.

schedule line   A subdivision, according to date and quantity of an item in a sales document. If the total quantity of an item can be delivered only in partial deliveries, the system creates schedule lines corresponding to each partial delivery and determines the appropriate quantities and delivery dates for each schedule line.

scheduling, network   Determines earliest and latest start dates for activities and calculates the required capacity, as well as floats.

scheduling agreement   A type of long-term outline agreement, with a vendor or customer that defines the creation and continuous updating of schedules. Schedules specify timing of partial deliveries for each item in schedule lines.

screen painter   An ABAP/4 Development Workbench tool that can be used to create, modify, display, and delete dynpros.

secondary cost element   Cost centers require services from other cost centers to their own produce activity. These are secondary costs. Planned assessment is used to plan the secondary cost quantities; activity input is used to plan the secondary cost values.

settlement parameters   Control data required for order settlement: allocation group, settlement cost element, and settlement receiver.

settlement rule   Consists of the sender and the settlement distribution rule, which includes the settlement receiving accounts, the distribution factor, the settlement type, and the validity period.

shipping conditions   A statement of the general strategy for shipping goods to a customer. If one of the shipping conditions states that goods must arrive at the customer location as soon as possible, the system will automatically suggest the shipping point and route that will deliver the goods the fastest.

shipping document　A document that defines a shipping transaction. SD shipping documents include delivery, material document containing goods issue information, and grouped deliveries.

shipping material　Material used for packing and transporting products. Shipping material includes crates, pallets, or containers. A shipping unit master record will normally specify a shipping material.

shipping point　Location that carries out shipping activities, such as a mail department or rail depot. Each delivery is processed by one shipping point.

shipping type　An indicator that shows which means and mode of transport are used to carry out a shipment of goods.

shipping unit　Combination of products packed together in a shipping material at a particular time. Shipping units may contain delivery items or items that are themselves shipping units.

ship-to party　Person or company that receives goods. The ship-to party isn't necessarily the sold-to party, the bill-to party, or the payer.

simultaneous costing　Process that displays the actual costs incurred to date for such things as an order. The process describes all costings of an order in the SAP system, including order settlement. These costings come in the form of preliminary costings and actual costings. The values can then be analyzed in final analysis.

sold-to party　Person or company that places an order for goods or services. The sold-to party can also perform the functions of the payer, bill-to party, or ship-to party.

spooling　Buffered relaying of information to output media, across multiple computers, if necessary.

SQL　Structured Query Language, defined by the American National Standards Institute (ANSI) as a fourth-generation language for defining and manipulating data.

standard cost estimate　Calculates the standard price for semifinished and finished products. Relevant to the valuation of materials with standard price control. Usually created once for all products at the beginning of the fiscal year or a new season. The most important type of costing in product costing. The basis for profit planning or variance-oriented product cost controlling.

standard hierarchy　Tree structure for classifying all data objects of one type. For example, the cost centers belonging to a company from a cost accounting point of view will be represented by a standard hierarchy copied from the R/3 Reference Model and customized.

standard price　Constant price with which a material is evaluated, without taking into account goods movements and invoices. For semifinished and finished products calculated in product costing.

static credit limit check   The customer's credit exposure may not exceed the established credit limit. The credit exposure is the total combined value of open sales documents, open delivery documents, open billing documents, and open items in accounts receivable. The open order value is the value of the order items that haven't yet been delivered. The open delivery value is the value of the delivery items that haven't yet been invoiced. The open invoice value is the value of the billing document items that haven't yet been forwarded to accounting. The open items represent documents that have been forwarded to accounting but aren't yet settled by the customer.

status   Order items with the item category TAK are made to order and have an object status that passes through the following phases:

- **1 Released**. The system sets this status automatically when the item is created to indicate that production can be initiated.
- **2 Revenue posted**. The system sets this status automatically, as soon as revenue is posted for an item for the first time.
- **3 Fully invoiced**. This status must be set manually, as soon as all revenues are posted for the item. After this status is set, no more revenues can be posted.
- **4 Completed**. This status must be set manually when the procedure is completed. If this status is set, no further costs can be posted.

stock   A materials management term for part of a company's current assets also known as *inventory*. Stock refers to the quantities of raw materials, operating supplies, semifinished products, finished products, and goods on hand in the company's stores or warehouse facilities.

stock transfer   The removal of materials from storage at one location and their transfer to and placement into storage at another. Stock transfers can occur either within a single plant or between two different plants. The removal of inventory from storage at the first location and its placement into storage at the other can be posted in the system in one or two steps.

style guide   A collection of the SAP design standards for uniform design and consistent operation routines for SAP applications.

subitem   An item in a sales document that refers to a higher-level item. Services and rebates in kind can be entered as sub-items belonging to main items.

summarization object   An object containing data calculated during order summarization, project summarization, or the summarization of a cost object hierarchy. A summarization object can, for example, contain the costs incurred for all orders of a specific type and a specific responsible cost center.

surcharge   Supplement, usually as percentage, used to apply overhead in absorption costing.

target costs   Calculated using the planned costs, along with the following:

- The planned activities divided by the actual activities (for cost centers)
- The planned quantities divided by the actual quantities of goods manufactured (for orders)

target document   A document to which the data from a reference document is copied.

tax category   A code that identifies the condition that the system is to use to determine country-specific taxes automatically during pricing.

tax classification   Specification of the method for calculating the tax liability of the customer based on the tax structure of the customer's country.

task list type   Distinguishes task lists according to their functionality. In production planning task lists, for example, a distinction is drawn between routings and reference operation sets.

TCP/IP   Transmission Control Protocol/Internet Protocol, the standard network protocol for open systems.

text   A system function that provides a note pad where you can store any related text about the current customer. The system indicates in the credit management status screen whether any text is already available about this customer.

text type   A classification for various texts that users can define in master records or in documents. Text types include sales texts, shipping texts, and internal notes.

third-party business transaction   Commerce in which goods or services are delivered directly from vendor to customer.

time interval   Time period between at least two activities linked in a relationship. The relationship type determines how start and finish times are used in the calculation.

total float   Time that an activity can be shifted out into the future starting from its earliest dates without affecting the latest dates of its successors or the latest finish date of the network.

transaction   The series of related worksteps required to perform a specific task on a business data processing system. One or more screens may be required. From the user's viewpoint, it represents a self-contained unit. In terms of dialog programming, it is a complex object that consists of a module pool, screens, and so on, and is called with a transaction code.

transaction currency   Currency in which the actual business transaction was carried out.

transportation lead time   Time needed to organize the transportation of goods. For example, the interval between the booking of the freight space (transportation scheduling date) and the loading of the goods onto the means of transport (loading date) is called transportation lead time. The transportation lead time may depend on the route.

transportation planning date   The date when the organization of goods transport must begin. The transportation planning date must be selected early enough so that the transport means is available on the loading date to load the goods.

transportation scheduling   Determination of all dates relevant for transportation, based on the delivery date. The system determines when transport activities must start to ensure meeting the requested delivery date.

transportation zone   The zone in which the ship-to party is located. The system uses zones to help determine the route. Transportation zones can be defined according to postal or ZIP code areas, or according to the territory conveniently covered by the means of transport.

unit costing   Method of costing where bills of material and routings aren't used. Used to determine planned costs for assemblies or to support detailed planning of cost accounting objects such as cost centers or orders.

unit of measure   A standard measurement recognized by the SAP R/3 system. Base unit of measure, unit of entry, unit of issue, order unit, sales unit, and weight group are examples of units of measure. *Grouping*, used in delivery processing, refers to the weight of a convenient quantity of a material. The weight group is one factor the system uses to determine the route. It's also used in delivery scheduling to determine the pick/pack time.

usage variance   Difference between planned and actual costs caused by higher usage of material, time, and so on.

user exit   An interface provided by an SAP R/3 application that allows the user company to insert into a standard R/3 component a call to an additional ABAP/4 program that will be integrated with the rest of the application.

user-defined field types   A classification code used to interpret the meaning of a user-defined field. For example, a user may designate a specific field as one of the following types:

- General field of 20 characters to be used for codes or text
- Quantity fields with a unit
- Value fields with a unit
- Date fields
- Check boxes

user-defined fields   Entry fields that can be freely defined for an activity or a work breakdown structure element (project system) or an operation (production planning).

valuation date   Date on which materials and internal and external activities are evaluated in a costing.

valuation variant   Determines how the resources used, the external activities, and the overheads are to be valued in a costing (that is, at what prices).

variance category   Distinguishes variances according to their causes:

Input	Price and usage variances
Yield	Scrap, mix variances, labor efficiency variances, schedule variances
Allocation	Fixed-cost variances, overabsorption variances, underabsorption variances

variance key   Controls how variances are calculated. Assigning a variance key to an object determines, for example, whether variances are calculated for the object by period or for the life of the object, which may be a cost center, an order, or a cost object ID.

variance version   Specifies the basis for the calculation of variances as follows:

- How the target costs are calculated
- Which actual data is compared with the target costs
- Which variance categories are calculated

view   A relational method used to generate a cross-section of data stored in a database. A virtual table defined in the ABAP/4 Dictionary can define a view by specifying how and what will be selected from whichever tables are targeted.

volume variance   Cost difference between the fixed costs estimated for the products based on standard capacity and the allocated fixed costs that are either too low or too high due to operating either below or above capacity.

WBS   See work breakdown structure (WBS).

WBS element   A concrete task or a partial task that can be subdivided.

work breakdown structure (WBS)   A model of a project that represents the hierarchy of actions and activities to be carried out on a project. Can be displayed according to phase, function, or object.

work in progress   Unfinished products, the costs of which are calculated by subtracting the costs of the order that have already been settled from the actual costs incurred for the order or by evaluating the yield confirmed to date.

work order   Generic term for the following order types: production order, process order, maintenance order, inspection order, and network.

work process   An SAP R/3 system task that can be assigned independently to, for instance, a dedicated application server—for example, dialog processing, updating a database from change documents, background processing, spooling, lock management.

workflow management   Tool for automatic transaction processing used in a specific business environment.

Index

Why Join the ASAP team?

We are a fast growing dynamic group of companies operating globally in an exciting new virtual environment. We have the simple aim to be the best at what we do. We therefore look to recruit the best people on either contract or permanent basis

If you are any of the following, we would like to hear from you.

1. Highly Skilled and Experienced SAP Consultant.

You will have been working with SAP systems for many years and will be a project manager or consultant of standing in the industry. If you are willing to assist in the training and development and perhaps recruitment of your team, then we will be able to offer you exceptional financial rewards and the opportunity of developing the career of your choice.

2. Skilled in Another Area and Looking to Cross Train

You may be a computer expert or a business person with expertise in a particular area, perhaps, logistics, finance, distribution or H.R. etc., and/or with a particular industry knowledge. If you are committed to working with SAP systems in the long term, we will be able to offer you SAP cross training and vital experience. You must have a proven track record in your field and must be prepared to defer financial advancement whilst training and gaining experience. If you have the commitment and the skill you will in time be able to receive from us the high financial rewards and career development choice above.

3. A Person who has worked in a functional job

for an End User Company and who has been involved in all aspects of an SAP project from initial scoping to implementation and post implementation support.
You will have an excellent understanding of the industry or business function you are in. You are likely to have a good degree, ambition, drive, flexibility and the potential to become a top SAP consultant. You will thrive on the prospect of travel and living and working in other countries, jetting off around the world at short notice and working as part of a highly motivated and productive team. You must be committed to a long term career working with SAP. We will be able to offer you an interesting and rewarding career, giving you training and experience in a number of different roles. If you can prove yourself, you can expect rapid career development, with excellent financial rewards. Your only limit is your ability and your aspirations.

How To Contact Us
ASAP World Consultancy, ASAP House, PO Box 4463,
Henley on Thames, Oxfordshire RG9 6YN, UK
Tel:+44 (0)1491 414411   Fax: +44 (0)1491 414412

ASAP - 24 Hour - Virtual Office - New York, USA
Voice Mail: (212) 253 4180 Fax: (212) 253 4180

E-Mail: info@asap-consultancy.co.uk

Web site: http://www.asap-consultancy.co.uk/index.htm

ASAP
WORLD CONSULTANCY™

ASAP Worldwide
Enterprise Applications Resourcing & Recruitment

The company established in July 1997 has ambitious plans to become the world's largest global recruitment company specialising entirely in "the placement of permanent, temporary and contract staff who will be engaged in the implementation, support, training and documentation of systems known as enterprise applications". These include: SAP, BAAN, Peoplesoft, Oracle Applications, System Software Associations, Computer Associates, JD Edwards, Markam, JBA etc.

The company benefits from:

- Detailed knowledge of the market, its requirements and dynamics.

- Use of one of the world's most advanced recruitment systems.

- Access to large databases of candidates.

- A global approach to the staffing problems of a global market.

- Unique and innovative solutions for solving the staffing problems of a high growth market.

- A commitment to offer clients and candidates a professional, efficient and high quality service that is second to none.

- A commitment to the continual development of the services that we offer.

- Reciprocal partnership arrangements with other recruitment companies worldwide.

A S A P
WORLDWIDE™

Services to companies looking for staff

Permanent, Contract & Temporary Recruitment

ASAP Worldwide has a deep understanding of the enterprise application resourcing market, its requirements and dynamics. Whether your requirement is for a single individual or a team of hundreds, we offer the best practices and standards of service you would expect from one of the world's most professional recruitment companies to solve your staffing requirements.

In such a high growth market where the right people are at a premium, it takes a very different approach to find and place candidates. We offer a unique range of services to companies of all sizes and in all sectors worldwide. We leave no stone unturned in our search for candidates and we have unique techniques for selecting the very best candidates to offer you. We offer originality and innovation that make us stand out from the crowd.

Service to people looking for work

We believe that there is far more to our work than simply trying to fill job vacancies. We believe that we are providing a service of equal value to both employers and candidates looking for work. We are genuinely interested in your personal and career development and we undertake to try our very best to find you the work that best meets your requirements. Because of the size of our network, we are able to offer a truly global service, so whatever part of the world you would like to work in, whatever the type of employer and whatever the type of work you would like, we believe that we are better placed to give you what you want.

Send us a copy of your C.V./resumé and receive a free copy of our "Career Development Programme" booklet, designed to help you advance your SAP career.

How to contact us:

ASAP Worldwide
PO Box 4463 Henley on Thames
Oxfordshire RG9 6YN UK
Tel: +44 (0)1491 414411
Fax: +44 (0)1491 414412

ASAP Worldwide - 24 Hour - Virtual Office - New York, USA
Voice Mail: (212) 253 4180 Fax: (212) 253 4180

E-Mail: enquiry@asap-consultancy.co.uk

Web site: http://www.asap-consultancy.co.uk

A S A P
WORLDWIDE™